PHILOSOPHY AND EDUCATION

PHILOSOPHY and EDUCATION:

A Total View

Adrian M. Dupuis, Ph.D., MARQUETTE UNIVERSITY
and
Robert B. Nordberg, Ed.D., MARQUETTE UNIVERSITY

With a preface by Reverend William Codd, S. J., Seattle University

THE BRUCE PUBLISHING COMPANY

Milwaukee

To Mary and Beverly

Library of Congress Catalog Card Number: 64–21063

Preface

AMERICAN culture is not particularly a philosophical culture. The authors of the present volume describe it as an extroverted culture, one finding the inner life of ideas pale and annoying. Most of the great debates in modern American education are not about philosophical things at all, but about factual things, about means and not about ends and ultimate goals. This characteristic was dramatically illustrated two or three decades ago in the National Cooperative Study of American Secondary Schools. In that study schools were evaluated on the degree to which they achieved their basic philosophy of education. It was discovered that the greatest weakness of the schools was their inability to formulate a clear philosophy of education for themselves. Conditioned by the relativity of American pragmatism, they had no absolutes, no ultimate goals to which to anchor their curricula. There is little evidence that the schools have made much improvement since that day.

In his book, *Becoming,* Gordon W. Allport claims that modern psychology is in a dilemma between two contrasting traditions, the Lockean and the Leibnizian. The Lockean tradition, named for the English philosopher John Locke, emphasizes mind as a *tabula rasa,* a mere passive recipient of stimuli and conditioning from the outside. The Leibnizian tradition, named for the German rationalist Leibniz, stresses the human mind as an active, self-propelling center of its own, independent of environmental stimulation. American and Anglo-Saxon traditions, claims Allport, are predominantly Lockean or passive and materialistic. As a result they omit the most significant aspects of human personality, such as the higher forms of reasoning and the capacity of the mind to transcend the immediate and the concrete and to make decisions in terms of long-range goals and of human freedom and ethical living. This is true not only of psychology, but is more evident in the field of philosophy. Because of their Lockean tradition Americans are much given to pragmatism and instrumentalism, which actually deny the essential nature of philosophy, i.e., concern with ultimates, with a philosophy of being. Consequently we have produced very few philosophers. The present book is an antidote against the philosophical bankruptcy seemingly prevalent in America. It aims to produce legitimate philosophers of education, not mere historians of education. It is concerned not with describing the means of education divorced from ultimate goals, but with establishing the ultimate goals themselves. Its aim is not mere information, but formation of the mind. Its ultimate aim is not only knowledge, but philosophical wisdom.

In his modern classic, *The Degrees of Knowledge,* Jacques Maritain clearly distinguishes the nature of philosophy from that of mathematics and natural science. Each is a separate discipline and has its own mode and level of thought. Science is called the first degree of abstraction, mathematics the second degree, while philosophy or metaphysics is the third degree. There should be no conflict among these disciplines if each is genuinely true to itself. The problem with modern philosophy, however, according to Maritain, is that much that parades as philosophy is not truly philosophy at all, but science, mathematics, or even poetry posing as philosophy. The fruit of this confusion is manifest in educational philosophy as a hodgepodge of conflicting theories and schools of education. Mortimer Adler, in one of his more popular lectures, stresses this point. In tracing the development of philosophy through the centuries he points out three critical problems. Plato and Aristotle distinguished philosophy from poetry and history; Thomas Aquinas separated philosophy from theology and freed man from the contradictory theory of the twofold truth; and in our time philosophy must be distinguished from physical (natural) science. Until this latter problem is solved satisfactorily we shall continue to have the jungle of philosophical systems that flourish in education. Before one can evolve an integral philosophy of education one must first be a legitimate philosopher. To provide a climate where philosophy can flourish is one aim of this book.

According to Maritain the mind of man is an instrument impelled by a drive which he describes by the phrase *"distinguer pour unir,"* i.e., by the urge to unite by distinguishing. This is the mark of a fine philosopher: precise distinctions. The true philosopher can analyze accurately and synthesize orderly and thus avoid the fallacies common to educational philosophy: oversimplification and false generalization. The present volume is an object-lesson in the philosophical habit of mind and in particular in the skills of fine analysis and orderly synthesis. Consequently it should form and strengthen the mind of the student. It is not merely factual and descriptive, a history of current philosophical systems, but a book that stimulates and guides philosophizing about education.

The book begins with fundamental self-evident principles and skillfully and luminously threads its way through the dilemmas of current educational philosophy. It starts with the problem of the one and the many and proceeds to an analysis of permanence and change, then works systematically and critically through the various schools of philosophy in education: traditionalism and modernism, realism and idealism, naturalism and supernaturalism, socialism and individualism, communism and existentialism, and finally ends with a synthesis under the title, "Philosophy of Education in Building the Future." The outcome for the student should be that he is enabled to formulate his own philosophy of education. This philosophy should be an integral system, a synthesis of the ultimate principles of education based on the fundamental and self-evident principles of metaphysics. It should embrace man's total life and his entire personality. It will properly relate both matter and spirit, nature and grace, the individual and the group and will incorporate any established contributions from science and mathematics.

Although this book is written mainly for students in Catholic colleges where it can be integrated with courses in classical scholastic philosophy, there is no reason why it cannot also be very profitable for students in non-Catholic and secular colleges. Granted that the bridge which unites philosophy with education is scholastic metaphysics, that philosophy is in its own right the "perennial wisdom" of the ages dating from the days of Plato and Aristotle. It is Catholic only in the sense that Catholic colleges and universities have adopted it. To study it is to come in contact with the integrated central tradition of philosophy in its purest form. This philosophy is the only philosophy deep enough and broad enough to embrace all other systems of philosophy and to synthesize them under the general virtue of wisdom. This is the synthesis which the field of educational philosophy needs so desperately today and the synthesis which this excellent book seeks to promote.

Concerned with ultimate goals.

WILLIAM J. CODD, S.J., PH.D.
Professor of Education
Seattle University
Seattle, Washington

Introduction

A NEW spirit, or the renewal of an old one, is stirring in the Catholic Church, both symbolized and stimulated by the second Vatican Council. It is a liberal spirit which seeks, among other things, *rapprochement* and understanding with other faiths, other outlooks.

One facet of this revitalized approach is that the student of philosophical thought should become acquainted with all the basic positions, metaphysical and anti-metaphysical, monistic and dualistic, ancient and modern, naturalist and supernaturalist, convinced Catholic though he be. Until now, there has been no text in philosophy of education intended basically for a Catholic readership but also embracing a variety of other outlooks. We have sought to fill that gap.

Again, American Catholicism has mostly outgrown the era when apologetics was confused with constructive scholarship, and didactic expositions of positions with philosophy. The Catholic philosopher works within the context of a belief in a Church which teaches infallibly within its sphere. Nevertheless, within that limit (or emancipation) there is no reason why he should not approach philosophical questions as creatively and inner-directed as any other man. We have also sought to use this approach to metaphysical, epistemological, ethical, and aesthetic problems as they bear on education.

The volume begins with a survey of some conflicts in modern educational controversies and the characteristics of education as a field of study. It then moves to an historical survey and evaluation of early Christian thought as exemplified by St. Augustine and by the medieval educational theories, chiefly of St. Thomas Aquinas and the Franciscans. Modern Catholic educational philosophies are then examined and evaluated.

Next attention is focused on modern non-Scholastic systems of thought: Instrumentalism, Idealism, Existentialism, Naturalism, and others. Finally, the role of educational philosophy in building the future of education and of society is considered.

Dr. Dupuis is responsible for chapters 6, 7, 8, 9, and 10, Dr. Nordberg, for chapters 1, 2, 3, 4, 5, 11, and 12.

ix

The authors acknowledge with appreciation those whose suggestions have helped us to shape the text. We cheerfully accept the
blame for whatever shortcomings remain in it.

ADRIAN M. DUPUIS
ROBERT B. NORDBERG

Acknowledgments

WE WISH to thank the following for allowing us to reprint copyrighted material:

The America Press, for passages from McGuken's *The Philosophy of Catholic Education*

Appleton-Century-Crofts, for citations from St. Augustine's *Concerning the Teacher* and *On the Immorality of the Soul,* translated by George C. Leckie (Copyright, 1938, D. Appleton-Century Company, Inc.)

The Catholic Education Press, for citations from Msgr. George Johnson's "Progressive Education" from the May, 1940, issue of *The Catholic Educational Review*

The Catholic University of America Press, for passages from G. Bettoni's *Duns Scotus,* translated by B. Bonansea

David McKay Company, Inc., for passages from F. J. Sheen's *God and Intelligence in Modern Philosophy* (Image Book edition)

Desclée Publishing Company, for material from J. Danielou's *The Christian Today*

The Educational Policies Commission, for citations from *Education for All American Youth*

George Allen & Unwin, Ltd., for material from *Religious Platonism*

Etienne Gilson, for passages from his *The Philosophy of St. Bonaventure,* published by Sheed & Ward, Inc., 1940

Harcourt, Brace & World, Inc., for material from *Fundamentals of Curriculum Development* by Smith, Stanley, and Shores

Harper & Row, Inc., for material from *Higher Education for American Democracy,* and from J. Donald Butler's *Four Philosophies*

Hawthorn Books, for passages from M. Nedocelle's *Is There a Christian Philosophy?* Vol. 10 of the *Twentieth-Century Encyclopedia of Catholicism*

D. C. Heath and Company, for citations from John Dewey's *How We Think*

Helicon Press, for material from Yves Congar's *The Mystery of the Church*

Holt, Rinehart and Winston, Inc., for material from W. G. Dennis *et al., The Planning of Change*

Houghton Mifflin Company, for citations from Counts and Lodge's *The Country of the Blind* and from Morris' *Philosophy and the American School*

The John Day Company, Inc., for passages from *I Want to Be Like Stalin* by G. B. Counts and Nuncia P. Lodge (Copyright 1947 by the John Day Company)

George Kneller, for citations from his article, "Education, Knowledge and the Problem of Existence," in *Proceedings of the Philosophy of Education Society,* 1961

The Macmillan Company, for material from John Dewey's *Democracy and Education*

Methuen & Co., Ltd., for passages from J.-P. Sartre's *Existentialism and Humanism*

The National Catholic Welfare Conference, for passages from Pope Pius XI's *Encyclical on the Christian Education of Youth,* from Pope Pius XII's *Humani Generis,* and from C. N. Lischka's *Private Schools and State Laws*

The National Society for the Study of Education, for citations from the National Society's Fifty-fourth Yearbook, Part I, *Modern Philosophies of Education*

The Priory Press, for material from T. Donlan's *Theology and Education,* published in 1952 by William C. Brown Co.

Random House, Inc., for material from Josef Pieper's *The Silence of St. Thomas* (Copyright 1957 by Pantheon Books); from John Dewey's *Human Nature and Conduct* (Copyright 1922 by Random House, Inc.); from Anton C. Pegis' edition of the *Basic Writings of St. Thomas Aquinas* (Copyright 1945); from Anton C. Pegis' introduction to the Modern Library volume, *Introduction to St. Thomas Aquinas* (Copyright 1948)

Henry Regnery Company, for material from J. V. McGlynn's translation of the *De Veritate* of St. Thomas, Q. 11; and from James Collins' *The Existentialists*

Sheed & Ward, Inc., for citations from J. Maritain's *An Introduction to Philosophy*

Yale University Press, for material from J. Maritain's *Education at the Crossroads*

Contents

PHILOSOPHY AND EDUCATION

CHAPTER ONE

The Conflict in Modern Education

MODERN psychology has presented no trait dichotomy of more widespread significance than Jung's introvert-extrovert categories. The introvert tends to look inward for satisfaction of his psychological needs. He lives largely in a world of thought and fancy. The extrovert is preoccupied with action, things, people, the environment, and finds ideas pale and even annoying.

Ours is, basically, an extroverted culture. Of late, American life manifests many signs of unwonted self-examination, but by and large we have been more interested in making things happen than in analyzing why they happen or what should happen. Accordingly, we have not been especially hospitable to philosophy or any other kind of theory.

The first task of a text such as this one, therefore, might be to show the relevance of theory. Your typical American is seldom happier than when he can say, "Yes, it's fine in theory, but it doesn't work" or "On paper, yes, but not in practice." What he basically means by this is that theory should be judged by practice, that it should be in a sense subordinated to practice. This view is itself, as we shall see, a theory, a philosophy.

Our task is complicated because education is a curiously confusing enterprise. To acquire one is usually a perplexing process, and to listen to theories about this process is sometimes baffling indeed. Suppose that an engineer, wanting to build a bridge, were told, "There are six theories on bridge building. You must, of course, use the right theory, or the structure will collapse." Suppose the engineer then asked, "Which *is* the right theory?" and were told, "Nobody knows." Such is approximately the dilemma of the fledgling

teacher. Among philosophies, he is offered instrumentalism, Platonism, Thomism, reconstructionism, positivism, existentialism, and
others, each claiming to be "the way, the truth, and the life." Among
psychologies, he has his choice of Gestalt theory, functionalism,
connectionism, behaviorism, Freudianism, and so forth.

This is, further, a time of great debate in American education.
Practices that held sway for a generation and more, nearly above
criticism, now are being examined, sometimes condemned, by the
man in the street. Most of this contention has been very practically
motivated, to be sure, by Cold War considerations. It has been
largely limited to the issue of how to produce more and better
scientists and technologists, and has not, as a rule, been carried on
at a very philosophical level. The disputed questions have mostly
been factual: Can children spell, read, compute, as well as formerly?
Are "fads and frills" being taught in "our schools"? Although the
controversy has not been mainly philosophical, educational philosophers have been enlisted to the fray. This is a time of many theoretical labels, of shifting grounds and realignments. Our problem is to
see all these variegated educational *isms* in perspective.

Modernism and Traditionalism

At first glance one might well assume that he is confronted with
dozens of theoretical systems standing in no clear interrelations.
Two basic patterns appear, however. We shall call them traditionalism and modernism and compare and contrast them in their
applications to various educational problems. In doing this, we do
not mean to imply that any schools of thought in education with
these two names exist, or that all philosophers who lean basically
to either of these positions would accept all that is cited as characteristic of the respective viewpoints. Neither do we mean that all
contemporaries accept the "modern" view or that all educators in the
past were "traditionalists." Rather, our aim is to simplify, to help
the reader get the "feel" of two fundamental ways of thinking about
education that have tended to persist with varying names and modifications throughout history. In general, the traditionalist believes
that man is a rational creature, able to know things as they are
independently of himself, and that the chief purpose of schooling is
to develop his mind. The modernist believes that man is qualitatively the same as any other animal, that thought is a biological,

adaptive function, and that the chief purpose of schooling is bio-psychological adjustment.

It might seem that these two names are poorly chosen. A traditionalist is, loosely speaking, one opposed to the new, while "modern" as a term is seldom applied to any time earlier than the Reformation. Yet we have said that both of these educational currents run through history. Remember that the distinction is simply one of dominance. The systems to be considered in our third, fourth, and fifth chapters were predominant until about the seventeenth century, at which time "modernism" gained the ascendancy.[1]

MAJOR ASPECTS OF THE CONFLICT

1. Permanence and Change

Philosophy is concerned with ultimates. The ultimate notion that arises every time we use the mind is that of being, and it is in terms of being that we resolve our judgments. One basic aspect of being is the baffling relationship between permanence and change. This is probably the most difficult and crucial of metaphysical problems, for it points up the tension between being and becoming, identity and otherness, and raises questions about the very *possibility* of many beings. Ordinarily, people think about change without any such metaphysical scruples. They simply observe that the grass which was short last week is long now, the pen which was full is empty, the candle which was unused is half burned. How could there be any great puzzle about the passing of things from one state to another, a phenomenon everyone has observed since infancy?

The trouble arises when we *think* about change. The grass which is now long is considered the *same* grass that was short. The full pen is the same pen that was empty; the half-burned candle is the same candle that once was new. Therefore, to say that something has changed is to say that it is, and is not, "the same" as before. But how can this be? The first principle of all thought and being is that a thing cannot both be and not be at the same time and under the same aspect. Change must violate this principle unless it can be shown that the thing changes under one aspect and endures

---

[1] The reader should be careful not to associate other connotations with these key terms. For example, "traditionalism" has a theological reference to the teachings of the Fideists, while "modernism" as a "synthesis of all heresies" was condemned in the encyclical *Pascendi* of Pius X. We are not concerned here with these teachings.

under another. The celebrated "problem of change" is to determine what abides and what does not, and how it is possible for these two elements to coexist in the same being. One extreme position, enunciated first by Heraclitus (circa fifth century B.C.) holds that reality is "pure becoming."[2] Change is not, upon this view, a passage of the same *thing* from one form or state to another. There is not, indeed, any "thing," there is only the passage. Heraclitus authored the oft-quoted observation that you cannot bathe twice in the same river or touch the same thing twice. As Sheen says, "He reduced the rational to the real, the spirit to the sensible, and God to the world."[3] Nobody has ever managed to go further than Heraclitus in the direction he took. His is a philosophy of pure becoming. Being, so far as it can be credited at all, is secondary to becoming. Change is the final reality. This is, basically, the philosophy of "modernism" in education, as in all other things.

The other extreme position, attributed to Parmenides (fifth century B.C.) holds that change is an illusion because it is impossible. If anything exists, it cannot have come into being. From what source would it come? It must come from something or from nothing. But it cannot come from nothing, for it is a contradiction in terms to speak of nothing producing something. A thing must exist before it can act as a cause. If it exists, however, then it cannot and does not need to *begin* to exist. *Ex nihilo, nihil fit.* So, if anything begins to be, it must have come from something that already was. This alternative, too, proves impossible, however. For, if *Y* "came from" *X,* then *Y* was already somehow present in *X.* But if *Y* was already in *X,* then *Y* is not new.

We cannot trace in detail the modifications by subsequent thinkers of the philosophies of pure becoming and of pure being worked out

---

[2] It is always possible to question whether a philosopher took exactly the positions popularly ascribed to him. In cases where no published writings are available or where one philosopher speaks through the pen of another, the question becomes rather impossible of settlement. One usually makes more distinctions within a system of thought he accepts than one he rejects. Partly for this reason, it is unlikely that Plato, Parmenides, etc., took precisely the positions usually attributed to them. From one standpoint, however, it does not matter whether a philosopher believed exactly what he is commonly alleged to have believed. This is a point of only historical interest, and always remains conjectural. What matters more is that there are certain basic views of reality which are philosophically possible and which are commonly associated with these men. Their names are offered here simply as handy "hooks" on which to hang certain essential viewpoints.

[3] F. J. Sheen, *God and Intelligence in Modern Philosophy* (New York: Image Books, 1958), p. 150.

by these two ancient Greeks. Plato (427–347 B.C.) supplied the concepts needed for a modification of Parmenides' position. He distinguished between concrete things and their nature or Idea, conceiving of the former as somehow "participating in" the latter. He misapplied the key, however, in holding that the Ideas existed independently of particular things, in a sort of superrealm.

Plato, Aristotle, and Parmenides, however, were as one in asserting that being is prior to becoming. This has been the position of the schools of educational thought we have called traditionalist. The modernist position (as ancient as Heraclitus) has been that becoming is the only final reality. All philosophies and, by that token, all philosophies of education must necessarily take some position on this issue, if only by implication.

2. Naturalism and Supernaturalism

This is a second aspect of the conflict. Nature is, loosely speaking, the physical universe, taken as a system in which all things have certain powers and can, under given circumstances, produce certain results. Some people believe that nature and reality are synonymous, that natural laws, known or unknown, account for all events. They are called naturalists. Others hold that "nature" itself is philosophically inexplicable unless one also recognizes as its creator, God. Since God is "above nature" we can, loosely speaking, say that all who believe in God are "supernaturalists." But the supernatural in the strict sense, as understood by those who accept divine revelation, refers to an order of being and activity which can be *known* only through faith, whereas God as First Cause of nature can be, theists hold, known by strictly philosophical reflection on the being of created things.

Those who reject supernaturalism sometimes think of the supernatural as a chaotic realm where anything might happen. This is not an accurate view. Theists believe in a supernatural *order,* that state in which man, aided by divine grace, exercises his powers toward his goal of eternal union with God.

What belongs to the supernatural? In general, the spiritual soul of man, miracles, prophecies, grace, angels belong here. Anything spiritual belongs essentially here, although "spiritual" and "supernatural" cannot be equated. That man's soul is spiritual is demonstrable on rational grounds, on a philosophical reflection over his actions and the *necessary* source for such operations as choice, commitment, understanding. A man is functionally indivisible, and lives simultaneously in the natural and supernatural orders. The supernaturalist usually belongs on the traditionalist side of the dichotomy adopted in this chapter, since he sees man as a rational creature with powers of knowing eternal truths. The naturalist usually, but by no means always, belongs on the modernist side, because most naturalists see man solely as an animal. Some leading naturalists are also educational traditionalists, however. Catholic educators are, of course, supernaturalists. Catholic education on the supernaturalist side and instrumentalism on the naturalist side have been the chief academic forces of our time in America. We must remember, however, that there are other groups on both sides of the issue.

To keep natural-supernatural relations in focus, we must remember that the one God is the source of all things. Man in the concrete is the subject, the person to be educated. Neither he nor his environment can be divided into natural and supernatural "parts." As Daniélou notes,

> The vocation to holiness is in no way opposed to the vocation to temporal tasks. First of all there is no danger that holiness will turn us away from temporal tasks. There is no danger of any exclusive concentration on the divine because God could never lead us away from the service of our brothers.[4]

Nevertheless, "The moving force, the animating principle, of everything Christian, everything holy, since Christ, is the Holy Spirit,"[5] and

> The key of the Catholic system is the supernatural. Not only Catholic theology, but Catholic practice, the Catholic attitude toward life, and most of all, Catholic education are insoluble mysteries if we exclude an understanding of the supernatural.[6]

Protestant and Jewish educational systems have also, for the most part, been based upon a belief in the supernatural.

3. *Nature of Man and Society*

Traditionalism is for the most part allied with a dualistic view of man as a rational creature compounded of matter and spiritual soul.

---

[4] Jean Daniélou, *The Christian Today* (New York: Desclée Co., 1960), p. 16.

[5] Yves Congar, *The Mystery of the Church,* trans. by A. V. Littledale (Baltimore: Helicon Press, 1960), p. 7.

[6] William J. McGucken, *The Philosophy of Catholic Education* (New York: America Press, n.d.), p. 15.

The soul is regarded as the vital force making the body *living* matter. Some postmedieval writers equated the soul with some narrow aspect of the person, such as consciousness, so that it is not surprising that many scientists have been unable to accept their views.

The soul-matter dualist admits that the soul so exists with matter in this life, but he holds that the soul is intrinsically independent of matter — that is, it is able to exist and function without material involvements, although it is extrinsically and indirectly dependent upon matter in the human condition.

The materialistic monist usually does not believe in God or in a supernatural order. He sees man as an animal, man's differences from brutes being only of degree. He sees education, therefore, as a form of animal-training. Since this term sounds a bit degrading, one is likelier to hear of "organismic adjustment," "social engineering," or the like. We should note in passing that there are certain organismic, holistic theories in psychology which are halfway houses between simple, nineteenth-century materialism and a matter-spirit dualism. Such are Gestalt psychology, field theory, and the like. These systems are Aristotelian to the extent that they postulate form as a reality irreducible to matter (though they do not usually use this terminology).

4. *Epistemology*

Two basic branches of philosophy are metaphysics and epistemology, or the studies of being and of knowledge. Epistemology never attains full stature unless it becomes defensive metaphysics. Traditionalists in education have usually been realists in the philosophical sense. That is, they believe that there is a real, extramental world, which we can know essentially as it is. They believe usually, as Thomists do, that our sensations present the concrete, material world, while our ideas present the natures and meanings of things. The intellect arrives at these from the sense data presented to it by a process called abstraction. This is the considering by the mind of the nature of a thing, aside from all material or individuating considerations. Abstraction is not some mechanical, inductive operation, but the use of a spiritual power. In principle, we can abstract as well from one case as from a thousand. The abstracting process seems somewhat artificial if we consider isolated concepts thus formed. The actual knowing process blends sensations and concepts in judgments and uses these judgments in deductive reasonings. Thus sense and intellect form, functionally, part of a single cognitive operation. St. Thomas never spoke of a "thinker," as moderns are prone to do, but of a *knower*. There is an organismic manipulation of many inter-related experiences and ideas.

The educational modernist is usually a pragmatist. He regards knowing in a drastically different way from the realist picture we have just presented. He does not believe in intellect as a distinct and irreducible power, nor in ideas as distinct and irreducible products of that power. He regards all knowledge as consisting in sense impressions and various elaborations, connections, and associations of sense impressions. He proposes that there are no non-material essences to apprehend nor any rational minds to apprehend them. What, then, is knowledge? It is a biological function, an instrument, as Dewey suggested. We form a judgment. We act on it. The results fit with our felt needs and with the rest of our experience, or they do not. They "work" or not and accordingly are retained or not. If a realist says, "There is a clock on my desk," he means, there *is* a clock on his desk. That is, aside from who knows it or not, who sees it or not, aside from every subjective consideration, there is a real clock on a real desk. His statement would, he believes, be true even if every finite knower should cease to exist. There is a *structural correspondence,* so to speak, between his judgment and the fact.

The pragmatist, if he says, "There is a clock on my desk," means something quite different. He means that if you perform certain operations you will get certain results. "If you look over there," he is saying, "you will have the experience commonly designated as seeing a clock." What *is* the clock, independent of experience or cognitive operations, or what is the desk? Nobody knows! Knowing is a relative, transactional process. We know how things are after they have passed through the complex and probably distorting machinery of becoming known, but it would be a contradiction to speak of knowing how things are before they are known.

Naturally the pragmatist rejects metaphysics because its arguments are not such transactional affairs. They are not "look and see" propositions, but depend heavily upon logic, which is meaningless apart from observation and verification. Truth, then, is not a structural correspondence between judgment and fact, but *a set of con-*

sequences of acting upon a judgment. A realist can grant, incidentally, that many kinds of truth are *tested* in this empirical, operational way, but he will not grant that the truth *is* the testing.

4. *The Search for Values*

The last facet of the conflict that we shall consider has to do with axiology — the search for values. But where do values come from? What, if anything, guarantees them? If being is prior to becoming, then to be is to be something, to have a nature. The aims of human education, further, should be shaped by a knowledge of what human nature is. Sometimes the existence of any human nature is denied on the grounds that fashions change, civilizations rise and fall, men change their habits, and so forth. But that is all beside the point. There are undoubtedly numerous incidentals of human nature that change incessantly — every time one breathes, for example. But what is the essence of man? And, to put it a bit loosely, what is he "for"?

Ethics is the branch of philosophy that studies the absolute good of man. It asks: What is it that is good, a value, not because of anything it is related to, but in itself? Aristotle found man's absolute good in happiness — which, for him, was largely a matter of developing what he called the speculative intellect. Christian doctrine has little quarrel with this. It simply adds that perfect happiness is not to be had in this life, but in eternal union with God, which is often characterized by a name suggestive of the cognitive area: the Beatific Vision!

The philosophers of pure becoming, the modernists, tend to say that values are changing, relative, and partly subjective. They usually find good in what has utility or in what the majority in a given time and place wants. When they speak of good (as of truth) in terms of consequences, however, they have difficulty answering: consequences for what?

Some Applications of the Conflict

The reader will notice a difference in our treatment of traditionalist and modernist systems, respectively. In dealing with the latter, we shall follow a plan of discussing methodology, agencies of education, curriculum, students, aims, academic freedom, and indoctrination. There is an obvious advantage in such a standardized frame of reference. There would, however, be a disadvantage if the same approach were taken in dealing with early and medieval Christian educational theorists, simply because they did not, on the whole, address themselves to precisely these categories. Rather than risk putting words in their mouths, therefore, we shall deal with the full sweep of philosophers such as Augustine and Aquinas, discussing pedagogical implications only insofar as they are clear and compelling. For the purpose of the present general comparison between modernism and traditionalism, however, these categories should be useful for making further differentiations.

Methodology.   The formula for the teaching method of modernists has become a cliché: "We learn by doing." This hypothesis fits well with the empirical philosophies to be discussed in our Chapters Six and Seven, with the view of thought as a biological, adjustive function. It argues for much drill and much activity. There are, indeed, some perceptual-motor skills in which the formula applies well enough. One does not learn to play tennis, typewrite, drive a car, without doing these things. They involve much sense-mind-muscle coordination. But what about academic content? What about ideas? Here the traditionalist gives a different answer: We learn by understanding, by insight, by getting the point.

The late Professor John Dewey, by far the most influential of the modernists, regarded learning as beginning with "problems." According to Dewey, a person has a goal, finds he cannot reach it by responses of which he is presently capable. Therefore, the learner forms hypotheses, tries them out, keeps them if they work. Sometimes, learning does happen that way. People often seem to learn, however, from sheer curiosity about what is in and behind the universe, from "a need we find mentioned curiously seldom in psychological literature — *man's need for truth.*"[7] Aristotle proposed that all men by nature desire to know. A person may learn a language he never expects to have to speak, simply because he enjoys doing so. This does not gainsay that he is motivated or that he has a goal, but it denies that he necessarily feels any special blockage, any "problem." Learning begins with insights as well as with problems! On the other hand, the modernist stress on doing has had a salutary influence in reminding teachers of the concrete and functional aspects of the materials they are teaching.

---

[7] R. B. Nordberg, "Developmental Needs of Man," Chap. 5, in *Knowledge for the Practice of Public Health Nursing,* ed. by Lucille E. Corcoran and Marjorie J. Corrigan (Washington, D. C.: Catholic University of America Press, 1962), p. 93.

A particularly important aspect of methodology is *generalizing*. It is surprising how many educational controversies boil down to the question of how much stress the curriculum should put upon generalizations. As a general semanticist might say, generalizing$_1$ is not generalizing$_2$. There are unconscious and vague carry-overs of habits, impressions, and so forth, on a hit-and-miss basis. There are hasty, rash, or childlike generalizations. There is also the systematic derivation of general conceptions or principles from individual cases.

Psychology can help us here. Some meanings are arbitrary. Sometimes, for instance, there is no chance for a learner to survey the whole choice-situation. He must explore, try out, in order to see how his choice fits his goal. There are, again, "brute facts," data which — at least for a given student at a given time — have no rationale; they just "are." Such are the English alphabet, the numbering system, the periodical table in chemistry. Where meanings are arbitrary, one must memorize. Arbitrary meanings do not constitute an education, but are at best the hooks on which, hopefully, an education might be draped. Other meanings, however, are rational. In some choice-problems, for instance, the elements can be surveyed so that their relations toward each other and toward the goal can be understood before the first choice. There are, in a broader sense, meanings that can be anticipated, deduced. They follow from something known. Where meanings are rational, one should generalize.

Mathematics provides handy examples. If there were no generalizations, no transfer of training, no rational meanings, the teacher would have to teach the child every combination of numbers that he might ever have to use. He would have to be taught 1754×4, 1756×4, and so forth. He would spend his whole life on simple computation and still not learn all of it. If the one problem he had never "had" were $16,482 \times 297$, and an occasion arose to do that computation, he would have to be taught "from scratch." We do not, of course, do this! We teach the numbering system, the rules and logic of computation, and turn the pupil loose. He can then solve any computational problem that comes along. Again, if generalizations were intrinsically impossible, a pupil would have to be taught every conceivable combination of words that could form a grammatically correct sentence. We do not do that. We teach him the *principles* of English grammar (a principle is general by very nature) and "turn him loose."

The traditionalist in general and the philosopher of being in particular tend to favor the search for generalizations, consistently with that viewpoint. The traditionalist believes in a world ruled by order and law and in the power of human intelligence to discover nature's laws at work. He believes that to exist is to have an essence and to have an essence is to be intelligible. Above all, he looks for *explanatory* principles, for *causes*. Some generalizations are more fundamental than others in the sense of containing the latter. Boyle's law is a straightforward empirical generalization about the volume-pressure relation of gas under certain conditions. Molecular theory contains more basic generalizations which explain Boyle's law. What we want above all in education is a *hierarchy* of understandings.

The modernist, the philosopher of pure becoming, consistently with his whole viewpoint, tends to be "leery of all generalizations, whether *a priori* or *a posteriori*."[8] First, generalizing is a function of the intellect, and intellect is in the modernist's eyes merely a function, and a dubious one at that. Second, the world about which we generalize is constantly changing, whereas a generalization is of its nature final, unless it be so qualified that, strictly speaking, it does not remain a generalization. Third, generalizing imparts an objective cast to thought, which would be deceptive.

Experience, the modernist reminds us, is very concrete and particular. Universals, he claims, are delusions. There is always a gap between generalizations and the real situations to which they allegedly apply. The most one can do is to form certain hypotheses which work successfully under some conditions and temporarily. The conclusion that they will work next time must always be provisional and, at best, probable.

We have dwelt somewhat on this aspect of the being-becoming argument because it is very basic at the practical level. Educational literature contains countless generalizations against generalizing. Empirical psychology has had much to say on this issue, too. It arises chiefly in discussions of transfer of training, the influence that learning one thing has upon learning another. Judd's and Orata's theory of transfer by generalization was played down and discredited in most educational psychology texts for a very long time. The whole trend of educational psychology, as of modern thought at large,

---

[8] J. Donald Butler, *Four Philosophies and Their Practice in Education and Religion* (New York: Harper and Brothers, 1957), p. 466.

might be said to be *a flight from generalizing*. In the 1950's, a counter-trend developed. Nearly every educational psychology text written within the past decade has emphasized Judd's theory and accepted it. It is still sometimes confused with the "formal discipline" or "mental muscle" theory of transfer, which proposed that the mind was like a muscle which could be strengthened by *any* sort of exercise so that it would then work better for any other exercise.

Some teachers and some students almost instinctively seek the general in the particular, which search is the heart of intellectualism. To refrain deliberately from doing so would be foreign to their whole way of thinking and perhaps impossible for them. Other teachers and students are endlessly fascinated with specifics and details. Other things being equal, more intelligent persons generalize more. Some people can generalize more effectively at one level of abstraction than at another. Thus some students do well at grasping descriptive principles but not mathematical ones. Others excel in mathematics but cannot seem to grasp metaphysical generalizations. Another factor is one's theory of knowledge. Still another is personality. Some persons seem to feel that the small is the definite and the definite is the safe. James Thurber's *Miss Groby* is an excellent example.

Generalization is of no value for its own sake. Overgeneralization is by definition bad, as is any hasty or sloppy jumping at conclusions. But the whole point of thought, education, inquiry, is to make valid generalizations where possible. The philosopher of being, the traditionalist, insists that much of the sickness of modern pedagogy has arisen from an ill-advised and debilitating fear of the general. He might add that valid generalizations, aside from their cognitive economy, are exciting! "All men by nature desire to know."

Agencies. Who has the right to educate? Who has the responsibility? The traditionalist has always stressed the role of the family as providing a natural and fundamental teaching-learning situation, and of religious authorities. He may or may not regard it as part of the essential function of the state to teach. If he does view this as a state function, however, he will insist that the educational rights of family and church are more fundamental, not to be usurped by government intrusions in this field. The modernist is apt to subordinate all claims of religious or family authority to the authority of the state. He regards education as a natural function of the state and believes that the state should have ultimate control over all schools and colleges, public or private, and final say in case of any disputes about pedagogical matters.

On the source and nature of the teacher's authority and on the proper agencies of education, the naturalist and supernaturalist differ radically. These differences have recently been felt in prolonged and heated controversy over federal aid to private and church-related schools. Naturalism tends to secularism, which finds the foundations of morality and religion only in nature. The English writers, George Bradlaugh and George J. Holyoake, helped to systematize this view in the nineteenth century. This viewpoint, in turn, is scarcely distinguishable from nineteenth-century liberalism, which subordinated all claims of religious authority to the authority of the state. The teacher is, on this view, a sort of civil servant.

The Catholic Church insists that "first of all education belongs preeminently to the Church, by reason of a double title in the supernatural order, conferred exclusively upon her by God Himself; absolutely superior therefore to any other title in the natural order."[9] She does not regard her right to teach as conferred by the state. The state may in some times or places take away her *power* to teach, but the state cannot take away her *right* because it did not confer that right.

Second, the Church holds that "the family . . . holds directly from the Creator the mission and hence the right to educate the offspring, a right inalienable because inseparably joined to the strict obligation, a right anterior to any right whatever of civil society and of the State, and therefore inviolable on the part of any power on earth."[10] Third, "it pertains to the State, in view of the common good, to promote in various ways the education and instruction of youth," but "by no means to absorb the family and the individual, or to substitute itself for them."[11]

Curriculum. The traditionalist regards a curriculum as a course of study, while the modernist regards it as the totality of the pupil's experiences under the conscious guidance of the school. The traditionalist sees curriculum chiefly as a body of facts and ideas to be taught. These facts and ideas do not depend for their validity or

---

[9] Pius XI, *Encyclical Letter on Christian Education of Youth* (Washington, D. C.: National Catholic Welfare Conference), p. 6.

[10] *Ibid.,* p. 12.   [11] *Ibid.,* p. 16.

importance upon the person who teaches or learns them or how successfully they are taught or learned. They are, with minor exceptions, objective. Education has some content, a "something" which is taught. The modernist is likely to view truth as successive experiences with ideas, so that he is logically led to a "sequence of potential experiences" and "This set of experiences is referred to as the curriculum."[12] If truth is so subjective and biological a thing, it is reasonable that the learner should, to a very large extent, make his own decisions, or that the learning group should decide what is to be learned and why.

Some latter-day progressivists have insisted strongly that John Dewey did not have in mind, and explicitly repudiated, some extremes of "the chosen curriculum," such as not teaching the children the alphabet unless they vote for it. In this they are correct. Dewey insisted upon consequences, yes, but consequences on the whole and in the long run. It would be unfair to accuse him of a narrow utilitarianism. Nevertheless it was precisely his position, and is in general the modernist position, that the test of value for anything in education is whether the learners find it helpful and to what extent they do so.

Education has a long and, in many ways, honorable history. The course requirements that seem arbitrary or pointless to the freshman were not invented this week. The liberal arts in their basic outlines go back to pre-Christian times in Greece and Rome and were reworked in a theological context in the medieval schools. But are there, can there be, any subjects, any issues, of unchanging importance? Is a required and permanent curriculum justified? Naturally, the philosopher of being will say "yes" and the philosopher of becoming will say "no." At more operational levels, the traditionalist will often see certain permanent and objective aspects of the curriculum, while the modernist is apt to press for the overthrow of anything that purports to be a standard or norm. English grammar provides a good example. The modernist argues that grammatical rules are arbitrary. They sprang from usage. Language predates grammar, the latter being something distilled from "a living thing." Language came from the people who, therefore, have a right to change it. There are no objective reasons why people should speak

---

[12] B. O. Smith and others, *Fundamentals of Curriculum Development* (Cleveland: World Book Co., 1950), p. 4.

and write one way rather than another. The essential thing is to communicate. If you can do this better by smashing the rules, by all means smash the rules!

The traditionalist may find certain valid points here, but he is apt to regard this argument as a specious collection of half-truths. He sees certain relations among grammar, logic, and metaphysics, important relations which pupils do not learn because their teachers have not learned them. Some things in English grammar are arbitrary in the sense that there is a function which might as well be performed in any of a number of ways. What finally matters is that there *is* the function and that reality itself is its source. This, the traditionalist will argue, is what the modernist does not see because he tends to skim the surface of any issue. Rules sprang from usage to the extent that usage already embodied an implicit awareness of certain principles, and usage is frequently corrected when one is more conscious of the principles. Language in its more profitable and effective uses was not developed by "the people" so much as by that small minority who have special feeling and skill in this area. They are the ones to whom its evolution should be entrusted. It is no accident that the state and style of grammar in any society at any time correlate quite highly with what might be called the anthropological health of that society. The English used in some quarters in America today is distressingly reminiscent of the types of verbal aberrations known in the decadent phase of ancient Rome! Even aside from the philosophic moorings of language, the modernist does not sometimes seem to understand the need for rules. In America, everyone drives on the right side of the road on most streets. In England, everyone drives on the left side. Either way works. What does not work is to drive on whatever side you happen to like at any moment.

Two chief currents stand out in naturalist thought about the curriculum. The first is that it should emerge from applications of scientific method. Some writers speak of "the most rigorous possible use of man's empirical reason, starting with the examination of all available evidence and reserving the final test of the conclusions so reached to the way these conclusions actually operate in human life."[13] There is also a strong social current to naturalist theories on curriculum. Reconstructionism, one of the newer philosophies, says

[13] *Ibid.*, p. 146.

that the curriculum should be based upon whatever a given society at a given time wants.

The supernaturalist, on the other hand, will be sympathetic with the remark attributed to Arnold Lunn: "The answer to the educational problem is a monosyllable: God." A curriculum should depend upon what education is for, and that depends upon what life is for. If God has chosen to reveal to us the essentials of His will and plan for mankind, then the vital truths contained in this disclosure should permeate everything taught. The supernaturalist does not, of course, want to base his curriculum exclusively upon theology. Philosophy also holds an essential place. The history of education shows, moreover, that the birth and flowering of the arts and sciences have been more from the Church to the world than vice versa. As regards scholarly development from naturalist origins, Pius XI suggested that "There the Christian teacher will imitate the bee, which takes the choicest part of the flower and leaves the rest. . . ."[14]

Students.   Who should be educated, how much, for how long? The traditionalist, because he stresses intellectual development, believes that, after the fundamental communicative materials and processes are learned, education should be for those who demonstrate sufficient intelligence to absorb it at their respective levels. He believes in a natural aristocracy — not a socially or politically privileged class, but simply those who have more capacity to learn. Accordingly, he believes that "standards" (admittedly a rather flexible term) should be kept high, and that it is better to have ten capable students than a thousand incapable ones. The modernist, since he views school as aimed more at "life adjustment," and since personality does not come in the same more-less dimension as intelligence, is apt to believe in education for everybody, limited only by one's desire to receive. No less influential a group than the President's Commission on Higher Education expressed regret over "the present orientation of higher education toward verbal skills and intellectual interests" and suggested that the colleges and universities concentrate on "many other aptitudes — such as social sensitivity and versatility, artistic ability, motor skill and dexterity, and mechanical aptitude and ingenuity."[15]

---

[14] Pius XI, *op. cit.*, p. 33.

[15] President's Commission on Higher Education, *Higher Education for American Democracy* (New York: Harper and Brothers, 1947), p. 32.

On the other hand, a supernaturalist will want all children to receive the essentials of a religious education. Beyond that, his attitudes toward universal education will not be a direct consequence of his supernaturalism. Supernaturalists, like naturalists, can be found on both sides of the question, "Higher education for whom?" Basically, however, if truth is primarily an intellectual function, and if intelligence is given in unequal amounts, higher education is chiefly for the more intelligent. If truth is an organismic, biological function, higher education is for everybody.

Aims. "What's it for?" That is the most important question about anything, and closely related to the first and indispensable question: "What is it?" Every educational philosophy has certain aims specific to itself. These will be considered in following chapters. Catholic education, for example, while it belongs basically to the traditionalist viewpoint as herein characterized, has certain aims which some other traditionalists, such as Messrs. Hutchins and Adler, do not share.

In general, however, traditionalists want to develop minds, while modernists want to adjust organisms. This does not mean at all that the traditionalist is not concerned with personality and character, or that he is unaware of the organic unity of man. He believes, however, that the mind is the focal point for accomplishing major human changes of any sort.

The term "dialogue," with certain pedagogical connotations, has been fashionable of late. It was fashionable with Socrates, for that matter. The traditionalist sees education as a dialogue with being. There is a hierarchy of principles within principles within principles. Just as theology teaches that the higher angels can comprehend more by fewer acts of the intelligence, so the historic purpose of liberal arts education has been to liberate the mind so that it can comprehend more and more under fewer and fewer generic laws. The philosopher of becoming, on the other hand, will reject any such flirtation with permanent truth. He holds adjustment or integration as his essential aim.

A naturalist will be concerned with preparation for "here" on the grounds that there is no "hereafter." The supernaturalist's educational aims include this life and the life to come. "The proper and immediate end of Christian education," said Pius XI, "is to cooperate with divine grace in forming the true and perfect Christian, that is, to form Christ Himself in those regenerated by Baptism. . . ."[16] While some Catholic writers have strongly opposed what is sometimes called a guidance viewpoint, and have even stated that it is contrary to the mind of the Church, they are not supported by the encyclical, which says that "Christian education takes in the whole aggregate of human life, physical and spiritual, intellectual and moral, individual, domestic, and social . . ." and also that " . . . the subject of Christian education is man whole and entire. . . ."[17]

Academic Freedom.   This concept was invented by modernists. It does not seem to have any definite or fixed connotations. It is sometimes regarded as the right of the teacher to teach anything he wants to teach, without qualification; or as his right to teach anything so long as it is demonstrably true; or as his right to teach anything he *thinks* is demonstrably true, sometimes with the added stipulation that he has investigated the matter. The modernist is inclined to deny that truth is either final or objective. Therefore, the teacher should be given maximum latitude to teach anything that will encourage the pursuit of truth to go on. Traditionalists are likely to stress academic *responsibility*. Since man can know things as they are, and since a teacher's job is to aid in this process, who, more than the teacher, has a sacred charge to present only established truth? If he wishes to present opinions, clearly identified as such, this is another matter. Naturalism often becomes secularism in reducing all religious teachers to the sphere of opinion (as against knowledge). Supernaturalists insist that some things in the religious sphere can be known with certainty and that the teacher has both the right and responsibility to teach these things.

Indoctrination.   The modernist slogan here has been, "Teach how to think, not what to think." This is understandable. If there is no objective truth, no one has any special right to force his conclusions on anyone else. If indoctrination means teaching conclusions, the traditionalist says that the teacher has not only a right, but a duty, to indoctrinate. But if indoctrination means teaching conclusions without teaching reasons for them, a traditionalist is likely to oppose it. We shall see, in our later treatment of St. Thomas Aquinas, how he always wanted instruction to proceed from the known to the

---

[16] Pius XI, *op. cit.,* pp. 35–36.
[17] *Ibid.,* pp. 23, 36.

unknown. The modernist wants to imbue the students with scientific method so they will know how to come to grips with a problem and work it through to their own conclusions. He will, in theory at least, be against indoctrination in any form. Yet there often seems to be an amazing unanimity of opinion among "modernists," sometimes called "the liberal line."

Theory seems only tenuously related to practice in this area. Tendencies to indoctrinate seem to correlate with the personality of the individual teacher more than with his philosophical commitments. Many teachers who indoctrinate a great deal do not seem to believe that they ever indulge the practice.

SUMMARY

We have introduced a conflict that exists in modern education and that, with varying applications, has always existed since formal schooling began. It is a division between those who see being as prior to becoming (traditionalists) and those who see becoming as the final reality (modernists). We have deliberately simplified the conflict so as to bring out its main roots more clearly. Certain basic facets of the issue were examined: naturalism and supernaturalism, the nature of man and society, the nature of human knowledge, permanence and change. Certain pedagogical corollaries were also examined: aims, methods, curriculum, agencies, students, academic freedom, and indoctrination.

To simplify is perforce to distort here and there. The view from the tower is not the view from the highways and byways. A student in the writer's class, after a summer of hearing about existentialism, phenomenalism, Thomism, reconstructionism, etc., asked in authentic despair, "How many schools of thought *are* there?" Perhaps the answer would be synonymous with the number of people who think about philosophical questions. Each philosopher will ask somewhat different questions than did his predecessors, shift his frame of reference slightly from theirs, which is probably good. It is bad only insofar as it confuses beginners. To eliminate as much of that confusion as possible, we have tried to show that, at bottom, there are two ways of thinking about the educational endeavor. They are opposed, impossible of reconciliation (despite much wishful thinking to the contrary), and fairly clear-cut in their procedural implications.

Where do these schools of thought come from? How are they arrived at? Our next chapter will explore these questions.

BIBLIOGRAPHY

Adler, Mortimer J., "In Defense of the Philosophy of Education," in *Philosophies of Education* (Bloomington, Ill.: Public School Publishing Co., 1942).

Butler, Donald J., *Four Philosophies and Their Practice in Education and Religion* (New York: Harper and Brothers, 1957).

Congar, Yves, *The Mystery of the Church,* trans. by A. V. Littledale (Baltimore: Helicon Press, 1960).

Daniélou, Jean, *The Christian Today* (New York: Desclée Co., 1960).

Dewey, John, *Experience and Education* (New York: Macmillan Co., 1938).

Henry, Nelson B., ed., *Modern Philosophies and Education,* 54th Yearbook, National Society for the Study of Education (Chicago: University of Chicago Press, 1955).

Kilpatrick, William H., *Education for a Changing Civilization* (New York: Century Co., 1926).

Maritain, Jacques, *Education at the Crossroads,* Yale paperbound ed. (New Haven: Yale University Press, 1960).

McGucken, William J., *The Philosophy of Catholic Education* (New York: America Press, n.d.).

Nordberg R. B., "Developmental Needs of Man," Chap. 5, in *Knowledge for the Practice of Public Health Nursing,* ed. by Lucille E. Corcoran and Marjorie J. Corrigan (Washington, D. C.: Catholic University of America Press, 1962).

Pius XI, *Encyclical Letter on Christian Education of Youth* (Washington, D. C.: National Catholic Welfare Conference).

President's Commission on Higher Education, *Higher Education for American Democracy* (New York: Harper and Brothers, 1947).

Redden, J. D., and Ryan, F. A., *A Catholic Philosophy of Education* (Milwaukee: The Bruce Publishing Co., 1942).

Sheen, F. J., *God and Intelligence in Modern Philosophy* (New York: Image Books, 1958).

Smith, B. O., and others, *Fundamentals of Curriculum Development* (New York: World Book Co., 1950).

CHAPTER TWO

Education as a Field of Study

WE HAVE examined a basic conflict in modern education. In later chapters, we shall see how this conflict is reflected in specific schools of educational thought. After viewing the overall tableau, however, it is good at this point to step aside from the issues and contemplate the ways of resolving them. Where do educational philosophies (in the broad sense) come from? How are they developed? If you will examine your own mind, you will doubtless find that you have certain views about education and that they come from a variety of sources, some more reliable than others. For one thing, you have been a pupil or student for many years, even if you have not taught. You have observed what other teachers did and have formed judgments about what techniques worked well and what goals were worth pursuing. If you were to begin as a teacher tomorrow, therefore, you would start with some theories or hypotheses from experience as a pupil. Chances are, however, that you would want to do some formal study of education to bolster this equipment. To what sources might you turn? What are the potential sources of knowledge about education? They are basically the same as the sources of knowledge about anything, but with some special applications.

COMMON SENSE

Common sense provides some of the knowledge the teacher needs. This, however, is a notion with shifting connotations, and almost everyone credits himself with a generous share of the virtue in question. We have in mind a more definite use of the phrase, however. There is a kind of unpolished metaphysics, a more or less vague apprehension of being and its manifestations, by which the common or universal consent of mankind to certain truths is won. "The natural, spontaneous, primitive, infallible judgments of the human reason constitute common sense."[1] A man who can see knows what, in general, his house looks like. He knows that if Mr. X was born before his brother, Mr. X is presently older than his brother. He knows that things equal to the same thing are equal to each other. The first principles to which ultimately philosophical questions must be appealed are perceived by the light of common sense, though philosophy can do much to sharpen and clarify them. By the same token, misguided philosophy can do much to dull and confuse them. Diogenes is said to have answered Zeno's arguments about the impossibility of motion by walking. This was a common-sense reaction and a rather good one.

A teacher knows many things about his working situation by common sense. He knows, for example, that the pupils exist, that he exists himself, that a pupil cannot simultaneously know something and not know it in exactly the same way. He knows that there is a difference between ideas that are true and ideas that are false and that it is part of his job to plant the true and uproot the false.

Philosophy is not simply common sense, but it is impossible without common sense. Any theory that flies in the face of common sense does so at grave peril.

FAITH AND THEOLOGY

Christians and Jews believe that God has entered human history, that He is actively engaged in shaping human events. For Christians, He has become man, revealing Himself to us in the person of Jesus Christ. Christians hold these truths on faith, that is, on an infused virtue enlightening the mind and enabling man to accept as certain the truths God has revealed; and among such truths the following are most important: God is a trinity of Persons, Father, Son, and Holy Spirit; God wills to communicate His life to man, both in this world and in the world to come; God created man to His image, that is, in a state wherein man shared in the life of God through grace; man rebelled against God of his own free choice, but in doing so lost his title to grace and to the supernatural life made possible through it; in Christ God became incarnate, true man, in

---

[1] F. J. Sheen, *God and Intelligence in Modern Philosophy* (Garden City, N. Y.: Image Books, 1958), p. 141.

order to redeem man from sin and again give him title to grace; Christ suffered, died, and rose gloriously, founded a Church to last to the end of time, and is *today* present to men in that Church which is His "Mystical Body."

All these truths a Christian accepts because of his faith. Many of these truths are mysteries and can never be known properly by reason. Yet these truths are not in conflict with the truths man knows by his unaided reason, and since faith is a virtue modifying in some way man's intelligence, the Christian is consumed with a desire to grasp these mysteries as much as he can. His faith is ever driving to an understanding of its object. This quest for understanding will be quieted in the afterlife, in the Beatific Vision, but here below it serves as the spark that ignites theology in the religious sense (as opposed to natural theology, or the philosophical quest for those truths which can be known of God and of man's end by the mind uninstructed by faith). Theology, thus, is a type of knowing, as is the faith from which it derives. The knowledge imparted by faith is common to the simplest peasant and the most erudite theologian, for through faith they each commit themselves to God, to Christ and His Church, and hope for the blessedness of eternal life with God. But the knowledge proper to theology is reflective, it is that of a faith grown conscious of itself and concerned with relating the truths man knows by faith to. the truths he hold on common-sense, scientific, and philosophic grounds.

To put it another way, we can say that one can learn by discovery or instruction. If it has pleased God to give to mankind a disclosure of His will and plan for us, then that body of knowledge is supremely important and should stand above all else in guiding us. Therefore, such a divine revelation should form the most important source of educational principles. Hence those who recognize such a revelation turn for major guidance to theology.

It is at once important to distinguish theology from other disciplines and to relate it to them. The special sciences are rightly concerned with "things," but their practitioners should go from things to God. The theologian, conversely, should go from God to things. It is fundamental in Catholic thought that faith and reason, properly understood and exercised, cannot contradict one another. All truth is finally anchored in one and the same God. Eugenio Cardinal Pacelli, later Pius XII, declared in a 1936 address:

God the Creator, Who is also the God of supernatural revelation, is the essential and inexhaustible font, embracing and sustaining all things, in which all truth, natural and supernatural, has its source. The Divine Word, Who operates in both spheres, speaks to us in different ways in the order of nature and in the order of grace, but the truths of one order can never be found in contradiction with the truths and mysteries of the other. In the consciousness of the harmonious coordination and subordination of the truths of the natural and supernatural order, the thoughtful Catholic student finds the origin of that sense of spiritual steadiness and inner security, which nothing in this world can replace, which constitutes his most precious heritage and is the privileged possession of those centers of learning whose breath of life is the Catholic faith.[2]

His predecessor, Pius XI, argued that

It is . . . as important to make no mistake in education, as it is to make no mistake in the pursuit of the last end, with which the whole work of education is intimately and necessarily connected. In fact, since education consists essentially in preparing man for what he must do here below, in order to attain the sublime end for which he was created, it is clear that there can be no true education which is not wholly directed to man's last end. . . .[3]

From theology the teacher can know where human beings come from, why they exist, what is their final destiny. Everything else, obviously, must be pondered and learned in that context.

It is never justified to answer a properly theological problem on a purely philosophical basis, because the data necessary to answer the problem are not known by man naturally. Catholic scholars have sometimes been careless here. On the other hand, the unity of truth implies that all we learn from theology, science, philosophy, aesthetic experience, common sense, is part of a single, harmonious mosaic. The Catholic who has seen the outlines of that grand mosaic can be pardoned if, like St. Augustine, he occasionally overlooks certain methodological distinctions in presenting his data. Reality is what it is, while the various disciplines as such, even theology, are abstractions. For St. Thomas, "sacred doctrine" is "an action, the instruction of men in the knowledge of salvation."[4] This operation "extends to all other things, even those considered in the philosophical disciplines, insofar as they are related to God as their principle

---

[2] Eugenio Cardinal Pacelli, address at The Catholic University of America, October 22, 1936.

[3] Pius XI, *Encyclical Letter on Christian Education of Youth* (Washington, D. C.: National Catholic Welfare Conference, 1936), pp. 4–5.

[4] Gerald F. Van Ackeren, *Sacra Doctrina* (Rome: Catholic Book Agency, 1952), p. 118.

and end."[5] At a later point in this chapter, we shall consider in particular the theology of education.

SCIENCE

Science is, in the classical sense, knowledge of things by their causes. The modern, empirical sense, while more in tune with this definition than is generally realized, adds implications of observation, induction, experimentation, testing, measurement, of "look and see."

The various sciences have contributed facts and theories which are useful or even essential to teachers. A teacher, of course, should keep generally abreast of developments in any science which he is teaching, such as biology, chemistry, or whatever. In addition, sciences such as sociology, psychology, anthropology, and economics give perspective about the learning process, the school as an institution, and so forth. Such information is valuable regardless of one's teaching field.

One of the modern sciences which is still developing is education. This science has the teaching-learning process for its formal object.[6] Strictly speaking, this pertains only to human beings. We sometimes speak of "teaching" brute animals, but "training" is a better term.

There are many things the teacher can learn by studying education as a science, important principles about learning which have not been known until recently: how children develop, the nature and functioning of intelligence, curricular adjustments for individual differences, the nature and functioning of motives in learning and remembering, creative and reflective thought, mental-health problems in the classroom — these and many other topics have been investigated empirically at great length.

AESTHETIC EXPERIENCE

Some writers postulate aesthetic intuition as a mode of knowing.

---

[5] *Ibid.,* p. 118.

[6] An object in philosophy is anything which can confront the senses, the mind, or any other power. The subject is that which perceives or knows the object. Two aspects of an object are commonly distinguished: The material object is the object in itself, in the concrete. The formal object is that in the object which makes possible its acting upon one or another faculty or power. In order to develop a science, one must establish what this science is to study — that is, specify its formal object. It is partly for want of attention to this problem — that some investigators in education have tended to be somewhat undisciplined and inexact in their questions, methods, and answers.

The term "appreciation," in one of its older and sadly uncontemporary uses, suggests perception of aesthetic values. Is this a qualitatively distinct manner of cognition? If so, how does it relate to philosophical knowledge? If beauty is order which is unity which is being, aesthetics belongs primarily to metaphysics and only secondarily to psychology.

The trouble is that there are many levels and varieties of aesthetic appreciation, some almost purely intellectual (e.g., an elaborate mathematical exercise) and some almost purely sensory (e.g., a sunset). The present writer views aesthetic perception in its typical manifestations as a beginning of ontological insight, a crude form of what comes to us in more ripened form in metaphysical contemplation. It may be helpful here to make Plato's distinction between the "lovers of sounds and sights" and the aesthetic philosopher "who recognizes the existence of absolute beauty and is able to distinguish the idea from the objects which participate in the idea, neither putting the objects in the place of the idea nor the idea in the place of the objects. . . ."[7]

A sense of taste, in matters large and small, will certainly influence a teacher's aims, material, and methods of presentation. Napoleon remarked that a man's palate can, in time, become accustomed to anything. There is little evidence that the educational process refines and elevates the tastes of most of its graduates in any substantial measure. If at any time we begin to feel inordinately proud of "our schools," we need but observe the cultural level of our environment to be restored to reality. Rock-and-roll music and a cynical and primitive exploitation of the emotions of the young prosper. "Westerns" and dramatizations of crass violence continue to dominate the television screen. What books sell best? Successful song writers advise the beginner, "Aim for the twelve-year-old mind."

Doubtless there are many reasons for this condition, but we cannot gainsay that the condition exists and that it coexists with a system of universal education going back almost to the foundations of the Republic. Schools, public and private, have often tended to be very concerned with the teacher's morality, moderately concerned with his knowledge, and almost completely indifferent to his tastes! For the most part, professors of education have lodged little protest against this state of affairs.

---

[7] Plato, *The Republic*, trans. Benjamin Jowett (Cleveland: World Publishing Co., 1946), V, pp. 201–202.

It would be pleasant to report that Catholicism in this country offers an oasis in this cultural desert, but grounds for the assertion seem to be lacking. We are feeling the beginnings of a sort of Catholic Renaissance in America, led by the observations of such astute observers as Msgr. John Tracy Ellis. This is just the dawn, however. The typical parish church and school and home are still decorated with religious art that may or may not be religious but is certainly not art. Books such as *The Little World of Don Camillo* have commanded a wider readership than the novels and stories of writers such as J. F. Powers or Morris L. West. It is impossible to name a Catholic among the top-ranking persons in some facets of our national cultural life. Critics in Catholic periodicals complain, and rightly, if a movie or play is immoral, but almost never do they protest banality, triteness, heavy-handedness, and the like. We must confess that our record in aesthetic matters is not, on the average, cause for satisfaction. The one consoling thought here is that non-Catholic education, on the average, does no better in elevating and refining taste.

PHILOSOPHY

There is another source to which the teacher may turn for light upon upon his craft: philosophy. What is philosophy? First, it is knowledge. This is its genus.[8] Second, it is a science in the classic sense: knowledge by causes. Philosophy, then, is a systematic, certain, and evident knowledge based upon some mode of demonstration. How does it differ from other sciences? Theology, we have noted, draws upon revealed truth, while philosophy depends entirely upon natural reason. Empirical sciences deal with various aspects of reality in a descriptive way, dealing with secondary and proximate causes, while philosophy is concerned with *ultimate* principles and causes — the final "why" of things, so far as it can be known by our reason.

Summing these elements, we can say that philosophy is a science

---

[8] Broadly speaking, the genus of a thing is the determinable part of its essence. The "difference" (from other species within the same genus) is the determining part of essence. The definition of a thing, strictly speaking, consists of proximate genus and ultimate difference. There is a stricter, mostly biological connotation of "genus" which is not intended here. In a strict sense, knowledge does not have a genus, but is an analogical notion.

which, by natural reason, studies things according to their ultimate principles and causes. The ultimate notion for human reason is being. This concept is in the background of every idea, judgment, deduction, every imagined thing or recollection. For that reason, metaphysics, or the study of being *as* such, is the zenith of human thought and sheds light on all else. Being is known by *all* men, and is indeed a "common-sense" notion. But the being studied by philosophers is the same being seen, however, for what it *is* and means as such, and not as the being of *this* or *that* individual or group or class.

It was suggested earlier that some confusion arises when writers fail to note carefully the formal object of their special science. This is true especially of philosophy. In books and articles on education, questions are often posed as philosophical which are psychological or sociological, or the other way about. This is quite a serious error, because psychological questions call for psychological methods to answer them, and philosophical questions need philosophical methods and answers. Much confusion could be avoided if philosophical and non-philosophical problems were more carefully differentiated.

In empirical science, statements must be worded with such definite reference to consequences and procedures that something can be done to test them and everyone can agree upon the exact test. "Is George intelligent?" would strike a psychologist as a nonscientific question because it is vague; it does not indicate exactly what information would constitute an answer. There are many possible criteria of intelligence. "What is George's Binet IQ?" is a scientific question because it refers to a definite test with a definite scoring system, etc. In science, the criterion of proof is verification. In philosophy, certain first principles become the regulative criteria.

The science-philosophy relation is not one of simple autonomy, however. A philosopher has a right to ask a scientist to reexamine a conclusion that is logically untenable, for philosophy establishes that one truth cannot contradict another. Metaphysical principles, moreover, are the first principles of all human knowledge. Therefore, the empirical sciences (psychology, physics, etc.) are dependent upon philosophy. This is not the direct sort of dependence that a conclusion has toward its premises. A scientist can usually make his case independently of metaphysics, and should, but his conclusions nevertheless presuppose metaphysical conclusions and can be resolved into them. Philosophy can, therefore, exercise a general and, so to speak, constitutional governance over the specialized empirical sciences.

We should also briefly note the relations between philosophy and theology. Since the latter entails man's participation in knowledge proper to God and transcending our natural powers, it is superior to any purely human science, including philosophy. By faith we know God, not merely in His abstract relations with us such as First Cause, but in *His own divine life* insofar as revealed to us and comprehensible by us. Where philosophy presents God as Being, dogmatic theology presents God as God. Theology can, therefore, judge and govern philosophy in something like the way that philosophy can judge and govern the special sciences. But just as the scientist is entitled to his own appropriate working methods and premises, so is the philosopher. It is confusing and unfortunate when, now and then, well-meaning apologists use Christian doctrine to prove a philosophical point or seek to establish either by science or metaphysics what revelation alone can establish. It is quite in order, however, for theologians to use certain truths proved by philosophy in their demonstrations. By the same token, the theologian needs the instrumental help of a valid philosophical system.

"Catholic Philosophy"

Some commentators object to this phrase on the grounds that Catholicism is a theology. Much of the philosophy historically associated with it predates Christianity by centuries. The word "Catholic," from the Greek *katholikos,* means "universal." It is used in designating the Church of Christ because He commanded that the Church should teach all of His doctrines in all lands in all times — that is, it should be catholic in scope, place, and duration. The creed refers to *unam sanctam catholicam et apostolicam ecclesiam.*

The question is what entities "Catholic" as an adjective (or "non-Catholic") can reasonably qualify. Stores in Paris used to sell what they called Existentialist hats. Sartre, the founder of Existentialism, objected that it is a philosophy and that, therefore, only philosophical positions can be called existentialist or nonexistentialist — not hats, eagles, battleships, or anything else one might think of. Catholicity, similarly, can reasonably be predicated or denied only of certain things. One can justly say of a book on religion that it is or is not Catholic, for example, but a novel cannot be so classified except that it can be written by a Catholic or deal with a Catholic issue.

Just as the phrase "Catholic truth" is awkward and redundant, truth being truth, so "Catholic philosophy" is not completely accurate. A system of philosophy can be Catholic in the sense that it has arisen within the Church and/or is compatible with revealed truths of theology. We shall see in Chapters Three through Five, however, that the notion of *a* Catholic philosophy is very false. "Christian philosophy" is a more common approach. It is strange to see all sorts of beliefs described as "the Scholastic view." Scholastic philosophy is defined more by chronology and aim than by contents. This was a series of efforts in the Middle Ages to harmonize faith and reason, especially in regard to the Platonic-Aristotelian heritage. As will be seen later, almost every metaphysical stance can be found among the Scholastics. The system that finally rose to preeminence is Thomism, to be treated in our Chapter Four.

It is no accident that the problem of relating theology and philosophy — or, more broadly, faith and reason — has exercised the best minds of the Church through the centuries and has given rise to divergent views. The problem is multifaceted and needs almost endless qualification of any statement. For example: It is necessary, especially for "interfaith dialogue," to preserve strictly the boundaries between philosophy and theology as we have discussed them. The Catholic, however, will be aware of certain other considerations which may be difficult to convey to those outside the fold. For one thing, from a psychological standpoint faith and reason are blended, like the ingredients in a salad, the taste of which is in nowise the simple sum of the tastes of its isolated ingredients. For another thing, the unity of truth is always a key factor. If faith and reason were taking us in opposite directions, the problem would be entirely different from what it actually is. In moments of deep insight, the torch of truth burns by its own brilliance. Methodological considerations, rightly important to beginners, are transcended.

Truth being one, we cannot rule out the possibility that natural reason might demonstrate to some men what others could not know without revelation. This is the case with some men and some doctrines. Again, as we have noted, these truths become blended for the individual in a single system. Thus,

A historian has a perfect right to speak of a Christian philosophy in a wide sense, or rather of an amalgam of Christian philosophies, to indicate systems which have arisen since the advent of Christianity and are formed in a Christian atmosphere. For example, the metaphysical notion of person has benefited from Trinitarian beliefs, which brought it home to people that a personal life is inconceivable without an interpersonal one, and Christianity encouraged the acceptance of a sort of intersubjective organism unknown to the ancients which gives an altogether fresh depth to the concepts borrowed by the Fathers from Greek philosophy.[9]

PHILOSOPHY AND ACTION

Having cited various sources of knowledge about education and discussed their interrelations, we are brought back to the important question with which we started: Is philosophy *relevant?* Philosophy texts often start by stating that, instead of being given an important body of truth, the readers will be given a prolonged quibble about its definition. Instead of being shown how matters stand, they will be told what positions various philosophers have taken, and nothing beyond this. There may even be a joke about blind men searching in dark rooms for nonexisting black cats. One could hardly blame a reader who pursued the book no further!

Some people insist on the value of knowledge for its own sake. Perhaps they do not mean quite what they say, but simply wish to disavow a utilitarianism which insists that the useful is the good and that information which "will not bake any bread" within a short time is wasted. Of *course* philosophy (and theology) should be expressed in action! To believe one way and live another is sin or schizophrenia. In the dialogue on the ideal state, Socrates' companion, Glaucon, questioned the value of the whole conversation on the grounds that, human nature being as is, the ideal state will never be achieved. Socrates asked, "Would a painter be any the worse because, after having delineated with consummate art an ideal of a perfectly beautiful man, he was unable to show that any such man could ever existed?" Having won Glaucon's acknowledgment that "He would be none the worse," Socrates pursued: "And is our theory a worse theory because we are unable to prove the possibility of a city being ordered in the manner described?"[10]

---

[9] Maurice Nedoncelle, *Is There a Christian Philosophy?* trans. by Illtyd Trethowan (New York: Hawthorn Books, 1960), Vol. 10, *Twentieth Century Encyclopedia of Catholicism*, p. 149.

[10] Plato, *The Republic, op. cit.,* p. 197.

When we know the ideal, at least we know in what direction we should be aiming. No baseball player always hits the ball. Each player settles for a batting average. Before achieving his batting average, however, he must understand that he is supposed to hit the ball. Philosophy cannot live the good life for us but it can play a major role in helping us know what the good life is.

The chief question here is whether principles are to be judged by practice or vice versa. Realism and pragmatism are, practically speaking, the two philosophic forces that between them divide up American education, as they divide up American life in general. The basic issue between them is whether principles are to be judged by practice, as pragmatists hold, or practice by principles, as realists hold. Judging is itself an intellectual function. Our chapter on Instrumentalism will discuss the pragmatist's plight of leaving himself no way to judge practices or consequences. For now, suffice it to say that suspicions of the relevance of philosophy usually derive from pragmatist thinking. Those who consider themselves realists but are very dubious of theory in general and especially of philosophy are advertising to the world that they are really pragmatists. There would be less confusion in their own minds and the minds of those whom they influence, if they would call themselves what they really are. Note again that the realist does not say that philosophy should not be carried out in action. He simply denies that its operational consequences constitute its ultimate validation or refutation.

"PHILOSOPHY OF EDUCATION"

What is the philosophy of education? What, for that matter, is the philosophy "of" anything? Even an abridged dictionary lists fourteen means for "of." "About or pertaining to," for all its vagueness, probably comes closest. The point may seem hairsplitting, but there is reason to believe that applications "of" philosophy to history, education, science, and the like, have often resulted in mixtures of the philosophical and nonphilosophical in such fashion that one cannot easily tell which is which or why.

Approximately, the philosophy *of* a branch of knowledge consists in a systematic statement of the philosophical principles underlying it, and in some tracing of issues in that division of knowledge to these principles. The latter do not come from the field to be treated, since philosophy is philosophy. There is today a widespread and seriously mistaken notion that this discipline can somehow be denatured, watered down into something much easier than itself, yet still remain itself. Many contemporary treatises on "school and society" and that sort of thing stem from this kind of wishful thinking. It is fine to write or read nonphilosophical treatises on education — but, again, let us call things what they are! The epistemology of education, for example, is no different from the epistemology, say, of history, if regarded intrinsically. The applications constitute the variable. There are divergent philosophies of education (or of any given field) not so much because philosophers in these fields see different specialized issues or work from different facts, as because they start from different metaphysical systems.

We defined education as the empirical science of the teaching-learning process. The educand is a human being. The philosophy of man is concerned with what, in the last analysis, it means to be a human being. Education aims at knowledge. Epistemology is concerned with the origin, nature, grounds, methods, and limits, of human knowledge. Education, again, leads students to accept certain attitudes, appreciations, values. Axiology and ethics are concerned with the nature, source, and grounds of values.

Almost every major debated issue in education leads directly into philosophy. You can demonstrate this for yourself. Think of some practical problem that seems to be of special importance in education today. Then call to mind the fundamental solutions which divergent groups have proposed for it. Then reflect upon what question, basically, the answer would logically turn. This will usually prove to be a philosophical question or to rest upon one. Academic freedom and indoctrination are examples. How do they differ? When, if ever, should a teacher indoctrinate, and why? To attempt to resolve such issues without philosophical analysis is to build one's house on quicksand.

THEOLOGY OF EDUCATION

We earlier remarked certain relations between philosophy and theology. To reflect upon these points is to see that a complete and satisfactory system of thought on education cannot omit theological premises. Most philosophies mirror either theism or atheism. If philosophy has something to say about the nature of man, so does theology, as also about the nature of knowledge, the aims of education, its proper agencies, and so forth.

The present volume is primarily philosophical. Nevertheless,

> Theology, as the wisdom of Christian life and thought, must have an essential relation to Christian education. It is imperative to understand the relationship existing between theology and Christian education in general before attempting to apply this wisdom to any particular educational problems.[11]

Theology affirms of man that his material body is governed by a spiritual soul, in virtue of which he was powers of understanding and free choice. It further affirms that he was created to know, love, and serve God in this life, so as to be happy forever with Him in the life to come. It further affirms that divine grace is a supernatural help which always helps man and yet never forces him in his relations with God, and that salvation would be impossible without grace. These are the essential truths about man around which everything in education, indeed, in life, should revolve. Philosophy and psychology may have much to say in defining free will and observing the factors that limit it, but they err if at any point they simply deny the phenomenon. Epistemology may teach us much about the limits and conditions of our knowledge of the objective world, but it errs if at any point it denies the possibility of such knowledge. Science may remind us repeatedly that we know nothing empirically about heaven, but it errs if it denies that the whole point of our existence is to get there. The encyclical of Pius XI on Christian education is a systematic theological treatise on education. For a larger study the reader is referred to Donlan's *Theology and Education.*[12]

Since we expect primarily a Catholic readership, we shall draw unhesitatingly upon theological sources whenever the point under consideration can profit thereby. One advantage of this is that philosophy can thus be rightly placed in the total unity and hierarchy of knowledge. There is then the hope of a Wisdom in the classical sense. Nevertheless, because of their distinct methods, questions, and purposes, and because we are addressing ourselves in part to non-Catholic readers, the two disciplines (theology and philosophy) will be carefully distinguished wherever there might be any doubt.

---

[11] Thomas C. Donlan, *Theology and Education* (Dubuque: Wm. C. Brown Co., 1952), p. 10.

[12] Donlan, *op. cit.*

In such instances, we shall also permit ourselves to make use of dogmatic facts and of the mind of the Church.[13] A dogmatic fact in theology is a truth not explicitly revealed but so connected with revealed dogmas that to deny it would be in effect to deny an article of faith. For example, it is not explicitly revealed that Paul VI is the legitimate successor of St. Peter, but to deny this would be to deny the doctrine of the Apostolic succession.

SUMMARY

Following our initial look at a basic conflict in American education, this chapter has sought to make the student method-conscious regarding educational philosophy as a field of study. This has been done by discussing the sources of knowledge about education, including philosophy, and their interrelations. The special problem of "Catholic philosophy" was discussed in this connection. Second, we talked about the exact character of the philosophy of education, its relevance to practical policies and actions, and the like. Our next chapter will apply the key notions encountered thus far to the bewildering contemporary educational scene. We now have a map to take along as we explore.

BIBLIOGRAPHY

Broudy, Harry S., *Building a Philosophy of Education*, 2 ed. (Englewood Cliffs, N. J.: Prentice-Hall, 1961).

Donlan, Thomas C., *Theology and Education* (Dubuque: William C. Brown Co., 1952).

Hocking, William E., *Types of Philosophy* (New York: Charles Scribner's Sons, 1929).

Johnston, Herbert, *A Philosophy of Education* (New York: McGraw-Hill Co., 1963), Chap. 1.

Lewis, Clarence I., *An Analysis of Knowledge and Valuation* (La Salle, Ill.: Open Court Publishing Co., 1946).

Nedoncelle, Maurice, *Is There a Christian Philosophy?* trans. by Illtyd Trethowan, Vol. 10, *Twentieth Century Encyclopedia of Catholicism* (New York: Hawthorne Books, 1960).

Pius XI, *Encyclical Letter on Christian Education of Youth* (Washington, D. C.: National Catholic Welfare Conference, 1936).

---

[13] The term "dogmatic" may confuse some readers, since one meaning it has come to have is "asserting opinions as if they were facts, or being overpositive in manner." When we speak of such matters as dogmatic theology, the term means "pertaining to dogma." A dogma, in this sense, is a revealed truth. There is an incidental relationship between the two senses, but one can certainly be dogmatic (treat of dogma) without being dogmatic in the looser sense. Dogmas are not matters of opinion, but of knowledge.

Plato, *The Republic,* V, trans. by Benjamin Jowett (Cleveland: World Publishing Co., 1946).

Sheen, Fulton J., *God and Intelligence in Modern Philosophy* (Garden City, N. Y.: Image Books, 1958).

Smith, Vincent E., *The School Examined: An Essay on the Curriculum* (Milwaukee: The Bruce Publishing Co., 1960).

Van Ackeren, Gerald F., *Sacra Doctrina* (Rome: Catholic Book Agency 1952).

CHAPTER THREE

Early Christian Educational Theory

THE PLATONIC STRAND

WITH the rise of Christianity, philosophy had a new competitor in the struggle for men's minds: faith. Faith is believing all that God has revealed *because* He has revealed it. This problem did not appear all at once, of course. The Old Testament records a gradual disclosure of God's nature and His plan for men to the prophets of the Jewish people. But the revelation entrusted to them was cumulative and incomplete. It culminated in Christ and His Church. Here, for the first time, the full outlines of God's covenant with man were seen. And here was something that, unlike philosophy, was more than human.

Those who accepted the divinity of Christ and believed His teachings had no further need to seek out *ultimate* truth. The Christian, in saying he "has the truth," does not mean that he knows all the secrets of heaven and earth, but that he has a basic disclosure from God of His nature and His plan for man. This knowledge is held with much residue of mystery. Revelation raises many questions besides those it answers. Nevertheless, the Christian knows where he came from and what should be his basic goal in life. Difficult epistemological questions remain, however: Now that we have the fullness of revelation, do we need philosophy? Do we need natural reason at all? If so, where does it fit in? How does it relate to revealed knowledge?

Two opposed viewpoints began to take shape. Antirationalists argued that it was unnecessary and presumptuous for man to exercise his puny mind much, now that God had spoken. Others argued that all knowledge is good, that faith helps us to grasp more

38

clearly and quickly what we know by reason. Why, they asked, did God give us this gift of reason, if not to be used?

One finds this disagreement running through the first few centuries of Christian education with special force. Tertullian (d. A.D. 230) typified the first, or antirational, viewpoint. Wrote he, "With our faith, we desire no further belief. For this is our . . . faith, that there is nothing which we ought to believe besides."[1] St. Basil said to his old teachers, the classics, "If ever I learned anything from you, I have forgotten it." Clement of Alexandria (150–215) and Origen (185–254) advocated the "intellectualist" viewpoint, a wedding of Christian wisdom and classical learning. St. Jerome (331–420), despite his antirationalism, gave us the Vulgate translation of Scripture, an unassailable model of scholarship that is still used. Ambrose (340–397) helped the intellectualist cause, not so much by an advocacy of classical literature as by showing that Christian teaching itself could and should be cast in scholarly form. Chrysostom (344–401), asked if Christians should "give up literature," replied negatively, but added, "we must not kill souls."

One could debate which faction won that "war." Indeed, it could be said that the struggle still continues. When we contemplate the extreme possibilities, however, and think in terms of basic metaphysical positions, it seems clear that the antirationalists lost ground. Evidence and reason play major roles in establishing that a divine revelation exists. Second, while divine assurance is necessary to establish beyond doubt that the mysteries of Christian doctrine are true, reason can show that they are plausible — that is, free from internal contradiction and harmonious with established knowledge. Third, reason can suggest metaphors and analogies which cast some light on revealed mysteries, though certainly not "explaining" them. In short, reason is with us the whole way. Since natural reason comes from the same God who provided the deposit of faith, why not trust it in all that pertains to its sphere? Since intelligence is the very thing that makes us human, why not exercise it to the full?

While the Christians pondered what to do with philosophy, some people sought to turn Christianity itself into simply another of the competing philosophies. Some pagan scholars of ancient Rome tried to water down Christ's teachings into a naturalistic and pagan

---

[1] *The Writings of Q. S. F. Tertullianus,* trans. by Peter Holmes (Edinburgh: T. and T. Clark, 1870), vol. II, p. 10.

system of thought, just as some writers do today. In those days, such writers did not have the audacity to call themselves Christians. Perhaps these ill-conceived efforts were valuable in an unintended way. They provided further incentive for the Church to emphasize that, while Christianity is not a philosophy, *anything that is true and good can be part of Christian education.* When, after the Dark Ages, peace was restored in Europe, the Church began to establish institutions of the sort now called universities. One saw the faith-reason controversy reflected in their activities and offerings, but the very fact that "secular" studies were offered at all showed that, in a larger sense, the controversy was over and the antirationalists had lost. In the beautiful cathedrals of the Middle Ages we sometimes see the relations of the various intellectual disciplines symbolized in stone carvings. Queen of the sciences was theology, the study of God and the things of God. These granite and marble portrayals show theology surrounded by the arts and sciences of the time — logic, arithmetic, grammar, music, and so forth. Natural science, social science, the liberal arts, and Christian doctrine, were all parts of the mosaic of Christian education that took shape.

But what philosophy was to be the handmaid of theology? It would have to preserve an irreducible distinction between God and creation, between matter and spirit, between natural and super-natural. Christian thought finds unity, perfect and absolute, in the Source of the universe, but not, as so much of modern thought does, in the universe itself.

Christian thought, that is to say, cannot logically be reconciled with monism, although such a reconciliation has often been attempted. Monism is any system of thought which regards reality as reducible to or explainable by one principle — whether mind, matter, energy, or something else. Catholics who seek to fit their faith into a monistic framework would do well to review the encyclical of Pius XII, *Humani Generis.* The encyclical criticizes those who, while scorning Scholastic thought,

> extol other philosophies of all kinds, ancient and modern, oriental and occidental, by which they seem to imply that any kind of philosophy or theory, with a few additions and corrections if need be, can be reconciled with Catholic dogma. No Catholic can doubt how false this is, especially where there is question of those fictitious theories they call immanentism,

or idealism, or materialism, whether historic or dialectic, or even existentialism, whether atheistic or simply the type that denies the validity of the reason in the field of metaphysics.[2]

Note that all of the philosophies mentioned as intrinsically contrary to Catholic thought are monistic.

At least in the sense indicated earlier, then, Christian thought must be dualistic. There are a number of varieties of dualism, however, which can be and have been applied to Christian thought. They all deny that God can be reduced to the universe, thought to extension. and so forth, and are therefore satisfactory in that important respect.

One variety of dualism is that of Plato (427–347 B.C.), who is usually held to have stated that the forms or natures of things exist apart from the things themselves, although he does not appear to have explicitly said that anywhere. Knowledge in the truest sense is concerned with these eternal forms or Ideas. By the same token, it cannot be either from or about the physical world presented by our senses, since that is a relative and ever fluctuating world. But if we do not know from the senses and from experience, what possibility remains? Plato concluded that we are born with certain innate ideas from a previous existence of the soul, and we learn by a reminiscing process, remembering what we already know. The most that the senses do is somehow start this reminiscing process, guide it a bit.

Aristotle kept Plato's Ideas as "Forms," but held that Plato did not make sufficient allowance for the material and concrete. Where modern thought has tended to give us a world without meaning, Platonism tends to meaning without a world. Instead of a real knower learning about a real world, Plato gives us a soul that pre-existed its union with the body and knows basically about a world other than the one in which the body lives.[3]

Among metaphysical positions predating Christianity, Platonism and Aristotelianism between them pretty well divide the field of

[2] *Humani Generis* (Washington, D. C.: National Catholic Welfare Conference, 1950), p. 15.

[3] Since Plato was a more subtle and poetic writer than the somewhat prosaic Aristotle, it is always difficult to be certain about his meanings. In any case, the writings of the man himself are probably more reliable than those of his commentators, as regards the question of what he "really meant." It is possible that Plato and Aristotle really held the same metaphysical positions, but that Aristotle expressed them more accurately and scientifically.

basic outlooks between which Christian thought can choose. For the most part, the first Christian philosophers leaned to Plato. This is understandable, since he had a sharper, deeper sense of the spiritual than did Aristotle, his pupil.

NEO-PLATONISM

Something called neo-Platonism also appeared. Perhaps it was poorly named, for it is not simply a slight modification of Platonic thought, but is quite a distinctive outlook, albeit a difficult one to fathom or describe. Neo-Platonists tried to harmonize Plato's views (and some of Aristotle's) with certain Oriental concepts. It is doubtful that the author of *The Republic* would have recognized his philosophy in much of this. As Feibleman suggests, "Plato's work casts a long shadow, and his name has not always been written on it."[4] Neo-Platonism made itself felt through the Jewish philosophers, then the Greeks, Moslems, and Christians. One writer insists that "Plato's own theology has never been tried in religion."[5]

Neo-Platonism is a difficult philosophy to expound because it verges upon mysticism. It has a seemingly pantheistic aspect in premising that God is "the One" above being, but conferring it upon finite things. The Platonic Ideas or Forms become thoughts in the mind of God. Matter, always a source of embarrassment for Plato, becomes the source of evil, somewhat as in Christian Science as developed by Mary Baker Eddy. The way that God "spills over" into things according to the neo-Platonists is called *emanation*. This was a major concept of Plotinus (205–270), an Egyptian philosopher. While poetry and philosophy are often indistinguishable in this school of thought, this concept of emanation reminds one too much of a physical process such as that by which uranium and certain other elements emit radiant energy.

CHRISTIAN PLATONISM

Neo-Platonism has been called both "the last of the pagan philosophies" and "a stage in the history of religion." It refuses to fit readily into any Procrustean bed. Plotinus, for example, although

---

[4] James K. Feibleman, *Religious Platonism* (London: George Allen and Unwin Ltd., 1959), p. 147.
[5] *Ibid.,* p. 148.

not a Christian writer, was concerned with how the human soul can regain its lost estate. Again, he thought of intellect as the image of God, which is similar to a point of Christian teaching.

In general, Plato's thought was a handy defense for Christians against pagan materialism. They also found help in Plotinus' view that there is a spiritual world more real than the world of matter. It was understandable, therefore, if sometimes Christian thinkers borrowed indiscriminately from both Platonic and neo-Platonic strands of thought. But neo-Platonism leads at last to pantheism. St. Augustine, who had the writings of Plotinus in Latin translation, excluded from his own "Platonism" some tenets he found incompatible with Christianity. It was mainly Platonism, as distinct from and sometimes opposed to neo-Platonism, that was seriously influential in Christian thought.

AUGUSTINE OF HIPPO

Early Christian thought was shaped by a number of men whose philosophies fell basically in the Platonic strain: Origen, Nemesius, Pseudo-Dionysius. But the great name here is St. Augustine's. Not to have read his *Confessions* is to have missed an authentic masterpiece. His writing is interesting, partly because, although he can be called a Platonist, he is constantly thinking for himself. He was equally capable of deathless maxims and of sophistical and irritating digressions.

Augustine's educational thought is chiefly summed up in two works, *De Doctrina Christiana* and *De Magistro*. In the former, he begins with the announcement that "The entire treatment . . . is based on two factors: the method of discovering what we are to understand, and the method of teaching what has been understood."[6] Of these two blades in the pedagogue's scissors, Augustine considers the first more difficult.

St. Augustine had reasons for subordinating the instructional half. He did not believe, first, that the principles for communicating revealed truth are different from those for communicating natural truth. Second, his Platonism distinguished a knowledge *about* things from a knowledge *of* things. Instruction gives the first, but this must take root in the more intimate knowledge "from the inside," as it

---

[6] *De Doctrina Christiana,* IV, sec. 1, tr. J. J. Gavigan, *The Fathers of the Church* (New York, 1947).

were. The Christian, with the help of divine grace, has a knowledge *of* God without which religious instruction would be valueless.

In Augustine's pedagogical ideas, we can see both his philosophy and his own career. He was for a long time a professor of rhetoric. His intellectual conviction of the limits of Ciceronian wisdom was in everlasting conflict with his constitutional inability to keep from appreciating a well-turned phrase.

Augustine was habitually concerned with the problem of language, the role of symbols in communication and thought. He makes certain points that might seem overstressed to us today, but he was combating a superstitious pagan outlook which saw signs in things. (Such superstition still exists somewhat today.) Augustine turned his full scorn upon all books of soothsayers and diviners, all amulets and charms. He criticizes various "magic" cures for hiccups, some of which are still in use at this writing.

Augustine wanted the Christian to use the things of this world, while keeping them always in a theological perspective. Above all, the Christian should, he felt, pay attention to languages. Hebrew and Greek are required to understand Scripture well, and thought in any realm is enlarged by linguistic expertise.

History was also stressed. Augustine saw history as a record of "things which have now passed away and cannot be revoked." Geography, natural history, and astronomy were also seen by him as important, though less so. Certain practical arts were included in his recommended curriculum as "signs of the times."

Both material and formal logic were recommended by the saint. One would expect him to advocate stress on grammar, and he does. Mathematics is recommended, and he insists on its objective character. Philosophy, chiefly Platonic, is recommended. He suggested the formula, "Nothing in excess,"[7] and context suggests that he considered the interest excessive when the learner was applying the material primarily for this-worldly purposes.

The *De Doctrina Christiana* also deals with the communication of truth, but Augustine's principles on this subject are more neatly summed in the *De Magistro*.[8] This dialogue between the fifth-century bishop and his 15-year-old son, Adeodatus, might be regarded as a

---

[7] *Ibid.*, II, sec. 58.

[8] St. Aurelius Augustine, *De Magistro* (Concerning the Teacher), trans. by George G. Leckie (New York: D. Appleton-Century, 1938).

negative answer to the question, "Can one man teach another?" Later, as we shall see, St. Thomas Aquinas penned a treatise to answer the same question affirmatively, but their positions are not so terribly far apart. Augustine's treatise was a reaction, largely, to the notion that knowledge is something the teacher somehow places inside the pupil. It was a somewhat one-sided reaction, and Thomas was concerned to correct the one-sidedness.

Since the *De Magistro* is a short and interesting work and one of the few great basic documents on education, the reader is urged to go through it completely. However, we shall pick up the main threads of its argument and evaluate them.

CAN ONE MAN TEACH ANOTHER?

One way to understand a detective story is to turn first to the back of the book and get the basic plot, then go back and weave through the hints tossed out by the author to challenge the reader's wits. At the end of the *De Magistro,* we find Augustine (who has been talking for a long time since his son interrupted) saying:

> men are mistaken, so that they call those teachers who are not, merely because for the most part there is no delay between the time of speaking and the time of cognition. And since after the speaker has reminded them, the pupils quickly learn within, they think that they have been taught outwardly by him who prompts them.[9]

Certain key terms here deserve note: *reminded*. Why not *told?* One recognizes Plato's reminiscence theory of learning. The teacher can at most cause the pupil to remember. But if the pupil does not know something he cannot remember it and the teacher will, in trying to impart it, fail. *Within*. The pupils learn within. Why this emphasis? Where else would they learn? Augustine is here pointing to the function of intelligence, which the learner supplies. Moreover, he is suggesting innate ideas learned by reminiscence. *Prompts*. This is the teacher's function: to remind, to feed cues to the forgetful actor.

The teacher does this chiefly by words and other symbols. Augustine calls them signs. Most of the dialogue is, accordingly, a discourse upon signs. It is Augustine at his best and worst. Sometimes he labors the obvious at length; then he may suddenly pounce upon us with some tremendous insight. Not until Chapter IX does Augus-

---

[9] *Ibid.,* p. 55.

tine begin to "zero in" on his target. He argues that an idea is more important than the sign of the idea, and in some sense *prior to it.* He suggests, indeed, that

> there is nothing which is learned by means of signs. For when a sign is given me, if it finds me not knowing of what thing it is a sign, it can teach me nothing, but if it finds me knowing the thing of which it is the sign, what do I learn from the sign?[10]

The argument is a telling one, similar to those encountered in some modern educational psychology texts, which stress that the child does not "get meaning from the printed page," but *brings meaning to it.* Anyone who regards this, as many do, as a modern discovery, would do well to read the *De Magistro.*

A hearer or reader is confronted with some actualized, concretized symbols. These have been spoken, written, stamped in braille, in some way materialized. The receiver identifies them as the symbols they are (not necessarily by a conscious process) and then associates meanings with them, not usually exactly the same meanings intended by the writer or speaker. Suppose you say to me, "cow." One of two things is the case: I know what a cow is, or I do not. If I do not know, the word you have spoken does not help me. If I *do* know, your word has simply pointed to something I already had within me. You might, however, say, "There is a cow eating your grass," and tell me something I did not know. To understand your statement, I must understand what grass is, what eating is, and so forth; I must understand *all the elements* of what you say. But you have *put them in a new set of relationships,* which is what most teaching amounts to. This aspect of communication is neglected by Augustine, as we shall see later in considering St. Thomas' comments on the same subject.

What was Augustine chiefly concerned to demonstrate here? He wanted to show that the learner provides the intelligence which forms the ideas, and that the teacher at most "assigns" the intelligence its specific tasks. The teacher does not provide either the truth to be known or the pupil's mind which knows it. At first blush, this position may appear curiously similar to that of the instrumentalists, who have tended to deny the teacher any significant causal role in the learning process. But St. Augustine's ideas of the nature of truth and of the man who gets the truth are radically different from those

---

[10] *Ibid.,* pp. 43–44.

of John Dewey and his followers. The *De Magistro* is a kind of hymn to the intelligence. It is as if the gifted saint is saying, "See how inexplicable all theories of teaching and of learning become until you postulate this fundamental spiritual power!"

The related distinction between knowledge "of" and "about" things, which figured in the *De Doctrina Christiana,* appears also in *De Magistro.* A human teacher, so far as he can be said to teach at all, does so from without. Christ teaches from within. The chief point here is a relation rather than a contrast, however: For

> even though I speak about true things, I still do not teach him who beholds the true things, for he is taught not through my words but by means of the things themselves which God reveals within the soul.[11]

A contrast is also made between the outward procedures by which men teach and the means by which souls in heaven are illumined. Adeodatus, if he has any doubts, applies a bit of his father's premises by saying that there is nothing "about which the inner oracle does not tell me what your words stated."[12]

AUGUSTINE'S THOUGHT AND APPROACH

There is a curiously contemporary tone to Augustine's *De Magistro* and to the portions of *De Doctrina Christiana* that deal with the role of signs. In our day, Susanne Langer, S. I. Hayakawa, Alfred Korzybski, and many others, have addressed themselves to his problem (Can there be meaning prior to the sign?) and have evolved methods of linguistic analysis remarkably similar to those of the early African bishop.

At the same time, St. Augustine's thought has been subjected to many inaccurate statements by naturalistic commentators. It has even been claimed that he denied the supernatural, which is nonsense. It is true that, in most of his writing, one does not get the painstaking differentiation of faith and reason, natural and supernatural, that was to mark some later writers. Augustine was much more concerned with the overall mosaic they formed, so preoccupied with its beauty and mysteries that he had little time for sorting out sources and methods.

It has been said of him and he said of himself that his thought revolved between two poles: God and the self. Augustine says in

---

[11] *Ibid.,* pp. 49–50.
[12] *Ibid.,* p. 56.

his *Confessions* that he found in the writings of Plotinus a bridge
to the doctrine of the Word as taught in St. John's Gospel:

> Thou procuredst for me . . . certain books of the Platonists, translated
> from Greek into Latin. And therein I read, not indeed in the very words,
> but to the very same purpose, enforced by many and diverse reasons, that
> In the beginning was the Word, and the Word was with God, and the Word
> was God.[13]

Basically, St. Augustine takes Plato's doctrine of innate ideas and
supernaturalizes it. One writer has said the gist of the *De Magistro*
is that all knowledge comes directly or indirectly from God. Centuries later, Pius XI wrote that "every form of pedagogic naturalism
which in any way excludes or weakens supernatural Christian formation in the teaching of youth, is false."[14] Augustine is not arguing
for infused knowledge.[15] But he is borrowing from Plotinus at
least to the extent that he sees knowledge as involving a divine
illumination.[16]

MODERN INFLUENCES OF AUGUSTINIAN EDUCATIONAL THOUGHT

It is very difficult to trace the influences of St. Augustine on education through the ages. First, some of his educational theories do
not have direct consequences for classroom procedure. Second, to
compare any two great Christian philosopher-theologians is to find
many basic similarities. One need but read St. Thomas Aquinas'
frequent and generous references to St. Augustine to see how much
the former borrowed (always with full acknowledgment) from the
latter. Some secularist writers have characterized as "Augustinian"
positions that are simply Christian. Nevertheless, some things can
be said.

Aims. Basically, the aims of Augustinian education are those of
Catholic education in general. In a more proximate sense, the Augustinian teacher will think of education as chiefly a drawing-out
(*educare,* to educe or bring out) of what is innate in the learner,

---

[13] Aurelius Augustine, *The Confessions of Saint Augustine,* trans. by Edward B.
Pusey (New York: Pocket Books), p. 115.

[14] Pius XI, *Encyclical Letter on Christian Education of Youth* (Washington, D. C.:
National Catholic Welfare Conference, 1936), p. 24.

[15] That is, knowledge independent of experience and directly provided by God.

[16] St. Augustine is also reminiscent of Aristotle in his steadfast repudiation of
skepticism. The former refuted the skeptics of the Third Academy by arguing that
probability (not such a modern concept!) is "like truth," and, therefore, whoever
speaks of probability shows that he has a concept of what truth is.

of what Christ teaches from within. He will rely heavily upon symbols and discourse and probably look with some scorn upon the "experience curriculum." Pius XI warned against stress on a drawing-out approach. Many people, he wrote, "with, it would seem, too great insistence on the etymological meaning of the word, pretend to draw education out of human nature itself and evolve it by its own unaided powers."[17] Significantly, however, the Holy Father pointed to St. Augustine himself to correct such a tendency:

> Such easily fall into error, because, instead of fixing their gaze on God, first principle and last end of the whole universe, they fall back upon themselves, becoming attached exclusively to passing things of earth; and thus their restlessness will never cease till they direct their attention and their efforts to God, the goal of all perfection, according to the profound saying of Saint Augustine, "Thou didst create us, O Lord, for Thyself, and our heart is restless till it rest in Thee."

Curriculum. We have seen how the liberal arts of Greco-Roman heritage were assimilated to Christian education, after the struggle between the rationalists and antirationalists was basically resolved. Classical humanism proved quite apt for a grafting of the golden branch of the order of grace. The basic idea became: Make theology central to everything. Then, take classicism and make the best of it. To a large extent, this has tended to be the pattern of Catholic education through the centuries. The Augustinian epistemology makes it reasonable to stress subjects with the greatest transfer value.

Methods. We have seen that Augustinianism logically calls for the drawing-out approach, the assumption that all knowledge the pupil will ever demonstrate is already in him. "Experience" is not so important in this drawing-out as thought. Perhaps the closest contemporary approach to Augustinian *method* is in the "great books" programs stimulated by Robert Hutchins and Mortimer Adler.

There is a methodological implication in a contrast between Augustine and Aquinas — not so much the Plato *versus* Aristotle issue as that of philosophical anthropology *versus* "pure" philosophy. Joseph Pieper suggests:

> A chance perusal of any of Augustine's writings, even a page from his most abstract work, *On the Trinity*, will convey the unmistakable impression: this was thought and written by a man of flesh and blood. But let someone take a similar glimpse into the tight structure of the *Summa Theologica* of St. Thomas Aquinas, and he will be tempted to ask: Were

---

[17] Pius XI, *op. cit.*, p. 4.

these sentences really set down by a living man or did not rather the objective content formulate itself undisturbed — neither blurred nor warmed — by the breath of a living thinker?[18]

Perhaps, *de gustibus, non disputandum est*. In any case, Pius XI stressed that good schools are not so much the result of "good methods" as of good teachers. A teacher who loves life and has a sense for beauty will doubtless "rub off" some of these enthusiasms and appreciations onto his pupils. Here the teacher can especially look to St. Augustine, of whom one professor said, "If he is not the greatest Latin writer who ever lived, he is certainly the greatest man who ever wrote Latin!" A writer of Instrumentalist persuasion acknowledged,

> The world that [Augustine] saw was quite a different place from Aristotle's: it was a cosmos of compassion and love as well as truth and reason. . . . To Augustine, however . . . the world was . . . a place where men are not merely 'rational animals' but spiritual creatures — creations of a divinely inspired act, possessed of a direct linkage to the Absolute.[19]

Agencies.   The Christian schools were in competition with others. It was in the latter days of the Roman empire that "public schools" as we now think of them in America became a common phenomenon. They were intended, however, mainly for the senatorial or knightly classes. Patronage of them by the emperors and local authorities was chancy. The Church at first was hesitant about setting up formal schools, but their need became increasingly clear. From the fifth to the eighth centuries the preponderance of educational effort shifted to the side of the Church. From this historical picture, perhaps, we can learn the lesson that operation of schools by the Church at all levels and in all fields is not an absolute obligation but depends upon local and shifting circumstances.

SUMMARY

This chapter has dealt with early Christian educational thought — its intellectual and cultural context, and the rise of Christian Platonism as exemplified in St. Augustine of Hippo. We considered the historic confrontation of faith and reason, and the problem that arose: Now that we

---

[18] Josef Pieper, *The Silence of St. Thomas,* trans. by John Murray and Daniel O'Connor (New York: Pantheon Books, 1957), p. 3.

[19] Van Cleve Morris, *Philosophy and the American School* (Boston: Houghton Mifflin Co., 1961), p. 61.

have the fullness of revelation, where does reason fit in? How important is it? We saw that the antirational outlook of Tertullian and others, while influential even until today, basically was replaced by a Christian intellectualism.

If philosophy has a place in Christian thought and education, however, what sort of philosophy? It was explained why absolute monisms, whether of pure being or of pure becoming, are incompatible with Christianity. A variety of dualistic systems was acknowledged as hypothetically tenable, and Platonic and Aristotelian systems were briefly contrasted. Neo-Platonism as a development in its own right was also considered.

We then turned to St. Augustine, greatest of the Christian Platonists, whose educational views are largely contained in his *De Doctrina Christiana* and *De Magistro*. We followed his reasoning on the recording of truth and on the meaning-sign relationship in communicating truth. We noted his stress on the role of the learner's spontaneous and God-directed intelligence. Implications of Augustinian education for aims, curriculum, and so forth, were traced.

Augustine represents, in a way, the beginning of the long struggle between Platonic and Aristotelian outlooks in Christian philosophy, educational and otherwise. We shall see in our next chapter what turn the struggle later took.

BIBLIOGRAPHY

Augustine, *The Confessions of St. Augustine,* trans. by Edward B. Pusey (New York: Pocket Books).

———— *De Doctrina Christiana,* IV, trans. by J. J. Gavigan, *The Fathers of the Church* (New York, 1947).

———— *De Magistro* (Concerning the Teacher), trans. by George G. Leckie (New York: D. Appleton-Century, 1938).

Cole, Luella, *A History of Education* (New York: Rinehart, 1950), Chaps. 5–7.

Drane, Mother Francis Raphael, *Christian Schools and Scholars* (New York: Benziger Brothers, 1924).

Feibleman, James K., *Religious Platonism* (London: George Allen and Unwin, Ltd., 1959).

Fremantle, Anne, *The Age of Belief* (New York: Mentor Books, 1954), Chap. 2.

Marique, P. J., *History of Christian Education,* I (New York: Fordham University Press, 1924).

Morris, Van Cleve, *Philosophy and the American School* (Boston: Houghton Mifflin Co., 1961).

Pieper, Josef, *The Silence of St. Thomas,* trans. by John Murray and Daniel O'Connor (New York: Pantheon Books, 1957).

Pius XI, *Encyclical Letter on Christian Education of Youth* (Washington, D. C.: National Catholic Welfare Conference, 1936).

Pius XII, *Humani Generis* (Washington, D. C.: National Catholic Welfare Conference, 1950).

Plato, *The Republic.*

CHAPTER FOUR

Medieval Educational Thought

THE earlier part of the period between the fall of the Roman Empire and the revival of literary learning is often called the Dark Age because of its intellectual stagnation. Like most historical clichés, this one is probably a mixture of fact and legend. For the most part, the medieval "rediscovery of learning" was a rediscovery of Aristotle. Perhaps the situation was never as bad as some writers have suggested. The early Scholastics did have Aristotle's *Organon* (Logic), which Boethius (480–526) had translated into Latin. There is also some reason to believe that some of Aristotle's other teachings had been passed on by word of mouth in Christendom, albeit probably with some distortions.

The Mohammedan conquests brought Aristotle's works into Western Europe. Christian, Muslim, and Jewish thinkers busied themselves from the tenth through the thirteenth centuries with integrating Aristotelian thought into their respective traditions. As might be expected, much confusion and debate ensued within each camp and among them. It was a time of much intellectual ferment and growing pains. One writer has aptly characterized it as "the transition from logic to metaphysics, or from Aristotle as the author of the *Organon* to Aristotle as the author of the *Metaphysics*, the *Physics*, the *De Anima* and the *Ethics*."[1]

However diverse the thought of Roger Bacon, St. Bonaventure, St. Albert the Great, and others of the time, what they all sought was to shed light on Christian faith, to relate it to the culture of their times and to meet the challenge posed by pagan philosophies.

---

[1] Anton C. Pegis, ed., *Basic Writings of Saint Thomas Aquinas* (New York: Random House, 1945), xxxvii.

Some historians and philosophers have complained bitterly that the Scholastics sought to make Aristotle into a Christian theologian, that they missed the real spirit of his ideas, and the like. These criticisms are true from the standpoint of those who make them; it is the standpoint itself that is in error. Such critics view philosophy as the loftiest form of knowledge and all religious doctrine as pure opinion. They see the Christian Church as having been on its last legs in the twelfth and thirteenth centuries, unable to survive the revival of Greek learning except by adopting Aristotle and baptizing him. There is no evidence that the Church would have had to close its doors had it not come to terms with Aristotle. Nor was there any intent on the part of the major Scholastics to misrepresent the positions of the Stagirite. Rather, they simply wished to take from the ancient Greek philosophers (with full acknowledgement) what was good, and fit it into a larger framework of truth. St. Ambrose reminded scholars, "Every truth, whoever said it, comes from the Holy Spirit." Maritain has suggested that "Between Aristotle as viewed in himself and Aristotle viewed in the writings of St. Thomas is the difference which exists between a city seen by the flare of a torchlight procession and the same city bathed in the light of the morning sun."[2] The small mind will wonder what a philosopher "meant in the context of his time," and the like; the large mind simply asks, "What does he *mean?*" To understand St. Thomas' treatment of the ancients, we must understand that this latter was his approach. "He made the thinkers of the past his contemporaries by seeing them in that present which is reality itself."[3] As Pieper notes:

> Thomas would have thought it unbearably self-important had anyone spoken of his "victory" over Averroes or Siger of Brabant. For him, an intellectual dispute was a common striving for the victory, not of one of the contenders, but of truth.[4]

Looking at the history of philosophy in this way, however, it was inevitable that St. Thomas and the other major Scholastics should see it as basically a struggle between the Aristotelian and Platonic

---

[2] Jacques Maritain, *An Introduction to Philosophy* (New York: Sheed and Ward, 1947), p. 99.

[3] Pegis, *op. cit.,* xli.

[4] Josef Pieper, *The Silence of St. Thomas* (New York: Pantheon Books, 1957), p. 22. Cf. St. Thomas Aquinas, *Commentaria in Metaphysicam Aristotelis,* lib. II, lect. I.

viewpoints, so far as natural metaphysics is concerned. The world
might be as Plato had said, it might be as Aristotle had said, but it
could not be both ways. In short, it is pointless and mistaken to

> argue that the Aristotle of St. Thomas is not the Aristotle of history, or
> even the Aristotle of any of the Greek and Arabian commentators. St.
> Thomas knows this, and he has criticized Aristotle often enough to make
> it perfectly clear that he was not proceeding in ignorance of the Aristotle
> of history. He preferred to ignore the failures of such an Aristotle in order
> to save what was true in him.[5]

The primary task of this chapter will be to sketch two major
systems of Scholastic thought and their applications to education:
Thomism and Franciscanism. They are the major, though not the
only, philosophical fruits of the latter Middle Ages, and the two
lasting strains of medieval educational thought.

"THE SPIRIT OF ST. THOMAS"

Our plan will be to present as briefly as possible the metaphysics
of St. Thomas, then his general philosophy of education, and last to
make applications, as in our second chapter, to methodology, agencies, aims, academic freedom, and indoctrination.

Some commentators have found the essence of St. Thomas'
thought in his distinction between possible being (potentiality) and
actual being (act) and his insistence that nothing can be reduced
from potency to act except by something already in act. Others
have found it in his position that essence and existence are really
distinct (although inseparable) in all things except God. One could
find it in either of those places perhaps or even elsewhere. If one
has to make a choice, it might be that his treatment of potency and
act is slightly more fundamental than anything else, since it is the
basis even for his proof of the existence of God.

More profitable than picking out any one such "key" is to realize
that there is a single pattern of thought here. Once one sees it he
can predict what St. Thomas will have to say on any philosophical
subject. Thomas' treatment of potency and act is a study of being
from the standpoint of change; his treatment of essence and existence
studies being from the standpoint of intelligibility. He takes the same
position in both places.

The present writer finds the "spirit of St. Thomas" in his *carefully*

---

[5] Pegis, *op. cit.,* xiv.

qualified dualism. "Modernist" philosophers have thought to solve the mind-body problem when all they have done is to dodge it by grasping only one or the other horn of the dilemma. It is easy to "solve" the mind-body riddle by simply denying either mind or body, but this denial flies in the face of all human experience. Philosophers in the Platonic strain, on the other hand, accommodate the various dualities of experience, but do not reconcile them, do not bring them into adequately explained harmonious relationships. St. Thomas consistently maintained the essential differences between God and creation, nature and supernature, matter and spirit, universal and particular, substance and accident, and so forth, but he *welded* all these dualities into an accordant whole. He gave us a universe in which no phenomenon need be a metaphysical fugitive.

St. Thomas' Philosophy of Man

We have seen in earlier chapters that theories of knowledge depend rather directly upon theories about human nature, which in turn depend upon metaphysical and theological positions.

The gap that appears in Plato's thought between the worlds of being and of becoming is reflected in a corresponding gap between body and soul. Platonism tends to identify the man with his soul, his body something that he is "using," but which is not necessary to make him a man. For St. Thomas, man was preeminently *one* being, although composite. How can this be? Man can be "one-though-two," said St. Thomas, if the whole substance is governed or determined by one cause or principle. This principle is the soul. He did not see the soul, as Descartes and some later thinkers did, as equated with some fragment or aspect of the person, such as consciousness. Rather, it was the governing agency of the entire organism. The body exists in and through the existence of the soul. "That is why we may say that, existentially considered, it is the body that is in the soul, not the soul in the body."[6] Perhaps some philosophers have sought to make this subtle relationship "simple" in a zealous desire to defend it. The best defense is that what is, is possible. Man is not simply matter; he is not simply spirit; he is not matter *plus* spirit. Although St. Thomas held that man's soul is immortal (because it is the principle of operations which transcend

---

[6] Anton C. Pegis, *Introduction to Saint Thomas Aquinas* (New York: Modern Library, 1948), xxii.

matter and which are intrinsically independent of matter), he stead-
fastly held that the state of the separated soul is an unnatural one,
and that if the soul is joined to the body this union is for the good
of the soul, or, better, for the good of the *person,* the whole man,
who knows, *through* his soul and its power of intellect, the essences
and inner being of the things he experiences *through* his body. St.
Thomas was not a Greek philosopher who saw man's end as an
endless contemplation of God by a separated soul, but a Christian
saint who saw man's end as the union of the whole man, body and
soul (remember the Creed tells us of the "resurrection of the body"),
with God. True, this union is brought about by a vision, a knowing,
and hence is primordially achieved through man's spiritual power
of intellect, but we must remember that this "knowing" is a *"loving-
knowing,"* one that spills over into the will of man and, indeed,
completes his whole personality.

From the point of view of epistemology, the important factor of
St. Thomas' thought is that it is *man* who knows, not a disembodied
spirit or brute matter, but a living organism, a spirit-matter composite who is truly *one.* Thus the Angelic Doctor never referred
to man as a *thinker,* but as a *knower.* Pegis suggests that:

> what we call the decline of mediaeval philosophy was really a transition
> from man as a knower to man as a thinker — from man knowing the world
> of sensible things to man thinking abstract thoughts in separation from
> existence. What is thinking but dis-existentialized knowing?[7]

THOMISTIC EPISTEMOLOGY

St. Thomas' epistemology is the facet of his philosophy that leads
most directly into his educational views. For brevity, we shall leave
out of account his treatments of God's perfect Self-knowledge, of
angelic knowledge, of human mystical experience, and some other
special phenomena, and treat of two basic topics: what knowledge
is and how we get it in the ordinary cognitive process.

In a sense, the knower becomes what he knows, for the known is
reproduced in him according to his own nature. Its concrete aspects
are reproduced in his sensations and images, and its substantial and
accidental natures in his ideas. And through judgment he truly becomes *one* with the known, which he *expresses* in a vital act of the
mind. Knowledge is a penetration into being in the sense that the

---

[7] Pegis, *Introduction to Saint Thomas Aquinas, op. cit.,* xxiv.

true and being are convertible. Truth is being as related to a mind, to an intelligence. And everything is knowable insofar as it has being, for nothing cannot be known. Thus Aristotle's epistemology suggests that "the soul is in some manner all things."[8] Both goodness and truth are convertible with being.

Like being, truth is analogical. For,

> when anything is predicated of many things analogically, it is found in only one of them according to its proper nature, and from this one the rest are denominated.[9]

Truth resides in the human intellect, but also in things insofar as they are designed and sustained by the divine intellect. If, then, we speak of truth as residing in the human intellect, there are many truths in many created intellects, or even in any one intellect according to the number of things known. If, however, we speak of truth as residing in the divine intellect, then there is one primary truth which each thing reflects in its own way.

By the same token, truths are eternal only insofar as they exist in the mind of God. If there were no eternal intellect, there would be no eternal truth. Truth has eternity in God's intellect, not in man's.

St. Thomas' theory of how we obtain knowledge is, while profound, rather "uncluttered" in comparison with some theories. Through our senses we know particulars, through our intellect we grasp universals and can compare individuals, *relate* one thing to another. We can then utilize these abstracted universals (concepts) in judgments and deductions. Thomistic epistemology sees being and knowledge as correlative, whereas modern thought tends to see knowledge as a process turned mostly inward upon itself.

There is a mode of experience rather directly referable to immediate stimulation of our sense organs, and analytically distinguishable from our interpretations of things. This is *sensation:* seeing, hearing, touching, etc. In the world are concrete things, *particulars*. A particular is in a place at a certain time. If you prefer to say it occupies a point in space-time, that is all right. It has weight. Potentially, it provides a basis for sense-experience. The *intellect* is a power of the soul (more broadly, of the person), the power of thought. It has both passive and active roles. Intellect is a nonmaterial power which grasps the nonmaterial essences (natures) of

---

[8] Aristotle, *De Anima, ed. cit.,* III, 8 (431b 21).

[9] St. Thomas, *Summa Theologica, ed. cit.,* I, Q. 16, Art. 7.

things. These "things" may be either *substances* (able to exist in themselves) or *accidents* (requiring a substance in which to exist).

A *universal* is any trait or relationship which is able to characterize more than one particular.[10] To abstract is to apprehend mentally the nature of something, apart from all material and individuating conditions.

Abstracting is the heart of human cognition. It deserves to be studied with the utmost care. Nor can it be overstressed that this is a supra-sensuous, spiritual function, and an active one. Various modern philosophies often seem to be viewing abstraction more nearly as the Thomists view it than they really are. Materialistic and induction-dominated notions creep into their thought, with the result that they see abstracting as a sort of additive, piecemeal process. One notices, they say, that certain experiences have certain common elements. One also notices that they have certain differences. By stripping off these differences, layer by layer, and stressing similarities, one arrives at the common denominator. The essential condition according to this view is that *there must be repeated experiences*. (Much of the logic of modern research methodology is based upon this premise.)

But abstracting is not at all like that. As Sheen writes,

> One experience only — that is, one object — is sufficient to form an intelligible species. The idea of metal can be formed from one experience of gold, and is not necessarily dependent on our experiences of brass and iron. . . .[11]

Since this point is surpassingly important and has great bearing on contemporary researches into insightful learning, it is best to let St. Thomas speak for himself on it: ". . . the intellect is not in error concerning [the nature of something]; whereas it may go astray as regards the accompaniments of the essence or quiddity in the thing, either in referring one thing to another, in what concerns composition or division, or also in the process of reasoning." Again, ". . . as regards simple things, in whose definition there is no composition, we cannot be deceived; but if we fail, we fail completely in under-

---

[10] There are other, disconcertingly similar meanings of the term in logic and philosophy with which our present usage should not be confused.

[11] Fulton J. Sheen, *God and Intelligence in Modern Philosophy* (New York: Image Books, 1958), p. 111. This work is very highly recommended for its treatment of intelligence and abstraction.

standing them. . . ."[12] In more contemporary terms we could say that a meaning is indivisible, and that error arises in predication.

The intellect, then, forms concepts by abstracting the universal from the particular. We use these concepts (e.g., "horse") in *judgments*: "This is a horse." *This* (particular, which I can see and touch) *is* (has the nature of) horse-ness (a universal found wherever there are horses). Notice how this judging function combines particular and universal, sense and intellect, concrete and abstract. *A whole person knows a whole thing.* This is different from the Platonic conception of innate ideas, learning by reminiscence, and the essential irrelevance of sense-experience to the real world. Third and last, we make deductions: "This is a horse; therefore, it can be tamed."

Plato had insisted that knowledge, since it ends as intellectual, must surely begin the same way. David Hume, many centuries later, was to insist that, since knowledge begins as sensory, it must surely end as sensory. Thomas sees it as having a sensory beginning but an intellective ending. The abstractive function makes this transition; that is why it is of such great importance. Intelligence is the power that does the abstracting; that is why St. Thomas' epistemology is a kind of hymn to the intelligence.

THOMISTIC PHILOSOPHY OF EDUCATION

With this minimal background we can turn to St. Thomas' directly expressed views on education.[13] One can glean his views on the various facets of the subject from assorted writings which were not specifically devoted to education. Conway has done this in a very admirable text.[14] There is always the danger in such an approach, however, of drawing more, fewer, or different conclusions than the

[12] St. Thomas Aquinas, *op. cit.,* Pt. I, Q. 85, Art. 7. Cf. Aristotle, *Metaphysics,* VIII, 10 (1052a I).

[13] To call this background minimal is perhaps an understatement, but it is difficult not to say too little or too much about a general philosophy with which one is concerned in a derivative way for a purpose such as ours. The best way to deal with St. Thomas is to read him. Like most great writers, he is much easier to understand than his commentators, certainly including the present one. In these days of undisciplined writing and unlabored reading, it may startle the reader of the *Summa Theologica* to be told in its prologue that St. Thomas is writing "in such a way as befits the instruction of beginners." He wants "to set forth briefly and clearly the things which pertain to sacred doctrine," and quotes St. Paul: "As unto little ones in Christ, I give you milk to drink, not meat."

[14] Pierre H. Conway, *Principles of Education — a Thomistic Approach* (Washington, D. C.: The Thomist Press, 1960).

original author would have sanctioned. St. Thomas discussed educational issues in many of his writings, but one in particular will be our chief source.[15]

We can best understand St. Thomas' treatise on education as a commentary on St. Augustine's *De Magistro,* reviewed in our previous chapter. You will recall that Augustine pitched that dialogue to the question, "Can one man teach another?" For the most part his answer was *no,* for reasons which Aquinas accepts in general. But the latter's answer to the same question is *yes,* for reasons that go beyond Augustine's treatment.

St. Thomas starts with the fact that people undeniably do learn many things without any instruction or guidance. The teacher, moreover, cannot impart any new knowledge except by utilizing what the learner already knows. The first grader, learning to count, uses apples. He is familiar with apples. Later, learning to add, he takes counting as a matter of course, as he does still later with adding when he learns to multiply.

Since this process can and does go on sometimes without instruction, the teacher should be concerned with helping the learner to do better, faster, more economically, what he could do alone if need be. Teaching is another case where art imitates nature, "by developing and extending it, not by copying it."[16] St. Thomas uses the analogy of a physician. The patient sometimes cannot heal himself unaided. Yet neither does the physician heal him. The physician gives him the necessary help to heal himself, rearranges the forces of a living body so that it can restore itself to normalcy. A teacher is a physician of the mind, dependent upon its natural operations.

WHAT DOES THE TEACHER PROVIDE?

One way to pinpoint the teacher's role is to list and describe carefully the things that are necessary or helpful in learning, and see which of them the teacher can or does provide. One necessary thing is *the intelligence of the learner*. St. Augustine, you will remember, had denied that one person can teach another, chiefly on the grounds that the learner supplies the mind that learns. With this,

---

[15] St. Thomas Aquinas, *De Veritate,* trans. by James V. McGlynn (Chicago: Henry Regnery Co., 1959), Q. 11, "On the Teacher."

[16] Vincent E. Smith, *The School Examined, An Essay on the Curriculum* (Milwaukee: The Bruce Publishing Co., 1960), p. 21.

Aquinas heartily agrees. We have seen how much his epistemology stresses the intellect's role. He also agreed with Augustine that God should be called always the principal teacher because He provides man's spiritual intelligence:

> Now this light of reason . . . is placed in us by God, as though a certain likeness of the divine truth taking up its abode in us. Whence, since all human teaching cannot have efficacy except from the power of this light, it is clear that it is God alone who internally and principally teaches, as nature also is the principal healer.[17]

A cause which produces an effect by its own power is called a principal cause, while one which produces its effect only by some power borrowed from the principal cause is called instrumental. St. Thomas is saying, basically, that the pupil is the principal cause of his own learning, and the teacher is an instrumental cause. For, after observing that the chief force of learning is from within, he adds: "Just as the doctor, although he works from without while nature alone works from within, is said to produce health, so man too is said to teach the truth although he enunciates it externally while God teaches from within."[18]

Another necessary element in education is *the known*. Here again, the teacher is of no help. He did not design or construct the world. A geography teacher may teach that the Arkansas River rises in central Colorado. This would be true if that teacher had never lived. Even the ideas that correspond to this truth about the Arkansas River (or any truth) are the result of the activity of the *pupil's* mind, and therefore cannot be said to be supplied by the teacher.

In short, the teacher supplies neither the mind that knows nor the reality that is known. Then of what use is he? Hardly any, concluded Augustine, who nevertheless continued to teach and write voluminously all his life. Thomas, however, found two roles the teacher can play. (1) He can *present selected* sense-data to help the learner's mind to abstract the correct ideas. Nowadays we call such data audio-visual aids. They are undoubtedly valuable at some levels and for some purposes, though it seems highly probable that their value has been greatly overstressed by educational psychologists, many of whom seem to be excessively attracted to the concrete.

---

[17] St. Thomas Aquinas, *De Veritate*, q. 11, a. 1, c.
[18] *Ibid.*, q. 11, a. 1, ad 7.

(2) Most important, the teacher can *suggest order in proceeding.* In this way, as Vincent Smith suggests, the teacher is a logician of sorts. That is, he leads the learner from the known to the unknown by rational discourse. That is the heart of teaching. Let us consider a very simple example. Suppose someone says to you, "There is a cow in your yard." As Augustine pointed out, there must be meanings already in your mind, prior to all these verbal symbols, or the symbols will convey nothing. You must know what cows are, what yards are, what "there is" means, and so forth. To that extent, the statement tells you nothing you did not already understand. But the way the words are arranged points to *a new set of relationships;* it tells you something you did not already know, namely, that there is a cow in your yard.

This grossly simplified example illustrates in what, essentially, all teaching consists. If you did not understand the statement of the person who told you about the cow, you and he might discuss it in other terms. If you still did not understand, he might take you to the window and show you the cow. Again, someone says, "The price of milk has increased." You know what a price is, what milk is, what it is to increase, and so forth. Now all of these elements are synthesized into a new judgment, a new piece of information. The one who performed this service for you was teaching you. *Teaching is ordering.* One might discover without being told that there is a cow in his yard or that (*non sequitur*) the price of milk has increased. Anything one learns by instruction, one might possibly have learned without instruction, though people are very little inclined to make certain types of discoveries without the conscious guidance of another.

St. Thomas stressed the role of first principles in this didactic process. Everyone has the beginnings of systematic knowledge in himself, in the form of first principles, self-evident truths from which he can derive conclusions either mediately or immediately. Self-evident principles are not *innate,* but they are known immediately and with certainty as soon as the *terms* in which they are formulated are known. Thus everyone knows that one being cannot at one and the same time *be* and *not be* in the same way, e.g., a chicken cannot simultaneously *be* and *not be* a chicken. As much as possible, said St. Thomas, the teacher should use these axioms as points of departure in moving from the known to the unknown:

Now the process of reason in arriving at the knowledge of the unknown in *finding* [independent discovery] is that it apply the common self-evident principles to determine matters, and proceed thence to certain particular conclusions, and from these to others. Whence it is according to this that one is said to *teach* another, in that the discourse of reason which he carries out in himself, he expounds to another *through signs,* and thus the natural reason of the student, through such things proposed to him, as through certain instruments, arrives at the knowledge of things unknown.[19]

Aristotle had similarly written, "All teaching and all learning are constituted out of pre-existing knowledge."[20] Having provided two functions for the teacher not included in the analysis of the saintly Bishop of Hippo, Aquinas makes bold to offer a different answer to the question, "Can one man teach another?"

Therefore, just as the doctor is said to cause health in the sick man when it is nature which is acting, so likewise one man is said to cause science in another through the action of the natural reason of the other — and this is to *teach.* Whence one man is said to teach another, and to be his master.[21]

There is food for thought in St. Thomas' conclusion, as in the way he goes about reaching it. Only after the most painstaking analysis does he presume to disagree with St. Augustine on a specific point. It is significant, too, that, since Thomas devoted only one work directly to education, this question of the respective causal roles in it of teacher and pupil was the one he took up. None of his writings shows much concern with *methods,* except insofar as methodological conclusions can be derived from his statements on more generic matters. Probably St. Thomas considered it obvious that, if the pupil does not understand what the teacher means, the pupil will say so and the teacher will keep saying it in different ways until the pupil *does* understand. Entire chapters are produced nowadays on this rather elementary point.

INTELLIGENCE OF THE LEARNER

If the pupil is the principal cause of his own learning, then his intelligence (i.e., the quality of it) will be a major differentiating factor. As the physician can make the patient no healthier than he has an innate capacity to be, neither can the teacher convey to the student more than he has an innate capacity to learn.

[19] *Ibid.,* q. 11, a. 1, c.
[20] Aristotle, *Posterior Analytics,* I (71a).
[21] St. Thomas Aquinas, *De Veritate,* q. 11, a. 1, ad 11.

TEACHER AS SCIENTIST

The chief connotation of "science" in St. Thomas' time was systematic knowledge of things by their principles and causes. Since the teacher has chiefly an ordering or arranging job to do, it is important that the teacher possess science. The master leads the pupil from known to unknown in two ways. First,

> by proposing to him certain helps or instruments which his intellect may use to acquire science, for example, when he proposes certain *less universal propositions* to him which nevertheless he is able to judge from what he previously knows; or when he proposes to him certain *sensible examples,* either similar or opposite, or other such, by which the intellect of the one learning is led to the knowledge of the unknown truth.
>
> He does so in another way by strengthening the intellect of the one learning, not indeed by any active power as though being of a higher nature . . . but insofar as he proposes to the student the *order* of the principles to the conclusions, who perhaps would not have of himself a power of inference sufficient to be able to deduce the conclusions from the principles.[22]

Another way to say this is that the teacher should have the science "in act" which the student has potentially. You cannot teach what you do not know. By the same token, if someone learns something without instruction, it is questionable semantics to say he taught himself, since this would require him to know and not know at the same time.

Lest there be any doubt, St. Thomas stressed that the "known" with which the teacher should begin is not simply that which is widely known or established, but presently known by the pupil or pupils to be taught. Hence diverse backgrounds within a class so often cause such severe problems in teaching. What is long since obvious to one is eternally unattainable to another! In any case, the teacher must strive to move from what is known best to the pupils to what is best known in itself. Aristotle, in stressing the same point, had used this analogy: "For as the eyes of bats are to the blaze of day, so is the reason in our soul to the things which are by nature most evident of all."[23]

Aims. Ultimately, the aims of St. Thomas, Duns Scotus, and the other great medieval educators were those of the Church. Education

---

[22] St. Thomas Aquinas, *Summa Theologica,* I, q. 117, a. 1, c. Cf. *Summa Contra Gentiles,* II, c. 75.

[23] Aristotle, *Metaphysics,* II, 993b 5.

is for whatever life is for, and Catholic teaching leaves no ambiguities on *that*. Scattered throughout Thomas' works are various references to passages from Aristotle's *Ethics* in which the latter said things applicable to this problem. As a rule, St. Thomas agreed with the Aristotelian positions in this area, simply reminding the reader here and there of union with God as the absolute good. Nowhere does St. Thomas take up the controversy of intellectual development versus the "whole person" aim. Insofar as he concerns himself with the matter, he seems to be saying what the oft-misunderstood Newman was to say much later: Of course we are concerned with the whole person, but the best route to him is through his intellect.

Methods. To look to St. Thomas for "how-to" treatises on teaching is to be disappointed. Indeed, there is no period of history when writers had less to say about pedagogical methods than during the Middle Ages. It is difficult to say whether this is because sound basic theory made methodology a somewhat redundant concern or whether teachers simply tended to accept conventional teaching methods uncritically.

It is also difficult to tell just how good or bad a job the typical medieval teacher did. Many writers seemingly have allowed their pro- or anti-scholastic sentiments to sway their judgment on the point. It has been claimed that there was much reliance upon textbooks and memorization of them, and that the whole curriculum revolved chiefly around ability to read Latin and take part in church services. The sort of reader who looks for evidence will be disappointed, though. We can also read that "severe physical punishment was common," but we must conjecture just how severe, how physical, and how common.

There is some reason to believe that memorization (from wax tablets) was often substituted for comprehension in medieval schools, and repetition accepted as proof of learning, rather than teachers demanding application and paraphrase. On the other hand, the medieval *disputatio* seems, in principle, an excellent teaching device, although chances are that it was often misused. In this technique, a student advanced a thesis (proposition), argued for it, then defended it against all objections raised by those present. It was similar to formal debate, still a common practice in schools and colleges.

If we simply ponder St. Thomas' basic beliefs about education, however, we can see methodological implications. We can see that the teacher should study the natural learning process that children use in independent discovery and simply help them to do the same thing better. One can see that the teacher should possess a scientific, organized grasp of the field to be taught, should know the present state of mind of the pupils and lead them step by step from what they know now to what they ought to know. St. Thomas had enough to say about the role of differences in intelligence that it seems probable he would advocate ability-grouping.

Still, what he says as "advice to the teacher" he could have as well said as "advice to the writer." Was there no distinction in his mind between telling and teaching? It is difficult to say. Either the saint considered the processes of discussion and testing so obvious as to need no comment, or he tended to accept the "telling-teaching" equation.

Agencies.   St. Thomas lived centuries before Pius XI wrote on this subject, but there is no reason to suppose that the great Dominican would have objected to anything in the encyclical — which, indeed, quotes extensively from him in arguing the rights of the family in education.

Education was dominated by the Church in the Middle Ages, but she did not have a monopoly on schools. In Italy, especially, municipal authorities continued to maintain school systems on a local basis. Civil authorities of the time usually operated through the clergy in educational matters, however.

Curriculum.   Our third chapter discussed how the antirationalistic view that Christian education should not include the fruits of Greco-Roman culture gradually lost out, how a "Christian curriculum" gradually took shape in which natural and supernatural knowledge were fused.

By the time of St. Thomas the medieval curriculum was fairly well standardized into three phases which can be outlined as follows:

I. LIBERAL ARTS
  A. Grammar, rhetoric, logic — the *trivium*
  B. Arithmetic, geometry, music, astronomy — the *quadrivium*

II. PHILOSOPHY (in a broad sense)
  A. Natural science, including medicine
  B. Social or moral science, including law
  C. Metaphysics, including natural theology

III. SUPERNATURAL THEOLOGY

One factor in this curriculum at an operational level was the "Latinizing" of Western Europe. Medieval Latin has been criticized as "decadent," but some classical scholars insist that it was more flexible and forceful than classical Latin, decadent only in the sense of being different. The humanism of the twelfth century as exemplified in John of Salisbury, involving much respect for classical literature, was another operational factor in the curriculum. We must be cautious, however, in interpreting the remarks of some secularist writers who miss the real spirit and significance of this educational pattern and thus judge it from the standpoint of incidentals and accidentals.

The licensing of teachers was largely controlled by the Church. Granting of the *licentia docendi* was first done by the bishop or chancellor of cathedral schools. After the rise of the university system, it was done by university officials — specifically, by professors. The medieval insight that professors are not "employees" of a university but rather *are* the university is one we might do well to recapture today! Some historians see the rise of the prescribed curriculum as connected with this licensing of teachers, but the relation is indirect. After finishing the liberal arts course, the student was granted a baccalaureate degree, bachelor of arts, which implied that he was an assistant teacher. After three more years of studies in the areas in Sections I and II of the above outline, he was a "master teacher," a master of arts. Something of the influence of the medieval guilds can be seen in this whole pattern. Again, however, we must not confuse correlation with causation. It is probably best to say that the same sense for order permeated both.

The *spirit* of the classical-Christian curriculum has been grotesquely misunderstood (or not understood at all) by many modern commentators. If they showed evidence of comprehending this spirit and chose to disagree with it for stated reasons, or even for unstated reasons, this would be one thing. But they usually show evidence of not comprehending the nature of the thing they are criticizing. To grasp a Thomistic concept of curriculum we must grasp the Thomistic concept of man and his intellectual light. Fundamentally, a liberal education aims to free this "light" from the impediments of matter and circumstance, to use the biological mode to rise above the biological mode, to enable the light of man's spiritual intellect to shine more strongly and, as it were, more purely.

Those later philosophers who saw in human thought only a bio-logical, adaptive function were consistent in wanting to remove from the curriculum any definite, prescribed content. The Christian realists who saw in human thought the possibilities for correspondence with objective reality were likewise consistent in insisting that a curriculum *must* have such content. The undefined jargon of many contemporary educators suggests that a curriculum is a series of "experiences," "life decisions," "existential responses," and what-have-you. This is their way of saying that a curriculum is *not* a course of study, not an objective thing that has some legitimate status as an abstract possibility even before the cooperative work of teacher and pupil turns it into a concrete actuality. We might compare what a painter does with what a composer does for this purpose. A painter starts with a blank canvas. (Our analogy is imperfect since probably he also starts with something in mind to produce.) He paints a picture, a concrete thing. What he produces is in a certain place; it has weight; it is a particular. A composer, on the other hand, starts with some lines on a sheet of paper and makes some marks on them. These marks do not have their definitive significance in themselves. They are a sort of blueprint, pointing out to the musician a certain abstract possibility. The musician or singer makes it concrete, actual. Strictly speaking, the song does not "exist" except when somebody is singing or playing it.

Modern educators tend to see the teacher's work as akin to what the artist does. The former makes "curricular decisions" much as the artist decides what to paint and how — more or less by spontaneous inspiration. Thomists and other realists see the teacher as doing more nearly what a musician does — actualizing an abstract possibility. It is fine to talk of curriculum as "the experiences of the child under the school's guidance" in reference to the actuality, so long as we also acknowledge curriculum as a course of study, in reference to the abstract possibility or plan. Over several centuries, this modern tendency to conceive of a curriculum as consisting more or less in whatever spontaneous inspirations a teacher happens to have, has robbed many generations of their academic birthright, has produced many people who have earned degrees without being particularly educated.

Academic Freedom and Indoctrination.   It could reasonably be claimed that Thomas Aquinas spent most of his life fighting for academic freedom. His ideas were often opposed, officially and un-officially, in various places where he was teaching. He was sometimes a storm center despite his peaceful intentions. Yet one who had long observed him under these conditions remarked, "We never knew him to lose his composure." It was not St. Thomas' way to make a noisy to-do about his rights as a scholar. Instead, like nearly all really great scholars, he simply went quietly ahead teaching and writing as his mind and conscience led him, with careful reflections upon the wisdom of the past. He would probably have been puzzled by some professors of the sort who seemingly have so little to say and make such a commotion about their right to say it.

There can be no doubt that he took his responsibility as a teacher seriously. It is recorded that he often prayed his life would not outlast his teaching, a wish that was granted. Since St. Thomas so often quoted from men with whom he disagreed, and since their arguments in his hands often had greater force than in their own, one can presume that he would not have wished to silence them, to prevent their having their "day in court."

We can also gather between the lines what Thomas probably would have had to say about indoctrination. From his emphases about what he wanted we can conclude what he did not want. He wanted the learner so far as possible always to understand "why." Knowledge of things by their causes and principles, scientific knowledge, this was the immediate goal in education. It was achieved by the teacher's starting with the pupil's present store of understandings and leading him forth systematically.

The opposite approach would be to teach conclusions without teaching reasons for them. That is the real evil of indoctrination and we can reasonably assume that St. Thomas would be against it both in theory and practice. Much of his writing was done to explain things to those who requested explanation. Prince or peasant, the supplicant always got his reply. Once a young student submitted thirty-six questions to the Angelic Doctor and asked to have them fully answered within four days. St. Thomas put aside pressing duties to meet the request, even reformulated some of the questions more precisely.

FRANCISCANISM

Although the founder of the Franciscans was not inclined to regard formal education highly, the early leaders of the order he founded quickly saw that the spirit of El Poverello could not be carried on and furthered without a carefully developed philosophy and system of education. It is not difficult to understand why St. Francis himself was opposed to many of the things which education in his day reflected. Too often the educated person was proud and overbearing. More often, the life of the educated aristocracy was a contradiction of the intellectual knowledge they assumedly possessed. In rebelling against these evils, St. Francis appeared to rebel against the intellectualism of the times, and perhaps he did.

St. Bonaventure set out in earnest to develop a religious and educational philosophy which would incorporate the mystical insights of St. Francis. Although the Bonaventurian movement was at its height in the late thirteenth century, it still remains the nucleus around which Franciscan education was built. The great Duns Scotus, who will be discussed later, took his lead from the thought of Bonaventure.

Franciscanism deserves serious study by today's student of Christian education because so many elementary and secondary schools and colleges are staffed by those following the rule of St. Francis. Franciscanism also has an affinity to Augustinianism in educational theory and practice, and as a result a study of Franciscan educational theory and practice gives the student greater insight into the spirit of early Christian education.

FRANCISCAN PHILOSOPHY

A central point in the Franciscan philosophy is found in Bonaventure's notion of wisdom. For him, wisdom consists in "passing over from vanity to truth." Truth is viewed as participation in "the Truth," God. Thus only that knowledge which is immutable is true. Vanity, which is the opposite of wisdom, consists in attraction to something which is transitory and mutable. Therefore, any educational activity which has the acquisition of "knowledge for its own sake" or development of intellectual powers as its basic goal is vanity. Wisdom, then, can be attained only when sanctity and knowledge have been harmonized. No one can be considered wise unless he first "lives as the true Christian ought; no one can acquire true knowledge unless he leads a holy life."[24]

---

[24] Etienne Gilson, *The Philosophy of St. Bonaventure* (New York: Sheed and Ward, 1940), p. 476 ff.

It is in prayers and devotion that knowledge is transmuted into love, and knowledge, whether it be of God or of creatures, apart from love, dries up the soul and makes man but a shadow of a man; in a word it kills personality.[25]

This notion of wisdom is most essential to understanding Franciscan education. Before one can even begin to acquire knowledge, he first must understand his own weaknesses, master his passions, control his thoughts, and order all his desires. In other words, the *will* takes precedence over intellect in the knowing process as well as in action. All true education will adapt secular as well as religious knowledge to the love of God. Man, then, should seek knowledge which will strengthen the foundations of his faith, build his character, deepen his love of God — in short, assist him to live the true Christian life. Love of God, then, must be the purpose of all activities involving the acquisition of knowledge, skills, and attitudes.[26]

John Duns Scotus was perhaps the outstanding spokesman of Franciscan ideals in the years following the deaths of St. Bonaventure and St. Thomas.[27]

It is very hard to put Scotism in a category. At first glance, Scotus might seem to be taking a step toward materialism. He says, for example, that matter is an entity in its own right and therefore is able to exist apart from form. He also seems to say that form arises from the potency of matter. He insists, however, that essences are real whether exemplified in any existing thing or not, a proposition which is hardly materialistic. What he really does to matter and to other things is to Platonize them. That is, everything he treats of tends to come out as a transcendent reality in its own right. Yet Scotus also has a strong sense of the functional unity of all things. One study suggests that "Scotistic philosophy is nothing but an attempt to offer more precise, more critical, and more scientific solutions to problems perceived in an Augustinian way and within the Augustinian tradition."[28]

---

[25] Rev. Cuthbert, O.S.F.C., "St. Francis of Assisi," *American Ecclesiastical Review*, LXXV, No. 5 (1900), 466.

[26] See Sr. M. Emma Healy, *St. Bonaventure's 'De Reductione'* (New York: St. Bonaventure College Press, 1940), p. 202.

[27] In recent years there has been something of a revival and reexamination of Scotism. One study, especially, is to be commended for attempting to put the *Doctor Subtilis* in a new light, namely Efrem Bettoni's *Duns Scotus: The Basic Principles of His Philosophy,* trans. and ed. by Bernardine Bonansea (Washington, D. C.: Catholic University of America Press, 1961).

[28] *Ibid.,* pp. 189–190.

Scotus, concurring with Bonaventure, left little doubt about the role the will plays in all knowledge-seeking activities. For him, it is the will that moves the intellect toward the object of knowledge. The essence of human freedom is found in self-determination, whether this be in terms of overt action or of seeking knowledge.[29] Thus the will actually embraces all rational powers; that is, the will decides what the intellect should seek to know. The will does not do the knowing, but it controls knowing. In the natural action of the intellect, the will must concur with it, since attention, which is a will-act, is a *sine qua non* of intellection.[30]

The Franciscan schools, then, are consistent when they place the greatest emphasis on the training of the will and character formation. A properly trained will can guide the intellect in its choices of that which is worth knowing. The decision of whether to know something or not is proper to the will. To put it more simply, the intellect does not go about knowing everything presented to it via the senses. Rather, guided by the will, intellect picks up only those elements of knowledge which fit the context of Christian life.

Scotus refuses categorically to subordinate one power to the other and insists that each influences the other. He goes on to say, however, that intellect and will are not on the same plane. Will is the superior cause in respect to acts of the intellect. The problem arises, of course, because free choice entails an element of rationality, which we ascribe to intellect. But this is the sort of difficulty which might arise from having made too sharp a cleavage in the first place. Duns Scotus solves it by saying that the will is rational by nature, it does not borrow rationality from the intellect. As the power of a rational being it is formally rational.

In any case, Franciscanism regards the will as the noblest human faculty. Love (charity), which is simply the expression of the harmonious operation of all rational powers (intellect and will), is the ideal "state of mind" for the Christian. For it is the possession of love of the Supreme Being which brings complete happiness and perfection to man as a person. For this reason, the uneducated person can be said to possess more wisdom than the brilliant scholar if the former loves God with all his heart and mind and if the latter

---

[29] Claude Mindorff, "Voluntarism versus Intellectualism," *Franciscan Educational Studies,* XI, No. 11 (1929), p. 34.

[30] Clement O'Donnell, "Voluntarism in Franciscan Philosophy," *Franciscan Studies,* XXIII, No. 1, p. 401.

possesses great learning about God's nature and attributes but is not moved by a burning love for God.

The life of St. Francis exemplified this basic principle. He made his life after his conversion a living witness of the harmony that can be achieved between the spiritual and temporal elements of life. Francis saw God in the animals (whom he called his brothers); his love of nature was a form of worship of God. He despised those elements of life which drew him away from God — riches and worldly pleasures. Chesterton found this outlook on life to be the key to understanding St. Francis' paradoxical views. It shed a new supernatural light on man's use of natural things. St. Francis has been accused of being a naturalist and a pantheist. Rather did nature stand transparent for him as a revelation of its Creator. He made life a love song to God. For him, happiness could be achieved by doing things that were not demanded, not for the sake of self-denial but for the love of God.

This Christocentrism might be regarded as the unifying principle of Franciscan education throughout the ages. All activities and knowledge must be related to Christian living; otherwise they are worthless. Knowledge has no *intrinsic* value. Without centering all knowing activities in Christ, man can never achieve true wisdom. Man's fallen nature precludes his becoming wise without divine grace. One cannot be considered a good student or a good artist or a good farmer unless he possesses a true love for Christ. As a Franciscan artist once said, "Christian art is that produced by one in the state of grace."

St. Bonaventure expresses the same Christocentrism as the creation of all things in and through Christ, modeling of all created things upon Christ, and, finally, the return of all to Christ.[31]

Another feature of Franciscanism was its emphasis on the worth of each individual, especially the lowly. All men, rich and poor alike, were deprived of the life of grace by the fall of Adam. Christ, by His redemption, returned all men, the lowly as well as the high, to their original position as children of God. Each person is priceless before God. Each has the same rights to the goods of the earth and the values of education.

St. Francis himself despised all class distinctions. To emphasize

---

[31] M. Meilach, "Jesus Christ: High Priest of Creation," *Cord,* XII, No. 9 (September, 1962), 265.

this point, he abandoned the privileges of his aristocratic family and expected his followers to do the same. They concentrated their educational efforts on the less privileged. When they went to the missions of the new world, they educated the children of the humble Indians in the same manner as those of the rulers. Chesterton points up this egalitarianism as one of the major contributions of Franciscanism to Western thought. To be a true follower of St. Francis, a true Christian, one must see the same God in all men. Man should not be lost sight of in the masses but should be held in the highest esteem. This must be a genuine love and respect, not merely a surface gesture.

> From the Pope to the beggar, from the Sultan of Syria to the ragged robbers, there never was a man who looked into the eyes of Francis without being certain that he was really interested in them. Francis was interested in everyone's own individual life from cradle to the grave. Each human being was valued and taken seriously. He treated the whole mob of men as a mob of kings. He demanded a great deal of human nature, not because he despised it, but rather because he trusted it and realized its potential.[32]

So far as education is concerned, we can summarize the main points of Franciscan thought as follows:

1. Wisdom, as contrasted with pure knowledge, is valued.

2. Priority is given to training the will as against intellectual development *per se*.

3. There is to be a Christocentric focus on all educational activities. The school is chiefly a place for shaping the Christian life. Love (charity) should be the guiding principle rather than learning and scholarship for their own sake.

4. Egalitarianism is advocated. There are to be no class distinctions and no distinction of intellectual classes. All children can attend school regardless of their social or intellectual "class."

FRANCISCAN EDUCATIONAL BELIEFS

St. Francis was not an educational theorist. However, one can discover certain guiding principles for educational practice in his example and in the works of his interpreters. Francis himself did

---

[32] G. K. Chesterton, *St. Francis of Assisi* (New York: George A. Doran Co., 1924), pp. 141 ff. and 188.

not believe in teaching within established schools. His antiaristocratic temperament urged him to use God's creation, the great out-of-doors, as his classroom. In this setting, the simplehearted and modest Francis taught the masses, chiefly by example, what it meant to love God. For him, this was true knowledge, true wisdom.

Methodology. In Chapter Three, the educational methodology of St. Augustine was discussed, and it is this philosophy which influenced Bonaventure. Vogel asserts that Augustine has applied the best principles of methodology and psychology in the *De Catechizandis Rudibus,* when he advises teachers not to confound the student with a multitude of facts so as to tire the memory. Rather, the pedagogue should emphasize the essentials and omit or pass over lightly all the trappings, etc. All instruction should be adapted to the individual differences of the learners using more examples and illustrations for slow learners. Whatever the teacher does, the love of God should clearly be the focus.[33]

One of the first things the Franciscans did was to eliminate Latin as the language of teaching. They felt the use of the vernacular lent itself well to the service of teaching religion and morals. Girard, a Franciscan contemporary of Pestalozzi, felt that use of the vernacular enabled the teacher to follow the same method a mother uses in instructing her children. The mother explains things to her children, thus connecting the symbol with the sense-impression the child has received from the environment. From these sense-impressions thus associated with symbols, the child forms ideas, or mental images. By association, then, the word is connected with the object. Each new learning is based on previous knowledge and experience. Once the child is able to go through this process, the teacher can lead him to a love of God by studying religion through the maternal method. The teacher could "form Christ in the hearts of pupils" — the central task of education.[34] When the Franciscans worked in the missions and were unable to use the vernacular of the Indians, they developed a picture language which incorporated the same principles as the maternal method. Father Valades, writing in 1579, claimed that the method of using pictures adapted to the intelligence and back-

---

[33] Claude Vogel, "Religious Instruction — Method and Text," *Franciscan Conference,* XIX (1937), p. 31.

[34] See A. Maas, O.M.C., *Pere Girard, Educator* (New York: J. Wagner, 1931), p. 13 ff.

ground of the Indians represents the first time in the history of education that such visual aids were used. Comenius was to propose a
similar technique a century later.[35]

Another technique used by the friars which was not used in the
schools of the times was creative expression. Music, painting, drawing, and sculpture were encouraged as means of self-expression and
as a way of showing one's honor and love for God. All students
were expected to develop some art or craft which suited their abilities
and interests.

One methodological outgrowth of the Franciscan conception of
the equality of all men can be noted in their use of mutual instruction. Girard introduced this method, basing it upon his own experience. As one of fifteen children, he was charged with the instruction of his younger brothers and sisters in reading, writing, and
reciting. His mother supervised the teaching of the older children and
the family was able to get a good basic education without the services
of a tutor. When he became director of a school with 300 children,
he put the method of mutual instruction to work. As he had only
four qualified teachers he put these master teachers in charge of a
class of seventy-five pupils. In addition, students were placed in
thirty-five groups according to their levels of ability and achievement. One of these small groups was placed in the hands of a
pupil who had mastered the work of that group. It was his responsibility to direct the learning activities of his group under the supervision of the master teacher. He, in turn, would attend the classes
of the master teacher at the level at which he was working. By using
this approach, Girard was able to accept all the children who wished
to attend the school. The method bears some similarity to the modern
plan of team teaching with the exception that all members of a
teaching team are fully qualified teachers.[36]

In addition to enabling the school to accept large numbers of
pupils, this method reminded young people of their responsibility
to help their fellowman for the love of Christ. It gave them valuable
experience in teaching and leadership. It gave them the opportunity
to develop their own talents and interests. It revealed to them both
their strengths and weaknesses.

[35] Pius Barth, *Franciscan Education and the Social Order in Spanish North America* (Chicago: DePaul University Press, 1950), pp. 209, 216.
[36] For a more detailed description of this mutual instruction method see Maas,
Pere Girard, p. 23.

The friars' use of audio-visual materials was not limited to "picture language." Dramatization was widely used to convey the meaning of the Christian religion to schoolchildren. Prayers and doctrines were set to music in the vernacular of the pupils. In fact, any audio-visual material which enabled the friars to communicate better with their pupils was utilized. In itself, this constituted a radical departure from the typical teaching methods of the time, which were abstract and often far removed from the life of the child.

Much has been written in recent years about the activity method of teaching. Rousseau, Pestalozzi, and the American Progressives all advocated the principle of activity as an essential element of true learning. But the Franciscans had employed the method with great success in their schools before the Progressives appeared on the scene. They taught the manual skills, arts and crafts, by working with the pupils on their projects. They used models and drawings from which the learners constructed buildings. The Indians became so proficient in such activities as weaving, drawing, tailoring, shoe-making, and carpentry that they broke the Spanish monopoly on the products of these skills.

The activity method was used in academic subjects as well. Even the teaching of religion was "activated" by dramatizations, musical performances, and the like.

Because of the emphasis placed on training of the will, Franciscan teachers attempted to base all learning on natural motivation. Unless the learner was moved to learn something because of his own choice, he was "just going through the motions" and no true wisdom would result. Consequently, the teachers were forbidden to use force to get pupils to learn their lessons. Experience had taught the friars that when pupils are interested in what they are doing, a friendly, cooperative, and mutually helpful atmosphere will pervade the school. Under such conditions, children are not only learning their skills and subjects, but are forming Christ within themselves. It is education of the whole child, not just his mind.

Aims of Education. From the above discussion of Franciscan philosophy and methodology, it is quite evident that the ultimate goal of education in general is the development within the educand of the love of Christ which will lead to the salvation of the soul. The Franciscans also insist, against Thomists, that the development of the perfect Christian also is the *immediate* objective of the school.

All education must be centered around Christ, the curriculum, daily classroom activities, recreation must be an exercise in Christian living. School life should not (and cannot) be separated from daily life; the intellectual life of the pupil should not be separated from his affective life. The school experience must be as Christocentric as the life in the family and the Church. The school's primary obligation, then, is character formation, of which intellectual formation is merely a subsidiary part.

The application of this view was evident not only in the Franciscan mission schools of the new world but also in the schools of Europe. In both places, the school was a place where the student was living in and for Christ. A perusal of statements of objectives in schools operated by the Franciscans today will reveal that there has been no change in this primary objective.[37]

The specific application of this objective demands that all basic skills, vocational and academic subjects, be wholly integrated with Christian living. All contact with nature should be related to God. The daily school schedule should be marked at all times by Christian practices arising from the pure love of God imbued with the simple faith of the Gospel and characterized by the perfect imitation of Christ. St. Bonaventure, in his *De Reductione Artium ad Theologiam,* devised a most ingenious plan whereby all subject matters and skills can be reduced to God as the first principle and center of all human activity.

Curriculum. In keeping with the primary objectives of Franciscan schools, religion is the only *essential* subject in the school. One can introduce whatever activities, subjects, or skills may meet the special needs or interests of the people being educated. The only requisite is that these latter be thoroughly integrated with Christian character formation. The pupil should look upon each subject or activity with the eyes of faith.

In arts and crafts, for example, the relationship to Christian living can be pointed up by impressing on the students that they should use their talents to their fullest since they are a gift of God. These talents should also be put to use in the service of God and His creatures. In literature study, the classics and other great productions of the human mind should be given a religious and moral dimension

---

[37] See T. Grassman, "The Implications of Franciscan Spirituality in Modern Life," *Franciscan Educational Conference,* XXIX (1948).

not found in secular or humanistic schools. The works of great Franciscan authors which exemplify the Christocentric outlook should be given special consideration.

In science, the teacher should stress the wondrous workings of God in the physical universe. The perfection in nature should be represented as the overflowing of God's perfection to be discovered in the natural and moral laws of the universe. Man's place as the highest corporeal being in the created universe should be pointed up along with the responsibility accompanying this lofty position in creation. Because of the influence of Roger Bacon, the great Franciscan scientist of medieval days, the schools of Francis' followers have not neglected science. The study of science is not directed by the objective of knowledge of the physical universe for its own sake, but for the honor and glory of God and the salvation of one's soul.

In the social studies, especially history, the emphasis should be on pointing up the finger of God in all events, rather than the study of historical data *per se*. History should be presented as a series of God-directed events leading to Christ's appearance on earth and the events since His death in relation to His kingdom. History should be a constant reminder of the eternal conflict between God and Satan. All events will culminate in the final judgment by Christ.

Agencies of Education. From the foregoing it is evident that the Church is the primary agency of education. Since religion is the domain of the Church and religion is the central focus of all educational activities, even the educational function of the family is to be guided by the principles of Christianity. Strictly speaking, there should be no separation of home, school, and Church — all are actively engaged in the pursuit of the same goal, Christian perfection. This application of unity was especially evident in the missions of the Franciscans. The mission was the center of all cultural, educational, and vocational activities. Children and adults alike geared their everyday activities to the religious and liturgical life of the mission. It was the seat of the transculturation from paganism to Christianity. Obviously, it was necessary for missionaries to counteract the pagan influences of the home or at least sublimate them to serve the purposes of Christian culture.

Students. We have seen that one of the more "radical" elements in Franciscanism was the rejection of the basic social inequality of human beings. This policy of mass education directed toward social change contrasted sharply with aristocratic ideals, which stressed court schools and the education of the children of nobles by tutors. St. Francis directed his teaching efforts to all classes but most especially the underprivileged. In like manner his followers offered the same educational opportunities to rich and poor. Every human being is "another Christ" who must be afforded all the opportunities to grow in the love of God. The individual differences of each person must be respected and each one given the opportunity to develop his talents and interests to the fullest. Because of his spiritual nature, man must never be viewed as just a number among the masses.

Further evidence of this democratic view of man is found in the Franciscan view of leadership. Pupils who are selected to assist other pupils should regard their work as a service to God and their fellow-man. Religious superiors and administrators are viewed as servants rather than masters. All of their decisions and actions must be for the good of their fellowmen, not for their own honor and glory. Because they hold a position of authority within the order or the school, they are not to consider themselves superior to any other person, be he beggar or thief.[38]

Another very democratic (and perhaps anti-intellectualistic) feature of Franciscan education was the inclusion of arts and crafts and vocational subjects in the school program. This practice was designed to meet the needs and interests of all the students, not just those with academic pursuits in mind. Furthermore, there seems to be no indication that any subject was higher in the prestige scale than any other. Religion alone received this honor. Each person was to develop in Christian perfection by using his talents, be they manual or intellectual.

Indoctrination and Academic Freedom. The rule of Franciscan schools that no student be forced to accept any belief or doctrine against his will suggests that "barefaced" indoctrination was frowned upon by the leaders of the movement. The pedagogical reliance on internal motivation seems to give further evidence that the Franciscans felt that indoctrination violated man's basic nature. Unless a child or adult learned some subject or skill or performed some act because he willed to do so, it would be worthless in the eyes of God.

---

[38] See James Meyer, *The Words of St. Francis* (Chicago: Franciscan Herald Press, 1952), p. 153 ff.

Franciscan historians have challenged anyone to point to an instance of forced conversion in the Indian missions. This approach seems to be quite consistent with the tenets of voluntarism.

That the Franciscans favored academic freedom for teachers can be concluded from their activities and teaching which ran contrary to those accepted by the political and educational majority. Duns Scotus battled against the dominance of Thomism. The friars opposed the stranglehold of the aristocracy upon the lower classes. Roger Bacon carried on his scientific experiments in an intellectual climate which was antiscientific. All of these scholars risked condemnation — and some got it. Girard dared to propose his educational theories which were later condemned as "unpedagogical, immoral, and irreligious." Perhaps, too, the "underdog" position which Franciscan philosophy has held in the Catholic sphere has motivated its practitioners to be more conscious of academic freedom.

SUMMARY

This chapter has summarized the philosophies of man and of knowledge, with applications to education, of the two great strands of thought produced by the Middle Ages. After Duns Scotus, Scholasticism began to enter what is called its decadent period. Various causes of this decline have been cited, all of which were probably involved. As much as anything, the cause may have been that everything of importance that could be said, given the state of knowledge at that time, had been said. Latter-day Scholastics explored byways of mysticism, empiricism, even anticipated some of the later work on language analysis, but none of it came to much of anything. The nominalism of William of Ockham may be cited at once as the end of medieval Scholasticism and the beginning of modern thought. Scholars became increasingly interested in *how* things happen, which would have been fine if *why* had retained its rightful place.

Scholasticism began to enjoy a vigorous revival in the past century, however, which is still going on. One can call it "neo" or not, according to how he feels about that dubious prefix. At any rate, it is to Catholic philosophy on the contemporary scene that we turn in our next chapter.

BIBLIOGRAPHY

Aquinas, St. Thomas, *Commentaria in Metaphysica Aristotelis,* Lib. II, lect. 1.
——— *De Veritate,* trans. by James V. McGlynn (Chicago: Henry Regnery Co., 1959), Q. 11, "On the Teacher."
——— *Summa Contra Gentiles,* II.
——— *Summa Theologica,* I.

Aristotle, *The Philosophy of Aristotle,* newly translated by J. L. Creed & A. E. Wardman (New York: Mentor Books, 1963).

Barth, Pius, *Franciscan Education and the Social Order in Spanish North America* (Chicago: DePaul University Press, 1950).

Bettoni, Efrem, *Duns Scotus: The Basic Principles of His Philosophy,* trans. and ed. by Bernardine Bonansea (Washington, D. C.: Catholic University of America Press, 1961).

Conway, Pierre H., *Principles of Education — a Thomistic Approach* (Washington, D. C.: The Thomist Press, 1960).

Gilson, Etienne, *The Philosophy of St. Bonaventure* (New York: Sheed and Ward, 1940), p. 476 ff.

———— *The Spirit of Mediaeval Philosophy* (New York: Scribner's, 1936).

Grassman, T., "The Implications of Franciscan Spirituality in Modern Life," *Franciscan Educational Conference,* XXIX (1948).

Healy, Sr. M. Emma, *St. Bonaventure's 'De Reductione'* (New York: St. Bonaventure College Press, 1940).

Maas, A., O.M.C., *Pere Girard, Educator* (New York: J. Wagner, 1931).

Maritain, Jacques, *An Introduction to Philosophy* (New York: Sheed and Ward, 1947).

———— "Thomist Views on Education," in Nelson B. Henry (ed.), *Modern Philosophies and Education,* I, 54th Yearbook of the N.S.S.E. (Chicago: University of Chicago Press, 1955).

Meyer, James, *The Words of St. Francis* (Chicago: Franciscan Herald Press, 1952).

Mindorff, Claude, "Voluntarism versus Intellectualism," *Franciscan Educational Studies,* XI, No. 11 (1929).

O'Brien, Kevin, *The Proximate Aim of Education — A Study of the Proper and Immediate End of Education* (Milwaukee: The Bruce Publishing Co., 1958).

Pegis, Anton C., ed., *Basic Writings of Saint Thomas Aquinas* (New York: Random House, 1945).

———— *Introduction to St. Thomas Aquinas* (New York: Modern Library, 1948).

Pieper, Josef, *Essays in Thomism* (New York: Sheed and Ward, 1942).

———— *The Silence of St. Thomas* (New York: Pantheon Books, 1957).

Plassmann, T., *End and Aim of Franciscan Education* (Milwaukee: The Bruce Publishing Co., 1929).

Sheen, Fulton J., *God and Intelligence in Modern Philosophy* (New York: Image Books, 1958).

Smith, Vincent E., *The School Examined, An Essay on the Curriculum* (Milwaukee: The Bruce Publishing Co., 1960).

Vogel, Claude, "Religious Instruction — Method and Text," *Franciscan Conference,* XIX (1937).

CHAPTER FIVE

The Philosophies of Modern Catholic Education

OUR treatment of Catholic educational philosophies to this point has been both systematic and historical. That is, we have considered certain schools of thought, but these are identified with certain times and historical movements. It remains to make an orderly review of "Catholic philosophy" of education as it stands presently, and to look tentatively to the future. The present chapter will do this under four headings: First, we shall note some common denominators, points of agreement among all Catholic educators. Second, some divergencies on such issues as methods and curriculum will be noted. Third, the main strands running through these differences will be isolated and analyzed. Last, we shall glance briefly at Catholic educational theory and the future.

COMMON DENOMINATORS

There are certain basic questions upon which the position of a Catholic flows necessarily from his being a Catholic. One of these questions is the nature of man. All Catholic educators will agree that man is a rational creature, a body-soul unit, and that he has powers of understanding and free will. They will agree that his soul is spiritual and immortal, that man's last end is happiness, and that this is achieved fully only by union with God in the Beatific Vision. This does not mean for a moment that all Catholic scholars agree in all details about what man is, how his mind works, and so forth. Indeed, there is no other topic more endlessly debated and probed by them. Not all Catholic scholars accept the hylomorphic theory which makes the soul the substantial form of the body. They disagree as to the extent to which man's innate rationality normally extends in the area of practical judgment. They disagree about the exact nature of abstracting, about the exact interrelations of intellect, will, soul, and body. They disagree about how much can be proved about the soul by natural reason alone.

This probing debate is good, but we must also occasionally back off from these minor differences and recall major similarities. No Catholic could believe that all human processes are mechanically determined and potentially explainable by laws of physics and chemistry, which is precisely what most psychologists and educators believe. No Catholic could believe that man has no material body and is merely "a thought in the mind of God," or that man is some sort of concentration of force or energy within a larger physical field, and nothing more. At minimum, a Catholic view must stipulate that man has a body, that he has a spiritual soul, that this soul is immortal, and that man has a kind of intelligence not found below him in the phylogenetic scale, and that he has free will.

Nature of Knowledge. All Catholic educators agree that truth consists in a correspondence between intellect and its object, and that it is possible in principle for man to know things as they are. Again, there are many minor variances within that basic framework. Some Catholic scholars lean to Augustinian epistemology, others to Thomism, Scotism, and so forth. At the practical level, one sees decided differences in opinions as to *just how easy* (or, if you prefer, just how difficult) it is to attain various kinds of truth. It has never been the mind of the Church that truth is simple and rather effortlessly attainable. Nevertheless, this thesis is advocated, directly or in effect, by numerous Catholic writers and lecturers, and many intelligent people are alienated by this "It's all so easy" approach.

One can understand it, perhaps. We live in a time when many schools of thought propose, in various ways and under various labels, that nothing can be known for sure and therefore it is reasonable to doubt everything. This conclusion (either undefended, or defended by rational procedures which presuppose it is not true) so pervades the modern scene that those of us who believe in any knowable truth are apt to go to the opposite extreme in reaction against this diffuse skepticism. Again, careless expression often causes people to mean one thing and say another. If one strong statement is permissible, we suggest that to regard truth as easily come by, and to suppose that those who have missed any part of it are therefore fools or knaves, is the mark of a simpleton. Indeed, it is doctrine that original sin (i.e., the sin concerned with man's origin) left as a legacy to all human creatures a certain darkening or clouding of the intellect, as well as a weakening of the will. The Catholic philosopher must maintain a careful course between a denial of the possibility of objective knowledge, and any assertion that such knowledge comes easily and without stringent intellectual discipline.

Agencies of Education. All Catholic educators will agree that the Church, family, and state have certain general roles in education. These are spelled out in the encyclical discussed earlier.[1] It is well to remember that this letter deals with *rights,* not necessarily with *powers.* From the fact that one has a just claim resting on natural law or otherwise, it does not follow that this claim always and everywhere be acknowledged. Neither does it follow that all of those who deny the claim are acting in bad faith. This was one of the difficulties in the current furor over proposed federal aid to church-related schools. Certain journals opposed this on grounds derived from the secularist premise that all claims of religious authority are to be subordinated to the authority of the state, which comes from the people. Catholic thought posits that the state's authority is not supreme in all spheres and that it does not derive ultimately from the people, though they may decide how, in general, it is to be exercised. It would be very difficult to convey to the secularist mentality of our day, without sounding "un-American," that the rights claimed in education and elsewhere by the Roman Catholic Church do not rest ultimately upon its being *a* church, but *the* Church. Where this claim is not recognized, however, it is perfectly reasonable for the Church to ask for her rights on other legitimate grounds.

Pius XI was clear enough that "first of all education belongs preeminently to the Church, by reason of a double title in the supernatural order, conferred exclusively upon her by God Himself; absolutely superior therefore to any other title in the natural order."[2]

---

[1] Pius XI, *Encyclical Letter on Christian Education of Youth* (Washington, D. C.: National Catholic Welfare Conference, 1936).

[2] *Ibid.,* p. 6.

He was equally emphatic that the family "holds directly from the Creator the mission and hence the right to educate the offspring, a right inalienable because inseparably joined to the strict obligation, a right anterior to any right whatever of civil society and of the State, and therefore inviolable on the part of any power on earth."[3] Finally, "The function . . . of the civil authority residing in the State is twofold, to protect and to foster, but by no means to absorb the family and the individual, or to substitute itself for them."[4]

A philosophical approach to the proper agencies of education might well operate through Plato's definition of justice as the doing and having of one's own, of what belongs to one's nature. For example, the proper end of the state is the temporal good of man. The state has rights in education insofar as this end is concerned and insofar as it does not conflict with the loftier end of man's spiritual good.

In his encyclical, Pius XI made considerable use of the philosophy of St. Thomas Aquinas, citing passages from the *Summa Theologica* and the supplement to it, on the parental origins of education and the parental rights to educate.

Purpose of Education. Here is another area where Catholic educators agree unanimously in general, but differ on specifics. The words of the encyclical are clear:

> The proper and immediate end of Christian education is to cooperate with divine grace in forming the true and perfect Christian, that is, to form Christ Himself in those regenerated by Baptism, according to the emphatic expression of the Apostle: "My little children, of whom I am in labour again, until Christ be formed in you."[5]

On the issue of schooling for good citizenship, the pope declared:

> The true Christian does not renounce the activities of this life, he does not stunt his natural faculties; but he develops and perfects them, by co-ordinating them with the supernatural. He thus ennobles what is merely natural in life and secures for it new strength in the material and temporal order, no less than in the spiritual and eternal.[6]

At more specific levels, however, we find some divergent opinions among Catholic educators as to the purposes of Catholic schools. These will be noted later.

---

[3] *Ibid.*, p. 12.
[4] *Ibid.*, p. 16.
[5] *Ibid.*, pp. 35–36.
[6] *Ibid.*, p. 37.

DIVERGENCIES OF CATHOLIC EDUCATORS

We have looked to the similarities; now for the differences.

Methods. There may or may not be, at a fairly general level, a methodology for teaching that flows necessarily from Catholic theology or Thomistic epistemology. Certainly, however, there is no specific way of proceeding upon which Catholic teachers agree. If anything, there seems to be a greater range of different techniques in Catholic than in public schools. Some teachers prefer lecture; others, discussion or a discussion-lecture combination. Some believe in frequent examinations and reviews, others minimize such procedures. The subject taught and grade level are, of course, variables here. But there is really not any "Catholic method." Educational psychology, which is an empirical science, rightly has much to say about pedagogical ways and means.

At a rather general level, though, there is probably an implied methodology in the philosophy of St. Thomas. Our third chapter showed how, according to St. Augustine, reality provides the intelligible and the learner provides the intelligence. Our fourth chapter indicated how, according to St. Thomas, the teacher nevertheless plays an important role by *ordering* the material. If there is a Thomistic "method" of teaching, we will find it in the saint's psychological principles and in his views on man's nature. To teach, we lead the pupil from what he knows to what he does not know, by pointing out new sets of relations among the things which he knows. One implication mentioned earlier was that the teacher is only an instrumental cause of the pupil's learning. We must get the pupil to *use his own mind* to understand what he did not understand before. That is the essence of good method, though its applications vary according to subject and maturity level of the learners.

Curriculum. While the liberal arts and certain other arrangements of subject matter are historically linked with the Church, there is no single "Catholic curriculum." Most Catholic educators insist that Christian doctrine must pervade everything that is taught. Chesterton somewhere expressed this when he said that there is a Catholic way to teach everything, even the alphabet. This is why most Catholics do not feel that the educational problem is solved by sending their children to secular schools, with a bit of "extra instruction" in religion.

Nevertheless, there is another viewpoint that is held by some as a theory and by more as a practice: curricular atomism. The defenders of this opinion argue as follows: Truth is truth. The truth in algebra or history is what it is, irrespective of the religious or antireligious convictions of the student. This argument is correct so far as it goes. It raises the question, though, of whether the proper and best use of natural reason in the special sciences can be made without the light that a valid theology and philosophy can bring. Truth is indeed truth, but to possess one truth may help one to grasp another one better. Pius XI insisted that no school can really be religiously neutral, but that "the so-called 'neutral' or 'lay' school, from which religion is excluded, is contrary to the fundamental principles of education. Such a school moreover cannot exist in practice; it is bound to become irreligious."[7]

We might suggest in passing that integrated subject matter is very easy to talk about and very hard to achieve. It is something one must work at very hard and long. It is, moreover, an endless task. Scarcely is a course of study put together when new discoveries or developments require modifications. And, since you cannot change part of an integrated thing without changing all of it, these changes require a new synthesis.

Indoctrination and Academic Freedom.   There is certainly no unanimity among Catholic educators on these matters. We have argued in an earlier chapter that Catholicism can make no peace with "freethinking" in the Voltairian sense, that Catholics will always insist on academic responsibility, responsibilty to truth. There are differences among Catholic educators, however, in the extent of their agreement with Jefferson's proposal that the occasional errors of reason need not be feared, as long as reason is left free to combat them. There seems to be general, though not unanimous, agreement that a certain freedom of *inquiry* is indispensable to scholars, and that, as discussed earlier, the teacher should present opinions as opinions and knowledge as knowledge. Some Catholic institutions seem not to have yet "got the feel" of vigorous intellectual controversy. Catholic education probably needs to get that "feel" as much as it needs anything. A scholarly synthesis such as that of St. Thomas is produced only after long and open scholarly debate.

Coeducation.   A dean of a Catholic men's college situated near

---

[7] *Ibid.*, p. 30.

a Catholic women's college remarked jocularly, "We try to keep the boys and girls apart, and give them plenty of chances to get together." This rather paradoxical observation seems to sum the attitude Catholic education has long taken toward the fact that there are two sexes. One hears occasionally that the Church is "against" coeducation, although, in some institutions, men and women take the same classes without any noticeable cataclysmic results. The idea that the Church opposes all coeducation may stem from a section of the encyclical of Pius XI, which says, "False also and harmful to Christian education is the so-called method of 'coeducation.' "[8] The reader who pursues the text, however, will see that this is no blanket indictment. What the author of the encyclical chiefly objected to is "a leveling promiscuity and equality" being mistaken "for the legitimate association of the sexes."[9] Shaw once suggested that, once woman became man's equal, she would ever after be his superior![10] To put it another way, equality is not identity. The gist of the arguments of Pius XI is that men and women have different roles in the family, and deserve schooling which prepares them for these roles. Whether it follows that they should be trained in separate classes, given present-day conditions is a problem for educational psychology.

Using Secular Schools.   Catholic education in America is faced with a new difficulty. It has not been possible to build and staff schools at a pace to match the growing population. Therefore, there has been much debate about various possible alternatives to the present Catholic educational system. One proposal has been that Catholic children attend public schools and receive religious instruction from Catholic sources. How one feels about such a program will likely depend upon how he feels about curricular atomism versus the notion of integrated subject matter. It has been argued, and rightly, that the situation has changed in public schools. One no longer finds texts in such schools, for example, in which the Catholic Church is characterized as "the whore of Babylon" and the pope as "the man of sin." This is merely a negative consideration, however. A more positive argument stems from the obligation to teach children to view everything from a God-centered

---

[8] *Ibid.,* p. 26.

[9] *Ibid.,* p. 26.

[10] Like most of Shaw's maxims, this one did not originate with him. It appears in the writings of Cato the Censor, *circa* 150 B.C.

perspective. It remains to be seen, however, how the Church will be able to provide Catholic education for all her children under present conditions. If compromises must be made, there are many views as to which are the least compromising.

MAIN STRANDS OF DIFFERENCE

If we back off from these specific points of difference, we can detect basic themes running through them. Two of these will now be discussed: intellectualism versus holism, and attitudes toward the concrete.

Intellectualism Versus Holism. If you want to start a rousing argument among teachers, ask whether schooling should be concerned with such things as personality and character. One attitude, exemplified by Admiral H. G. Rickover, is that education is for the mind. Personality, character, will, anything that is not directly pertaining to the intellect, these things can be handled by other agencies — home, church, psychologist, etc. Defenders of this theory will look in vain for support in the encyclical of Pius XI, which says that

> the subject of Christian education is man whole and entire, soul united to body in unity of nature, with all his faculties natural and supernatural, such as right reason and revelation show him to be; man, therefore, fallen from his original estate, but redeemed by Christ and restored to the supernatural condition of adopted son of God. . . .[11]

Again, he says that

> Christian education takes in the whole aggregate of human life, physical and spiritual, intellectual and moral, individual, domestic and social, not with a view of reducing it in any way, but in order to elevate, regulate and perfect it, in accordance with the example and teaching of Christ.[12]

As argued earlier, education is for whatever life is for. If life is for the salvation of one's soul, then education cannot be merely for intellectual development. One might wonder, thus, how the "intellectualist" thesis finds any Catholic defenders. The problem is not so simple, however; it has other facets.

First, it must be stressed that the usual *versus* here is a very dubious one. The opposite of intellectualism is not holism, but anti-intellectualism. The opposite of holism is elementarism, not intellectualism. In short, two things have been pitted against each

---

[11] Pius XI, *op. cit.*, p. 23.
[12] *Ibid.*, p. 36.

other which are not intrinsically opposed and do not even directly meet for comparison. We can understand this better by glancing at each of the terms of these comparisons. Pius XII, who took an active interest in empirical psychology, said in an address to a group of clinical psychologists:

> Man is an ordered unit and whole, a microcosm, a sort of state whose charter, determined by the end of the whole, subordinates to this end the activity of the parts according to the true order of their value and function.[13]

Man acts and reacts as a unit. What happens to part of him happens to all of him. What part of him does, all of him does. His unity extends, so to speak, both to the passive and active voice. This is the heart of holistic psychology. A holist would utterly reject, therefore, the notion that you can develop someone's mind and leave his personality untouched, or vice versa.

"Intellectualism" is, to say the least of it, conceived in various ways. In one context, it is a very old quarrel between Thomists and Scotists, the latter leaning to voluntarism. In a broader way, intellectualism is simply the stress and cultivation of the intellect. It is difficult to think how this could do any damage to personality or character!

The mainspring of the intellectualist position, probably, is the conviction that "God loves him who loves the intellect," this faculty being "the best thing in man." Aristotle had characterized the man "who exercises his reason and cultivates it" as "both in the best state of mind and most dear to the gods."[14]

And St. Thomas wrote:

> Supposing, therefore [i.e., in follow-up of Aristotle's argument] and as is indeed the case, that God has care and providence for human things, it is reasonable that He should delight with regard to men as to that which is best in them, and which is most akin, i.e., most like, to God. This indeed is the *intellect,* as is evident from what has preceded.[15]

O'Brien has developed a rather thorough and systematic treatment of what might be called Catholic holism in education.[16] Smith's text is equally thorough and systematic in building a case for an

[13] Pius XII, address to the 51st International Congress of Psychotherapy and Clinical Psychology, April 13, 1953.

[14] Aristotle, *Ethics,* X, 1179a 20.

[15] St. Thomas Aquinas, cited in *Principles of Education — a Thomistic Approach* (Washington, D. C.: The Thomist Press, 1960), p. 73.

[16] Kevin J. O'Brien, *The Proximate Aim of Education — a Study of the Proper and Immediate End of Education* (Milwaukee: The Bruce Publishing Co., 1958).

approach that can be called intellectualist.[17] These texts are best read firsthand to get something of the "flavor" of both viewpoints. The present writer cannot concede, however, that there is any necessary conflict between them, since (as has been argued) holism and intellectualism are not intrinsically opposed.

There has been a tendency for holistic practices to be fostered in Franciscan education, albeit with fluctuations and variations. St. Francis of Assisi (1182–1226) was not a scholar; indeed, he militantly opposed a life of books and disputations and bade his followers flee them. This facet of his teaching, however, was not observed in the order for very long.

Because Francis was not given to philosophizing, we cannot turn to him for an articulation of Franciscan holism. Yet it is found in many of his utterances in an informal way, and very much in his life. Attention and recollection in prayer, as stressed in the Franciscan rule, had they been written of in the twentieth century by a psychologist, might have been described as "integrative activity." Again, the pattern of life of the *Poverello* shows his absolute unwillingness to split intellect from emotion and action, even to the extent of entertaining an idea about which one did nothing.

Francis has often been called a nature lover, which he was, and even a nature worshiper, which he was not. Rather did nature stand always transparent for him, as is reflected in his frequent and truncated prayer, "My God and my All!" St. Francis saw the Creator in everything he observed and experienced. This is the end of the holist's road. James writes,

> Francis did not start from Nature. He set out from God and found Him everywhere. To start with Nature, it would seem, is to start at the wrong end. True, from Nature to Nature's God is a logical passage for the human mind. Indeed man has never been satisfied to remain at the sense level. For a truly aesthetic appreciation of Nature it is necessary to see it flooded with the light of the invisible.[18]

This writer has elsewhere suggested that capacity for aesthetic experience, for religious experience, and mental health are interrelated, that

> a rather consistent personality pattern tends to be associated with those who are sceptical of large wholes or simply fail to perceive them at all.

---

[17] Vincent E. Smith, *The School Examined: An Essay on the Curriculum* (Milwaukee: The Bruce Publishing Co., 1960).

[18] *The Franciscans* (New York: Macmillan Co., 1930), p. 54.

Many arguments on a variety of topics hinge on the level of abstraction where reality resides, the unconscious assumption of each arguer being that it resides in one place and in one place only! Those who find it only in the smallest elements of a situation are not likely to have much capacity for aesthetic (or religious) experience. An element of fear seems to be present in all such cases. There seems to be a feeling that "the definite is the safe, and the small is the definite." Hence, "Let's be objective" often means, "Let's not get very far beneath the surface of things."[19]

St. Francis was never concerned to be "objective" in that sense. On the whole, Franciscan education has followed him in this example.

Some developments of Christian holism in educational theory were also made in the opening decades of the present century at The Catholic University of America in Washington, D. C. The names of Thomas E. Shields, Edward A. Pace, and George Johnson loom large here. Their work has been followed up to an extent by Sr. Mary Nona McGreal, Sr. Janet, and the Commission on American Citizenship, as exemplified in the text series, *Guiding Growth in Christian Social Living.*

As one looks at the early "holists" at The Catholic University, there is no doubt that they advocated teaching "the whole child," that they repudiated any one-sided intellectualism, and that they were conscious of all major facets of the child's character. One finds virtually no reference, however, to the empirical work in Gestalt psychology and other organismic systems of the time, nor does one find much sense of applied holism at a descriptive level. The stress seems to have been on the idea, "Let's educate *all* aspects of personality," but with little hint that personality is not the sum of these aspects, that *it* governs *them* and not the other way about.

In 1917, Shields wrote of the concept of adjustment, "The only surprising thing about this educational doctrine is that so many educators of our time seem to regard it as a new thought, whereas it is the very central thought of Christianity."[20] In 1921 he anticipated something of the ideographic method and the "internal frame of reference" in writing:

It is vain to treat symptoms instead of disease, yet nothing more is possible until we fully understand the causes of the evils of which complaint is made. The problem is usually approached from the outside. The dullard is

---

[19] R. B. Nordberg, "Acceptance and Capacity in Appreciating Beauty," *Catholic Educational Review,* LVI, No. 7 (October, 1958), 437.

[20] Thomas E. Shields, *Philosophy of Education* (Washington, D. C.: Catholic Education Press, 1921), pp. 67–68.

observed as if he were a frog or a tadpole by the educationist who has no light to guide him but that derived from the memory of successful school days and a brilliant educational career.[21]

Two decades later, Msgr. George Johnson wrote of various psychological categories:

> What we are likely to lose sight of . . . is . . . that these are abstractions and that back of them are vital, pulsating realities — the joys and the sorrows, the hopes and the ambitions, the comings and the goings of individual men, women, and children. . . . Time and again, through the course of history, human beings have been nailed to the cross of an abstraction.[22]

Sister M. Nona, O.P., president of Edgewood College, wrote recently:

> One of the elements of mystery in the child is the astonishing unity which combines animal and rational in the one person. It is not his body alone that learns, nor his intellect abstracted from the body, but the single person as a whole. We may concentrate attention upon the physical or spiritual in him, but can never really separate the one from the other. His curriculum, therefore, must be planned to accommodate the learning child as a whole person, body and soul in one. It must provide for the development of all his powers — senses, imagination, memory, emotions, reason, and will — as a complete, unified personality.[23]

Again, a text in the *Christian Social Living* series declares that the goals of Christian education in America should include physical fitness, economic competency, social virtue, cultural development, and moral and spiritual perfection in Christ.[24]

One can find reiterated through the centuries the Church's stress on intellectual cultivation, just as one can find her advocating the development of the whole person. It is plain from these combined facts that the great minds of Christendom have seen no opposition here. What too many modern thinkers have forgotten is that *the intellect is the best focal point for holistic education.* This is, indeed, "the lost insight" of modern educational theory! When the instrumentalist teacher talks about "the whole child," too often it is a whole from which intellect has been screened out.

---

[21] Thomas E. Shields, *The Making and the Unmaking of a Dullard* (Washington, D. C.: Catholic Education Press, 1921), p. 15.

[22] George Johnson, *Better Men for Better Times* (Washington, D. C.: Catholic University of America Press, 1943), p. 17.

[23] Sr. Mary Nona, "Know You What It Is to Be a Child?" *Catholic Educational Review,* LVIII, No. 4 (April, 1960), 219.

[24] Srs. Mary Joan and Mary Nona, *Guiding Growth in Christian Social Living,* I (Primary Grades), (Washington, D. C.: Catholic University of America Press, 1944), p. 14.

The question is not really whether teachers should aim just for the mind or for the complete human development. It is more a matter of whether teachers shall be pro- or anti-intellectual. It is easy, in educational theorizing, to lapse into a preoccupation with words for their own sakes, so that one does not realize that his theories have no empirical consequences. Here is an example. Let the teacher ask himself: If I want to provide moral and personality training, how should I proceed differently than if I want only to train the mind? If I want to provide "will training," how shall I proceed? For the most part, any such project proceeds by conveying *ideas,* and how does anyone convey ideas except through the intellect? St. Thomas stressed that the will turns the intellect to the contemplation of truth in the beginning and the will delights in attainment of truth in the end. The other side of the coin can also be emphasized, however: the will plays no role in attainment of truth save insofar as it activates the intellect. O'Leary stressed, in an address to the American Catholic Philosophical Association:

> No dichotomy can be established between moral virtues and prudence which is an intellectual virtue. By this I do not mean that every command or advice must be rationalized, explained, or rendered acceptable: but I mean that there should be a simultaneous development of moral virtue and prudence.[25]

Attitudes Toward the Concrete.   A certain ambiguity of standpoint and attitude toward the concrete — toward immediate experience and particulars — has long marked Catholic thought, and, therefore, Catholic education. Perhaps it is reality itself that produces this ambiguity. The Aristotelian critique of Plato and the Thomistic critique of Augustine were alike designed to recapture the concrete, to allow matter its place in the universe and sensations and images their place in knowledge. Yet, Aristotle and St. Thomas have often been criticized for equating the abstract with the real, for getting away from the immediacy of experience and actual events.

How does this come about? For one thing, you will recall that Thomists see created reality as individually existing things, which can, however be classified and ordered because each in some way expresses a universal. The "real" is neither the particular shorn of

---

[25] Timothy O'Leary, *American Catholic Philosophical Association Proceedings,* 1949, p. 124.

its universality nor the universal as mentally abstracted from the particular, but the concrete thing that contains both aspects. The nominalist[26] acknowledges no universal in the particular, and therefore sees any abstractive procedure as getting away from reality. Thomists have been wont to insist that abstraction, rather, takes us *toward* reality. A more accurate (and Thomistic) statement is that it takes us toward the *intelligibility* of reality, toward its formal aspect. If we do not remain conscious of abstracting, there is always the danger of confusing the universal with the particular. We should remember that all parrots are alike only in what is necessary to make them parrots, all olives are alike only in what is necessary to make them olives, and so forth.

A Thomist will not be concerned if he is guilty of a false abstractionism in the eyes of those who deny the validity of all abstractions; but, if the Thomist is guilty as charged in terms of *his own* theory of knowledge, that is a more serious matter. Occasionally, some Catholic teachers seem to confuse the universal with the particular, as when they feel that anything "Catholic" must be defended, or when they make statements such as "Latin is a beautiful language."

One of the formal systems that has arisen chiefly as an attempt to keep a firm grip on the concrete is Christian existentialism. This has been very influential on the continent and many people feel that, in the ordinary course of things, its next operation will be to sweep through America. It deserves, therefore, a careful, if necessarily brief treatment herein.

Catholic Existentialism. Existentialism has had many interpretations. Jean-Paul Sartre has stated that it is an attempt to draw systematically all of the conclusions that follow from an atheistic position. Chief among these, as Sartre agrees, is that existence is prior to essence. Less technically, man is whatever he makes himself. Everyone would agree, of course, that man has modified his civilizations, habits, and so forth, but Sartre means more than this. He means that there is no human nature because there is no God to conceive of it. A bread knife can have a nature because it is a manufactured thing; someone designed it. No one designed man,

---

[26] One who sees in universals mere *nomina* or names. This amounts to a denial of essences. Sometimes it is accompanied by a denial that the mind can form any concept or image corresponding to a general term. But if the mind does form such a concept, it is held not to correspond to anything.

however; man designs himself as he goes along. A later chapter will deal with existentialism in general; our present concern is with "Catholic existentialism."

The first question one must ask is whether there can be such a thing. Pius XII included in his list of philosophies that are irreconcilable with Catholic thought, "existentialism, whether atheistic or simply the type that denies the validity of the reason in the field of metaphysics."[27] This makes sense. An ontology which denies God and essences is off to the worst possible start if its aim is to be Catholic! Most Protestant theologians would also raise vigorous objections. Yet there are men who are called Christian existentialists, and whose sincerity cannot be doubted: Kierkegaard, Jaspers, Marcel, Barth, Niebuhr, Tillich. How is such a thing possible?

The first conclusion is that obviously they are not atheists. It is debatable to what extent they are concerned with Sartre's essential thesis, that existence is prior to essence. Rather, they are chiefly concerned with certain by-products of existentialism: the individual's peculiar awareness of his contingency and free choice, his moral responsibility for making himself what he is, the whole subjective gamut of one's life as a creature of God.

These ideas, taken in themselves, fit well into a Christian context. The Christian existentialists want to recapture the immediacy of Christian life, somewhat as the early Franciscans wanted to. Jaspers speaks of self-realization through involvement with one's own self-made world. He speaks of "objective being" in regard to the environment. This is considered "as not merely the objective world wherein we feel, think, and act, but also one which *includes* our thinking, feeling, acting."[28]

Gabriel Marcel is probably the leading Christian existentialist. Marcel certainly cannot be accused of indifference to the transempirical. He has written that the most serious of modern repressions is repression of the "ontological need." This is partly the "Who am I?" problem and partly "What is reality?" "The truth is," he writes, "that neither of the two can be dealt with separately."[29] Marcel

[27] Pius XII, *Humani Generis* (Washington, D. C.: National Catholic Welfare Conference, 1950), p. 15.

[28] George F. Kneller, *Existentialism and Education* (New York: Philosophical Library, 1958), p. 51.

[29] Gabriel Marcel, *The Philosophy of Existence* (London: The Harvill Press, 1948), p. 7.

does not mean, however, that we are to accept the conventional ontology of the leading Scholastics or of metaphysicians in general. He speaks of an "intersubjectivity upon which I seek to ground my ontology." As for the ontology of the First Cause, "it is only the living witness, that is to say the believing consciousness, which can decide what can or cannot be regarded as God."[30] Marcel speaks of "participation" as the way to truth and to happiness. Abstractions are to be understood by living them.

> There is never any question for him of an experience of the spiritual structure of reality except in all the concreteness of immediate incarnate experience. "Eternal truths," "immutable essences," "pure intelligibles," are not phrases that spring easily to his lips. Even where he speaks of values, it is not something like justice-as-such that he has in mind; values are a certain way of meeting being, and are as singular as the transcendent whose voice they are.[31]

What implications does Christian existentialism have for education? On the one hand, it is likely that the movement (however unfortunately named) will grow and have influence on education; on the other hand, nobody can say for sure just yet what sort of influence it will be. Individual circumstances must be taken into account to make valid judgments. Here Catholic teachers may well learn something from existentialists and phenomenologists about how to describe individual situations. This might favorably affect the teaching of the moral aspects of religion. For, while it has ever been Church doctrine that the gravity of a sin depends upon one's state of mind and of will and on certain other circumstances, little of this relativism is usually reflected in catechetical instruction. Again, existentialism can be a healthy exercise in the connectedness of things, which is conducive to integrated subject matter. Some of the newer ways of teaching religion, with stress on commitment, conversion, active participation in liturgy and social life, as contrasted with the use of formal catechisms, have an existentialist flavor.

One of the less fortunate results might be a return to Dewey's theme that finality is ever to be avoided, that "objective, systematized

---

[30] Gabriel Marcel, *The Mystery of Being*, V. II (Chicago: Henry Regnery Co., 1951), pp. 10, 4.

[31] Kenneth T. Gallagher, *The Philosophy of Gabriel Marcel* (New York: Fordham University Press, 1962), p. 117.

knowledge can only be hypothetical, never decisive."[32] It is easy to see how this would influence curricula and methods.

Since we are presently concerned with the educational influence of *Catholic* existentialism, perhaps this question should be posed: Is it not possible to effect a "return to the immediate" within a Thomistic framework? Are the chronic abstractionists really Thomists in spirit? Most of the philosophical excesses or aberrations that St. Thomas opposed in his day derived from Platonic epistemology, metaphysics, and psychology. In a way, St. Thomas was an existentialist of his day, because the fundamental Platonic error, as he saw it, was a slighting of *existence*. Some contemporary writers have referred to "the existentialism of Thomas Aquinas."

It sometimes seems, as regards essence and existence, or the abstract and concrete, that teachers and pupils manage to get the worst of both worlds. On the one hand, an art teacher protested that few of his students could draw a particular human arm as it is, because they literally cannot see the arm. That is, their vision is distorted by their preconceptions about the human arm. Likewise, the student studying botany may find it impossible to wander through a garden and *enjoy* the flowers, so busy is he classifying them as carduaceous, contractile, and so forth. On the other hand, students and teachers are often equally short on abstractions that really go to the heart of anything, really yield deep or systematic understanding. If some sort of "Christian existentialism" can help to eliminate this peculiar state of affairs, so much the better!

ATTITUDES TOWARD LANGUAGE AND METAPHYSICS

One philosophical development about which Catholic scholars have done very little to date is the rise of analytic and linguistic philosophy. Since this outlook and methodology are very influential in British philosophy and increasingly so in America, it seems probable that they will influence educational practices in this country, although such influences cannot yet be traced.

Linguistic analysis is the child of positivism. Auguste Comte (1798–1857) held that the only kind of valid knowledge comes from forming a testable hypothesis and testing it. Many contemporary systems of thought are traceable to this viewpoint, operationism being

---

[32] Kneller, *op. cit.*, p. 57,

one. Rudolph Carnap and the Vienna Circle tied the testing of hypotheses closely with the language in which the hypotheses are couched.[33]

Ludwig Wittgenstein, whose *Tractatus Logico-Philosophicus* appeared in 1921, became the acknowledged leader of that branch of neo-positivism known as linguistic analysis. Stripped of niceties, Wittgenstein's philosophy is admirably summed in an admonition he put forth: "Don't think, but look!" Metaphysical problems, the analysts hold, are pseudo problems. They have all arisen because men were careless in using language, unconscious of assumptions involved in the subject-predicate habit of speech and other semantic elements, unwary of the shifts in meanings of words from one context to another. The way to deal with a metaphysical problem is to "expose" it, to explain it away.

If a philosophical question can be salvaged at all, this is done by specifying the procedure for getting an answer to it. "One of the principal tasks of the logical analysis of a given proposition is to find out the method of verification for that proposition."[34] A statement like "This is hot" has meaning because it can be translated, "If you touch this, you will experience the sensation commonly known as heat." A statement like "God exists" is meaningless because there is nothing that will happen any differently if God exists than if He doesn't.

The linguistic viewpoint, like any viewpoint, cannot be self-validating. It is essentially a metaphysical position and therefore needs a metaphysical support. But how can metaphysics support an attack on metaphysics? Wittgenstein was somewhat aware of this dilemma. Throughout his *Tractatus,* he had been insisting that only testable propositions have meaning. Toward the close, he acknowledged that this proposition, on which all the rest depended, is itself not testable. Wittgenstein's way out:

> My propositions are elucidatory in this way: he who understands me finally recognizes them as senseless, when he has climbed out through them, on them, over them. (He must so to speak throw away the ladder, after

---

[33] *The International Encyclopedia of Unified Sciences,* which began in 1938, gives a good indication of the flavor of this movement. Leading contributors were Otto Neurath, Niels Bohr, Bertrand Russell, John Dewey, Rudolph Carnap, and Charles Morris.

[34] Rudolph Carnap, as quoted by Morton White (ed.), *The Age of Analysis* (New York: Mentor Books, 1959), p. 210.

he has climbed up on it.) He must surmount these propositions; then he sees the world rightly. Whereof one cannot speak, thereof one must be silent.[35]

So far from "remaining silent," however, Wittgenstein wrote a very long book about these transempirical matters. Perhaps his analogy is its own best refutation: A ladder that isn't there may well lead to a window that isn't there, either!

It is clear that steadfast application of linguistic analysis, as it has developed in positivist hands, to the daily diet of students, would eliminate from their lives and thought anything supernatural, anything mysterious, anything not grounded very directly in observation, preferably controlled observation. One can understand the popular appeal of this mode of thought and related systems, such as general semantics and cybernetics. They deal with a very small segment of reality and equate it with the whole. They encourage the student to cast aside as meaningless great and important problems that have exercised the best minds of all the ages. Nothing pleases us more than to be told that the things we cannot understand are humbug. To believe this on a large scale, however, is conducive to living in a fool's paradise.

The writer believes that the guidelines are present in the writings of St. Thomas for a Thomistic approach to linguistic analysis. Part of this is found in Thomas' treatment of the relations of subject and predicate in declarative sentences.[36] Another aspect is contained in his treatment of the analogy of being. These principles should be spelled out in relation to the linguistic analysis camp, if only to show that Catholic scholars are aware of this school of thought and have their own answers to it.

Indeed, it could be said that the Scholastics were, on the whole, the most language-conscious philosophers the world has ever produced, as witness their familiar dictum, "Never deny; rarely affirm; always distinguish." St. Thomas' unvarying way of dealing with a problem was this: He would state a question or a hypothesis, then cite a few objections to its truth, then state and defend his own position, then answer the objections. Usually, his answer was a yes-and-no answer in the sense that he would show how the proposition is true if taken one way and false if taken another. He did this more

---

[35] Ludwig Wittgenstein, *Tractatus Logico-Philosophicus* (New York: Harcourt, Brace, 1922), p. 224.
[36] St. Thomas, *Summa Theologica*, I, Q. 13, Art. 12.

systematically than do most contemporary linguistic analysts. Wittgenstein's most ardent followers admit that his writing is sadly lacking in order and system.

We need to do more about linguistic analysis than provide a Catholic "answer" to it, however. The system as it stands, granted its positivistic basis, can be very useful in teaching us a heightened awareness of the *functional mediation of empirical propositions*. Many of our everyday expressions, including some nourished in Catholic quarters, prove curiously devoid of meaning when one tries to relate them to any series of operations and observations. Examples would be: "There's a lot of truth in that." "She has lots of personality." "The Church is against that movie." "We must preserve the American way of life." "Cary Grant is handsome."

CATHOLIC EDUCATIONAL THEORY AND THE FUTURE

While man's knowledge tends to go forward in season and out, certainly it does not do so at a steady pace. There are times when findings from the various sciences and technologies pile up mountainously, and nobody has found time or insight for the major breakthroughs that seem to lie hidden in the pile. Then, suddenly, new basic perspectives on things emerge; the mountain of data labors and a new theory is born.

The world is not in a quiescent time now as regards knowledge. The race for survival against the perpetual threat of Communism has tended to obliterate the line between science and technology. The team approach, the new role of the monetary research grant as a "status symbol," these and other factors have worked to obscure individual genius and individual initiative. Nevertheless, willy-nilly and a bit compulsively, knowledge continues to accumulate. There have been a few theoretical modifications to accommodate this accretion. The main insights, however, are yet concealed, the missing silver needles in the giant stacks of hay.

Therefore we ask: What can Catholic educational theory contribute to and receive from the future of knowledge? This question raises the issue of whether there can be such a thing as "Catholic educational theory," to which we suggested an answer in an earlier chapter. There can be, at least, educational theories and principles which apply Christian doctrines (e.g., the freedom of the will) to educational problems, do the same with Scholastic philosophy, and also incorporate the best of social and behavioral science, emerging with a harmonious whole of some sort.

Notice that the relations presumed by the question are reciprocal. It is presupposed (and has previously been argued) that Catholic thought as such can both give valuable understandings to scientific questions and be enriched by scientific findings.

SOURCES OF CHANGE

What are the possible or likely sources of change in Catholic educational theory for the future? One source is new doctrinal defini-①tions. The Deposit of Faith has been essentially complete since it was given by Christ to the Apostles.[37] From time to time, however, there are disagreements as to some point of doctrinal interpretation. "Does it mean this or does it mean that?" A doctrinal definition is a formal statement made by the pope or by an ecumenical council in union with him to clarify such an issue. It may or may not emerge after long, scholarly study by any number of theologians, but, when issued, it is part of the essential teaching of the Church. There is, therefore, no appeal procedure for reconsideration of such a statement. Henceforth it is part of the belief of Catholics.

It should be clear that such a pronouncement does not add to the Deposit of Faith, but rather affirms that a certain point has implicitly always been there and is now explicit. On a few occasions, indeed, there have been doctrinal definitions of points that had been explicitly taught from the first, but which the Church chose to reaffirm because of some current heresy.[38] We shall later consider what sorts of doctrinal definitions might in the future modify Catholic educational thought.

A second source of possible changes is refinement of philosophical ② positions. The encyclical *Humani Generis,* while warning against the dangers of flirtations with any and every system of philosophy, insisted that Scholastic thought is always susceptible of more refinement, terminological changes, integration with recent scientific findings, and so forth.

The social sciences provide a third source of possible changes in

---

[37] First Council of the Vatican, sess. iii, cap. 4: "And the doctrine of faith which God revealed is proposed, not as a mere philosophical discovery to be elaborated by human minds, but as the divine deposit delivered by Christ to His spouse, to be by her faithfully guarded and infallibly declared."

[38] Such was the definition of the divinity of Christ in A.D. 325.

Catholic educational thought, and they also stand to profit from Catholic thought. Education is vitally related to various problems about human society, its institutions, functions, and relations. Teachers need to understand how groups originate and develop, how a culture comes to be what it is and what role the culture plays in children's learning. They need to understand the outlines of the process by which men produce, distribute, and use material goods, and how states originate and are governed.

Psychology and psychiatry provide a fourth source of changes in Catholic educational theory, probably the most important source at this stage of history. A teacher needs to know as much as possible about human behavior, consciousness and unconsciousness, about emotions, motives, perception, all that is human.

SOME PROBLEMS AND POSSIBLE SOLUTIONS

Such are the sources of possible new light. What are some problems and likely solutions in each area? As regards doctrinal definition, almost any such clarification of the Deposit of Faith is likely to have consequences for education. Certain areas, however, are of special relevance. In general, whatever gives further comprehension of the nature of man has this character. While the interrelations of intellect, body, and will are basically known, this is a very recondite field where further understanding is, to say the least, always possible. We have seen, for example, that the extent of separation of intellect and will, as illustrated by the divergent positions of St. Thomas and Duns Scotus, and the primacy of intellect or of will as illustrated by the same authors, are points of current debate. The mind-body problem is one of perennial significance for psychology and education. One fruitful new approach from language analysis has consisted in a heightened attention to the various things people mean in referring to "mind": consciousness, the self, the soul, intellectual ability, memory, etc.

Social science could, on the whole, profit from some attention to Thomistic positions on the nature of society and its proper relations to the individual. There is a strong tendency in our time for sociologists to perceive the group as having the same mode of reality as the individual person. A group never acts of a single volition, whereas an individual, whatever his conflicts, ultimately does. Strictly speaking, one cannot teach "a class," but only individual students. The assumption that the individual exists for society, rather than vice versa, is an habitual supposition of sociologists that is similarly incompatible with Thomistic thought.

Social science also has quite a bit to contribute to Catholic thought on educational principles, however. How do group folkways influence the contents and method of children's learning? What are some characteristics of the school itself as a sort of miniature society? Without subscribing to the viewpoint that makes social consensus the criterion for everything, one can profit from the empirical studies that have been done of how human groups form and operate.

PSYCHOLOGY AND PSYCHIATRY

Again we have a reciprocal relation. Psychology has much to contribute to illumine the Faith, and vice versa. We shall consider these relations in regard to three leading schools of psychological and psychiatric thought and research.

Behaviorism and Connectionism. Behaviorism is supposedly a psychological methodology, not a school of thought. Some authors say that this methodology proposes that psychological theories should be based upon behavior as something publicly visible. It is difficult to see how anyone could, by this criterion, be other than a behaviorist, since there is nothing the psychologist can study in persons other than himself except behavior. There is the further implication, however, that introspective techniques should not be used and no references should be made, in seeking to explain one's data, to consciousness or mind. It was once customary to distinguish between methodological and radical behaviorism. The first kind rules out mind and consciousness only as objects of psychological study, and only on the grounds that *they cannot be observed*. Radical behaviorism rules them out on grounds that *they do not exist*. How the behaviorist can deny his own consciousness is something of a puzzle, since (*a*) he is more directly aware of it than of anything else, and (*b*) it is the means by which he is aware of everything else. Nevertheless, behaviorists tried to build "the psychology of stimulus-and-response."[39] The early behaviorists were candid enough in announcing their system as an application to psychology of materialism. One text declares:

---

[39] Edwin G. Boring and others, *Psychology — a Factual Textbook* (New York: John Wiley and Sons, 1935), pp. 6–7.

Materialistic monism asserts that the processes of the mind are in fact physiological processes; thus conscious behavior does not exist. This is the position of physiological behaviorism whose chief proponent was J. B. Watson. Its popularity, which was considerable in the 1920's, is now on the wane.[40]

One writer suggests:

The absurdity of attempting to build a psychology which is nothing more than the study of behavior is made clear by the following greeting from one thorough-going behaviorist to another: "You are fine. How am I?"[41]

This thesis surely need not be pressed with Catholics. In the first place, although behaviorism sometimes wears the guise of a methodological development, one need but to turn to its literature to find frequent explicit affirmations of its materialistic basis. In the second place, it simply is not possible to build a reasonably complete, rounded science of man while ruling out the inner life, all that *makes* him man. Indeed, what is sometimes called "rational psychology" (not the most felicitous phrase in the world) deals with the soul and its properties — its simplicity, spirituality, immortality, origin, relations with the body, and the like. Even in empirical psychology, we have many occasions to require introspective data. What role, if any, does imagery play in thinking? Obviously, if people's conscious states cannot be investigated (by having them note and report these conditions, or otherwise) this problem can neither be investigated nor even allowed any meaning. In certain experiments on reading, subjects were asked to press one key when they "saw" a word and another the instant they grasped its "meaning." This, too, is an introspective problem. Many questions of forensic psychiatry, even some involving the death penalty, turn upon one's intentions — e.g., a sentry falling asleep on duty "deliberately." What happens to such questions if the whole mental life must be abandoned as meaningless or nonexistent? It is true that consciousness in another cannot be observed directly, but speech is behavior too, and people can report their thoughts. Even the psychoanalysts, whose faith in the conscious mind tends to run very low, allow them that.

We have stressed this issue because psychology is no longer in

---

[40] Karl F. Muenzinger, *Psychology: The Science of Behavior* (New York: Harper and Bros., 1942), p. 414. Cf. C. D. Broad, *Mind and Its Place in Nature* (New York: Harcourt, Brace, 1925). H. Feigl, "Logical Analysis of the Psycho-physical Problem," *Philosophy of Science*, I (1934), 420. William McDougall, *Body and Mind* (New York: Macmillan, 1920).

[41] Floyd L. Ruch, *Psychology and Life* (Chicago: Scott, Foresman, 1941), p. 11.

its youthful phase when writers were wont to label schools of thought categorically. Today's behaviorist takes his behaviorism, more so his materialism, for granted. He does not argue it; often he does not even mention it. But there are quite a few technological and theoretical developments that come directly from behaviorist underpinnings and simply cannot have any place, short of drastic reformulation, in Christian thought. Osgood's "semantic differential" is an example, as are various attempts to "measure meaning," most of cybernetics and general semantics, and the uncritical acceptance of "teaching machines."

Gestalt and Field Theory. On the other hand, there are strong similarities between Thomism as such and psychological holism as such. It is true that some Gestalt psychologists have characterized themselves as materialists. It is difficult to see, however, how one can really be a materialist and a holist simultaneously, since holism consists largely in the affirmation of form as not reducible to matter, while materialism consists largely in a denial of this. Most Gestaltists, whatever they call themselves, come close to an *Aristotelian naturalism,* which, while it stops short of specific affirmation of the spiritual, at least has a feeling for form.

What difference if the Scholastic says, "Every act is an act of the person" or the Gestaltist says, "Man acts and reacts as a unit." At a descriptive level, they mean the same. Thomism and holism can meet on the bridge of this tremendous insight. Catholic educators can learn much from holistic, organismic psychologists in the way of functional, descriptive treatments of the unity of man. At the same time, we can lead them to the view from the theological side of that bridge. What psychology needs to rediscover and continue to describe is *the person.* The person is not the soul, not the body, but the functionally indivisible, substantial union. The functional unity that Gestaltists, field theorists, and organismic psychologists find so interesting and significant is an empirical, fluctuating kind of unity, but it stems ultimately from the metaphysical unity of the being, which both governs and determines the psychosomatic unity which is personality.

There are two theoretical areas where Thomism as such and holism as such can make common cause in future theoretical development. One concerns person and personality, as just noted. The other concerns insight. In contrast to the emphasis of connectionistic psychologists upon trial-and-error learning, Gestaltists stress insight, which Bayles defined as "a sense of, or feeling for, pattern."[42] More technically, the term

> connotes a grasp on the part of the learner of an entire situation, particularly of the interrelationship of parts of the situation to each other. . . . It holds that the learner . . . is aware more or less clearly of the *why* of his action.[43]

Most of the naturalistic holists have not distinguished brute from human insight. Indeed, some of their work has tended to obliterate the line. Kohler, for example, reported experiments dealing with the ability of anthropoid apes to learn by insight. Less well known is his declaration that "It may be taken for granted as positively proved that their [chimpanzees'] gamut of phonetics is entirely *subjective* and can only express emotions, never designate or describe objects."[44] Not to differentiate the "insight" of man and beast can be fatal to understanding the whole issue. Once that differentiation is correctly made, however, all that the holists have had to say about insight joins hands beautifully with the Thomistic analysis of abstraction and judgment. Insight in the psychotherapeutic sense, i.e., self-understanding, is not philosophically different, though complicated by ego involvement.

Maritain has insisted that "thinking begins, not only with difficulties, but with *insights,* and ends up in insights which are made true by rational proving or experimental verifying, not by pragmatic sanction, that human thought is able to illumine experience, to realize desires which are human because they are rooted in the prime desire for unlimited good, and to dominate, control, and refashion the

---

[42] Ernest E. Bayles, "The Idea of Learning as Development of Insight," *Educational Theory,* II (April, 1952), 66.

[43] Charles E. Skinner, ed., *Essentials of Educational Psychology* (Englewood Cliffs, N. J.: Prentice-Hall, 1958), p. 213. Cf. Jacob W. Getzels and Philip W. Jackson, *Creativity and Intelligence* (London: John Wiley and Sons, 1962), pp. 83–86. J. Hadamard, *The Psychology of Invention in the Mathematical Field* (New York: Dover Publications, 1954).

[44] Wolfgang Kohler, *The Mentality of Apes,* trans. by Ella Winter (New York: Harcourt, Brace, 1925), p. 221. Cf. Robert M. Yerkes and Ada W. Yerkes, *The Great Apes* (New Haven: Yale University Press, 1929), p. 546: "It may not be asserted that any one of the anthropoid types speaks."

world."[45] He says this because of his acceptance and deep grasp of *abstraction* as treated by St. Thomas. Abstraction cannot be equated with insight, because human trial-and-error learning involves abstraction. But sometimes we are able to abstract, not merely *an* essence (in the broad sense, as corresponding to any possible idea), but *the* essence of a situation, a problem.

Materialistic notions often creep in, unnoticed, to interpretations of the mind's abstractive act. Even some self-styled Thomists occasionally regard abstraction as primarily a negative process of peeling off nonessentials by repeated experiences of something, until at last the pure heart of it is exposed, shining and clear. Understanding, however, is not a negative act of sweeping away misunderstandings, but *a positive act* of "getting the point." *We can in principle abstract from one case as well as from a thousand.* That is the "insight about insight" that contemporary educational theory urgently needs. An infant does not learn to recognize his mother's nose, then her ears, then her eyes, and so forth, and put them together to make a face. He recognizes her face before he can discern any part of it.[46]

Those who have understood the spirit of Catholic education well have always stressed teaching for insight. Pius XII, in an address to students of Rome, said:

> In order to study seriously, you must beware of the belief that the number of things learned is the fundamental element in building your educational edifice. What is necessary is not a great number of materials, but rather learning well, understanding profitably, and examining thoroughly everything that is necessary and useful.

He counseled against "an excess of matters which are purely mnemonic, which are quite distinct from serious and satisfying study, from a true and profound educational formation, and by which the school risks transforming itself into a game which saddens the parents and irritates the students."[47] A Jesuit writer deplores "the Catholic's ready answer" and "a merely defensive psychology," and suggests that "the function of the Catholic college is not merely to

---

[45] Jacques Maritain, *Education at the Crossroads* (New Haven: Yale University Press, 1960), p. 13.

[46] See St. Thomas, *Summa Theologica,* P. I, q. 85, a. 3; *Commentary on the Posterior Analytics,* Bk. I, 1. 4, n. 43.

[47] Pius XII, "The Bases of Sound Education," address to students of Rome, March 24, 1957. Reprinted, *The Pope Speaks,* IV (Summer, 1957), 14–20.

teach the formulas of the Catholic religion, but to impart in a thousand ways, which defy formularization, the Catholic attitude toward life as a whole."[48]

Depth Psychology. The third major school of psychology and psychiatry to be considered, and the last, is psychoanalysis. This is at once a theory of human development and behavior, a method of research, and a system of psychotherapy, the whole system developed basically by Dr. Sigmund Freud. Its method is simple in essence. By free association and interpretation of dreams, recently by other related techniques also, emotions and behavior are traced to repressed instinctual drives in the unconscious. By bringing unconscious drives and conflicts into awareness, the analyst hopes to help the patient modify his emotions and behavior in a healthy direction. Freud preferred that the term "psychoanalysis" be limited to the strict interpretation and practice of his ideas. The broader expression, "depth psychology," refers in general to the psychology of unconscious mental life. Included would be the "analytic psychology" of the late Carl Gustav Jung, which minimizes sexual factors in emotional disorders and stresses a "collective unconscious" and certain quasi-mystical elements. Alfred Adler's "individual psychology," which stresses compensation and overcompensation for inferiority feelings, also comes under the category, as do some more recent systems, such as those of Karen Horney and Harry Stack Sullivan. It is somewhat problematical how much one of these systems differs from another. As is usual in such matters, they are seen as radically different by their respective proponents, and as strikingly similar by those who stand somewhat aloof from the whole movement.

The relations between religion and depth psychology were somewhat strained at first. It is often said that this is because clergymen saw a threat to their beliefs and livelihood in the new system. The giant's share of the blame, however, appears to belong to Freud himself, who was militantly, almost offensively antireligious. Also, the early psychoanalytic movement was to a very large extent a Semitic development, and characterized by marked anti-Christian feelings. Also, in the late 1940's and early 1950's certain Catholic orators widely regarded as "official" made a number of strong statements against psychoanalysis, followed by some retractions which

---

[48] George Bull, *Why a Catholic College?* (New York: America Press, 1956), pp. 7, 13, 14.

the newspapers, as is their wont, buried in the inside pages. This controversy bore fruit, though. Catholic scholars went into the issues carefully. The Holy Father made a number of statements outlining the mind of the Church on this subject.[49] His attitude toward depth psychology was one of encouragement tempered by caution. The pontiff pointed out certain "danger zones" in the theory and practice of psychoanalysis: Freud's pansexual orientation, denial by some therapist's of the patient's fundamental moral accountability, occasional probing of conscience without permission, unwarranted intrusions into innermost layers of personality, deliberate provocation by some therapists of violent emotions in the client for therapeutic reasons, possible injuries to a third party through counseling and psychotherapy, the degrading of human dignity for experimental purposes, and confusing of guilt with guilt feelings. He stressed, however, that the notion that there are some processes in the soul that never become conscious is not in itself incompatible with Catholic thought.

A great deal of contemporary educational theory is based upon depth psychology. Some things have been taken over uncritically by educational psychologists. Other riches of psychoanalytical insight have been left unutilized, however. Now that the guidelines have been laid down for a harmonious relating of depth psychology with Christian thought, it is to be hoped that educational theorists will profit further from depth psychology.

We have given one answer to the question: What can Catholic educational theory contribute to and receive from the future of knowledge? The rapidly expanding state of knowledge at the descriptive level, and the probability of new insights in many areas in our time, were cited as reasons for considering the outlines of a new synthesis of Christian knowledge, especially as regards points that could become part of educational theory. New doctrinal definitions, philosophical refinements, social sciences, and psychology and psychiatry were cited as possible sources of such new knowledge. Some possible problems and general lines of solution in each area were included. Under the "psychology and psychiatry" category we looked at behaviorism, holism, and depth psychology.

---

[49] E.g., Pius XII, discourse to delegates, Fifth Congress of Psychotherapy and Clinical Psychology, *Linacre Quarterly*, XX (1953), 97–105; Cf. Francis P. Furlong, "Peaceful Co-existence of Religion and Psychiatry," *Bulletin of the Menninger Clinic*, XIX, No. 6 (November, 1955), 210–216; James H. VanderVeldt and Robert P. Odenwald, *Psychiatry and Catholicism*, 1957, Chap. 14, "Religion and Psychiatry."

SUMMARY

This chapter has attempted to review Catholic philosophies of education as they stand presently, and to look tentatively to the future. This was done because of the number of important issues on which Catholic teachers differ and as a means to help distinguish the essential from the incidental.

Certain common themes and positions were pointed out on the nature of man, the nature of knowledge, the agencies of education, and its purposes. Divergencies were also discussed in the areas of methodology, curriculum, indoctrination and academic freedom, coeducation, and use of secular schools. Two main strands running through these differences received special discussion: intellectualism versus holism (a dichotomy we tended to reject) and attitudes toward the concrete, especially as exemplified in Christian existentialism. Finally, a look was taken at Catholic educational theory and the future.

Now we have brought Catholic educational philosophy, which is supernaturalist, from the foundation of the Church (circa A.D. 29) to date. But naturalism is even older. Thales of Miletus held this viewpoint six centuries before Christ, concluding that everything was made of water. Through Hobbes, Rousseau, Spencer, Dewey, and others, the naturalist stream has continued until our day, when it threatens to become an all-devouring river. To that vista we next turn.

BIBLIOGRAPHY

Ashley, Benedict M., and Conway, Pierre H., *The Liberal Arts in St. Thomas Aquinas* (Washington, D. C.: Thomist Press, 1959).

Avalos, Beatrice, *New Men for New Times* (New York: Sheed and Ward, 1962).

Boring, Edwin G., and others, *Psychology — a Factual Textbook* (New York: John Wiley and Sons, 1935).

Brennan, Robert E., *Thomistic Psychology* (New York: Macmillan Co., 1941).

Broad, C. D., *Mind and Its Place in Nature* (New York: Harcourt, Brace, 1925).

Bull, George, *Why a Catholic College?* (New York: America Press, 1956).

Ellis, John Tracy, *American Catholics and the Intellectual Life* (Chicago: Heritage Foundation, 1956).

Feigl, H., "Logical Analysis of the Psycho-physical Problem," *Philosophy of Science,* I (1934).

Gallagher, Kenneth T., *The Philosophy of Gabriel Marcel* (New York: Fordham University Press, 1962).

Getzels, Jacob W., and Jackson, Philip W., *Creativity and Intelligence* (London: John Wiley and Sons, 1962).

Hadamard, J., *The Psychology of Invention in the Mathematical Field* (New York: Dover Publications, 1954).

International Encyclopedia of Unified Sciences, The.

James, *The Franciscans* (New York: Macmillan Co., 1930).

Johnson, George, *Better Men for Better Times* (Washington, D. C.: Catholic University of America Press, 1943).

Kneller, George F., *Existentialism and Education* (New York: Philosophical Library, 1958).

McCluskey, Neil J., *Catholic Viewpoint on Education* (Garden City, N. J.: Doubleday and Co., 1959).

McDougall, William, *Body and Mind* (New York: Macmillan Co., 1920).

McGucken, William J., "The Catholic Philosophy of Education," Chap. 6, *Philosophies of Education,* I, 41st Yearbook of the N.S.S.E. Reprinted by The America Press.

Marcel, Gabriel, *The Mystery of Being,* Vol. II (Chicago: Henry Regnery Co., 1951).

———— *The Philosophy of Existence* (London: The Harvill Press, 1948).

Maritain, Jacques, *Education at the Crossroads* (New Haven: Yale University Press, 1960).

Mary Joan, Sister, and Mary Nona, Sister, *Guiding Growth in Christian Social Living,* I (Primary Grades), (Washington, D. C.: Catholic University of America Press, 1944).

Muenzinger, Karl F., *Psychology: The Science of Behavior* (New York: Harper and Bros., 1942).

O'Brien, Kevin J., *The Proximate Aim of Education — a Study of the Proper and Immediate End of Education* (Milwaukee: The Bruce Publishing Co., 1958).

O'Leary, Timothy, *American Catholic Philosophical Association Proceedings,* 1949.

Pius XI, *Encyclical Letter on Christian Education of Youth* (Washington, D. C.: National Catholic Welfare Conference, 1936).

Pius XII, "The Bases of Sound Education," address to students of Rome, March 24, 1957. Reprinted, *The Pope Speaks,* IV (Summer, 1957).

———— discourse to delegates, Fifth Congress of Psychotherapy and Clinical Psychology, *Linacre Quarterly,* XX (1953).

———— *Humani Generis* (Washington, D. C.: National Catholic Welfare Conference, 1950).

Ruch, Floyd L., *Psychology and Life* (Chicago: Scott, Foresman, 1941).

Shields, Thomas E., *The Making and the Unmaking of a Dullard* (Washington, D. C.: Catholic Education Press, 1921).

———— *Philosophy of Education* (Washington, D. C.: Catholic Education Press, 1921).

Skinner, Charles E., ed., *Essentials of Educational Psychology* (Englewood Cliffs, N. J.: Prentice-Hall, 1958).

Smith, Vincent E., *The School Examined — An Essay on the Curriculum* (Milwaukee: The Bruce Publishing Co., 1960).

Vander Veldt, James H., and Odenwald, Robert P., *Psychiatry and Catholicism,* 1957, Chap. 14, "Religion and Psychiatry."

Wittgenstein, Ludwig, *Tractatus Logico-Philosophicus* (New York: Harcourt, Brace, 1922).

Yerkes, Robert M., and Ada W., *The Great Apes* (New Haven: Yale University Press, 1929).

look for critical 'holes' in the idea

Naturalism

INTRODUCTION

RUNNING through most of the educational literature today one finds a dominant thread. The importance of this fact is for life as well as for education. The central theme of this thread is expressed in such terms as "continuous progress," "the perfectibility of mankind," and "perpetual betterment through scientific advances." The underlying philosophy of this outlook is signified by the term "naturalism."

As a philosophy of life (perhaps the oldest one) it maintains that nature is the only reality worthy of the serious consideration of man, and that man himself is the apex of this reality.

Naturalism, like most other philosophies, is not a simple, unitary system — there are many kinds, just as there are several brands of pragmatism, realism, and idealism. But there is one common denominator for all kinds of naturalism, namely, the explicit or implicit denial or disregard of any reality above nature. Using this negative definition one might include all modern philosophies (and some very ancient ones) in the family of naturalists except the few theocentric systems of the Eastern and Western world. Thus pragmatism, instrumentalism, reconstructionism, Marxism, logical positivism, and atheistic existentialism are all naturalistic.

For the purposes of this chapter, however, naturalism is limited to a set of beliefs proposed by philosophers who have had significant influence on education in the nineteenth and early twentieth centuries. The other schools of related thought will be considered in succeeding chapters.

METHODOLOGY

It is in the area of methodology, perhaps, that naturalism has had the greatest effect on education. Since this philosophy constitutes both a reaction against traditional educational methods and a proposal for substituting "natural" methods in their place, it might be well to indicate what both facets are.

In the first place, the naturalist is opposed to the formalized, teacher-centered methods of the medieval and Renaissance scholars, many of which persist to this day. (And we should recall that these teacher-centered methods were *opposed* also by the great thinkers of medieval times, Augustine, Aquinas, and Scotus.) In such methods the teacher was viewed as the active agent in the teaching-learning process, whereas the student was presumed to be the recipient of the knowledge presented to him. In their worst form such approaches made of the pupil's role a very passive one, indeed. His only activity was "giving back" to the teacher that which he had learned from the teacher or from books.

This pupil activity usually took the form of recitation or written and oral examinations. It might be argued that such passivity on the pupil's part was not in harmony with the basic philosophy of traditionalism. Nevertheless, it was a characteristic of all traditional teaching methods. A second characteristic was the repression of the pupil's natural instincts and desires. As will be shown later in this chapter, the naturalist objected to the Hebrew-Christian conception of man's fallen nature. Much of traditional teaching and discipline was designed to repress the evil tendencies of youthful nature. In some instances educators such as Cotton Mather believed that education's most important task was to "drive the devil out" of the pupil. Therefore, the naturalist objected to all harsh methods of discipline; he opposed the view that "Children are to be seen and not heard"; he considered "miseducative" the attempts to make all pupils conform to one norm of behavior.

One final aspect of traditional education violently opposed by the naturalist might be termed "authoritarianism." As will be pointed out later, all authority upon this view rests within nature, not in God. Therefore, teachers have no right to appeal to any outside authority such as God or the Church for their own authority as teachers. It rests with all the people, including the pupils.

What, then, does the naturalist propose as substitutes for the methodology of the traditionalist? First, he maintains that all teaching methods should be based on experience. Since he relies on the inductive method, he insists that the first criterion for judging the value of a teaching method should be based on self-activity of the pupil finding the answers for himself. The pupil himself must observe nature in order to find facts and discover answers to his problems. To *tell* the pupil all the facts, to *show* him the procedures, to *give* him the answers, merely makes him a recipient of reports of others' experiences. The child has not *learned* but merely memorized or "absorbed" what he has been told. Thus all teaching methods should be characterized by pupil activity involving direct or at least vicarious experience; the pupil must educate himself.

A second characteristic of naturalistic teaching-learning methods is found in their conformity to the natural development of the pupils. A modern application of this principle is stated in terms of *readiness* of the organism for any given learning. Negatively stated, this principle means that it is not the teacher or society that determines what the child should learn, but his own developmental level. Positively stated, it means that when the organism is ready for a certain type of learning activity it will seek it *naturally,* that is, without being forced by the teacher or by adult society. Thus the pupil will learn about his physical environment when his interests and instincts lead him to such learning; boy-girl relationships will be developed when children reach the age for such relationships; pupils will learn to read when they are *ready*. Consequently, any attempt to forge ahead of the "natural time" or to repress at that time the youthful desires for these activities defeats the whole purpose of education.

A third characteristic of naturalistic methodology is that all educational activities should be enjoyable to the child. The tasks assigned by traditionalist teachers were designed to discipline the student and therefore were considered unpleasant by the student, but the naturalist felt that any task that went "against the grain" for the pupil should be avoided. Note how quickly and easily children (or adults) learn what they enjoy. Number games, word games (Scrabble), reading interesting stories, studying plants or animals in their natural habitats, the skills of woodworking, household arts, dramatics, and the like, constitute real enjoyment for the learner. Any teacher of a subject which students elect because they *like* it will testify to the great amount of effort that is put forth in comparison to that displayed by students in required courses. Thus any teaching-learning methods which make the material distasteful to the pupils should be avoided.

Since classroom discipline usually is associated with methodology, the naturalist asserts a fourth characteristic of sound teaching, namely that all discipline should derive from the natural elements of the situation. The situation will provide a form of innate discipline that should replace that of the teacher. To illustrate, a child learns to avoid hot objects because he has experienced the discomfort and pain which follow his touching them; the pupil learns to cooperate with other pupils when he finds himself ostracized by his classmates. An exception is made to this principle (utilizing the natural consequences of unacceptable behavior) only in cases where the first test may be the last, especially with young children. Playing with a sharp knife, darting in front of vehicular traffic, taking arsenic, lead to natural consequences from which the person might never recover. Accordingly, the child must learn by indirect means that such behavior is dangerous for the organism. Perhaps the parent or teacher might take the child to the scene of an accident or show pictures of a mangled child who had dashed into the path of an automobile.[1]

PESTALOZZI'S SCHOOL

The first attempt to put the naturalistic view of methodology into practice was in the experimental schools of the great educator, Pestalozzi. Even though his schools failed because of his own lack of administrative ability, they were in operation long enough to give visitors a chance to view the new methodology. His experimental schools generally were boarding schools. Thus education was an experience *in living* rather than a preparation for life. Learning took place in the fields, carpenter shops, the kitchen, before the fireplace, or in any other natural setting. The formal classroom atmosphere of the traditional school was avoided. Sense-perception constituted the foundation of learning rather than verbal definition or explanation; verbal formulations always were connected with objects of sense; exercises were developed so they proceeded from the simple level of the child's experiences to the more complex levels. The

---

[1] See H. Spencer, *Education* (New York: D. Appleton Co., 1907), p. 172. Cf. also his *First Principles of a New System of Philosophy,* 2 ed. (New York: D. Appleton Co., 1896), p. 229. In the first reference, Spencer proposes the "natural consequences" theory of discipline. In the second, he indicates how it should be modified, especially with young children, for instances involving serious harm to the child.

"object lesson" was used extensively as a means for developing perception and facility to describe correctly what one had perceived.[2]

Learning by experience is evident throughout the curriculum. To illustrate, geography was learned by field trips within the vicinity of the school. The children would get a general view of the river valley from some vantage point and follow this with a special study of each sector of the same valley. Then they would bring back samples of the soil from the valley and surrounding hillsides, from which they constructed their own relief map of the area. Only after the children had completed their own project would they be shown a professional map of the area. Then the map "made sense" literally to them, because it was based on firsthand experience.

Other areas which lent themselves especially well to this natural method were singing, physical education, nature study, and local history. There were no formal music classes because the children sang while they were on their hikes in the fields, while they walked the corridors of the old castle which served as their school and home, and while they sat before the fireplace in the evening. Physical education was a very informal and natural type of activity consisting mainly of playing games, hiking, and some gymnastic exercises. Nature study was not organized around books but around the specimens the children collected in the environs of the castle. Local history was reenacted by the students, who made snowforts and fought the battles around these forts.

Most striking, perhaps, was the absence of the harsh discipline usually found in schools of the time. The children's love and trust in their teachers replaced rules and regulations; there were no special rewards and no punishments; the children loved their games and their lessons because they were all made pleasant and enjoyable. Discipline in the sense of rigid control by the teacher was unnecessary because the children were happy and permitted to develop according to their natural tendencies. Their natural desire to be active was not thwarted by unnatural regimentation.[3]

The American Progressive Education movement learned its methodology from such schools as Pestalozzi's. The use of the field trip,

---

[2] The simplest form of the object lesson consists in having the child describe some object that is placed before him.

[3] For descriptive anecdotes about the Pestalozzi schools see R. DeGuimps, *Pestalozzi: His Life and Work* (New York: D. Appleton Co., 1895), pp. 209–275.

J. Parker — father of Progressivism

the emphasis on knowing the nature of the child, the replacement
of harsh discipline with pupil freedom, the stress on pupil activity,
and many other characteristics of the Pestalozzi school were observed firsthand by Francis Parker, the father of Progressivism. It
was this movement that tried to adapt this methodology of naturalism
to the American classroom.

AGENCIES OF EDUCATION

From the chapters on Christian education it is quite evident that
the Church as an educational agency plays a predominant role. The
school, during the Christian era, is viewed as an arm of the Church.
In reality, there were few schools that were not Church schools.
Even Rousseau's education (a "classic" naturalistic position) was
"Christian" despite the fact that all his writings on education were
condemned because of their antireligious beliefs. One might expect
that Rousseau would give to the school that role of which he divested
the Church. Such, however, was not the case. His celebrated work,
Emile, proposes that formal schooling is both unnecessary and harmful to education "according to nature." Even the tutor's role must
be subordinated to that of the home and nature. His function is a
negative one: to keep the child and youth from the evil influence
of corrupt institutions and society. Of these three educational agencies
(home, church, and school) Rousseau would recognize only the
home. The foundations of good physical and mental health are laid
during infancy (ages one to five).[4] If the child is spoiled by faulty
home training during these formative years, his tutor will have great
difficulty in correcting the errors.

It might be argued that Rousseau recognized the school as an
agency of education in the person of the tutor. Perhaps so! Certainly,
though, Emile's tutor is a far cry from the formal classroom of
Rousseau's day or of modern times.

That the Church's role as educator was excluded from Rousseau's
plan is evident from his recommendation that the student be introduced to religious ideas only during the last phase of education,
just before he enters society. To talk of the supernatural before this
time "is the method of superstition, of prejudice, of error";[5] for the

---

[4] See J. Rousseau, *Emile,* in the R. L. Archer ed., *Rousseau on Education* (London: Edward Arnold Co., 1916).

[5] *Ibid.,* Chap. VII, p. 201.

child must know thoroughly the nature of the physical universe before he can be expected to comprehend the nature of the spiritual universe. When the pupil is able to grasp the abstract concepts found in religion, then he should be allowed to make his choice among the various religious sects.

Other naturalists were not as naïve or idealistic about the role of the family as a unique educational agency as was Rousseau. Although they believed that the parents' role is very important in the child's education, one should have formalized institutions (schools) whose very existence is rooted in nature. The period of infancy for animals was very brief, so the parents could furnish all the training the young animal would need to preserve his life. The infancy of the human species, however, is greatly prolonged and thereby demands extended training which the parents usually are not able to provide. Consequently, it is quite "natural" for man to create institutions which will enable him to learn the manifold habits, skills, and knowledge necessary to live a full human life.

Pestalozzi and Spencer recognized this and accepted the school as one of the fundamental educational agencies. Pestalozzi conducted his "natural education" within the setting of the boarding school. Spencer, too, placed upon the formalized school the responsibility for educating the "whole child." He disclaimed the view, accepted at his time, that the school's primary job consisted in nourishing the mind. Spencer's recommendation that the school assume responsibility for health and physical education, vocational and social education, as well as intellectual training, seems to indicate that he makes the school the primary educational agency.[6]

Furthermore, Spencer's religious agnosticism aligns him with the complete secularization of the school, relegating to the Church little or no educative function. The rise of the modern secular school, especially in America, might be traced in part to the influence of the great naturalists, especially Rousseau and Spencer.

Naturalism, in summary, recognizes only two primary educational agencies, the *home* and the *state* (through the state-sponsored secular school). Of course, a twentieth-century naturalist undoubtedly would acknowledge the important function that secondary educational agencies serve. Mass communication media such as radio, television,

---

[6] See subsequent sections on curriculum and aims in this chapter.

movies, newspapers, all play important parts in the modern child's education.

CURRICULUM

Since the naturalistic philosophy of education was never applied as the sole thought system underlying any large modern educational enterprise, it is difficult to list the curricular offerings in great detail. One can glean from the literature of the great naturalists and the practices of their disciples, nevertheless, certain basic principles of curriculum-construction and subject-matter offerings in harmony with these principles.

Just as in other areas of educational philosophy, the naturalistic approach to curriculum represents a revolt against the traditional view of education. Rousseau, Pestalozzi, and Spencer all rejected the highly abstract, verbal content of the traditional curriculum. Rousseau's rejection of the kind of society which existed at his time included a repudiation of the kind of education that society fostered. Rousseau sought to tear down the bastions of reason and sophistication which the schools represented. Development of "reason" isolated from the harmonious development of emotion and instinct truly is miseducative. Rousseau believed there should be no curriculum until the child was twelve years old. Living with nature and in harmony with nature should constitute the core of the child's educational experiences. In the first period (infancy up to five years of age) the child should be allowed to grow as nature directs. He should be permitted to be active when he "feels like it," to rest when he wishes; he should be hardened gradually to the hardships which nature provides so that he will grow up "healthy and hardy." In other words, those natural activities which promote physical well-being should constitute the curriculum at this developmental stage.[7]

During the second period (ages five to twelve) one notes the same absence of anything resembling the curriculum of a school of the times. These seven years stress physical development carried on in a natural setting, in which the child is protected from the evil influences of society. Rousseau argued that this would keep the child from acquiring prejudices, vices, or bad habits which might interfere with later attempts to educate him. But, during this period of awakening, nature provides an ever widening scope of curricular

---

[7] Archer, *op. cit.,* Chap. IV.

content. The child observes with great interest the things his natural environment places before him. He does not need books or lessons from which to learn geography and natural science. The fields, rivers, plants, animals, and the heavens are adequate subject matter for his inquiring mind. Because his maturity level is more advanced than it was during infancy, his observations are systematic. To use the jargon, this curriculum is exclusively "experience-centered."[8]

The next three years are to be spent on learning useful skills (vocational education) so the child might provide for his livelihood. Nature study and physical fitness activities still constitute a major portion of his educational work. At this stage he is introduced to the world of books for the first time. The books should be characterized by their concern for man's natural needs and the means of satisfying them. Even for this stage, Rousseau exclaims:

> I hate books; they teach people to talk about things which they do not understand. . . . Since we must have books, there is one which, in my opinion, affords a complete textbook of natural education. . . . What is this wonderful book? Is it Aristotle? Is it Pliny? Is it Buffon? No; it is *Robinson Crusoe*.[9]

For all practical purposes, then, Rousseau is against the entire school curriculum as it existed at his time for the age group twelve to fifteen.[10]

Only after the child has reached fifteen does education assume a more academic nature. At Rousseau's time, this was the age when formal education ended for most youth, but the sort he favored should just begin at fifteen. Prior to this age, the child is concerned only with himself. His parents and elders strengthened this propensity by serving the child in all his needs and desires. At fifteen, however, the child learns that to be loved by others he must show by his words and deeds that he is worthy of such love. It is this natural tendency which provides the stimulus for training youth for life in society. History, even though Rousseau felt it was poorly written at his time, offers youth the best source for the study of society, because it is a study of men. The ideal history is that which gives facts and causes of the facts and events. A good history is not to be vitiated by the opinions of the historian, as so many are — Polybius, Sallust,

---

[8] *Ibid.*, Chap. V.
[9] *Ibid.*, p. 161 f.
[10] *Ibid.*, Chap. VI.

Livy, the standard texts of the time. Rousseau considers Thucydides, Xenophon, and Herodotus much closer to his ideal of "good historians."

Literature is another area of study which Rousseau recommends for this final educational period. The student should read agreeable books and be taught to analyze them. Through such activity he will develop aesthetic taste and learn grammar. Rousseau believed the student would profit most from reading the ancients, simply because they are "nearer to nature."

As one might expect, this is the period of education when sex education should be introduced, since this is the age of sexual awakening. Rousseau supplies many recommendations for teaching teen-agers about sex. Suffice it to indicate that all recommendations are "according to nature."

The final task of education during this period consists in facilitating the youth's actual entrance into society. Rousseau admits that man cannot live for himself and by himself. Since the child has been protected from the evils of society during the first fifteen years of his life, his choices about men and society after that time will not be clouded by these evils. His choice of a wife, companions, and leaders will be based on unbiased natural inclinations, he will judge his fellowman with purity of heart and mind. Now he is a finished product prepared to live in harmony with nature and his fellowman.[11]

Like many creators of new ideas, Rousseau had neither the ability nor the inclination to put them into practice. Pestalozzi's experimental schools at Burgdorf and Yverdon represent short-lived attempts to apply Rousseau's principles of curriculum construction in the school. Since Pestalozzi worked within a much more realistic framework of a school and classroom, however, he did not utilize the age groupings recommended by Rousseau. The curriculum of his school, though, was nature-centered rather than subject matter-centered. All of the activities of the school were based upon experiences and materials appropriate to the developmental pattern of the pupil. All the artificiality and bookishness were removed from the studies of the elementary school years. Children studied nature as nature, not as described in books. They were given boundless freedom to satisfy their own needs and interests through free-play activities, drawing, singing, dancing, or whatever they wished. Reading, writing, and

---

[11] *Ibid.*, Chap. VII.

numbers became part of the child's curriculum when he was ready
for them rather than a predetermined activity for a certain grade
level or age group. Apparently, Pestalozzi looked upon these "subjects" as something the child would want to learn simply because
they were so much a part of his natural environment. To him there
seemed to be no need for a formalized, lockstep curriculum, since
the child would move naturally from objects of sense to words,
numbers, and ideas.

Spencer, the systematic philosopher of naturalism, is much more
specific than Pestalozzi in his application of naturalistic theory to
curriculum construction. Since "complete living" is the purpose of
education, the curriculum of the school must be chosen in accordance with this purpose. In the order of importance, the ingredients
are:

1. Those activities which directly minister to self-preservation;
2. Those activities which, by securing the necessaries of life, indirectly
minister to self-preservation;
3. Those activities which have for their end the rearing and discipline of
offspring;
4. Those activities which are involved in the maintenance of proper social
and political relations;
5. Those miscellaneous activities which make up the leisure part of life,
devoted to the gratification of the tastes and the feelings.[12]

Stated in modern terms, Spencer's curriculum (for any school)
must contain health and physical education. When this basic content is assured the next obligation of the school lies in vocational
education so that the student can earn a living. Those studies which
enable the person to become a good parent, such as homemaking,
cooking and sewing, child-rearing, and the like, claim the next place
of importance in the curriculum. Education for "citizenship" ranks
fourth in the hierarchy of curricular offerings. When the student
knows how to keep himself physically fit, to earn a living, to be a good
parent, then he should learn how to be a good citizen. Only when all
of these topics have been satisfactorily covered in the curriculum, can
the school indulge the students in the content areas such as literature and philosophy.

Ideally, complete preparation in all areas should constitute the
goal of the school. But since this ideal cannot be achieved, even in

---

[12] H. Spencer, *Education: Intellectual, Moral, and Physical* (New York: D. Appleton and Co., 1866), p. 16.

a lifetime, the school should preserve a proper balance between the areas. Spencer's vehement opposition to the humanistic curriculum of his time did much to influence the rise of the natural and social science to a position of eminence in the schools. The practical arts were given precedence over the fine arts, especially in the early days of American progressivism.

Perhaps no educational movement gave passage to Rousseau's, Pestalozzi's and Spencer's views on the curriculum as did early American progressivism. Although progressivism is usually associated with the flowering of Dewey's instrumentalist philosophy, this phase comes well after the movement was under way in America. One characteristic of the early progressive curriculum which allies it closely with the curricular theories of Rousseau, Pestalozzi, and Spencer is its child-centeredness. A study of child nature, it was argued, will reveal the nature and content of the curriculum. This child-centeredness later gave way to the society-centered curriculum of the instrumentalists. Since this phase of progressivism will be treated in the next chapter, it is enough here to point out that the early reform of progressivism can be traced to the naturalistic theories of these "big three": Rousseau, Pestalozzi, and Spencer.

STUDENTS

When the naturalistic philosophy of education was first expounded, universal schooling was unknown. Beyond the most elementary level, it was limited to the intellectual and/or economic elite. In fact, educational elitism had been taken for granted since Plato advocated that youth be educated according to the role they would play in society. A very small number would receive advanced education: these should rule the people. Others should be trained to be guardians or defenders of the people: these would constitute the military forces. The lowest class should be trained in the skilled crafts: these would be the servants of society.

Throughout the ages, the last-named group constituted the great majority of the population, even in highly civilized countries of Western Europe. Even though political liberalism, with its origins in the Greek experiments in democracy, had succeeded in gaining acceptance among many leading statesmen and political theorists, educational liberalism was not put into practice. Thus the cry of "equal educational opportunity for all" had the ring of radicalism to the traditionalist educators of the times. But the naturalists, who were advocates of political liberalism, also became opponents of educational elitism. Rousseau, as R. L. Archer points out, opposed every facet of traditional education.[13] He wanted all children to reap the benefits of "education according to nature." Pestalozzi's schools were open to the rich and the poor, the bright and the dull. Spencer, too, in rejecting the fundamental beliefs of traditional education, advocated that all youth receive an "education for complete living." Early American progressivists placed their full support behind the movement to educate "all the children of all the people."[14]

Certainly, other educational theorists besides the naturalists bolstered the movement against elitism, but it is to the credit of the naturalists that they held liberal views about education in harmony with the political liberalism which they preached.

AIMS OF EDUCATION

As "naturalism" indicates, the purposes of education are found within nature. The explicit denial of any goals outside man or the physical world in which he lives constitutes a radical departure from traditionalism, which usually had some ultimate supernatural goal. Chapters Two through Five on Christian education show very clearly that there was no question about the ultimate aim of education from the third century to the present among the educators of theocentric persuasion.

Since the naturalist denies the validity of any aims outside the natural sphere, his concern must be with immediate or proximate aims. Perhaps these aims might be summed in the dictum that schools should develop the "whole child," that is, the entire natural organism. Whereas traditional education had placed major emphasis upon intellectual functions, the naturalist proposes that the child be given opportunity to grow physically, mentally, socially, emotionally, aesthetically, vocationally, *under the auspices of the school.* What is so radical about this proposal? Was the traditionalist against physical, social, emotional, and vocational adjustment? Certainly not! But the traditionalist maintains that the development of these

[13] Archer, *op. cit.,* p. 2.
[14] See R. H. Beck, "Progressive Education and American Progressivism — Felix Adler," *Teachers College Record,* LX, No. 2 (November, 1958).

areas of human behavior is not the responsibility of the school but that of other agencies such as church, family, and state. An essential difference, then, between naturalism and traditionalism in regard to aims lies in the school's assuming the role of educator in all phases of human activity. Even though Rousseau had intimated the objective of naturalistic education in his *Emile,* the first specific statements of such objectives did not appear until Herbert Spencer's *Education: Intellectual, Moral and Physical* was published in 1866. He states categorically: "To prepare us for complete living is the function which education has to discharge; and the only rational mode of judging of any educational course is to judge in what degree it discharges such function."[15]

According to Spencer this end can be achieved by "that education which prepares for direct and indirect self-preservation; that which prepares for parenthood; that which prepares for citizenship; that which prepares for the miscellaneous refinements of life."[16] In this same context Spencer points out that the order of precedence or importance of the aims listed is the order in which they appear in the statement. Thus the school's most important job as an educational agency is to see to it that the child learns how to preserve his own physical health and well-being. Preparation for citizenship and leisure-time activities appear at the end of the list and are of lesser importance.

In most respects the naturalistic hierarchy of educational objectives represents a complete reversal of traditional purposes of the school, chiefly, perfecting of man's highest powers *via* study of literature, philosophy, and the classics.[17]

ACADEMIC FREEDOM AND INDOCTRINATION

Since academic freedom was not a major issue when naturalism initiated the great educational ferment of the nineteenth century, only indirect reference can be made to the position of the naturalists on this point. It must be noted, however, that the religious-oriented education of the times implied a certain adherence to the basic theological outlook of any school. Thus the teachers in state schools, and independent ones as well, were expected to teach doctrines in harmony with the accepted religious beliefs of the community or

---

[15] Spencer, *op. cit.,* pp. 14–15.

[16] *Ibid.,* pp. 18–19.

[17] The section on curriculum in this chapter points up the relationship between naturalistic objectives and content.

state in which the schools were operated. Also in many of the European countries of the times there was an established religion (usually Lutheran or Catholic) to which all civil servants, including teachers, adhered.

In addition to a commitment to a theological creed, most states demanded of teachers a rather strict conformity to the political beliefs of those in power. Consequently, in these two areas, religion and politics, there was relatively little academic freedom in the sense in which we speak of it today.

Because of this relatively rigid adherence to accepted religious and political beliefs, indoctrination of youth in these areas was considered quite acceptable. Granted that teachers gave students the reasons for accepting the doctrines of religion and politics, all students were expected to master these basic views. This was the case especially in the lower schools, where *memoriter* learning was the rule. At the university level, however, there was much more academic freedom for the teacher and much less indoctrination of the students.

The naturalists, then, became the champions of free thought for both teachers and students. Rousseau, for example, insisted that students be given an opportunity to select their own religion when they reached maturity.[18] Even in the early phases of education, the child is not to be told the answers to questions, but should be allowed to discover them. At no stage in the process should the tutor impose his views on young Emile. Spencer also rejected the authority of Church and state in the educational enterprise and recommended that the student appeal to his own experience and that of experimental sciences for acceptable truths. Under no conditions should the teacher dictate the truth to his students.

The early progressives advocated the same approach in their teaching methods. The child was given the freedom to choose those activities and studies in which he was interested and for which he felt some need. Teachers were admonished to give pupils (even very young children) encouragement to wander from the beaten path of "accepted truth" in search for truths that would be meaningful and useful to them. Teachers themselves demanded the freedom to hold ideas not commonly accepted in the communities in which they taught. Further, they insisted that students be encouraged to espouse and defend unpopular political and social theories if they so desired.

---

[18] Archer, *op. cit.,* p. 200 ff.

In general, naturalism in education, because of its revolutionary character, rejected all authoritarian controls on education and in their place enthroned complete freedom of thought for teachers and their pupils.

PERMANENCE AND CHANGE

As pointed out in Chapter Two, most modern thought systems fall into the category of *philosophies of change*. It is true that the naturalists of the pre-Christian era believed that the final substance underlying all reality was some form of matter such as earth, fire, air, or water, but the naturalists of the modern era (who are our primary concern) were not so naïve. For them, nature is what scientists tell us it is, a world of continuous change. Of the several alternative views within the latter category of naturalists, the one which has affected educational thought most is evolutionism. To be even more specific for the rationale of this book, evolutionism will be analyzed from the human standpoint, since our concern is with the education of men, not animals.

Bertrand Russell states the position of naturalism regarding man's origin and nature quite categorically when he says that "man has developed out of the animals and there is no serious gap between him and the amoeba," and that "from the protozoa to man there is nowhere a very wide gap either in structure or in behavior. From this fact it is a highly probable inference that there is also nowhere a very wide mental gap."[19]

Thus the modern naturalistic hypothesis asserts that the only pathway to an understanding of man is the biological. It rejects that crass materialism which views man as a machine and replaces it with the conception of man as "organism." Moreover the naturalist finds traces of those activities of man which traditional philosophers attributed to the power of a spiritual force in animal life. He does not, however, stop with man in his present state of existence, for man's nature is marked by plasticity and flexibility. Man in his present state is not the best possible being for he, too, can be improved and perfected, just as his animal brothers before him became better by natural mutation and selection. Nature itself fosters the trend to betterment and progress within the human species.

---

[19] B. Russell, *The Analysis of Mind* (London: George Allen and Unwin, Ltd., 1921), p. 40 ff.

Herein lies the task of education. If nature itself contains those ingredients necessary for the improvement of the species, it behooves the educator to formulate his aims, devise educational methods and procedures, create a curriculum, and strengthen educational agencies according to the natural tendencies found within man. Then and only then can one be assured of the continued progress of the human race. Any appeal to sources outside nature for improvement of the educative process is miseducative since it violates the very foundations upon which education should be built. Nature must be accorded free play if there is to be improvement in the child. Nature itself seems to guarantee progress! This optimistic view of man is evident in the educational writings of Rousseau, Spencer, and Pestalozzi, who advocate a form of education based upon nature.

If change is a generic trait of all existence for the naturalist, "Are there no ultimate, final, changeless, or absolute aspects of reality?" There are none, unless perhaps one wishes to posit nature itself as the ultimate matrix of all existences and events. Even the most cherished truths of traditional philosophy are subject to change. The values of past generations might still be esteemed but they lose their tone of finality.

SUPERNATURALISM VS. NATURALISM

The family of naturalists becomes exceedingly large, especially in modern times, when one uses the label of naturalism to denote any person who denies (implicitly or explicitly) the existence of anything above nature, or those who disregard the supernatural. Thus Rousseau, who was a deist, fits into this category, even though he believed that God had created the world. Spencer, the agnostic, falls into the same class since he believed that even if the supernatural realm existed, man could know nothing about it. Of course, the militant atheist is right at home in the naturalist camp. The most prevalent type of naturalist in the twentieth century is the secularist, and it is his influence that has been felt most in the schools. For all practical purposes the secularist is concerned only with the physical and social world around him. Usually he will not raise any objections if one of his fellowmen wishes to believe in the supernatural or to practice some religious rites, provided these beliefs and practices do not intrude upon the private or public lives of others. Any such attempt on the part of the supernaturalist is met by forceful rebuttal by the secularist. The enmity between these two groups has produced some of the most violent verbal and legal battles in education during this century.

The effects of secularism on the curriculum have probably been both negative and positive. On the negative side of the ledger, secularism has succeeded in eliminating from the public schools (and even from some private schools) any overt traces of commitment to any religious beliefs. The teaching of and about religion cannot be a part of any curriculum or even take place on public school property. Bible reading and the recitation of prayers are now judged unconstitutional for public schools, inasmuch as they formally commit the state to the profession of a specific religious creed.

On the positive side, secularism has helped elevate the natural and social sciences to the same position of prestige and importance formerly held by the sacred subjects.

That the aims of education have been affected by secularism is evident in the various statements of the objectives of education. Except in the stated aims of religious schools one cannot find any reference to a final or ultimate end of education such as "union with God" or the "salvation of the soul," "spiritual peace," or the like. Instead, all objectives are this-worldly and are pointed to securing happiness in this life and purely on the psychological-social plane. Even when these objectives are mellowed and sublimated by social altruism there is no mistaking the fact that supernatural aims are not the motivation for such altruism. As noted above, the role of the Church as an influential agency in education has been either minimized or completely eliminated. The growth of secularism and the augmentation of the role of the state in education have coincided. Some believe that the former has caused the latter.

NATURE OF MAN AND SOCIETY

Twentieth-century man is so accustomed to hearing that "there is no such thing as a *bad* boy" (or girl) or that parents are to blame for the delinquency of their children, that he cannot appreciate fully the furor caused by the naturalistic assertion that man is not morally evil. In order to understand the shock such a statement would give the intellectual world one must remember that Christian theology dominated the thinking of the Western world from the third century after Christ until the present. Although Protestants and Catholics disagreed upon the extent to which man's nature was affected by the "fall," there was agreement between them that man was not in a state of original innocence. True, all God's creation was *good,* but man's own free acts had ushered in sin and evil.

No small wonder, then, that the following statement by Rousseau fell upon Christendom like a bombshell:

> Everything is good as it comes from the hands of the Author of Nature; but everything degenerates in the hands of man. . . . He will leave nothing as nature made it, not even man. Like a saddle-horse that must be trained for man's service, he must be made over according to his fancy, like a tree in his garden.[20]

This statement presents the basic thought of all naturalistic education. The adaptations of the Spencerian school, the Pestalozzians, and the American progressives, contain the same essential assumption. Of course, none of them (even Rousseau) contended that the child could do no wrong, but when evil was committed the blame should be placed upon the environment rather than upon the child, for youngsters are corrupted by the environment. In harking back to education according to nature, all of the philosophers of naturalism were revolting against some of the absurd and artificial content and methods of education. But, more than that, they were asserting something about man's nature which was wholly repugnant to the prevailing thought of the times — namely, that man had within himself all the power and resources necessary to achieve happiness and did not need the assistance of grace or the Church.

Education, thus — especially secular education — is constructed upon a view of man completely divorced from the theological foundations of Western education. The effects of this concept of the "emancipated man" upon educational aims, content, and methods have been profound and far-reaching. In the first place, those engaged in the educational enterprise must learn all about child nature in order to understand the child and his problems. This belief was reflected in teacher-education programs in the nineteenth and twentieth centuries, when the emphasis began to switch from knowledge of subject matter to be taught to knowledge of child nature. Professional courses in child and educational psychology became the center of the educational program for teachers. "Know the child and you will know

---

[20] J. J. Rousseau, *Emile,* translated by W. Payne (New York: D. Appleton Co., 1896), p. 1.

what to teach" became the slogan of the newer professional programs in education.

Second, great emphasis was placed upon the study which teachers should make of the environmental background of each student, since unacceptable behavior was rooted there rather than in the pupil's ill will. Teachers were advised to learn of the racial, natural, and religious backgrounds of their students. If a pupil caused trouble or lacked initiative in school, the home conditions should be studied to see whether a home broken by divorce, death, or marital conflict is responsible for the child's difficulties. If a teacher were unable to manage a class, he was held responsible because he lacked insight into child nature. Or, perhaps, the curriculum was "traditional" and therefore devoid of anything interesting to the pupils or meeting their needs. All of these innovations in pedagogy were based on the revised view of the nature of the child. He was innately good or, at worst, neutral, and one must seek the source of bad behavior in the environment rather than in the child.

Third, the aims of education and curricular content were to be determined in the light of the child's needs and interests rather than to be based upon the preconceived notion of adult behavior and interests. When the child reaches adulthood, he, too, will have mature interests and will put away the things of childhood. Thus, as with the older philosophies of man, the new philosophy of naturalism based its educational theories on the dictum, "Know the nature of man and you know the nature of education."

From the nature of man one must move to the nature of society, for only the most naïve of philosophers would view man as an island. At the outset, the generalization might be made that the naturalists of the eighteenth and nineteenth centuries were individualistic in their interpretations of society. As naturalism gradually was absorbed by the pragmatism of the twentieth century, society, rather than the individual, became the dominant context for the understanding of man. This latter phase of naturalism will be examined in the next chapter.

Taking their cue from Rousseau, early naturalists believed that the highly moral relationship between man and nature should be preserved. This relationship was one of innocence and simplicity based upon an innate goodness which could be corrupted only by an immoral society. It is not surprising that Rousseau had this attitude toward society of his time, for it was shot through with duplicity, extravagance, artificiality, and chauvinism, especially among the aristocracy. But even an idealistic dreamer like Rousseau was not against society *per se*. He was against the type of society he knew, that of the middle eighteenth century. Note how he sets aside a certain phase of education to introduce Emile to society.

Borrowing from earlier writers such as Locke and Montesquieu, Rousseau proposed his plan for a regenerated society which would not violate nature. His study of Greek and Roman civilization and the information on the lives of the American Indians seemed to bolster his view that man in his natural state could achieve happiness and contentment. From these sources he attempted to discriminate what belongs to nature and what to the artificial accretions of society. To pure nature he attributed man's desire for self-preservation and his fear of hunger and pain. As reason evolved in man, he developed the power of speech, family life, and the practical arts. With these, he was able to live the placid and happy life of the "noble savage." These developments, however, did not impair his freedom or his status of equality with his fellowmen.

But man did not remain in this simple state of nature. He was prodded by his imagination to seek more goods than he needed, thus creating artificial need. He began to emulate his fellows in an attempt to acquire more wealth and prestige than others. It was this development in early society that brought about the degeneration of man. Social distinctions were sought so one man could consider himself superior to another. Man became the enemy of man. He used his fellowman as an instrument to achieve his own selfish artificial needs. Greed, avarice, injustice became the rule of society rather than the exception.

If such was man's state at Rousseau's time how did he propose to correct the man-to-man relationship in society? Did he demand the abolition of society and a complete return to primitive institutions? Strangely enough, he did not. However, he gave to society, or the state, the duty of preserving for all men in society that freedom and equality which he possessed in the state of nature. The task of any government, then, is "to find a form of association which will defend and protect with the whole common force the person and goods of every associate, and in which each, while uniting himself with all, may still obey only himself, and remain as free as before."[21]

Here Rousseau poses the paradoxical view that mass cooperation would place no limitation upon individual freedom and that states exist only by virtue of the "general will," but should not limit the individual will. In the last analysis his view seems to harmonize well with the statement that "he who governs least, governs best." It is, perhaps, this conception of organized society (state) which was popular among the early naturalists. Society remains a somewhat artificial, albeit necessary structure. Man is considered the basic unit rather than a part or member of a social organism. Society is made up of individuals; individuals are not sparks or offspring of society. The only reason for the latter's existence flows from the need of protecting the individual from hostile forces or assisting the individual to achieve more happiness, security, and contentment by cooperation with his fellowman.

EPISTEMOLOGY

Following the lead of Plato, Aristotle, and the Scholastics, traditional philosophers centered their speculations around the problems of metaphysics. The discipline of metaphysics was the heart of philosophy, its central focus, and epistemology was a specialized aspect of metaphysics. Metaphysical speculations, of course, relied heavily upon reason in addition to sense-experimentation. It is true that some of these traditional philosophers did not advocate radical or extreme rationalism, did not assert that reason *alone* was the source of all valid knowledge, but held that its role, especially in the metaphysical realm, was paramount.

The naturalist rejected the role that intellect or reason plays in the knowing process and put forth the claim that the only valid form of knowledge is that derived from *experience*. For the early naturalists, "experience" chiefly meant that mode of acquiring knowledge based on direct contact of the organism with the physical world through the senses. The more sophisticated naturalists included the refined modes of knowing used by the empirical sciences. Both, however, imply a denial of reason as a source of knowledge. In practice, both types of experience are evident in naturalistic educational theory.

---

[21] J. J. Rousseau, *Social Contract and Discourses* (New York: Everyman's Library, E. P. Dutton Co., 1914), p. 45 ff.

Education's methodology perhaps exemplifies this shift from traditionalism most clearly. All of Rousseau's recommendations on "how to teach" Emile flow from the belief that experience is the only teacher. He ranted against the teaching methods of the time because they were not aimed at giving the student any personal, direct experience with the world; they used abstract reasoning alone as the avenue to learning. Pestalozzi's approach, similarly, was based upon direct experience. Spencer, the scientific naturalist, enthroned experimentation, the usual method of empirical sciences, as the only valid method of teaching. The methodology of the early American progressives was wholly experience-centered.

In like manner the curriculum of the naturalists might be classified as experience-centered. All of the theorists mentioned above rejected the rationalistic curriculum of the Renaissance humanists because it lacked any connection with the natural world. In fact, naturalists, especially Spencer, are credited with displacement of classical and humanistic studies from the curriculum of nineteenth- and twentieth-century schools. In its place one finds studies designed to meet the personal and vocational needs and interests of the students. Modern languages replace classical ones because they are useful. Health and physical education become an integral part of the curriculum because they contribute to "self-preservation." Household and industrial "arts" take their place in the curriculum because they meet the legitimate demands of the students. The role of humanistic studies becomes minor, for these studies find their reason for existing in the curriculum only insofar as they contribute to "preparation for the worthy use of leisure time." In other words they are recreational rather than essential.

Since the theological mode of knowing is not experimental, there is no place in the curriculum for religion except insofar as it might be viewed as an historical curiosity. Also, because of this rejection of theology as a legitimate discipline, the function of the Church as an educational agency is negated. In its place one finds the secular state assuming the major responsibility for educating youth. Indoctrination, usually associated with teaching of religion, is rejected and replaced by the pupil's freedom to discover those truths which nature in her outward manifestations presents to him.

The most highly developed applications of the epistemology of experience to education were produced by the instrumentalists.

Whereas the outstanding theorists of naturalism, such as Rousseau and Spencer, did much to weaken the position of traditionalism in education, it was left to the followers of John Dewey to make full-scale applications of that basic philosophy to the classroom, school administration, educational psychology. The succeeding chapter will point up the major tenets of this new school of thought.

Before leaving this section on the epistemology of naturalism it might be well to indicate the part it has played in the development of education as a science. Prior to the advent of naturalism, education in general and teaching in particular were looked upon as "art" rather than "science." However, with the naturalistic emphasis upon experience and empirical science as the only modes of knowing, education itself began to seek answers to its problems through scientific means. Educational psychology developed along empirical rather than speculative lines. The preference for one teaching method over another was based upon "research" using statistical evidence rather than any metaphysical beliefs about the nature of the pupil. In reality, all of the traditional practices and beliefs in education were submitted to the scrutiny of science. Only those which could meet the demands of empiricism were considered acceptable. The great educational controversies of the first several decades of the twentieth century can be traced to this central issue, the "scientizing" of education.

SEARCH FOR VALUES

As noted in our Chapters Two through Six, traditionalists believed that there were at least some values that were permanent. However, in the hierarchy of values, those related to the spiritual realm were considered most significant. Those values closely associated with nature, that is, man's lower physical nature, were definitely on the lower end of the scale of values. There have been movements throughout the Christian era which looked upon any values associated with the purely natural as false ones. For this reason, some early Christian writers looked upon Greek and Roman learning as essentially evil because it was not based upon the supernatural structure of Christian theism.[22] Even the great lover of nature, St. Francis of Assisi, found value in the things of nature only because they were reflections of divine goodness.

---

[22] See Chapter Three, pp. 38–39.

It was against this essential unity of all values with the super-natural that the naturalists revolted. For them, all *real* values are rooted in nature. There is no need to call upon the supernatural realm to "sanctify" values since nature possesses its own inherent values, is its own good! Whatever man enjoys in nature is good whether this enjoyment involves ethical or aesthetic experiences.

Perhaps the simplest way to illustrate the naturalists' view of value is to contrast it with the Christian view in ethics. For the Christian, man's highest good is the attaining of his eternal goal. Any words, deeds, thoughts, which might deter him from attaining this final goal were considered evil. Nature itself might, under certain conditions, distract man from his final end. For the naturalist, the opposite was true. Desirable behavior was that which enabled man to harmonize his life with nature. Any behavior which thwarted natural needs and desires was not good, but evil. Thus, whereas the Christian was expected to guide his moral behavior by following a code based upon divine revelation (or reason illumined by revela-tion), the naturalist argued that nature itself provided its own code through the medium of man's innate desires and needs. The natural-ist's fundamental principle of ethics, then, was not "Do good and avoid evil," but "Seek pleasure and avoid pain," since man's natural tendencies were in this direction.

This hedonistic principle is very evident in Rousseau's writings and was, of course, the only criterion of value that remained after the supernatural had been rejected. Even the intemperate Rousseau, however, did not advocate crass hedonism, for if a person indulged himself to extremes, pain would inevitably result. Thus one should not gorge oneself with culinary delicacies even though there might be some *immediate* pleasure in doing so. The pain and discomfort that would follow upon such gluttony would outweigh the pleasure. Also, Rousseau wanted the child to experience pain and displeasure so that later he might avoid those acts which cause the unpleasurable results. In other words, nature itself dictated moderation rather than unbridled self-indulgence.

A much more sophisticated and social-centered theory of natural-istic value was developed by the instrumentalists. It reinterprets the principle of hedonism in the light of the social realities of the twentieth century. This extension of naturalistic ethics will be con-sidered in the next chapter.

The principles enunciated above regarding the ethical values of naturalism hold also for aesthetic values. They, too, are rooted in nature and do not depend on any source outside nature for their validation. Nature itself provides the criterion for beauty; there is no need to call upon universal principles such as unity and proportion to judge beauty. A landscape is beautiful simply because it *is* nature. A painting is beautiful because it *reflects* nature, not because it elevates man above nature.

The educational implications of the naturalistic theory of value are not difficult to discern. The most obvious one constantly appears in modern educational literature: good education is pleasurable. Thus, methods of teaching should be based upon the belief that the child is not averse to learning, but enjoys it. Teaching methods and materials will appeal to students' natural inclination to learn. The curriculum will consist of those experiences which meet pupils' needs and interests rather than a collection of subjects which adults believe children should master. Difficult tasks are not to be excluded, however, for even they can be made pleasant. (Note how hard children work at learning difficult games.)

Since the aim of naturalistic education is to assure complete living (natural happiness) all students should be afforded and should profit from such an education. Nature provides values for all, not for just an intellectual elite. Certainly if there are no absolute or immutable values, indoctrination in any form is unacceptable and academic freedom for teachers is essential.

EVALUATION OF NATURALISM

Throughout this chapter it has been noted that naturalism constituted a revolt against the theocentric philosophies which had dominated the Western world for fifteen centuries. It should come as no surprise, then, that Christian leaders, both Catholic and Protestant, promptly condemned those doctrines which violated Christian faith and moral principles. The following are some of the areas in which Christianity and naturalism are in basic conflict:

1. Naturalistic metaphysics is incomplete since it denies the existence of any realities above or beyond nature. God, angels, grace, man's immortal soul, and the like, are relegated to the category of myths.

2. Because it posits no ends outside nature, naturalism negates

any purposefulness *in* nature. Process rather than purpose becomes the central theme of philosophy.

3. Naturalism's philosophy of man is only a half philosophy since it views man solely as a biological organism.

4. Naturalism's view of man as morally good denies the reality of a fallen or wounded nature inclined to evil.

5. Since man is merely a biological organism for the naturalist, all of his needs can be met by nature itself. The supernatural assistance derived from the sacraments, prayer, and grace is viewed as a concoction of the "established authorities" of Church and state, designed to keep man in chains.

6. Because experience and/or scientific method are the only valid means of arriving at knowledge recognized by the naturalist, his epistemology is incomplete. Reason and revelation are valid means of attaining truth, for the Christian.

7. By rooting all values in nature alone, naturalism repudiates the highest values which civilized man has attained, viz., religious, aesthetic, moral.

8. Because the naturalistic view of man is incomplete, his theory of social organization likewise must be incomplete.

From the philosophical inadequacies of naturalism listed above, the following educational errors can be pointed up:

1. Education has no ultimate or final end. There is no final goal upon which education can set its sights. Education is its own end.

2. By insisting on experience as the sole source of knowledge, naturalism limits itself to one educational methodology, the experimental method. Thus it fails to capitalize on many of the methods used in traditional education which had proved their worth and have passed even the "test of experience."

3. In equating animal and human nature, naturalists have reduced education to "training" (with all the materialistic and pragmatic connotations of that term).

4. The elevation of pupil freedom to the status of a dogma led naturalists to the denial of the value of discipline imposed by the authority of the teacher, church, or community.

5. The secularization of education fostered by naturalists defrauded the curriculum of those studies such as religion and the humanities which enable man to see beyond his physical needs and

desires. Pleasure was substituted for virtue, freedom from pain replaced sacrifice and charity.

From this list of shortcomings one might conclude that, from a Christian point of view, naturalism contributed nothing to education. It must be remembered, however, that revolutionary movements are nourished by weaknesses or deficiencies in existing institutions. A few of the most significant contributions of naturalism to educational theory and practice should be cited.

1. Perhaps the most significant educational reform proposed by the naturalists flows from their belief that the natural growth pattern of children should determine the content and method of education. The modern concept of "readiness," accepted by educators of all persuasions, is a result of this principle.

2. A corollary of this generalization reminds the educator that content and method should be adjusted to the individual differences of the pupils. Rousseau, Pestalozzi, and the early progressives recognized the failure of traditional education in regard to this rather obvious fact and offered both theoretical and practical means for adapting content and method to individual differences.

3. Yet another principle advocated by the naturalists and generally accepted by all modern educators stresses the pedagogical value of "learning by doing." Much of traditional teaching was highly verbal and abstract, even when the occasion did not call for such an approach. The naturalist reminds all educators to utilize direct experience whenever possible to insure meaningful and lasting learning.

4. One final contribution suggested by naturalistic theory which has been of value to all educators can be traced to the dictum that "learning is *naturally* pleasurable." Too often, the traditionalists preached that learning was pleasant, but their practices belied their principles. In many traditional schools, especially at the lower levels, it was assumed that "good education" must be unpleasant because children were unwilling to learn. But the naturalist argued that if education utilized the natural interests of students as the starting point for learning, even the most difficult tasks could become pleasant.

SUMMARY

Naturalism, in all its variants, differs from "traditionalism" in that it either denies absolutely the supernatural order or holds that this order is totally irrelevant to life and to the task of education. The naturalists of the 19th and early 20th century — Pestalozzi, Froebel, Spencer — advocated teaching methods which make the pupil, not the teacher, the central figure. The content of the curriculum is selected to help pupils achieve growth in their *whole* person, not merely their intellectual abilities. Education is to prepare them for life, for earning a living, for attaining all their potentialities.

Discipline should come from within and not be imposed from without. Man, the naturalists hold, is naturally good. Thus the process of education is to facilitate the growth of natural virtues; it has no ends extrinsic to human nature. For the naturalist, man is the measure of all things.

BIBLIOGRAPHY

Archer, R. L. (ed.), *Rousseau on Education* (London: Edward Arnold Co., 1916).

Beck, R. H., "Progressive Education and American Progressivism — Felix Adler," *Teachers College Record*, LX, No. 2 (November, 1958).

Cole, Louella, *A History of Education* (New York: Rinehart & Co., 1950), Chaps. XVI–XVIII.

DeGuimps, Roger, *Pestalozzi: His Life and Work* (New York: D. Appleton Co., 1895).

Franklin, Benjamin, *The Works of Benjamin Franklin* (New York: John Bigelow, 1904), 12 vols.

Froebel, F. W., *Education of Man* (New York: D. Appleton Co., 1887).

Honeywell, R. J., *The Educational Works of Thomas Jefferson* (Cambridge: Harvard University Press, 1931).

Maritain, Jacques, *Three Reformers* (New York: Charles Scribner's Sons, 1929).

Mayer, Frederick, *A History of Educational Thought* (Columbus, Ohio: Charles E. Merrill, Inc., 1960), Chaps. 18, 20.

McCormick P. J., and Cassidy, F. P., *History of Education* (Washington: D. C.: Catholic Education Press, 1946), Chaps. XXVI–XXIX.

O'Connell, G., *Naturalism in American Education,* (Washington, D. C.: Catholic University of America Press, 1936).

Rousseau, Jean J., *Confessions* (New York: D. C. Health, Penguin Books, 1953).

——— *Emile,* trans. by W. H. Payne (New York: D. Appleton Co., 1896).

——— *Social Contract and Discourses* (New York: Everyman's Library, E. P. Dutton Co., 1914).

Russell, B., *The Analysis of Mind* (London: Allen and Unwin, Ltd., 1921).

Spencer, H., *Education* (New York: D. Appleton Co., 1907).

——— *Education: Intellectual, Moral and Physical* (New York: D. Appleton Co., 1866).

——— *First Principles of a New System of Philosophy* (2 ed.) (New York: D. Appleton Co., 1896).

Thorpe, F. N., *Franklin's Influence in American Education* (Washington, D. C.: U. S. Bureau of Education, 1903).

CHAPTER SEVEN

Progressivism and John Dewey's Instrumentalism

INTRODUCTION

THROUGHOUT the preceding chapter, periodic reference was made to the influence of naturalism on the early phases of progressivism. Too often, in the popular press, progressivism is associated solely with the philosophy of John Dewey. However, it must be remembered that the progressive movement was well underway before Dewey entered the educational arena. In reality the progressive movement was at least three decades old before John Dewey lent the support of his philosophical system to the movement.[1]

If any one parent philosophy is to be assigned to pre-Deweyan progressivism, naturalism, perhaps, provided the hereditary genes of the infant philosophy. For the sake of brevity and simplicity, then, let us assume that the important philosophical beliefs of early progressivism with their attendant educational implications have been discussed in the preceding chapter. This present chapter will be devoted to the advanced stages of progressivism, especially as it has been affected by the philosophy of Dewey and his followers. Dewey's philosophy is called *Instrumentalism* for reasons that will be given later. However, the terms *experimentalism* and *pragmatism* are also used to designate the same general theory of education and its philosophical underpinnings.

As one might expect, though, there are many differences of opinion among writers calling themselves instrumentalists, progressivists, ex-

---

[1] See L. A. Cremin, "The Progressive Movement in Education: A Perspective," *Harvard Educational Review,* Vol. 27, 251–280, Fall, 1957.

perimentalists or pragmatists. Obviously, all of these differences cannot be accounted for in one chapter which purports to cover them all. Therefore, an attempt will be made to synthesize the different views or to state those of the best-known spokesmen such as Dewey, Childs, Kilpatrick, and a few of the more recent ones. Also, it is worth noting that the differences among the members of this school of thought are more apt to appear in the areas of educational practice such as curriculum, methodology, and aims, rather than in the philosophical bases of the system.

METHODOLOGY

Like their naturalistic forebears, the theorists of "matured" progressivism made some of their most significant educational changes in the field of methodology. The naturalists, however, were content to center their methodology around such generalized concepts as "experience" or the "scientific method." But Dewey and his disciples devised a very specific set of operations for conducting learning activities. This systematic approach to the methodology of experience has come to be known as problem-solving. The epistemological bases of problem-solving are considered in another section of this chapter; our concern here is with the classroom adaptations of this theory of knowledge.

Unlike the epistemologies of traditional philosophies, that of instrumentalism was designed for classroom use. Few classical philosophers looked upon their theories of knowledge as having much bearing on school methodology. But the instrumentalist believes that education is philosophy's first concern. In fact, Dewey defines philosophy as a theory of education. It is not surprising, then, that one can see a direct relationship between the epistemology and classroom methodology of this philosophy.

Before providing a description of the problem-solving method it might be well to indicate how the role played by the teacher in this method differs from that of the traditional teacher. Generally speaking, a teacher following the traditional pattern would be assigned to teach a certain subject. In some instances the amount and sequence of the subject matter to be taught was decided by educational authorities above the teacher, whereas in others the teacher himself might make the decision. In either instance, however, the pupils were given no choice in the selection of subject matter to be learned; the decision rested with the teacher.

In the problem-solving method, the teacher assumes the role of a helper and guide; the pupils become the central figures. The teacher does not become thereby inferior to the pupils, but neither is he to be considered superior. Perhaps a realistic way of describing this most important relationship between teacher and pupils is: the teacher is a more mature and experienced equal of the pupil. Often the critics of problem-solving miss the whole point of the relationship between teacher and pupil by inferring that the instrumentalist makes the teacher subject to his pupils.

Mindful, also, that no subject matter is sacred to the instrumentalist (see section on "Curriculum" below), teachers and pupils work within a framework of a relatively free choice of topics that interest them.

Let us now proceed to our description of the teaching-learning method of the instrumentalist. First of all, whose problems are to be solved in problem-solving? Those prepared by the teacher? or those which arise in the pupil? W. H. Kilpatrick, Dewey's disciple, answers this question thus: "It is from the pupil's action that the pupil learns. Therefore, it is the pupil's problem that we wish."[2] Therefore, no meaningful learning will take place unless the student is personally involved in some difficulty. This, then, is the starting point of the method — the pupil (or pupils, for there are group problems, also) has a real difficulty or problem that he wants to solve. He has no patterns of behavioral responses that will remove the difficulty he feels; there is a mental block disturbing the equilibrium of the organism. Now learning can begin. Once the student has felt some difficulty the next step consists in moving from the rather hazy state of feeling a difficulty to one of clear recognition of the nature and scope of the problem. Without a definite statement of the problem any further work on it will be of a "trial and error" nature or like fighting an unknown and unlocated enemy in the dark. At this juncture, the role of the teacher becomes most important. Young and inexperienced problem solvers will need assistance from the

---

[2] W. H. Kilpatrick, *Foundations of Method* (New York: Macmillan Co., 1926), p. 246. See also pp. 232–250 for an analysis of Deweyan methodology. Kilpatrick is the author of the well-known *Project Method* which is an adaptation of the problem-solving method of Dewey. See W. H. Kilpatrick, *The Project Method* (New York: Teachers College, Columbia University Press, 1921).

teacher in locating and defining the problem. The "feeling of difficulty" may be present, but determining just exactly what the difficulty
is may be a well-nigh insurmountable task for the student. When
the problem has been defined, the student is prepared to begin his
search for any relevant data which might be of assistance in suggesting solutions to the problem. This search will take him far beyond
the confines of any one subject matter. Again, the assistance of the
teacher might be called for to assure accuracy and thoroughness in
the quest for pertinent facts and information. If the student coming
from a traditional classroom is accustomed to use only a single
text or reference, he must be trained in the use of a wide variety
of source materials. Because of the multitude of sources, the pupil
must learn to evaluate the reliability and adequacy of each one.
He should be advised of the bias that exists in the various publications, be they of a scientific, political, economic, or religious nature.

Perhaps the reader has surmised that this step in problem-solving
might require a great deal of time on the part of the students. Would
it not be more reasonable for the teacher to provide the bulk of
the data that the student might need to suggest solutions? Certainly
not! Problem-solving involves pupil activity. Even if the teacher
would provide in one class period what it takes the student a month
to ferret out for himself, the responsibility lies first and foremost
with the student. The teacher's goal at this stage is to teach research
skills and techniques, not subject matter.

Only after the learner has completed a thorough search for data
about the problem is he prepared to suggest possible solutions to it.
This broad background will enable him to see pertinent relationships between what at first might have seemed like piecemeal bits
of information. When relationships become clear the learner should
be able to produce many fruitful inferences or hypotheses. Here
again the teacher serves the important function of encouraging the
pupil to propose hypotheses which might be put to the test. But
note, the teacher does not propose the hypotheses or possible solutions — the pupil does. Slow learners might need more teacher
assistance than rapid learners but both must solve their own problems within the limits of their own abilities. Also, the teacher committed to instrumentalist methodology will encourage the student to
make the leap into the unknown in proposing solutions rather than
remain with the stereotype solutions of the past, for truths are

created, not discovered. Herein lies the creativity of which the instrumentalist speaks so much. Creativity is measured by the variety and meaningfulness of the hypotheses proposed, for it is from such hypotheses that new knowledge is born.

When a sufficient number of possible solutions has been proposed the learner must evaluate each of the hypotheses in relation to their anticipated outcomes. Dewey called this process "reasoning."[3] This implies a scrutiny of each hypothesis to determine if it might meet the demands of the problem situation. The pros and cons of each hypothesis will be weighed against each other to ascertain the possible ill effects of applying one of the hypotheses. Again the teacher's task consists in preventing the student from making a hasty and unwarranted choice of a solution to be tested. The teacher might even have to warn the student that one of the hypotheses presented might result in serious harm to the individual or society. But, as in the other steps of problem-solving, the teacher is not the one to decide which suggested solution will be put to the test first. The learner must make this decision after due deliberation about the anticipated results of each hypothesis.

The final step in problem-solving is, of course, putting the hypothesis, which the learner ascertains to be the most likely to solve the problem, to the acid test of experience. If the suggested solution is never put to the test of experience, no knowledge will result from the entire exercise. In some respects, all the effort will be as meaningless as the rote exercises of traditional education which were "mastered but never learned." Thus, for the instrumentalist, all true learning (and knowledge) is an outgrowth of the experimental test of ideas or hypotheses. If a hypothesis actually solves the problem the feeling of difficulty will vanish. If the difficulty does not disappear, the hypothesis must be rejected and another one selected for the test of experience. If the learner "runs out of hypotheses" to be tested, he may have to check back on the entire process. Perhaps the problem was not properly defined or limited. Perhaps his search for relevant data was incomplete, shoddy, or hampered by prejudices or bias. Or he might not have been thorough enough in using the data garnered as a basis for creating hypotheses.

As described above, the problem-solving process is viewed as a complete mode of knowing, not merely a teaching technique. There

---

[3] See below, section on "Epistemology."

are teachers, however, who view it as only one of many teaching techniques. These teachers, however, view problem-solving as a method of learning traditional subject matter. Most often, the teachers themselves divide the subject into problems and put the students to work solving them. But the goal of mastery of the subject has not been abandoned.

In summary, the salient features of this teaching-learning method which make it radically different from the traditional approach to teaching are:

1. The origin of the problem, the execution of the process, and the final testing are primarily pupil activities.

2. The purpose of the method is to find new means of solving difficulties, rather than to defend the beliefs and values of the past.

3. No solution is final. The problem solver must always be prepared to cast aside any solution which does not satisfy the demands of the situation. Old truths must be cast aside in favor of more up-to-date ones.

4. The final appeal is always to "experience" rather than to any external source of truth.

EDUCATIONAL AGENCIES

Earlier in this book it was made clear that each of the three primary educational agencies (the family, the Church, and the state) were assigned very definite roles in the complex undertaking called education. The family is responsible for moral and physical training, the Church chiefly for moral training, and the state for civic training. To some extent, the school was the one institution to which all three agencies delegated certain educational tasks, the most important of which was developing the intellectual powers of youth. The roles of the three agencies in education, however, were kept quite distinct (at least, theoretically).

Such a clear definition of roles is impossible for the instrumentalist. For him, education is life — it is living. It is a process which cannot be divided into parts with each part parceled out to one or the other institution in society. The section on "Curriculum," below, demonstrates that the school, the community, and the home are all doing the same thing albeit at different levels. But there is no differentiation of roles in the strict sense.

Yet the traditionalist might still ask the instrumentalist with whom the ultimate responsibility rests in educational matters. Obviously it cannot rest with the Church since the instrumentalist is a secularist. Can the family, then, be designated as the ultimate authority in such matters? Perhaps in primitive societies the family can care for the educational needs of youth. However, in complex societies such as ours, the family is wholly unequipped to shoulder this responsibility. By a process of elimination, then, the civil authority is designated as the only agency which can bear the ultimate responsibility for education. But, the instrumentalist is quick to add, the state is not to be considered the *goal* of *education*. Dewey, for example, rejects the nationalistic notion that the state is the goal of education when he criticizes German educational ideals of "education for the state."[4] He does not believe that it is incompatible for the state to provide all the facilities for free public education and yet not make the state the primary goal of education. He says: "This conclusion is bound up with the very idea of education as a *freeing* of *individual capacity* in a progressive growth *directed to social aims*. Otherwise a democratic criterion of education can only be inconsistently applied."[5]

Certainly Dewey was attempting to avoid the Scylla and Charybdis of statism and rugged individualism in the sponsorship of the vast educational enterprise in American democracy. On the one hand, if education is to be directed to social aims, it cannot be left under the control of authoritarian institutions (such as the Church or ruling powers). On the other hand it cannot be left to the whim of individuals nor serve purely individual goals. The instrumentalist escape from the dilemma seems to lie in the position that *society* is the primary educational agency, and the state, as the arm of society, must provide all the opportunities necessary for the educational process to be carried on within a democratic context.

This resolution of the dilemma makes sense only when related to the instrumentalist notion of society as an organism (see section below on the "Nature of Man and Society"). If the relationship between individuals and groups is truly an organic one, the setting apart of specific educational agencies with specialized responsibilities is unwarranted. If education is equated with living, then the responsi-

---

[4] J. Dewey, *Democracy and Education* (New York: Macmillan, 1910), pp. 108–112.

[5] *Ibid.*, p. 115. (Italics mine.)

bility for promoting the educative process must rest with society since it is the context for living.

The unsympathetic reader still might demand an answer to the query: "Who shall educate?" "Society" is an abstraction. "Decide which of the traditional agencies you consider the most important and responsible for the control of education."

When pressed in such a manner, the instrumentalist might admit that the state, as the concretization of society, is the primary agency of education. And, so long as the state is democratic, there should be no fear that the state will become the goal of education.

CURRICULUM

For one who is accustomed to think of the curriculum in terms of subjects such as history, English, mathematics, and the like, it is difficult to conceive the instrumentalist's notion of curriculum. Perhaps the best way to emphasize the difference is to state what he does *not* mean by the term. In regard to the elementary school curriculum, he *does not* make the skill subjects (reading, spelling, writing, and computing) or the content subjects (children's literature, geography, history, science, and mathematics) the center of learning activities. For the high school level, he *does not* believe that the traditional subjects (mathematics, science, foreign and classical languages, history, and the like) constitute the basic curriculum. Does this mean that the instrumentalist does not want the student to learn anything about these fields? The answer is both: Yes! and No! Let us try to explain this ambivalent answer.

Since the instrumentalist rejects the traditionalist notion of the curriculum he must have some definition or delimitation for the term. Kilpatrick defines the curriculum as *all* of those activities of *living* for which the school accepts responsibility, or everything that the pupils or students do under the auspices of the school.[6] This definition implies the inclusion in the curriculum of all activities formerly considered extracurricular. Thus, athletics, dramatics, club activities, recreational activities, and the like are just as essential as the "subject-matter" classes in the organization of a good curriculum. Also note that the curriculum is equated with *living*. In

---

[6] W. H. Kilpatrick, "The Experimentalist Outlook," *Philosophies of Education,* 41st N.S.S.E., Yearbook, Part I (Chicago: University of Chicago Press, 1942), p. 76 ff.

other words, the curriculum is the sequence of events in the school life of the pupil; it is not a preparation for adult life, but life itself. This notion is consistent with the instrumentalist view of knowing (learning), namely, the people learn what they live. One might ask how children of elementary school age can *live* arithmetic or spelling? The instrumentalist answer is that if the school provides a real-life environment, children will learn these skills simply because they are such an integral part of the culture into which they are born. In order to communicate with others, children will learn the fundamentals of language. After all even those children who never attend school learn to speak their native tongue mainly because they find it necessary to communicate with their fellowmen. Reading, writing, and spelling, too, will be learned because these activities are so much a part of modern living. Why do so many children learn to read before they go to school? Simply because it adds another dimension to living. The environment is such that they want to learn to read; they find it useful.

It seems, then, that the instrumentalist has no serious difficulty in accounting for the "skill subjects" of the traditional elementary school curriculum.[7] But what of the so-called content subjects? Will the realities of everyday living prompt the student to master geography, science, and history? Perhaps not. But is it necessary for a pupil to absorb all the factual material contained in these traditional subjects? Dewey answers this question very clearly:

> We violate the child's nature and render difficult the best ethical results by introducing the child too abruptly to a number of special studies, of reading, writing, geography, etc., out of relation to this social life. The true center of correlation on the school subjects is not science, nor literature, nor history, nor geography, but the child's own social activities.[8]

Although the content of the isolated subjects is not considered sacred by these theorists, they do believe that children will learn much of the material treated by the traditional elementary school. This feat is to be accomplished through the medium of pupils' problems and interests. For example, no child of the late twentieth century can escape the impact that space travel has made upon our world. He hears of it from all sides; he viewed the launching of

[7] *Ibid.*, p. 76.

[8] J. Dewey, *My Pedagogic Creed,* pamphlet of the Progressive Education Association (Washington, D. C., 1929), p. 9. Reprinted from *School Life* LIX, No. 3 (Jan. 16, 1897), 77–80.

space vehicles on TV; he hears rumblings of the possibility of intercontinental missiles falling on his city. All of these factors cause problems and arouse the interest of youngsters which in turn will motivate them to learn geography and science (even history). A visit to the zoo or a farm will motivate them to study nature.

The instrumentalist goes the traditionalist one better when he argues that the proper use of children's interests, problems, and needs can result in much more real knowledge than the traditional school could transmit. The artificial boundaries of the subjects are eliminated; pupils are given the freedom to study whatever relates to their problems or interests; and what they study they *know* because it was learned in a context which makes sense to the pupil. The physical and social environment is so pregnant with incentives to pupil learning that at times it behooves the teacher to "get out of the pupils' way."

The other activities of the elementary school — singing, dancing, physical education — will be as essential to school life as the areas mentioned above. They should not be looked upon as frills, for they are as much a part of living as reading and writing. In fact, many of these activities will engage the intelligence of students just as much as the so-called "academics" — and in a more interesting and meaningful way.

The reader might wonder to what extent the instrumentalist concept of the curriculum affected the elementary school program. There seems to be little doubt that the period from the beginning of World War I to the end of World War II witnessed wide acceptance of this view. Very few public schools did not incorporate some of these notions in this period of educational ferment. Even after World War II, when many secondary schools returned to a modified traditional curriculum, the elementary school retained most of the characteristics of the instrumentalist curriculum. Some of these are: (1) the emphasis on pupil activity; (2) greater freedom for pupils to select those activities which interest them; (3) the absence of subject-matter barriers, replaced by the "integrated curriculum"; (4) the presence of many nonacademic subjects centered around the interests and needs of pupils.

Adapting the secondary school curriculum to the new definition posed far greater problems for the instrumentalist. Even the traditional elementary curriculum, especially at the primary level, was entwined with the real needs of children. But the secondary curriculum still was geared to college-entrance requirements rather than to the vocational or social interests of the majority of its clientele. It was this very lack of breadth of curricular offerings that gave the instrumentalist the opportunity to attack the traditional curriculum and offer his own version of the "emerging curriculum."[9]

The same philosophy of the curriculum explained above in connection with the elementary program holds for the secondary level. Recall that the curriculum is *living,* and more specifically social living. All subject matter must be learned in a social context. Again Dewey is very explicit in his rejection of curricular offerings divorced from their social context.

> History is of educative value in so far as it presents phases of social life and growth. It must be controlled by reference to social life. When taken simply as history it is thrown into the distant past and becomes dead and inert.

> Literature is the reflex expression and interpretation of social experience; that hence it must follow upon and not precede such experience.

> The only way to make a child conscious of his social heritage is to enable him to perform those fundamental types of activity which make civilization what it is.[10]

Because of their empiricist bent one might expect the instrumentalists to argue for the value of science *as science.* But even here the emphasis is on the social aspects of science.

> Education cannot be unified in the study of science or so-called nature study, because, apart from human activity, nature itself is not a unity.

> The study of science is educational in so far as it brings out the materials and processes which make social life what it is.

> One of the greatest difficulties in the present teaching of science is that the material is presented in purely objective form, or is treated as a new peculiar kind of experience which the child can add to that which he has already had. It should be introduced, not so much as a new subject matter, but as showing the factors already involved in previous experience and as furnishing tools by which that experience can be more easily and effectively regulated.[11]

These statements seem to give the instrumentalist position on the three basic areas of the secondary school curriculum: social studies,

---

[9] W. H. Kilpatrick, "The Experimentalist Outlook," *op. cit.,* p. 77.
[10] J. Dewey, *My Pedagogic Creed,* p. 10.
[11] *Ibid.,* pp. 9 and 12.

the sciences, and literature. What of the vocational subjects? Dewey says:

> They are not special studies which are to be introduced over and above a lot of others in the way of relaxation or relief or as additional accomplishments. I believe rather that they represent, as types, *fundamental forms of social activity;* and that it is possible and desirable that the child's introduction into the more formal subjects of the curriculum be through the medium of these activities.[12]

Certainly, the prestige granted to the academic subjects in traditional education has been revoked by the instrumentalist. In their stead he places the creative, expressive, and "socializing" activities. Of course, it took some time for this new outlook to affect the curriculum of the high school. At first it lent support to the movement, already underway, to dethrone the classics and the humanities from their dominant position in the curriculum. The instrumentalist could not accept the belief that these subjects trained the mind and livened the spirit. It also reinforced the tendency to place the vocational and recreational subjects on a par with the academic, since the former were the activities that the majority of youth would continue after leaving high school. The instrumentalist gave his support to the elective system which had been almost unknown prior to the twentieth century. Under this system the student is allowed (and encouraged) to select those studies which meet his vocational and personal needs as well as his interests.

Even when the "progressive" high schools of the 1920's and 1930's retained certain subject areas from the traditional curriculum, the organization of the content centered around real-life problems in that area rather than in any systematic coverage of the area. For example, there was a rapid rise in courses like *Problems of Democracy, Current Events, and Social Problems.* In these courses the students and teacher mapped out a series of problems which were of interest and concern to them. For example there would be no systematic, formal treatment of the constitution of the United States, but this topic would be treated in connection with some social problem. Even science and mathematics classes became problem-centered.[13]

One characteristic that all these new courses had in common was the objective of "democratic living." A perusal of texts in the Prin-

---

[12] *Ibid.,* pp. 10 and 11. (Italics mine.)
[13] See above section on "Methodology."

ciples and/or Methods of Secondary Education which appeared from 1920 to the present time will demonstrate the extent to which the objective of democratic living was expected to permeate all the activities of the secondary school.

It was mentioned earlier that the secondary school clung to the traditional conception of the curriculum more tenaciously than the elementary school. Most of the influence of instrumentalism came about quite gradually and was felt chiefly in the few ways mentioned above. Finally, one secondary curriculum, called the Core and designed to incorporate the principles of instrumentalism, was developed by "experts" in the field of curriculum. This curriculum should be clearly differentiated from any of the traditional patterns of subject-matter courses. The Core curriculum applies to "that part of the experience curriculum which refers to those types of experiences thought necessary for all learners in order to develop certain behavior competencies considered necessary for effective living in our democratic society."[14]

Quoting an expert in the field, Bossing agrees that the true Core curriculum must be characterized by the following:

1. It must be based upon the problems of personal and social development of all youth of high school age.

2. These problems must be developed outside the context of the separate subject-matter fields such as history, geography, literature, and the like. Rather, the common problems selected should be a result of the enlightened consensus of teachers, students, and the community.

3. The problem-solving method (described above) should be the controlling teaching-learning method.

4. The Core program is the arena for individual and group guidance. Teachers must have a thorough understanding and knowledge of the groups with which they work so they can assist them in solving personal as well as group problems.

5. The majority of the teachers in the school have the "developing of social competence" through the medium of problems as their major goal. The rest of the school program, such as electives in the special fields, should supplement the Core activities.[15]

---

[14] Nelson Bossing, *Principles of Secondary Education* (rev. ed.) (Englewood Cliffs, N. J.: Prentice-Hall Co., 1955), p. 403.
[15] *Ibid.*, pp. 406–407.

This program seems to represent the flowering of Dewey's recommendations (which he made more than a half century before)
for a curriculum for "social living." It is based upon his belief that
experiencing is learning; it presupposes that mental powers are
socially built, not innate; it is democratic, for it utilizes pupil-teacher
planning in all phases of the activities; it presupposes that all truth
and value are relative to time, place, and altered circumstances; it
recognizes individual interests and needs only when these do not
conflict with or supercede common interests and needs.

The extent to which this *pure Core* has been accepted in secondary
schools is difficult to determine, since at least three or four curricula,
all using the name Core, are found in the schools. Many of these
simply are reorganizations of the traditional curriculum designed to
integrate studies that have a natural affinity; e.g., history and geography. However, it seems safe to say that it has been used very
extensively, especially at the junior high level. It is also difficult to
list the activities of the pure Core, simply because they are not pre-
planned or predetermined. Each Core program will contain the common problems of those involved in it. Thus a rural high school Core
program will be quite different from that found in a large metro-
politan area such as New York. Perhaps the best advice to the reader
is to locate such a program and observe it in action.[16]

As mentioned above, the instrumentalist concept of the curriculum
made its greatest inroads on the elementary school, but much less
on the secondary school. Its effect on the college program is even less
direct. Some of the indirect effects, however, are worth noting. First,
the demise of the humanistic studies as the center of the curriculum
was assured by the reinforcement given by instrumentalism to scientific and sociological movements. Second, the college curriculum became almost completely elective at this time. This type of curriculum
was much more in harmony with the instrumentalist view of meeting
the needs and interests of students. Third, the predominance of practical (vocational) courses and the addition of what the traditionalist
calls "fresh air" courses (social dancing, sports, personal grooming,
social adjustment, and the like — all for college credit) is sometimes
laid to the influence of instrumentalism.

Apart from these indirect influences it is possible to point to

---

[16] See N. Bossing and Faunce, *The Core Curriculum* (New York: Prentice-Hall,
1951).

some college curricula supposedly constructed on instrumentalist principles. One such is found at Antioch College. Although it was founded as a traditional liberal arts college in 1853, its first president, Horace Mann, incorporated certain notions of higher education which later would be promoted by the instrumentalists, such as the shift from liberal to practical studies, health and physical education, the sciences, and admission of all students regardless of race, color, creed, sex, or economic status. During the heyday of progressivism the curriculum was revised to meet the needs and interests of its clientele as well as to make college an "experience in living." In this "school of life," the students and faculty cooperatively devised the new curriculum to contain the following areas: (1) activities designed to assist the student to become vocationally competent; (2) activities affording the student the opportunity to explore career interests in real-life situations; (3) opportunities for the individual to develop into a responsible, mature, and confident person; (4) activities designed to give the student a realistic rather than an "ivory-tower" understanding of the physical and social world; (5) opportunities to live democratically with fellow students in order to make effective and creative adjustments to society.

In order to make the curriculum a true "exercise in living" one half of the five-year program is spent living off campus. Students are assigned to different off-campus jobs in their freshman year in order to explore the job opportunities before selecting a career. Then students alternate living on and off campus every other school term. There is no college supervision while they live off campus; they must plan their own budgets and schedule their own time. On campus, students get experience in democratic living by making their own regulations in regard to dress, behavior, social life, and the like. In general, letter or number grades are not used and a student is deemed ready to graduate when he has achieved a certain level of competence in "living intellectually, socially, and vocationally."

During the 1920's and 1930's a relatively large number of colleges made serious attempts to revise their curricula in accordance with the then popular progressive view of education. Though the trend in colleges after World War II was away from this philosophy, many institutions still maintain a curriculum in harmony with instrumentalism.

Perhaps a more significant development in higher education reflecting the direct influence of instrumentalism is the community college movement. Although there were many community colleges prior to World War II, the movement received great impetus from the 1946 Report of the President's Commission on Higher Education, *Higher Education for American Democracy*.

As envisioned by the President's Commission, the community college should be primarily an institution to provide terminal education of a general and vocational nature. As such it will serve the needs and interests of the post-high school population who do not plan on following the programs of colleges and universities in the professional and preprofessional areas. The curriculum, then, should contain all of the vocational subjects which will prepare the student to find profitable employment or improve his present job status. A second category of offerings might be classified as life-adjustment subjects such as homemaking, practical arts and crafts, recreational or leisure-time activities. A third classification would resemble the general education courses found at the freshman and sophomore levels of most four-year colleges, such as the humanities, social sciences, and physical sciences. But even in these courses, the emphasis would be on students' problems, interests, and needs rather than the established content of the area. In the social sciences, for example, the most important social problems of the community and the world would be stressed instead of a chronological or logical treatment of any one of the social sciences. As much as possible then, all the courses would be related to "living." It should be the "college of democracy."

In summary, the following characteristics of the instrumentalists' curriculum can be detected at all educational levels: (1) It is centered around student activities rather than subject matter. (2) Current problems and issues are considered most important: the study of the past is of use only insofar as it might facilitate the solution of current problems. (3) The remote goal of the study of current problems is the control of future events. (4) The needs and interests of students are given precedence over the prescriptions of adult society. (5) All activities should have a social as well as an individual purpose. (6) Democratic planning, learning, and cooperation are essential attributes of any curriculum at all educational levels. (7) Vocational subjects are given a status equal to that of the formal academic studies. (8) Constant change and revision in the curriculum must accompany changes in the physical and social universe.

STUDENTS

It will be emphasized in the next section that the aim of instrumentalist education is education itself. It is inconceivable, then, that education beyond the elementary level should be limited to an intellectual or socioeconomic elite. Furthermore, the instrumentalist's commitment to democracy as a way of life with all its egalitarian implications affords additional grounds for extending the availability of advanced education to all who wish to take advantage of the opportunity.

Early in his career Dewey lashed out against "educating the few" and giving the masses a narrowly utilitarian training in vocational subjects.[17] Obviously, the traditional curriculum could not be maintained if all the children of all the people were to receive as much as fourteen years of schooling.[18] To adjust to this necessary change the instrumentalist, as noted previously, constructed a "living curriculum" which would meet the needs and interests of all students.

That the instrumentalist was successful in his attempt to break down the traditional belief that only the intellectual or socioeconomic elite were to receive advanced education is evident from the attendance data of the 1960's. Over 90 percent of the youth of high school age are attending high school and nearly 40 percent of the youth of college age are in various types of college programs. It is true that other factors, such as automation and labor legislation, have contributed to this condition, but the instrumentalist always has agitated for more and more education.

It seems, then, that the instrumentalists were the first philosophers to challenge successfully the Platonic conception of education according to intellectual classes. The student will recall that Plato recommended that only a very small percentage of the population should receive higher education. These few, the intellectual elite, would become the rulers. These were to be selected from all classes and given the best education the state could offer. By far the greatest majority of the children would be trained in the practical arts and crafts; they would be the servants of society. Those who were neither

---

[17] J. Dewey, *Democracy and Education,* p. 225 ff.

[18] See Educational Policies Commission, *Education for All American Youth* (Washington, D. C.: N.E.A., 1944), p. 21. Also, President's Commission on Higher Education, *Higher Education for American Democracy* (New York: Harper & Bros., 1947), Chap. IV.

rulers nor servants would be the guardians or defenders of the state, viz., the military.

Plato believed that this was the only way education could be organized simply because children were born with the mental equipment to rule or they were born without it; this is how God and nature wanted it. That this view dominated education since Plato's time is evident from the history of education. In fact, it is still widely accepted in both the East and the West (even in most Western democracies).

Obviously, Dewey and his followers could not accept the Platonic theory.[19] First, they denied that man is born with a ready-made mind with a certain pattern of traits and abilities. Rather, they believed that these are derived from living in society. Therefore, education (which is living) is one of the main sources of creating the mental equipment of the individual, and *all* should be given the opportunity to create their abilities through education.

Second, the individual differences which the instrumentalist recognizes in constructing educational programs also are a result of the environmental forces playing upon the organism. The greater the educational opportunities, the greater will be the contributions of the individual to society. To prove this theory, some instrumentalists point to the improvements in mental abilities that come from improvements in the environment. Also as the educational level of a nation rises so does its technology and standard of living. In reality, some instrumentalists believe that more and more education will eventually reduce individual differences to a point where they become inconsequential.[20]

Perhaps the clinching argument used by the instrumentalist for extending educational opportunity to all youth is the one mentioned above, namely, the new conception of democracy as a process, a way of life. If democracy is the most fundamental value, the instrumentalist, to be consistent, must demand that all youth be afforded the opportunity to receive advanced education in free public schools; free elementary education will not suffice. He is faithful to his principles when he backs free compulsory education at all levels.[21] He is consistent when he argues that education must change to meet the

---

[19] J. Dewey, *Democracy and Education,* p. 102.

[20] T. Brameld, *Patterns of Educational Philosophy* (New York: World Book Co., 1950), pp 645–647.

[21] J. Dewey, *Democracy and Education,* p. 114.

demands of the people rather than those of the intellectual or socioeconomic elite. He is true to his commitment to democracy when he battles for federal aid to public schools.

The Educational Policies Commission of the N.E.A. summarizes this position well in the following statement:

> Schools should be dedicated to the proposition that every youth in these United States — regardless of sex, economic status, geographic location, or race — should experience a broad and balanced education which will (1) equip him to enter an occupation suited to his abilities and offering reasonable opportunity for personal growth and social usefulness; (2) prepare him to assume the full responsibilities of American citizenship; (3) give him a fair chance to exercise his right to the pursuit of happiness; (4) stimulate intellectual curiosity, engender satisfaction in intellectual achievement and cultivate the ability to think rationally; and (5) help him to develop an appreciation of the ethical values which should undergird all life in a democratic society. It is a duty of a democratic society to provide opportunities for such education through its schools. It is the obligation of every youth, as a citizen, to make full use of these opportunities. It is the responsibility of parents to give encouragement and support to both youth and schools.[22]

The President's Commission on Higher Education echoes the same sentiments when it demands that many more students (with other than purely academic ability) be cared for in institutions of higher learning. They insist that all barriers to equal opportunity be removed, including the barrier of the "restricted intellectual curriculum."[23] Throughout their report the members of the Commission (with some exceptions) demand that the government — local, state, and national — provide the means necessary to enable all to attend institutions of higher learning without any great expense to themselves or their families. The instrumentalists have always favored such assistance, especially in the form of federal aid to public institutions.[24]

In conclusion, it seems evident that the philosophical beliefs of the instrumentalists as well as the public support given by them to expanding educational opportunity leave little doubt regarding their position on this issue. They favor, without reservation, more and more education for more and more people. It must be, however, that kind of education which meets the demands of changing times;

[22] Educational Policies Commission, N.E.A., *Education for All American Youth* (Washington, D. C.: N.E.A., 1944), p. 21.

[23] President's Commission on Higher Education, *op. cit.*, pp. 27–33 and 67–70.

[24] J. Dewey, *Democracy and Education*, p. 114.

education must incorporate the changes in society which will remake man; and as man reconstructs society he must reconstruct education.

AIMS OF EDUCATION

Traditional philosophers from Plato to the modern era seem to have no difficulty determining the aims of education. True, there might be a great variety of aims stated by proponents of different schools of thought. But in all instances the philosophical system itself contained definite guideposts for determining educational aims. Thus the Christian philosopher very categorically affirms that the ultimate aim of education is identical to the ultimate aim of life itself — union with God. The rationalist might designate the development of the rational powers of man as the ultimate aim of education. In both cases the end or aim is definite and fixed. All other aims are subsidiary to the ultimate one.

For the instrumentalist, the philosopher of change, the statement of the purpose of education is much more difficult. Dewey did not simplify the task when he said that ". . . education as such has no aims."[25] But he was too realistic to deny that people who educate have aims and throughout his writings he constantly refers to educational aims.

One thing is certain, says the instrumentalist, there is no ultimate aim for the educational process. Obviously a philosopher who denies the existence of immutable truths, changeless reality, and absolute values cannot point to an ultimate purpose for life itself. It follows that he cannot propose any final goal outside the educational process:

> In our search for aims in education, we are not concerned, therefore, with finding an end outside of the educative process to which education is subordinate. Our whole conception forbids this. We are concerned with the contrast which exists when aims belong within the process in which they operate and when they are set up from without.[26]

This position leaves Dewey with only one choice,[27] "There is nothing to which education is subordinate save more education." And, as indicated above, the realization that education is a continuous process should prompt educational leaders to guarantee every man, woman, and child the opportunities to continue his formal and informal schooling throughout his life.

---

[25] J. Dewey, *Democracy and Education*, p. 125.
[26] *Ibid.*, p. 117.
[27] *Ibid.*, p. 60.

Simply because the instrumentalist denies the existence of ultimate ends of education, it does not follow that he cannot espouse immediate ends. Before pointing out some of these immediate ends, it might be helpful to devote some time to the instrumentalist's conception of aims or ends. Dewey, again, will be the spokesman on this most crucial of educational issues.

First, he distinguishes an end or aim from a result. A person throws a stone which breaks a window. The result of this action is the broken window. But this may not have been the purpose of the person throwing the stone. His purpose might have been to test his strength. Animals, too, display purposive behavior when they store food for winter use: they have a definite aim for their activity. Of course, results usually follow such purposive actions. The main difference, then, between simple results and purposive action is that purposive action is characterized by "intrinsic continuity." The ant working on his winter food supply is acting purposively since he performs a series of acts which are intrinsic to the job he is doing. The results may or may not be fully realized. Dewey draws a parallel for the classroom when he says that "it is nonsense" to speak of an educational aim when the teacher or the assignment dictates the sequence of the pupil's acts or when the pupil merely performs a series of disconnected acts prompted by his own whims. A true aim "implies an orderly and ordered activity, one in which the order consists in the progressive completing of a process. Given an activity having a time span and cumulative growth within the time succession, an aim means foresight in advance of the end or possible termination."[28]

Second, an aim must give direction to the activity before it can be considered valid. This is achieved by the use of the method of problem-solving (see section above on "Methodology"). Unless one follows the method of intelligence, one cannot be considered to perform purposive acts. Here, again, the unity of the instrumentalist's conception of educational aims, methodology, and epistemology is evident.

After analyzing purposive behavior, Dewey suggests criteria by which one can choose good aims. First, aims must be derived from the problematic situation itself (not from without). Thus it is a false educational aim to have the student learn something that he will be able to use only as an adult. Similarly an aim or goal set up by the

---

[28] *Ibid.*, p. 119.

teacher cannot be considered a true educational aim since it is not intrinsic to student activity.

The second criterion of good aims is flexibility. In some respects, this is a corollary of the first since situations might change while the problem solver is working toward a resolution of the difficulty. New evidence, broadened perspective, and altered circumstances all make it mandatory that the aim of the particular activity might be changed even during the course of the activity. "The aim is experimental and hence constantly growing as it is tested in action."[29]

The final criterion to be applied in the selection of an aim is the extent to which it frees the person or group to perform other acts for other ends. Simply stated, this connotes that there can be no final or ultimate end for an activity; each immediate aim leads to other aims. In other words, means and ends are not separable but form the links of an endless chain. One activity (a means) is directed to another activity (an end) which, in turn, will be a means directed to yet another end.

It seems evident from the foregoing discussion of "means and ends" in education that the instrumentalist does have immediate ones although he has no ultimate goal for education.

At the risk of putting words in the instrumentalist's mouth, let us attempt to list some of these immediate or proximate goals:

1. Education should develop in the student the method of experimental inquiry (problem-solving).

2. Educational activities should foster flexibility and openmindedness in the pursuit of solutions to problems.

3. Change and growth are prime goals of the educational process.

4. Since education is "socializing the individual" it should assist the student to adjust to his physical and social environment (social efficiency), or, as Kilpatrick says "to lead the good life."

Some recent instrumentalists feel that the last objective, "social efficiency," includes all the others. There is ground for this conviction in Dewey's early writings. In his *Pedagogic Creed,* for example, he avers that "education is social process" and the school is an institution designed to assist the child "to use his own powers for social ends." In *Democracy and Education* he devotes an entire chapter to natural development and social efficiency as aims. After pointing out what he felt was inadequate in Rousseau's conception

[29] *Ibid.,* p. 123.

of natural development as the end of education, he proceeds to show how the proper balance between natural and social development might be achieved through education. This feat is realized "when we recognize that social efficiency is attained not by negative constraint but by positive use of native individual capacities in occupations having a social meaning."[30] Thus ". . . social efficiency as an educational purpose should mean cultivation of power to join freely and fully in shared or common activities."[31]

Certainly, such statements of purpose are quite theoretical and one might ask that they be translated into workable objectives. This task was performed by those of Dewey's followers who were interested in the practical affairs of running schools as well as in the elaboration of his theoretical views. One such statement of objectives, *The Purposes of Education in American Democracy,* seems to reflect Dewey's view regarding the proper balance between natural development and social efficiency. The following categories of objectives are used: (1) self-realization; (2) human relationship; (3) economic efficiency; and (4) civic responsibility.[32] Each of these categories is divided into eight (or more) specific objectives. Since every student of education is well acquainted with these objectives, there is no need to reproduce them here. It may be well, however, to point to some of the more significant aspects of this most influential statement of objectives for American public education especially as these relate to and are derived from the philosophy of instrumentalism.

The first chapter of the report is devoted to the nature and sources of educational objectives. One important point mentioned is that educational objectives are not discovered. Rather, they "evolve" from the individual social living of the people and reflect the values in esteem at the time. They form, then, a part of the social policy of a people and, as such, should reflect the trends in society.

The second chapter is devoted to an explanation of the nature of democracy and the implications of the new conception of democracy for education. The view that democracy is a social process, a way of life, is explained and defended. The proposal that the school

---

[30] J. Dewey, *Democracy and Education,* p. 139.

[31] *Ibid.,* p. 114.

[32] Educational Policies Commission, *The Purposes of Education in American Democracy* (Washington, D. C.: N.E.A., 1938).

be a miniature democracy is shown to be in harmony with the new conception of democracy. The reciprocal relation of rights and duties in a democracy is set forth.

The third chapter gives the rationale for the new statement of objectives with some historical notes on the development of the objectives of modern education. With these preliminaries completed, the Commission proposes and explains each of the categories of educational objectives.

The objectives of self-realization refer to such knowledges and skills as thinking, reading, writing, computation, speech, listening, health, recreation, ethical and esthetic interests. In introducing the second category, the objectives of human relationship, the Commission indicates that this has been the neglected area in American education. In reality, the Commission believes these relationships should have priority over all other purposes in education. Unless the schools foster such goals as cooperation, democracy in the home and school, friendship, respect for humanity, and the like, all other achievements will be in vain. The objectives of economic efficiency and civic responsibility are similarly directed to the socialization of the individual.

The closing chapter of the report discusses the difficulties involved in achieving the objectives of democratic education and suggests ways of solving these difficulties.

There are more recent versions of the Educational Policies Commission objectives, but no major philosophical changes can be detected.[33]

The instrumentalist conception of educational aims represents a radical departure from those of traditional education. (1) There is no ultimate objective for education; all aims are immediate. (2) Education is its own end; it cannot posit an end outside its own process. (3) All educational goals must change as times, conditions, and people change; there are no immutable goals for education. (4) All aims must incorporate the belief that the socialization of the individual takes precedence over the development of the individual for his own sake. In other words, education must *free the individual* to cooperate with others for the general welfare. (5) Education must develop the whole child rather than any one faculty such as intellect.

---

[33] See Bulletin of the National Association of Secondary School Principals, *Imperative Needs of Youth* (Washington, D. C.: N.E.A., 1947).

(6) All educational aims must be judged in the light of democratic principles. Any purpose of education which is not in harmony with the view that democracy is a way of life must be rejected. (7) Educational aims cannot be separated (theoretically or practically) from the aims of the community, the nation, and the world.

ACADEMIC FREEDOM

In the succeeding section of this chapter the instrumentalist view on indoctrination and pupil freedom is explained. It is emphasized that although the pupil should not be expected to accept the beliefs of his teacher, he is not completely free to think and act as he pleases. The same principle can be applied to the issue of the academic freedom of the teacher.

Certainly, the instrumentalist is gravely concerned with academic freedom. He has both philosophical and practical reasons for this concern. Philosophically, he is bound to the defense of academic freedom by his notion of truth. As will be noted below (see section on "Epistemology") he denies the existence of absolute and changeless truth. Truth is not to be "discovered," but created by putting hypotheses to the test of experience. Therefore the teacher, just as every other person involved in the solution of problems, must be free to create those truths which will effect the needed changes in the world of physical and social events. A teacher should not be restricted by the defenders of the *status quo* in his search for new ways of living, thinking, or acting.

Another philosophical presupposition which places the instrumentalist on the side of almost unlimited academic freedom is his espousal of the doctrine of endless change. Life itself has no permanent goals. Since education is life, it, too, has no permanent goals. Change and growth can never take place in education if teachers are not free to try new ways of solving problems and to teach and publish these results even when they run contrary to the beliefs and standards of the society in which they work. On the contrary, the teacher (or researcher) who is completely free to create new truths and bring about needed change is rendering far greater service than one who merely teaches what, in most instances, is the minority opinion of some pressure group.

A final philosophical consideration militating against the limitation of academic freedom lies in the instrumentalist's commitment to democracy as a way of life. If democracy is the prime social value, then freedom of expression for teachers must be applied in all fields — science, religion, and politics.

In addition to these philosophical reasons for defending unlimited academic freedom, the instrumentalist might suggest some very practical arguments against limiting such freedom. For example, once the wall of protection of academic freedom has been weakened by any restrictions, there is no known means of stopping the march toward complete muzzling of teachers. Examples of this procedure are rampant in our own times not only in the dictatorships but even in some of the democracies.[34] The post-World War II era saw many attempts to dictate to teachers what they should teach and how they should teach it.

A second practical argument against the limitation of academic freedom of teachers rests in the difficulty of deciding who should determine what is to be taught. The school board? The American Legion? The American Medical Association? The Socialist Party? The predominant religious sect in a community? The board of regents of the university? The faculty of a school or university? The instrumentalist would argue that, regardless which organization (or combination of organizations) is given authority over what is taught, someone's freedom will be encroached upon. The only solution to this difficulty lies in giving academic freedom to all engaged in the educative process.[35]

One might get the impression from the foregoing discussion of academic freedom that the instrumentalist favors "lawless thought." Such however, is not the case. Dewey believed that freedom is not an absolute. Freedom from physical and intellectual restraint always must be coupled with freedom *for* something. For the instrumentalist this freedom is *for* the good of society. The individual exercises freedom of thought so that he can make his contribution to group interest.[36] The first limitation, then, put on freedom is that it have a social purpose: freedom is not its own end.

Yet another criterion of true academic freedom is the extent to which the teacher or researcher adheres to the canons of the experimental method. No teacher is allowed to propagate doctrines, or be-

---

[34] H. K. Beale, *Are American Teachers Free?* (New York: Scribners, 1936).

[35] J. Dewey, *Democracy and Education*, p. 352. Cf. also *How We Think*, p. 149.

[36] J. Dewey, *Democracy and Education*, pp. 351–353; *Experience and Education*, Chap. V.

liefs (even relative ones) unless they have been arrived at by means of experimentation (scientific method).[37] It is for this reason that the instrumentalist objects to the teaching of sectarian religion and certain ideological tenets of the various "isms" in the public schools. These beliefs, he considers, lack empirical grounds and represent simply unfounded preferences of their proponents. But, one might ask, "What is to be done about the many religious, political, and economic doctrines which are prevalent today, all battling for the control of man's mind? Are these to be completely ignored by educators? Are they to be suppressed by those in government? Should teachers not be allowed to join any of these religious sects, political parties or ideological movements?"

The instrumentalist has no objection to membership in these various groups as long as the teacher does not use education as the means of converting the young to his point of view. The teacher is not expected to conceal his convictions, but he should never use his position to indoctrinate for his own biases. Teachers should band together to defend the rights of their fellow teachers to teach the truth as they see it. If freedom of speech is denied to teachers it will eventually be denied to all.

Dewey himself always was the champion of academic freedom. For example, when Bertrand Russell was to teach in the United States, an attempt was made by certain groups who opposed his moral philosophy to prohibit him from fulfilling his teaching assignment. Dewey came to his defense even though Russell and Dewey were philosophical opponents.

Of course the instrumentalist faces the same dilemma as any liberal. Simply because he is a liberal, he must grant freedom of speech even to those who would destroy freedom of speech. If he denies freedom of speech to anyone he is no longer a liberal. If he grants it to one who would eradicate freedom of speech he might lose his own freedom. But he is optimistic, in the long run, that the forces of freedom will win. One of the best ways to weaken the forces of autocracy and dictatorship, he argues, is to challenge them in the arena of free debate. Therefore, allow Fascists and Communists to speak their piece; present all sides of the issues involved in the struggle between these "isms" and democracy. The pragmatic method of intelligence, especially the final step — the

---

[37] For a description of the experimental method, see section on "Epistemology."

test of experience — will show that such "isms" will not solve the problems of modern society.

In conclusion, it can be asserted that the instrumentalist favors academic freedom in the broadest sense of the term. For both philosophical and practical reasons he considers it wrong to limit the freedom of teachers to teach the truth as he sees it. The teacher, however, must not use his position to indoctrinate his charges for they, too, have the right to free testing and expression of ideas. The only qualification that the instrumentalist puts on academic freedom is the demand that the teacher apply the "method of intelligence" to the solution of the problems at hand.

INDOCTRINATION

A glance at the sections on "Epistemology" and the "Search for Values" (see below) will reveal why "indoctrination" is a topic which must be of grave concern to the instrumentalist. His rejection of the immutability of truth and values and his insistence upon the experimental method of knowing leave little doubt about his opposition to indoctrination.

As early as 1896 Dewey objected to the teacher's telling students what was true and false, right or wrong:

> The teacher is not in the school to impose certain ideas or to form certain habits in the child, but is there as a member of the community to select the influences which shall affect the child and to assist him in properly responding to these influences.[38]

This statement is very significant for two reasons. On the one hand it bids the teacher to refrain from implanting in the young the notion that there are any absolute truths or values and especially to avoid imposing his own biases and preferences on the pupils. On the other hand, the teacher is expected to "select the influences" which shall initiate the child into the social living of the school (which is itself an integral part of the larger social context). Thus the prescription against indoctrination does not imply the absence of social direction — there is no such thing as *absolute freedom*. Dewey clarified this view of pupil freedom in *Democracy and Education*:

> The essence of the demand for freedom is the need of conditions which will enable an individual to make his own special contribution to a group

[38] J. Dewey, *My Pedagogic Creed*, p. 8.

interest and to partake of its activities in such ways that social guidance shall be a matter of his own mental attitude, and not a mere authoritative dictation of his acts.[39]

This reciprocal relationship of individual freedom and social authority contains the theoretical refutations of the "child-freedom" practices of some progressive schools. Neither Dewey nor his followers (who understood this relationship) ever preached that the child should act or think just as he pleases.[40] In fact, such an extreme view is completely out of harmony with the instrumentalist belief that mind and personality are a product of social inheritance rather than of inherited faculties or powers.

It might appear, then, that the instrumentalist is arguing for the preservation of the *status quo* in all matters. Such is not (and cannot be) the case. His insistence upon the changing character of the physical and social universe prohibits him from defending the *status quo* in any realm of human endeavor. The important problem, then, for the instrumentalist is how to avoid the extremes of indoctrinating the student in any one scientific, political, or religious creed and the complete *laissez-faire* philosophy of some early progressives.

The resolution of this dilemma seems to lie in the use of the problem-solving method. If the young are disciplined in this method of critical thinking, they need not be told what to think by the teacher or community authorities. As difficulties arise in the physical and social environment, the young will apply the methods of intelligence to the solution of these problems. They will have mastered the methods of collecting and analyzing data, they will *know how* to discover and state hypotheses or plans of action as well as to put them to the test of experience. The possession of these skills will enable each new generation to decide whether to retain or reject the truths and values held by the present generation. We cannot and should not expect our children to retain our chosen beliefs unless these same beliefs can stand the test of critical intelligence. However, there is some "indoctrinating" and most instrumentalists will admit that their program does involve a deliberate attempt to implant in the youth the "rightness" of the method of experimental inquiry.

---

[39] J. Dewey, *Democracy and Education*, p. 352. Cf. also *How We Think*, p. 198.
[40] J. Dewey, *Experience and Education* (New York: Macmillan Co., 1938), Chaps. IV and V.

Should teachers not be allowed to indoctrinate for democracy? One of Dewey's disciples, Kilpatrick, was very explicit in his rejection of even this form of indoctrination. He believes it is just as miseducative to indoctrinate children in the principles of democracy as it is to indoctrinate them in the foundational beliefs of any political or religious "ism."[41] Kilpatrick stated this precept with the full realization that his own beliefs about democracy might be rejected by future generations.[42]

It would appear that the instrumentalist has left nothing for the school to do except "training in the method of problem-solving." After all, if there are no truths or values of a permanent nature in which the school can indoctrinate its clientele, why waste time teaching or learning that which will be of no use to the next generation? The instrumentalist admits this and, as we have seen, believes that there should be no hard and fast curriculum. But he also realizes that problem-solving cannot be carried on in a complete vacuum. Therefore some subject matter is needed with which (or upon which) to solve problems. But the important point, at least as far as indoctrination is concerned, is that *all* points of view should be examined in connection with the study of a certain problem.

To illustrate this approach, let us assume that the students are seeking solutions to the religious conflict in American life today. Their search should lead them to the study of all religious beliefs; the religious commitment of the teacher, of the community, or of the "majority" should not influence their judgment. Only after they have exhausted all sources of data should they proceed to suggest solutions. If a problem involves economics, the students should be given the opportunity to study communistic, socialistic, and capitalistic theory and practice, not just the one to which their teachers and elders happen to subscribe.

In summary, the following points might be made about the instrumentalist's view of indoctrination:

---

[41] W. H. Kilpatrick, *Philosophy of Education* (New York: Macmillan Co., 1951), pp. 124–126.

[42] One of the "left-wing" movements among the followers of Dewey, the Social Reconstructionists, argues that the school should indoctrinate for a "new social order." For a justification of their position see G. S. Counts, *Dare the School Build a New Social Order?* (New York: John Day Co., 1932). Cf. also T. Brameld, *Toward a Reconstructed Philosophy of Education* (New York: Dryden Press, 1956), Chap. 6.

1. The student should never be expected to accept any statement solely on the authority of the teacher.

2. All points of view on any issues must be presented "objectively," that is, free from the biases of those holding the view.

3. The "reasons for" each view are as important as the statement of each view.

4. The student is not free to think and act just as he pleases. He is always bound by the canons of the method of intelligence (problem-solving).

5. Intelligent behavior or thinking is learned, not innate. Therefore the student must be challenged by real problems which will bring about or create his mental equipment. He is not to be told what to think.

6. The social environment provides the context in which critical thinking will take place, for such activity cannot be carried on in a vacuum.

PERMANENCE AND CHANGE

In Chapter Two we pointed out that modern philosophies are basically "philosophies of change." Naturalism, naturalistic realism, existentialism, and Marxism fit quite well into this category. But none of them is as pervaded by the notion of change as instrumentalism — it is the philosophy of change *par excellence*. One cannot comprehend its epistemology or value theory without the previous recognition of this dominant theme of the entire system. If one were to point to any one metaphysical belief as essential to the instrumentalist philosophy, it would be the doctrine of change. Kilpatrick states categorically that change is *inevitable*. "As inevitably as civilization continues to exist and thought continues to be itself, just so inevitably will changes come. We face, then, a world of inherent and unending change. . . . The only thing we can assert with certainty is that we face rapidly changing forces which are shaping an unknown future."[43] Why can one call the doctrine of change a metaphysical presupposition of the instrumentalists? Do we not observe change all about us in the world of physical and social events? Indeed we do! And most traditional philosophers also recognized that

---

[43] W. H. Kilpatrick, *Sourcebook in Philosophy of Education* (New York: Macmillan Co., 1926), pp. 258–259.

change was evident in the universe. But for them change was only
one aspect of reality; the other was permanence.

Thus, when the instrumentalist affirms that all reality is constantly
changing he is making an assertion about the nature of things which
goes beyond his experimental data. He, then, is as much a metaphysician as the Platonist, Aristotelian, or Hegelian, albeit an "experimental metaphysician." Perhaps the escape from the dilemma
of the modern philosopher who tries to avoid metaphysics (or
claims to be antimetaphysical) lies in the espousal of a negative
metaphysics; he denies the metaphysical beliefs of other philosophers.
Dewey, of course, put forth much effort in the attempt to debunk
traditional metaphysics. But it seems he could not escape completely
his early metaphysical training.[44]

Even if Dewey himself was not willing to admit the metaphysical
nature of his emphasis on change, some of his followers saw no dis-
grace in such an admission.[45] Furthermore the philosophies of change
found a congenial atmosphere in the age of evolution. The world of
philosophy had just been shaken to its foundations by the proposal
that the world was very old — much older than the biblical story
told. The species extant in the nineteenth century were believed to
be the result of a long evolutionary process rather than static types
as Aristotle had claimed. The theories of classical physics, chemistry,
biology, and the applied sciences of medicine and the like were
being rejected in favor of new theories based on recent findings.
It is evident, then, why modern philosophies like instrumentalism
espoused the "cause of change" and denied any permanence in the
world.

It must be noted that the instrumentalist does not limit the
application of the doctrine of change to the physical and biological
universe. Dewey made applications of the doctrine to the fields of
logic, epistemology, and ethics. To illustrate, he argued that Aristotle's
logic was designed for a static universe and should be rejected

---

[44] It might be of help to the reader in understanding Dewey's philosophy if he
keeps in mind that Dewey's early philosophical training at the University of Vermont
was given by the realist H. A. Torrey. A few years later he completed work on his
doctor's degree in philosophy under the tutelage of the Hegelian (idealist) G. S.
Morris, at Johns Hopkins.

[45] See John L. Childs, *American Pragmatism and Education* (New York: Henry
Holt and Co., 1956), pp. 52–54. *Education and the Philosophy of Experimentalism*
(New York: Century Co., 1931), Chap. III, Sidney Hook, *The Metaphysics of
Pragmatism* (Chicago: Open Court Co., 1927).

because it no longer can serve a purpose in a universe characterized by change.[46] Similarly, his theory of knowledge (problem-solving) is designed to solve difficulties arising in a milieu of uncertainty, flexibility, and plasticity. The conclusions arrived at by this method are tentative, relative, and lacking all the characteristics of certainty or immutability (see section below on "Epistemology"). The field of morals, in which the traditionalist argues so vehemently against mutability, does not escape the onslaught of the instrumentalist doctrine of change. All conceptions of right and wrong will vary as man and his environment move from one stage of development to another (see below, section on "Values").

Thus, it appears to this author, the central metaphysical belief of the instrumentalist is the doctrine of change. But this doctrine has other metaphysical corollaries. One, the denial of the supernatural, is discussed below in the section on "Naturalism versus Supernaturalism." Since the traditional concept of God and the spiritual realm are inextricably bound with immutability any consideration of them is impossible within the instrumentalist framework. Also, the body-soul dualism of Aristotle and the Hebrew-Christian belief in spirit and man's life of spirit must be rejected. Man and all manifestations of his being are of a purely natural origin, and, moreover, are ever changing.

Other cherished beliefs of the traditional metaphysician suffer a like fate at the hand of the instrumentalist. The teleological emphasis of the traditionalist cannot be countenanced if one believes in the all-pervasiveness of change. In place of a world governed by certain laws and designed for certain ends, the instrumentalist posits an indeterminate, insecure, and goalless one.[47] In a world of this type the problem-solving method enables man to adjust to and assist in the control of the environment — a metaphysics of change calls for a logic of change.[48]

There is one aspect of instrumentalism that is worth noting (especially for the hostile reader), namely, the theoretical agreement between the various principles enunciated in each of the areas of philosophy. Using change as the central metaphysical doctrine, the in-

---

[46] J. Dewey, *Logic, The Theory of Inquiry* (New York: Henry Holt & Co., 1938), p. 65.

[47] J. Childs, *American Pragmatism and Education* (New York: Henry Holt & Co., 1956), pp. 60–64.

[48] *Ibid.*, pp. 64–69.

strumentalist constructs a new logic, a new epistemology, a theory of ethics, aesthetics, and politics which harmonize with this basic starting point. Dewey, the mastermind of the system, accounted for all the areas of traditional philosophy. Perhaps Dewey's bent for "system" is part of the "Hegelian hangover" of which he is often accused. But this same thoroughness will not be as evident in the philosophy of the Marxists, existentialists, and analysts. For this reason Dewey is sometimes referred to as the last of the great "system builders."

NATURALISM VS. SUPERNATURALISM

We pointed out above that the early manifestations of naturalism in education were somewhat negative; i.e., they were *against* most beliefs that theologians and traditional philosophers held dear. Although a certain amount of this negativism might be found in instrumentalism, the concern of this philosophy was to construct a theory of radical naturalism which incorporated an explanation for the phenomenon of the Hebrew-Christian tradition. Thus instrumentalists do not close their eyes to the hard fact that belief in the supernatural is part of the warp and woof of Western education. They realize that belief in the supernatural has been tied to belief in the brotherhood of man. But they do reject the notion that the acceptance of these supernatural doctrines is essential to the continued acceptance of the fundamentals of democratic living. That the instrumentalist must reject most of the doctrines of theology and theodicy is evident from his basic assumption about knowledge. (See below, section on "Epistemology.") His sole reliance upon empirical procedures, his assertion of the relativity of all truth and the tentative nature of all knowledge, preclude any acceptance of the absolute and immutable truths from the theologian or the philosopher.

What, then, is to be done with the many doctrines (especially those of a moral nature) which are found in American culture? They, too, must be put to the test of experience and judged in the light of their consequences for the public good. For example, the Christian tradition fostered the performance of acts of charity toward one's fellowman. Those blessed with earthly goods were to help their less fortunate fellowman, be he friend or foe. Many religious men and women devoted their entire lives to assisting the sick, the orphan, the prisoner, and the poor. These noble acts are good, the instrumentalist holds, not because they find their source in the mandate of some supernatural authority, but because they have met the test of experience: the consequences are acceptable to human society; they solve, to some extent at least, the problems of human misery. The truth or acceptability of such beliefs and practices is justified in human experience, not in divine mandate.

For all practical purposes, then, the instrumentalist can have no truck with any of the purely traditional theological beliefs of the Western world. All that remains (from these beliefs) for his scrutiny involves ethical norms, for these can be submitted to the test of human experience. These latter are what the instrumentalist is making reference to when he speaks of "spiritual values." One should never associate the term "spiritual" (when used by the instrumentalist) with belief in a Triune God, the existence of angels, devils, the immortal spiritual soul of man, and original sin.[49] Therefore, it seems that any attempt to harmonize the basic beliefs of Christianity with those of instrumentalism is pure wishful thinking.

Are instrumentalists militant atheists, then? Probably not, since atheism itself involves certain presuppositions which cannot be put to the test of experience. Perhaps the best term characterizing the instrumentalists' views would be "secularism." Their concern is with the problems of the world of work, politics, human relationships, of living. The dreamer and the poet might wish to soar from the realities of everyday living to the world of chimera and myths, but let the man of action concern himself with the multitude of problems which deprive man of contentment and peace. This is the "new religion" of mankind, the cult of the "public good."

To determine the educational import of this radical naturalism is not difficult. The aims of education will be this-worldly, flexible, and practical — questions of man's final end, of God, and of everlasting life are of no crucial moment. The curriculum must be stripped of theological trappings and be centered on those activities which will better human existence. Indoctrination in any set of religious or

---

[49] One might say that William James allowed for religious experience. But a close scrutiny of his work, *The Will to Believe*, will reveal that his conception of religion is basically different from that of the Hebrew-Christian faith. Also, Dewey and his followers rejected James's semimystical interpretation of religious experience. See Dewey, *Essays in Experimental Logic* (Chicago: University of Chicago Press, 1916), p. 319.

social doctrines must be abandoned. Teacher and pupil freedom
are essential to any instrumentalist outlook. The community or state
through its arm, the secular public school, is the prime agency of
education. Because of its antihierarchical bent, instrumentalism favors
the education of all students to the full extent of their capabilities.

NATURE OF MAN AND SOCIETY

In the foregoing section it was pointed out that the instrumentalist
rejected the dualistic view that man is composed of a material body
and a spiritual soul. Does it follow that he holds a purely mechanistic
view of man? No! He contends that one can argue for a naturalistic
conception without committing himself either to mind-body dualisms
or a lifeless mechanism. In trying to understand this view the reader
is asked to recall the gist of the foregoing section on permanence
and change, especially those parts referring to evolution.

Man is a product of evolution, just as are all other manifestations
of reality. Man, then, can lay no claim to powers, faculties, or traits
which place his origin in a world beyond nature. This both simplifies
and complicates matters for the instrumentalist. On the one hand,
he does not have to seek explanations for the interaction of spiritual
and material functions in man. On the other hand, he must account
for those functions traditionally attributed to mind. In any theory of
education, this latter concern is all-important.

What, then, is the instrumentalist's conception of mind? Dewey's
thesis on this most basic question is that man's rational powers can
be accounted for by a theory of human behavior (including what
the traditional philosopher called "mental") based upon the principles
of the natural evolutionary process; there is no need to have recourse
to transcendental forces. This thesis does not affirm that man has
no rational powers above those of animals, but that the origin of
the very advanced and complex forms of behavior can be traced to
simpler types of "adjustment behavior" found in animals. In other
words, animal attempts to adjust to the environment are foreshadow-
ings of the human use of ideas or hypotheses to serve the same end,
i.e., adjustment to environment by the solution of problems arising
in it. Obviously, this view rejects the traditional notion of a mind
endowed from the beginning with rational and volitional powers.
Also, it gives no solace to those who hold that the human body might
be a product of the evolutionary process but deny that mind finds

its origin in biological evolution. Mind is not different from body, but is merely another aspect of it.[50]

How the monistic theory of man's nature affects human thinking is described in some detail below in the section on "Epistemology." Here it is sufficient to note that for the instrumentalist *thinking is a biological process*, just as seeing, breathing, walking.

The question of the origin of mind, however, which the traditionalist attributes to a supernatural force, has yet to be answered by the instrumentalist. To affirm that it *simply evolved* seems gratuitous. How did we get from the stage of the monkey using various objects to get his bunch of bananas, to Einstein developing the theory of relativity? Dewey recognized this problem, as did his friend, George H. Mead. They knew that the strictly biological, cause-effect interpretations of the mechanists could never raise the amoeba to an Einstein, or to the level of an ordinary ten-year-old child, for that matter.

To extricate themselves from this very real difficulty, instrumentalists have proposed the theory that "mind" finds its origin in "social behavior" rather than in physical and biological processes. They have not, however, rejected the notion of continuity between the three levels — physical, biological, and social. In this theory of the origin and development of mind, the social level is just as "natural" as the biological, even though much more intricate. The social level involves association and communication of the beings functioning thereat. It also views these beings as participating in activities involving small and large groups. It appears that these three kinds of activities are responsible for those functions we are wont to call "mental."[51]

To show that there is some continuity between human behavior and animal behavior, Dewey points to the ability of animals equipped with eyes, ears, and noses to "sense danger" and avoid it. This ability, he believes, contains the basic ingredients of mental behavior since the animal has mastered a more advanced method of adapting to the environment for its own preservation than lower organic forms are able to achieve. But this is not yet rational behavior, because animals do not know that they have these reactions to the stimuli of danger. Man, on the other hand, knows that he has these reactions,

[50] John Dewey, *Creative Intelligence* (New York: Henry Holt and Co., 1917), pp. 30, 35.

[51] John Dewey, *Experience and Nature* (Chicago: Open Court Publishing Co., 1925), pp. 270–272.

and can use abstract symbols in place of the original sensations. The shrill cry of the blue jay in the forest is not a symbolization of danger in the same sense that the flashing red lights at a railroad crossing symbolize danger. That is, the organism had to be developed well beyond the responses found in animal (including "herd") behavior before one can speak of mind or intellection. Truly rational behavior, as Dewey and Mead view it, is found only in those groups characterized by communication through abstract symbols, which convey meaning not contained in themselves. The first sign of mental activity in the evolutionary process lies in the use of language. Thus we have the first two ingredients of "mind": association (beings in groups) and communication (use of language). The third, participation (conscious cooperation with other members of the group) is a characteristic of full-fledged human society. Because all human infants grow up in this highly developed environment and act in the same manner as adults, the instrumentalist feels no compulsion to posit an inborn faculty of mind. For him, the converse is true: mind is an acquired way of acting, socially built.[52]

One other topic of classical philosophy related to our discussion on the nature of man involves the age-old problem of free will. Since the instrumentalist rejects the notion of an antecedently existing mind (or soul) in which the faculty of will might be rooted, he must either deny the existence of free will or propose a new theory to explain human choices. At first glance, it might seem that a fatalistic view of human behavior might be acceptable to the instrumentalist, since he places such great emphasis on environmental forces in man's life. Dewey writes:

> The essence of habit is an acquired predisposition to *ways* or modes of response, not to particular acts except as, under special conditions, these express a way of behaving. Habit means special sensitiveness or accessibility to certain classes of stimuli, standing predilections and aversions, rather than bare recurrence of specific acts. *It means will.*[53]

With will thus equated to habit, and habit an *acquired* mode of response to the environment, it might appear that environment, in the long run, predetermines choice. Dewey attempts to temper this deterministic notion:

---

[52] W. H. Kilpatrick, *Philosophy of Education,* p. 37.
[53] Dewey, *Human Nature and Conduct,* p. 42. (Italics mine.)

> The medium of habit filters all the material that reaches our perception and thought. The filter is not, however, chemically pure. It is a reagent which adds new qualities and rearranges what is received.[54]

It seems, then, that the instrumentalist is espousing the paradoxical position that the will (not as a faculty but as a way of *reacting*) is determined, yet free. Man is determined insofar as the initial motivation for choice is found in environmental and hereditary factors which limit the scope of his activities; he is free insofar as he can rearrange or redirect these forces into novel or modified patterns of behavior.

To illustrate this view of will let us examine the case of a very influential person such as Abraham Lincoln. Can it be said that Lincoln's choice was the cause of events which took place at the time of the Civil War? No! The social conditions of the times provided the primary impetus for the events which took place. Thus it cannot be maintained that Lincoln's free choice was the cause. One cannot say, then, that these events would not have taken place if Lincoln had not willed them. Does this mean that the biological organism we call Lincoln simply responded to certain social stimuli in the sense that he did nothing to them? Not quite so, because these stimuli precipitated a "felt difficulty" in Lincoln and he proceeded to interact with them in such a manner that the course of events might be altered. He tried to state the possible directions events might take; he attempted to predict what the consequences of each direction would be; he reacted in such a way that one of these possible directions should be tried as a solution to the difficulty. Therein rested Lincoln's freedom — the freedom to interact with and redirect events of which he was not, strictly speaking, the cause.

This conception of man's mind as the resultant of social processes has a direct bearing on the instrumentalist view of the nature of society. If there are no antecedently existing minds that could band together to form societies, a new theory of the origin of society was needed. Actually, the foregoing treatment of the origin of mind contains implicitly the instrumentalist theory of the origin of society. The evolutionary process itself accounts for the existence of families, groups, communities, states, and nations.[55] It is proper, then, to speak of communities or societies only when the characteristics of

---

[54] *Ibid.*, p. 32.
[55] This position is sometimes referred to as social evolutionism or social Darwinism.

association, communication, and participation are present in groups of beings.

Although there are many other considerations of the instrumentalist view of the nature and origin of society, time can be devoted only to one of them: the relationship between members of society. This relationship is organic, similar to the relationship found within a biological organism. That is, the members of groups, communities, societies, are parts of an interrelated and interdependent organism from which the member receives its lifeblood, rational powers, its entire *modus vivendi*. The educational import of this view of society is far-reaching and is discussed at some length above.

How does the instrumentalist translate the notion of "society as organism" into a practical formula for managing the affairs of men? Since instrumentalism is a twentieth-century philosophy, one would expect that the democratic way would be selected by the instrumentalist as the best means of securing the optimum good of the social organism. Indeed such is the case. But certainly the conception of democracy as a representative form of government, current in the past two centuries, did not embody the characteristics of an organic union among the members of society. In reality, representative democracy was constructed on the premise that *independent individuals* selected other individuals who would *represent* them in the legislative halls. As independent persons, they possessed rights antecedent to the organization of any government or societal structure.

But the instrumentalist cannot begin with this premise, since individual minds or persons are formed (created) by membership in communities and societies. Consequently, for the instrumentalist democracy itself must be viewed as a way of living involving interrelated and interdependent parts of the social organism. It is a way of managing not only the affairs of government but *all* human affairs — family life, economic life, religious, recreational, and educational activities; democracy must pervade living itself.[56]

Since democracy should be lived, one might ask how democracy can be related to knowing. Is not knowing itself a phase or aspect of living? The method of problem-solving embodies democratic

---

[56] Most of Dewey's works exemplify this new conception of democracy. See especially, *Democracy and Education* (New York: Macmillan Co., 1916). Perhaps the clearest and most brief exposition of this view is found in Boyd H. Bode, *Democracy as a Way of Life* (New York: Macmillan Co., 1950).

methodology, especially when group problems are the concern. When a group of people cooperate for the solution of a common problem and follow the methodology of problem-solving, they are "living democratically." Perhaps for the first time in the history of philosophy, a democratic methodology is organically linked with a theory of knowledge. The effect of this marriage of knowing and living will be most evident in the instrumentalist theory of values (see below, section on "the Search for Values").

Any theory of man and society which introduced such radically new conceptions might be expected to remain in the ivory tower of philosophical speculation for many years, and have little or no effect upon education or any other practical aspect of living for a long time to come. Such was not the case, however, for instrumentalism. Dewey and his followers, unlike most philosophers before them, recognized that the shortest avenue to the acceptance of new ideas was via education. By defining philosophy as a theory of education they demonstrated their conviction that philosophy is a practical rather than a contemplative concern. Even their most abstract and theoretical treatises are directed to school practice. They tell the administrator and teacher just what should take place in the classroom if they want to conduct it in accordance with certain philosophical beliefs. St. Augustine's *On the Teacher* (*De Magistro*) is perhaps the only example in classical philosophy of a writer concerning himself with recommending classroom procedures that will harmonize with a specific theory of knowledge.

One of the most dramatic educational innovations derived from the instrumentalist view of man and society is the switch from the traditional emphasis on the role the individual plays in learning to that of the group or society. The learning context should be social because the individual mind is a product of society. Because the student does not bring an antecedently existing mind to school with him when he begins his ascent of the educational ladder, it is the school's job to "make a human being of him." Dewey is very specific in his demand that "social living" be the heart of the educative process.[57] Thus the curriculum should not be a collection of independent subjects but an integrated pattern of activities involving social living (especially democratic living).

Because instrumentalism rejects all dualistic interpretations of

---

[57] For the first statement of this view, see J. Dewey, *My Pedagogic Creed*.

man, the school's concern is for the whole child, not only his mind. After all, mind is a creation of living rather than a faculty for living. Then education cannot point to any end outside itself — it is its own end. The end of education is not even a *preparation* for living, as Spencer believed, but democratic living itself. As such, it is a continual process, *a process without end*.

To summarize, it seems that the two most radical changes brought about by the instrumentalist conception of man and society affect the curriculum and aims of education. That the areas of methodology, agencies, students, academic freedom, and indoctrination are quite definitely influenced by this new notion of man's nature and that of the society in which he exists is evident. But a more direct relationship to these facets of education can be traced to the epistemological or axiological beliefs of instrumentalism.

EPISTEMOLOGY

The traditionalist believed that the prime motivation for learning was founded in what might be called a natural desire to know. This belief implies that intelligent beings want to know and learn, whether or not such knowledge may have any practical, immediate value or usefulness. Of course, traditionalists recognized that some kinds of knowledge which man seeks do have a "bread and butter" usefulness. To illustrate, Plato recommended that the lowest social stratum be trained in those skills which will provide food, clothing, and lodging for the workers themselves and for the upper levels of society. Even the education designed for the rulers was to serve the practical purpose of making wise rulers of them. But the educational program for rulers did not consist in courses on "how to" govern but rather in a program of studies that were designed to develop "wisdom." The wise man, then, would make a good ruler.

John Dewey and his followers rejected this traditional conception of the purpose of knowledge. For them, the motivation for knowing was not derived from any innate desire to learn but rather from some block or difficulty which the organism experienced in everyday living. It might be well, then, to trace the method of arriving at knowledge which Dewey proposed in the first edition of *How We Think*.[58]

---

[58] This is one of Dewey's most influential treatises of a theoretical nature, since it has had such wide applications in education and the social sciences.

Upon examination each instance (of thinking-knowing) reveals, more or less clearly, five logically distinct steps: (i) a felt difficulty; (ii) its location and definition; (iii) suggestions of possible solution; (iv) development by reasoning of the bearings of the suggestion; (v) further observation and experiment leading to its acceptance or rejection; that is the conclusion of belief or disbelief.[59]

A more detailed exposition of the steps in this "complete act of thought" is essential to an understanding of the problem-solving method of teaching and learning.

Step I: A Felt Difficulty

The most important point in understanding the first step in the knowing process is acceptance of the statement that there would be no thinking if there were no perplexity or problem. Thus the animal or human organism would never launch into the act of knowing if there were no events to disturb the equilibrium of that organism. If an organism suffered no blocks or difficulties in satisfying its needs or meeting the demands of a new situation, or, in other words, if the means for achieving a desired end are at hand, there is no difficulty and the organism is not motivated to thought. But if the means to the desired end are not immediately at hand, the organism is prompted to discover the means to achieve the end. Dewey illustrates this starting point with the following incident. While in the downtown section of New York, a man is reminded, on seeing a large clock, that he has only forty minutes to reach a place quite distant. In fact, it had taken him an hour to travel the same distance by streetcar.

Now the man is perplexed because the means immediately at hand (the streetcar) will not enable him to achieve the desired end (his appointment) on time. If the man had an hour or more to get to his destination, there would be no problem or perplexity; there would be no motivation for thinking. This particular situation, then, is the first step, which Dewey calls the "felt difficulty," in the knowing process. But note, the difficulty must be felt or recognized by the organism. Without such cognizance, there would be no perplexity, no problem, and no thinking.

Step II: Its Location and Definition

As Dewey indicates, the second step, locating and defining the

[59] John Dewey, *How We Think* (Boston: D. C. Heath & Co., 1910), p. 72. The revised edition of 1933 contains a somewhat different statement of these five steps but retains the same logical structure.

problem, often fuses with the first step, especially when the situation is not strikingly novel. But when the case involves a perplexity not hitherto experienced, the location and definition of the problem becomes a separate step. In such a case, one must pause and ponder the situation to determine just where the difficulty lies. If this is not done, any further deliberation or actions will be merely trial-and-error behavior which may or may not solve the difficulty.

To impress upon the reader the importance of this second step Dewey cites the manner in which a physician behaves when summoned by a patient. He hears what the patient has to say about his illness (and not all the patient tells is correct). Also, the physician notes other indications of a certain disease. Does the physician immediately prescribe the remedy? No! He makes a much more thorough analysis of the difficulty and only after extensive study of the case (especially in novel ones) does he state what the trouble is. He may call in several consultants before he gives the final diagnosis. This procedure is necessary, Dewey insists, in all novel and complex problems.

> The essence of critical thinking is suspended judgment; and the essence of this suspense is inquiry to determine the nature of the problem before proceeding to attempts at its solution. This, more than any other thing, transforms mere inference into tested inference, suggested conclusions into proof.[60]

Step III: Suggestions of Possible Solutions

After the problem has been located and defined (with some assurance that the person is "on the right track") by procedures capable of some sort of experimental verification, the organism is ready to move from "what is present to something absent." This step involves suggesting possible solutions or hypotheses, a somewhat speculative activity since it projects into the unknown. Because of the uncertainty of this inferring to the future there can be no assurance that any of the suggested solutions will solve the problem. These tentative solutions constitute what Dewey calls an idea (conjecture, guess, hypothesis, or theory). Ideas, then, are tentative solutions to or instruments for solving problems which arise in the environment.[61] Of course, the presence of alternative suggested solutions enhances

---

[60] Ibid., p. 74.

[61] The term instrumentalism, applied to Dewey's philosophy, is derived from this conception of "ideas."

critical thinking because the organism is not tied to any one course of action in its attempt to extricate itself from the difficulty. To return to the example used in Step I, the more alternative solutions the person can propose that will get him to his destination on time, the better are his chances of solving his difficulty. Because the streetcar is definitely out of the question, the alternatives of subways, interurban trains, taxis, and the like give the person a better chance of selecting one that is likely to get him to his appointment on time. If there is only one suggested solution, obviously he must try that one.

Step IV: Development by Reasoning of the Bearings of the Suggestions

This step involves the search for the implications of each of the ideas or suggested hypotheses. Note the difference in the meaning of the term *reasoning* as used by Dewey from that found in Chapters Three to Five (and in classical philosophy, in general). For Dewey, reasoning has its beginning in an idea or suggested solution. Each hypothesis must be scrutinized closely to determine the consequences that such a course of action *might* have. Thus a hypothesis that seems plausible at first glance might, at closer scrutiny, be found unsatisfactory or even absurd when the "full consequences are traced out." The reverse may also be true, for example, when a hypothesis that at first sight might appear utterly ridiculous, might later, upon closer examination of the possible results, be accepted as the one for the first test.[62]

To illustrate this fourth step, return to example of the physician. Once he has made the diagnosis (i.e., located and defined the problem — Step II) and proposed several kinds of treatment (Step III) he reasons about the possible consequences of each. If treatment with drugs or immediate surgery are the two alternatives, he must decide, on the basis of anticipated results, which is the better course of action to follow.

Step V: Further Observation and Experiment Leading to Belief or Disbelief

The last step in the knowing process demands that the hypothesis, which has been selected as the one most likely to succeed in resolving

---

[62] The current practice of "brainstorming" perhaps is derived from this concept of reasoning. Each member of the brainstorming team is encouraged to suggest any possible solutions that come to mind, regardless of their seeming remoteness. Sometimes these wild conjectures produce ideas which later serve as solutions.

the difficulty, be put to the experimental test (or the test of experience). The reasoning which took place in Step IV requires experimental corroboration to confirm it. Step IV is conjectural; Step V is empirical. The solution becomes acceptable only when the empirical results of Step V agree with the anticipated results spelled out in Step IV.

For example, if the physician anticipated that administering certain drugs would cure the patient (Step IV) and discovered that the patient did not get well after he had administered the drugs, the discrepancy between the anticipated results and empirical results would force him to reject this solution. Then he must try one of the other suggested solutions or he might wish to go back to Step II to determine the acceptability of his original diagnosis — he might have gathered additional information in the process of making the empirical test.

If the anticipated results and the actual results are the same, the person then is able to accept the conclusion or assert that the problem has been solved. But such acceptance is not final or absolute. Further testing or experimentation might suggest a revision or even rejection at a later date.

The importance of observation both at the beginning and end of the knowing process is emphasized by Dewey. It is essential at the beginning to define the exact nature of the problem; it is essential at the end to determine the acceptability of one of the hypotheses.

The reader might ask whether Dewey insisted that each formal step be followed in every problem situation. As pointed out above, Steps I and II often fuse when the problem situation is not completely novel. Further, the trained or disciplined "problem-solver" will be able to discern readily how much time and effort must be spent at each stage of the process. Also, Dewey warns that in some cases a whole lifetime might have to be spent on the solution of a single problem.

In summary, the main points of Dewey's epistemology are:

1. All thinking (learning or knowing) is initiated by the feeling of some difficulty.

2. The organism then locates and defines the exact nature of the problem.

3. Possible solutions (hypotheses, ideas) are sought for resolving the difficulty.

4. These suggested solutions are scrutinized for their anticipated consequences.

5. The one most likely to solve the problem is put to the test of experience.

Finally, it must be remembered that this method of knowing applies to the problems of everyday life as well as to those of the complex sciences.

At this point, a very important consideration concerning the nature of the conclusions of the Deweyan approach to knowing must be treated. What resemblance do they bear to the "truths" which the traditional philosopher holds in such esteem? The answer is quite simple. For Dewey and his followers all conclusions are tentative; all knowledge is subject to constant revision. Each variation in a problematic situation will call for variations in solutions. The "truths" of one era will be the falsehoods of another. The resolution of each problem will constitute a "new truth." In other words, the organism creates truths as the need arises. It does not accept a ready-made truth as the solution to a new problem (or an old problem for that matter). There are no self-evident truths from which other truths might be derived.

What philosophical presupposition underlies this Deweyan conception of relative truth? Earlier in this chapter it was indicated that instrumentalism was the philosophy of change *par excellence*. If change is a characteristic of all reality it must *ipso facto* be a characteristic of truth, for truth reflects the reality it portrays. This belief, then, suggests a criterion for truth quite different from that proposed by "traditionalists." Perhaps, for the first time in the history of philosophy, the consequences or results are given as the criterion for truth. Only after a hypothesis has been tested in experience and the results prove to be the solution of a difficulty can one speak of an idea or a theory being "true." Dewey himself recognized the difficulty involved in using the term "truth" as a synonym for a tentative solution which had met the test of experience. He felt that the term was so associated with concepts like "immutable" and "absolute," that a more accurate connotation of his conception of truth might be given by the term "warranted assertability."[63] Stated in

---

[63] See *The Philosophy of John Dewey*, Library of Living Philosophers, Vol. 1, P. A. Schilpp, ed. (Evanston: Northwestern University Press, 1939), p. 567 ff. For a critique of this view, see Bertrand Russell, *An Inquiry Into the Meaning of Truth* (London: George Allen and Unwin Ltd., 1940), pp. 318–326.

another way it means that after the problem-solver has proceeded through the logical steps of the knowing process (the complete act of thought) and has accepted the solution as meeting the demands of the situation, then he is warranted in asserting that the anticipated and actual results are congruous. And that is as near as one can get to truth.

Further, the instrumentalist contends that the "quest for certainty" which so engrossed traditional philosophers is not in harmony with the modern scientific mentality. Prescientific man needed the security which was derived from certainty, but modern man has reached that level of maturity which enables him to act confidently even when he has no assurance that the predicted results and actual results will be the same.

One final consideration about this most important matter of truth relates to the origin or source of truth. For the Christian philosopher, the source of truth is the Author of all truth, God. But Dewey rejects any external, transempirical source. The interaction of man and nature might be pointed to as the source; that is, neither nature alone nor man alone create truth but man acting upon nature and nature acting upon man do so. Nature is to be viewed as constituting both physical and social reality — the world of rocks, plants, animals, persons, communities, and nations. Problems arise involving all of these manifestations of nature and must be solved before equilibrium can be restored to the individual or social organism. Most emphatically, though, these *alone* are the sources of knowledge and relative truth.

The *educational implications* of the Deweyan theory of knowledge bear a direct relationship to the teaching-learning process. Unlike some of the other philosophies discussed in this book, the student can observe instrumentalist "epistemology in practice" in the classroom. A detailed description of the applications of this system was given above in the sections on "Methodology," "Aims," etc. We can here point up once again the most salient features. Unless the teaching-learning process roughly follows the pattern of problem-solving logic no significant learning will take place. If this new pattern is not employed, meaningless memorization and parroting of timeworn and outmoded facts and formulas will be mistaken for true learning. This latter approach, the instrumentalist believes, constituted the central failure of traditional education.

Since solving real problems lies at the heart of living (as well as learning-knowing) the instrumentalist does not point to any goal or purpose for education which reaches beyond the educative process itself. In other words, education is its own end. It is worth noting that nowhere in the history of education has education been viewed as its own end except in this system. For the Christian, the ultimate aim of education is the salvation of the immortal soul and/or unity with the Godhead. For the secularistic humanist knowledge or development of intellectual powers is viewed as the end of education. For a naturalist like Spencer, *preparation for* complete living as an adult constituted the goal of education. For other naturalists, pleasure was viewed as the final goal of all educational activities. In all of these instances, there is some goal outside of education which gives meaning and purpose to all educational activities. But the instrumentalist contends that these external ends are either false or, at best, misplaced. Thus the Christian view of educational aims is false whereas Spencer's aims should be considered subsidiary to the educative process itself, in instrumentalist thought.

The instrumentalist conception of truth implies that no subject matter shall be sacred in the school curriculum. An "emerging curriculum" designed to meet the needs of the pupils will replace the traditional curriculum. If one were to point to any one core of curriculum content, it would consist of student problems rather than any systematic collection of truths (subject matter).

Similarly, if truth is a dynamic concept involving constant change, academic freedom for the teacher is essential for progress. The educator must not be shackled by adherence to an accepted system of truths and values but must be free to search for solutions to problems. Pupils, too, should be free to work toward solutions to their problems with the assistance of their teachers. But under no conditions should teachers attempt to indoctrinate youth with their own views. Certainly, the student has as much right to *create his own truth* as the teacher.

THE SEARCH FOR VALUES

There are two questions about values in general that should be answered before proceeding to an explanation of the instrumentalist's interpretation of ethical and aesthetic values: "What is the nature of value judgments?" and "How are value judgments reached?"

In response to the first question, the instrumentalist affirms that value judgments find their origin in the same context as judgments of fact — the interaction of the individual or social organism with the environment. To state it another way, a judgment of right and wrong is just as *scientific* as any statement about the nature of the physical universe. As such, the principles of freedom, equality, and justice have just as much right to the claim of "objectivity" as do the principles of the empirical sciences. For this reason the instrumentalist cannot subscribe to the notion of some modern philosophers (logical positivists, for example) that value judgments merely are expressions of moral preferences with no grounding in experience or reality.[64]

In this respect, then, the instrumentalist is closer to the traditional philosophers than to the modernists. However, since all knowledge, scientific or otherwise, is relative and all values are characterized by change, he cannot accept the traditionalist's conception of the immutability of values. Even the most ancient and prized ethical and aesthetic norms of mankind are subject to revision. Does this mean that the instrumentalist wishes to throw out all the values of the past? He claims not! Rather he believes that a gradual, and at times almost imperceptible, change is taking place in man's conception of ethical norms and standards. For him, this is as it should be, for each encounter of man and his environment presents a novel situation which calls for a reinterpretation and adjustment of value judgments to meet the demands of the new situation. The new statement of a value judgment may be similar to a previous one but is seldom identical to it. Of course, some values persist for a longer time than others because they are realized in those areas of human experience where change is less rapid. In other areas, on the other hand, a constant and rapid revision of values is to be expected. For example, social values have seen many changes in the past one hundred years simply because the social structure itself has undergone such radical change. But the changes have not been radical enough to suit the instrumentalist.[65]

Should this theory of value be classified as utilitarian? Dewey claims it is not:

> The utilitarian theory of equation of acts with consequences is as much a fiction of self-conceit as is the assumption of a fixed transcendental world

[64] J. Dewey, *Theory of Valuation* (Chicago: University of Chicago Press, 1939), pp. 6–8.
[65] J. Dewey, *Democracy and Education*, pp. 298–305.

wherein moral ideals are eternally and immutably real. Both of them deny in effect the relevancy of time, of change, to morals, while time is of the essence of the moral struggle.[66]

In like manner, he rejects the claim of individualistic hedonism which makes the pleasure of the individual the criterion of value. The Deweyan view of the social origin and nature of values precludes the acceptance of any criterion of individual pleasure as the key to making value judgments. The individual acquires his values by virtue of his membership in social groups.[67]

Perhaps the best way to describe the instrumental theory of value is to say that, like the other aspects of that philosophy, it represents an attempt to build a new theory. That this "new" theory has vestiges of older ones is to be expected, for no thinker can escape completely from the cultural streams from which he acquired (consciously or unconsciously) his intellectual meanings and content. The answer to the second question, also, will illustrate the novel aspects of this theory of value; for the manner in which one arrives at values will affect his view of the origin and nature of values.

The second general question is concerned with the method of arriving at values. It has been mentioned that the instrumentalist contends that value judgments are just as objective as are judgments of fact. If such be the case, then the same method used to arrive at scientific judgments will be employed for the acquisition of value judgments. This is the method of problem-solving delineated above in the section on "Epistemology."

First, this means that there are no preexisting values which are part and parcel of a ready-made natural or eternal law. Second, there are no values contained in the mind or conscience of man at birth. Thus there would be no values, just as there would be no knowledge, if there were no problematic situations. The only difference between the two is that value statements involve the moral or aesthetic aspects of the relationship of man to man which have disturbed the equilibrium of the social organism.

The first step in *creating* a value will be occasioned by a difficulty for which those involved have no ready answer: no means immediately at hand to extricate themselves from the difficulty. The

[66] J. Dewey, *Human Nature and Conduct* (New York: The Modern Library, 1930), p. 51.
[67] *Ibid.*, p. 58 ff.

very existence of this real difficulty prompts them to get to the heart of the matter by locating and defining the problem. After a thorough search for all relevant data, various hypotheses are proposed as solutions to the problem. The anticipated consequences of each hypothesis are scrutinized and the one most likely to resolve the indeterminate situation is selected for the test in experience. If the difficulty disappears, equilibrium is restored to the social organism. Then, and then only, a value judgment is warranted. Specific examples of this procedure and the status of conclusions will be discussed below in the context of ethical and aesthetic situations.

ETHICAL THEORY

Because of the empirical bent of their epistemology and their insistence upon the relativity of all knowledge and values, instrumentalists have been accused by traditionalists of having no great concern for ethics. However, a perusal of the works of Dewey and his followers will reveal that they seem to be much more concerned with ethical issues than with those of a purely scientific nature. This concern is reflected in the shift of emphasis in the schools from the abstract sciences and mathematics to the "social studies." Under their leadership, these studies pertaining to living received an impetus hitherto unknown in the history of education. Even the study of the natural sciences is given an ethical slant, for they are not to be learned for their own sake but for the value and enrichment they might contribute to human well-being. This great concern for ethical matters might be considered another aspect of Dewey's "Hegelian hangover."[68]

The first question to be answered in the analysis of instrumentalist ethics is: Would there be any ethical norms if there were no social groups? Could an isolated individual ever make a value judgment? From what already has been said about instrumentalism it seems highly improbable that an individual might ever utter a value judgment. Remember, there is no antecedently existing mind: mind is socially built. Further, there are no antecedently existing values: they, too, are socially built. Fundamentally, moral standards are simply the statement of customs which themselves are socially built. Dewey says, "For practical purposes morals mean customs, folkways — But always and everywhere customs supply the standards

---

[68] See Chapter Eleven for an analysis of the idealistic emphasis on value theory.

for personal activities."[69] It seems fair to assert that all values are fundamentally social values (for the instrumentalist). It is only when a number of beings are in association and communication that difficulties might arise which involve matters of right or wrong. Ethical statements, such as "It is wrong to steal," "It is good to care for the aged," "Parents should love their children," are meaningless outside a social context.

Let us use the first situation, stealing, to illustrate how the ethical prohibition against stealing arose. Is it wrong to steal because God's commandments make such a prohibition? Is it wrong because it is written in the minds and hearts of men? For the instrumentalist, neither of these explanations is acceptable. But he might account for the existence of this ethical norm in the following manner. A group of primitive people were living in a land with ample food for all which could be had with little or no effort. Due to some catastrophe such as a flood or drought, a shortage of food ensued, leaving some with an inadequate supply to satisfy normal needs. When the pangs of hunger became too great, those without sufficient food took some from a fellow tribesman. This action upset the equilibrium of the tribe, resulting in a feeling that something "was out of kilter" (the felt difficulty). The tribesmen got together in an attempt to determine just where the difficulty lay (locating and defining the problem). At this stage it was not the problem of ownership or private property, since up to this time all members of the group were able to get all the food they needed without actually "owning" the trees or plants from which the food was picked. Stated in question form the problem is: "How can we avoid difficulties arising when one tribesman takes food which is in the possession of another tribesman?"

With the problem thus defined, the tribesmen offer possible solutions to it. After due consideration of all the conceivable consequences of each of the solutions the tribesmen felt that a strict prohibition against taking what was in the possession of another would be the hypothesis most likely to solve the difficulty. This one was put to the test of experience and found satisfactory. The entire process may have taken many decades. But if no such difficulty had ever arisen there never would have been an ethical statement: "It is wrong to steal."

---

[69] J. Dewey, *Human Nature and Conduct*, p. 75.

As most examples, the one above represents an oversimplification of the instrumentalist view of the origin of ethical norms. But it serves to illustrate the important characteristics of ethical judgments. Paramount among these is the belief that actions are not right or wrong in themselves: they are judged to be right or wrong only when they cause a difficulty in the social realm. Another important consideration is that no ethical norm is valid for all times and under all conditions. For example, the statement "It is wrong to steal" might be meaningless under conditions of pure socialism. Finally, it seems that ethical norms can never be individual or personal — they are always social in nature and origin.[70]

If morality is basically social, it is evident that a "Do as I say!" or "Do as you please!" criterion will not suffice for determining what is right and wrong. To illustrate, a powerful person or group of persons (such as political or ecclesiastical authorities) decide that a certain kind of behavior is right or wrong. For an instrumentalist, this can never be considered a valid value judgment since it satisfies only a few people. Similarly, no individual can say, "This form of behavior pleases me, therefore it is right." Thus both moral authoritarianism and anarchism are unacceptable to the instrumentalist.

Since no external authority (God or man) nor the individual involved in a moral action is the source of moral judgments, the instrumentalist appeals to the "authority of the situation." This means that a value judgment is valid only when it resolves the problematic situation. But how are we to know when the problem is solved? When equilibrium has been restored to the social organism, or when *all* involved in the problematic situation are satisfied. In other words, the appeal is to the *authority of the people* — democratic authority.

Again the significant role that democracy plays in the entire instrumentalist system is brought to the fore. A democratic ethics is integrated with a democratic metaphysics and epistemology.

AESTHETICS

Thus far, it has not been difficult to perceive the theoretical agreement between instrumentalist epistemology and ethics. The method of problem-solving yields ethical as well as scientific judgments;

---

[70] Although Dewey speaks of the individual in connection with moral behavior, the individual is never acting in isolation. In fact, Dewey rejects the "good intention" aspect of individual morality. See Dewey, *Democracy and Education,* Chap. XXVI.

both have the same objective nature for both are rooted in experience; both are intended to reduce or resolve the tension existing between the organism and the environment. However, the whole emphasis of problem-solving is on the application of intelligence to real-life problems. How do the concerns of the traditional philosopher about value judgments involving beauty fit into the pattern of real-life problems? On the surface, it seems that there is no place in instrumentalism for a guiding theory of art. But, as was indicated above, Dewey attempted to incorporate all of the areas of traditional philosophy into his system and aesthetics was not slighted. One of his lengthier works (355 pages) is devoted to the subject of art.[71]

The first characteristic of instrumentalist art is that it is rooted in experience. It is derived from the same interaction of organism and environment as are other products of human intelligence. It does not find its origin in any innate ability of a gifted person nor in the inherited characteristics of any race or ethnic group. It has the same biological source as other forms of thought.[72]

The second characteristic of this theory relates to the response of the artist and the one observing the product. Negatively stated this means that unless the artist enjoys producing his art form and those who observe it enjoy this product it simply is not art. Thus the factory worker who assists in the production of a beautiful car is not an artist. Likewise, the portrayal on canvas of a sunset which no observer enjoys is not a work of art. In this sense they are useful.[73]

A third characteristic of the theory is that all art products as well as aesthetic judgments about them arise in the same *social context* as all other human products and value judgments. Just as there would be no knowledge or values if there were no association, communication, and participation of beings, so there would be no art and no art appreciation if these social conditions did not exist.[74] To state it simply, the instrumentalist believes it is inconceivable to have either art or an artist if only one person were involved — if there were no groups or societies, there could be no art.

A final characteristic of this aesthetic theory is its thoroughgoing

---

[71] J. Dewey, *Art as Experience* (New York: Minton, Balch and Co., 1934).

[72] *Ibid.*, pp. 29, 65, 78.

[73] J. Dewey, *Democracy and Education*, pp. 240 and 279. Cf. *Art as Experience,* p. 21.

[74] J. Dewey, *Art as Experience,* p. 261,

relativism. And this characteristic, like the three listed above, is true of all the conclusions of inquiry. Applied to aesthetics it means that there are no criteria which can be applied to the art forms by which one can make an absolute judgment about their beauty. Traditionalists used such criteria as symmetry, unity, and the like to evaluate the products of art.[75] But the relativist cannot apply such absolute standards. Therefore such judgments as *"Hamlet* is better than *The Death of a Salesman"* are quite meaningless since this evaluation of the two plays is based on certain immutable criteria.

This example suggests another aspect of aesthetic relativism. What art works one era enjoys, another might despise; art forms will change as modifications are made in the environment and in man. Michelangelo's works are (or were) beautiful; Picasso's works are considered beautiful in the twentieth century. In the thirtieth century, the works of both might be considered the aberrations of psychopathic minds. Thus, to each generation its own likes and dislikes; to each race its own preferences; it is senseless to argue whether the art works of one time are better (or worse) than those of another time.

The instrumentalist theory of aesthetics presents many difficulties, even to some of Dewey's disciples. The reasons for some of these problems of interpretation have been pointed out above. The most basic one lies in the experimental nature of the instrumentalist doctrine of the origin of all knowledge and values.[76]

One way of pointing up the educational implications of instrumentalist value theory might be by contrasting them with those of traditional education. Whereas the traditional curriculum contained the ethical and aesthetic values deemed to be of lasting worth, that of the instrumentalist would be concerned with reinterpreting old values in the light of changing times and conditions and with creating new values. The traditional school would have as one of its major aims the conservation of the values of the cultural heritage; the instrumentalist goal would avoid conservation and emphasize the creation of new values. In the traditional school, academic freedom

---

[75] Dewey occasionally mentions something like "unity" but he seems to be referring to the unity of experience rather than a unity in the piece of art. Cf. *Art as Experience,* pp. 35, 160, 183.

[76] Perhaps the best brief statement of the ambiguity of instrumentalist aesthetics (by an author quite sympathetic to the philosophy of Dewey) is found in the article by H. B. Dunkel, "Dewey and the Fine Arts," *School Review,* Vol. 67 No. 2, Summer, 1959, 229–246.

was limited by the value commitment of the culture in which it existed; in the new school there should be no limitations to academic freedom in regard to value commitment. The traditional school did not hesitate to indoctrinate the student in those values deemed to be true values; the new school opposed indoctrination in any set of values regardless of their prestige: students should be free to select their own value systems.

EVALUATION OF INSTRUMENTALISM

In the preceding chapter naturalism was evaluated from a Christian point of view. Since instrumentalism is one of the naturalistic philosophies all of the limitations of naturalism listed apply as well to instrumentalism. In addition to these, the following might be cited:

1. The belief that man's mental faculties are created by society is wholly unacceptable to the Christian philosopher.

2. Difficulties which arise in the environment certainly start the thinking process on its way. But the Christian philosopher maintains that thinking may be initiated in other ways. For example, the native desire to know, regardless of the presence of a felt difficulty, might initiate the thinking process.

3. The Christian educator will admit that there are relative truths and values, but he must reject the notion that all truths and values are relative.

4. The Christian educator cannot accept the view that all values are derived from problematic situations involving the adjustment of individuals to society.

5. The emphasis upon change as the underlying metaphysical principle of all reality makes it impossible to speak of either the goals of man, society, or life in general. The absence of any ultimate purpose in life reduces the activities of life to a sequence of disconnected, aimless events.

6. The "consequence theory of truth" is inadequate. Consequences may be one of the considerations in a theory of truth, but, because of the uncertainty derived from such a criterion, radical agnosticism can be the only result.

7. The intermingled strains of realism, idealism, and scientism found in instrumentalism result in logical inconsistencies which are repugnant to the traditional philosopher.

In spite of the many limitations of instrumentalism, it, like naturalism, has made significant contributions to education. Msgr. George Johnson points to what he considers the most important of these: *Contributions that Exp. has given to education.*

> Yet not a bit of attention would it receive and no progress would it make were it not for the fact there lurks in it a truth concerning the educative process that has been largely forgotten, a truth which has been protesting, vainly for the most part, against the regimentation, the standardization, the routine and the artificiality that have been the concomitants of our effort to provide and administer an education that would reach all the children of all the people.
>
> . . . What is this vengeful truth? It is a simple truth, rather obvious as a matter of fact. It is generally accepted in the field of formal education. It is accepted as a matter of course in family life, in ordinary social relations, wherever men and women and children learn from one another out of school. Dr. Shields gave expression to it when he wrote, "The temptation of the teacher is to ignore the fact that the temple of life and mind can be built by none other than the inward dweller."

Msgr. Johnson then asserts that "action, activity, living, doing" are essential conditions for learning. Traditional teachers wrongly "put a premium on pupil passivity" and ignored the "fact that personal experience is the only sound basis for learning."[77]

Since activity is central to the instrumentalist educational system, the study of teaching-learning methods is given major consideration. Dewey's problem-solving method and Kilpatrick's adaptation of it, the project method, are used widely in all schools. Certainly, they should be given credit for developing these useful methods.

Yet another contribution of Dewey and his followers lies in their extensive use of the behavioral sciences for the purposes of education. True, other educators have done the same, but the instrumentalist gave great impetus to the development of the science of education.

Finally, instrumentalism in applying the principles of democracy to classroom management has shown that pupils can develop self-discipline by being made responsible for their own behavior. Of course, the Christian educator cannot accept the view that the teacher's authority is limited by that of the students. But he can utilize the worthwhile experience which pupils gain in shouldering some responsibility for their own behavior. Pupils are more apt to obey those rules which they participated in making and, cer-

---

[77] Msgr. George Johnson, *Progressive Education* (Washington, D. C.: Catholic Education Press, 1940), pp. 4–5.

tainly, pupils will achieve a better understanding of democracy by practicing it.

SUMMARY

Progressivism and the Instrumentalism of Dewey have been the dominant forces in American education during the twentieth century. The progressivists hold that reality is in ceaseless flux, constant ongoing evolution, and that evolution reaches its peak in the development of society. Man is pre-eminently a social being, and the task of education is coextensive with the task of life: an ongoing process whereby man socially evolves and strives, through collaborative effort, to master the universe for the goals freely chosen by a democratic society.

Perhaps the chief influence of the progressivists has been in the area of curriculum construction, in revising the concept of what the school is for. The school is not meant to develop merely intellectual powers, nor is it simply to be a *preparation* for life. Rather it is to be itself an *experience in living,* providing the environment whereby pupils can achieve the skills and exercise those skills necessary for life in a democratic society. The teacher is meant to be a guide, a helper, and is there not to teach content but rather to initiate pupils to the techniques and methods whereby they can determine their own goals and work out the solutions to the problems they encounter in daily life.

Progressivists reject the supernatural and hold that there are no goals of education extrinsic to the educative process itself: education is its own goal, and has for its proximate ends the direction of biological and social evolution in the manner best suited to advance democratic living.

BIBLIOGRAPHY

Beale, H. K., *Are American Teachers Free?* (New York: Scribners, 1936).

Bode, Boyd, *Democracy as a Way of Life* (New York: Macmillan Co., 1950).

Bossing, Nelson, *Principles of Secondary Education* (rev. ed.) (Englewood Cliffs, N. J.: Prentice-Hall Co., 1955).

Bossing, N., and Faunce, J., *The Core Curriculum* (Englewood Cliffs, N. J.: Prentice-Hall, 1951).

Brameld, Theodore, *Patterns of Educational Philosophy* (New York: World Book Co., 1950).

———— *Toward a Reconstructed Philosophy of Education* (New York: Dryden Press, 1956).

Butler, J. D., *Four Philosophies* (New York: Harper Bros., 1957). Part V.

Childs, John, *American Pragmatism and Education* (New York: Henry Holt & Co., 1956).

———— *Education and the Philosophy of Experimentalism* (New York: Century Co., 1931).

Counts, G. S., *Dare the School Build a New Social Order?* (New York: John Day Co., 1932).

Cremin, L. A., "The Progressive Movement in Education: A Perspective," *Harvard Educational Review,* Vol. 27, Fall, 1957, pp. 251–280.

Dewey, John, *How We Think* (New York: D. C. Heath & Co., 1910).
——— *Art as Experience* (New York: Minton, Balch & Co., 1934).
——— *Creative Intelligence* (New York: Henry Holt & Co., 1917).
——— *Democracy and Education* (New York: Macmillan Co., 1910).
——— *Essays in Experimental Logic* (Chicago: University of Chicago Press, 1916).
——— *Experience and Education* (New York: Macmillan Co., 1949).
——— *Experience and Nature* (Chicago: Open Court Publishing Co., 1925).
——— *Human Nature and Conduct* (New York: Modern Library, 1930).
——— *Logic, The Theory of Inquiry* (New York: Henry Holt & Co., 1939).
——— "My Pedagogic Creed," *School Life,* LIX, No. 3 (Jan. 16, 1897) pp. 77–80.
——— *Theory of Valuation* (Chicago: University of Chicago Press, 1939).
Dunkel, H. B., "Dewey and the Fine Arts," *School Review,* Vol. 67, No. 2, Summer, 1959.
Educational Policies Commission, *Education for All American Youth* (Washington, D. C.: N.E.A., 1944).
——— *The Purposes of Education in American Democracy* (Washington, D. C.: N.E.A., 1938).
Hook, Sidney, *The Metaphysics of Pragmatism* (Chicago: Open Court Publishing Co., 1927).
Johnson, Msgr. George, *Progressive Education* (Washington, D. C.: Catholic Education Press, 1940).
Kilpatrick, W. H., "The Experimentalist Outlook," *Philosophies of Education,* 41st N.S.S.E., Yearbook, Part I (Chicago: University of Chicago Press, 1942).
——— *Foundations of Method* (New York: Macmillan Co., 1926).
——— *Philosophy of Education* (New York: Macmillan Co., 1951).
——— *The Project Method* (New York: Teachers College, Columbia University Press, 1921).
——— *Sourcebook in Philosophy of Education* (New York: Macmillan Co., 1929).
National Association of Secondary School Principals, Bulletin, *Imperative Needs of Youth* (Washington, D. C.: N.E.A., 1947).
President's Commission on Higher Education, *Higher Education for American Democracy* (New York: Harper & Bros., 1947).
Russell, Bertrand, *An Inquiry Into the Meaning of Truth* (London: George Allen and Unwin Ltd., 1940).
Schilpp, P. A., ed., *The Philosophy of John Dewey,* Library of Living Philosophers, Vol. I (Evanston: Northwestern University Press, 1939).

CHAPTER EIGHT

Scientific Realism

INTRODUCTION

IN THE early chapters of this book, scholastic realism, based chiefly upon the philosophy of Aristotle and St. Thomas, was given extensive treatment. The modern realists of the nonscholastic types hold some fundamental views in common with their traditional fellows. The most significant of these is the independent existence of things, objects, or elements; that is, these "reals" exist whether there is a human mind to perceive them or not. When one acquires knowledge, it is of a preexistent world, not a world which exists only when I perceive it. In general, however, they have abandoned most of the philosophical views held by the scholastics. This aspect of modern realism will become very evident when the basic philosophy of this school is discussed below.

The name "scientific realism" has been chosen because of the empirical orientation which is common to these thinkers.[1] They share this scientific outlook with other modern philosophies such as instrumentalism, positivism, and Marxism. Thus they regard philosophy as essentially one with science. Philosophy does not provide a special kind of knowledge different from that obtained in the empirical sciences. In the main, then, philosophy is the servant of science.

Another important consideration, for purposes of this text, is that scientific realism was not given to philosophizing about education. In reality, it seems that the educational philosophy was developed as a reaction to or rebuttal against Dewey's philosophy of education. However, simply because this brand of educational realism be-

---

[1] Other names often used to designate the same school are naturalistic realism, evolutionary realism, or the new realism.

gan as a reaction against an existing scheme of education, it does not mean it has no relevance for or influence on modern education. On the contrary, the post-World War II demand for more "solid subject matter," especially in the sciences, can be traced in a large part to the indirect influence of the scientific realists. The present-day demand for scientists and scholars can only boost the stock of this school of thought.

METHODOLOGY

One might begin the discussion of the realists' conception of methodology by asking whether they would align themselves with the lecture-recite-assign approach of the traditional school or the experience-centered methods of the progressive school. Their answer is quite unanimous, since they believe that the exclusive use of either approach is inadequate. The traditional school methods emphasized rote memorization, resulting, as Whitehead says, in the accumulation of "scraps of information and inert ideas."[2] But the progressive school errs, they argue, in maintaining that only activity methods (problems, projects, etc.) or direct experience are truly educational. Breed, Russell, Whitehead, and Broudy all maintain that realists can never admit the exclusive domination of activity since it is rooted in a subjective philosophy. The exclusive use of such teaching-learning methods assumes that the learner does not begin from objective things and events but actively "creates" them. Activity methods presuppose that there is no content (subject matter) which "preexists" the experience of the learner. Russell, for example, believes that the young child needs "to do" what he is learning but learning by doing becomes both inadequate and superfluous for the older student. The pupil who has been properly educated can extract meanings from abstractions and manipulate these abstractions to further his learning without the assistance of direct experience.[3]

Broudy, it seems, reverses the order of the process. He believes that methods which ensure the mastery of subject matter should

---

[2] A. N. Whitehead, *The Aims of Education* (New York: Mentor Books, 1949), p. 13. Whitehead's educational theories are similar to those of the realists. His philosophical doctrines are treated in Chapter Eleven since they appear more akin to idealism.

[3] B. Russell, *Education and The Good Life* (New York: Boni & Liveright, 1926), p. 246.

precede the use of problem-solving techniques. When the student knows enough about a subject, only then can he set about intelligently to solve problems involving that subject matter.[4] But, he adds, the exclusive use of memorization certainly is not the proper way to achieve mastery of the subject.[5]

One might conclude that realists would favor the use of any teaching-learning method which will enable the teacher to assist the student in developing his intellectual powers and acquiring an integrated knowledge of the world about him. In practice the realist shows much less concern for method than he does for content.[6]

In all their discussions of the method, one basic notion seems to underlie their conclusions on the subject, namely: scientific method provides the exemplar for teaching-learning methods. Indeed, modifications are needed to fit the maturity, needs, and interests of pupils. But these modifications should never replace the fundamental steps of the scientific method.[7]

If pupil interest is not to play a major role in the determination of instructional methods, what is its purpose? Intrinsic interest, certainly, has great motivational value because the pupil will get about learning the subject or skill because he sees it as an end in itself. Most youngsters do not need prodding to learn games, songs, and dances. But if educators were to rely solely on intrinsic interest to get pupils to learn something, obviously there is much they *should* know about the world which they never *would* know. Here the realist calls upon the value of extrinsic interest (discipline). Thus a student must learn mathematics (which may have no immediate interest for him) if he wishes to become an engineer. He must submit to the discipline of rigorous and often distasteful study if he is to achieve his goal. Since the realist holds for the value of extrinsic interest he must employ teaching methods which accord with the discipline of the subject taught. This view suggests that special subjects will provide their own method based upon the logic of the subject itself.[8]

One other point often included in the realist's consideration of

---

[4] H. Broudy, *Building a Philosophy of Education* (Englewood Cliffs, N. J.: Prentice-Hall, 1961), p. 292 f.

[5] *Ibid.*, p. 302.

[6] See section on "Curriculum."

[7] See section below, on "Permanence and Change" and "Epistemology."

[8] F. Breed, "Education and the Realistic Outlook," *Philosophies of Education*, 41st N.S.S.E. Yearbook (Chicago: University of Chicago Press, 1942), p. 102 f.

method is evaluation. The measurement movement in America usually is attributed to realists, of whom E. L. Thorndike is the best known. As will be seen in the section on "Curriculum," the realist maintains that the content of education should be composed of *that which* is *known*. If such be the case, quantitative measurement of what the student has learned is not only possible but essential if the teacher and the student are to know whether this content has been mastered. Early attempts at achievement testing, it is true, consisted chiefly in "memory items" but great strides have been made in developing items which test understanding, interpretation, synthesis, and other complex intellectual functions. Obviously, the instrumentalist would have to repudiate the realist's philosophy of measurement, for the instrumentalist denies the objectivity of facts and principles as well as the stability of knowledge.

AGENCIES OF EDUCATION

Since the new realists have rejected the authority of the Church in matters involving "acceptable knowledge," certainly the Church can lay no claim to any authority in education. Russell considers organized religion the "font of stupidity." Breed and other realists are not quite as outspoken against the role of the Church in education, but their claim that all true knowledge is rooted in experience and science seems to negate the claims of the Church to the right to educate.

But what of the rights of the family as an educational agency? Russell feels that its primary responsibility lies in building the character of the child, which he feels should be nearly completed by the age of six. A generally wholesome school environment will be adequate to maintain the level of morality which was acquired before the child entered school. The family cannot be held responsible for the intellectual education of its children simply because it is not equipped, in most instances, to fulfill this obligation.[9] Santayana also believes that the family is not fitted to perform the primary functions of education such as developing intelligence, breaking down prejudices and biases.[10]

If neither the family nor the Church is a legitimate or adequate educational agency, it falls to the state to see to it that its citizens receive a good education. But the realist, at least in the Western

[9] B. Russell, *Education and the Good Life,* p. 239 f.
[10] G. Santayana, *The Life of Reason* (New York: Mentor Books, 1960), p. 111.

world, is quick to add that the state should dictate neither the curriculum and methods nor even the aims of education. These purely educational matters should be left to the judgment of professional educators whose training equips them for their job just as that of the medical doctor prepares him for his. The state has performed its proper function when it provides adequate facilities needed by educators in their most important task of developing the minds of youth and transmitting the fund of knowledge.

One aspect of the state's responsibility for education, most realists would agree, consists in affording free education to all those who can profit from it.[11] Since the realists seem to take it for granted that all should be educated to the limits of their ability, the section on "Students" will be omitted from this chapter.

CURRICULUM

We observed, in the section on "Methodology," that the realist has more concern for the content of education than the methods of teaching the content. The realist seems to have no other choice since what is to be known is outside the knower. It is the educators' responsibility to construct a curriculum from those "reals" which are worth knowing. Most readers will have little difficulty surmising what the realist considers worth knowing, since in all probability it will bear great similarity to the curriculum of the elementary and secondary schools which he attended. If one has attended a liberal arts college, its curriculum probably was constructed along realistic lines. In addition to the basic skills taught in elementary schools (and sometimes in high schools and colleges) the realist would insist that the curriculum contain subjects (or blocks of subjects) covering the areas of mathematics, natural and social sciences, and the humanities. With Russell, the realists would argue that all students "should learn the bare beginnings of subjects which need not be further pursued by those who are bad at them."[12] American realists do not seem to object to the inclusion of vocational subjects in the upper elementary and secondary schools.

Just how these areas are organized in the curriculum does not seem to be important as long as sufficient heed is paid to their proper

---

[11] C. Weber, *Basic Philosophies of Education* (New York: Holt, Rinehart & Winston, 1960), p. 229.

[12] B. Russell, *Education and the Good Life*, p. 262.

integration. Lack of integration of subjects leads to what Whitehead refers to as "scraps of information and inert ideas."

The logic underlying this curriculum is quite simple. Men have learned much about the world, themselves, and others. All of this knowledge is contained in the "cultural heritage" of the people. Each generation wishes to convey what is already known to the rising generation. True, each new generation cannot expect to know everything contained in the heritage of the past. But those in charge of the educational enterprise must select the most significant knowledge and organize it in a manner which will enable youth to learn it. Each generation will add to this storehouse of knowledge and each generation will have to select that knowledge which it considers of "most worth." One will find, then, something old and something new in the realist curriculum; it will have its permanent and changing aspects. Of course, some disagreement is to be expected among realists about curriculum content just as one finds no complete agreement among other philosophers.

What is the realist's reaction to the activity curriculum of the progressives and instrumentalists? Obviously, he must reject the principle of pupil activity as the sole criterion for curricular content. Is he opposed, therefore, to any learning by doing? Not so! As long as "doing" draws the student to a knowledge of the real world it is quite acceptable. Should the students be active in making the curriculum? Most probably not. It is the student's job to acquaint himself with the real world, not a world of his own creation. The curriculum, then, should be made by experts, not children. The student should be encouraged to go beyond that required in the basic curriculum, but he must master first the essentials which the educators of the older generation have designated as recognized truths worth knowing.

The reader might ask where one might find the realist philosophy of curriculum applied in a national educational system. Certainly, the most thoroughgoing scientific realism has been realized in the Soviet education system. The student is expected to master the content of the basic natural and social sciences, mathematics, art, music, languages, and all the rest. In addition he must acquire a mastery of the use of the tools of learning and research. Even such emotionally laden subjects as literature, art and music are taught from the perspective of "social realism."[13]

---

[13] See Chapter Nine, "Marxism and Education."

In the United States, realism might be considered the philosophy which dominates the majority of college-preparatory secondary schools and most colleges. As mentioned earlier in this chapter, since World War II scientific realism has been making tremendous gains in educational circles (as Breed predicted in 1942).[14] The highly popular scholarship and college-entrance examinations are thoroughly realistic in orientation and content. Certainly, the "space age" will encourage greater emphasis on knowledge and the power that knowledge provides to the nation which possesses it.

AIMS OF EDUCATION

Realists, just as other philosophers, have expressed the aims of education in various forms. Breed, Russell, and Whitehead have given serious consideration to this most important factor in educational theory. Each of their views will be presented but it might be well to begin with the rather general statement of aims given by John Wild, as this seems to distill the essence of all realists' statements. For him, the aim of education is fourfold: ". . . to discern the truth about things as they really are and to extend and integrate such truth as is known; to gain such practical knowledge of life in general and of professional functions in particular as can be theoretically grounded and justified; and, finally, to transmit this in a coherent and convincing way both to young and to old throughout the human community."[15] Thus all educational activities from elementary school through university work should aid the learner to acquire and integrate the truths (knowledge) which the human race has acquired and be able to apply it in practical situations (utility). In addition the schools, especially at the higher levels, should push forward the frontiers of knowledge.

Breed, expressing similar sentiments, avers that "the chief function of all education is direction of the learning process. . . ." Education should guide the student in discovering and knowing the world around him as this is contained in the school subjects (the "truth tradition"). Education should also train the student in the methods

---

[14] F. Breed, "Education and The Realistic Outlook," *op. cit.*, p. 91 f.

[15] John Wild, "Education and Human Society: A Realistic View," *Modern Philosophies and Education,* 54th N.S.S.E. Yearbook (Chicago: University of Chicago Press, 1955), p. 31.

of acquiring knowledge (primarily, the scientific method).[16] As long as the school makes the acquisition of knowledge and the mastery of the methods of acquiring knowledge its primary objectives, Breed probably would not object to making development of physical fitness, training in economic and social competency as secondary objectives. Thus it appears that Herbert Spencer's objectives of education could not be acceptable to either Wild or Breed as *primary* functions of the school.

Russell follows the same line of reasoning in his discussion of educational objectives. He, too, would not object to the school's assisting the child to become a healthy, happy, and well-adjusted *individual* (the emphasis is on individuality). But he insists that the prime goal of all school activities should be the development of intelligence. The well-educated person is one whose mind knows the world as it is. Intelligence is that human function which enables one to acquire knowledge. The school should do all in its power to develop intelligence. The student can acquire true knowledge only when he possesses a highly developed intelligence. Highly developed intelligence has its practical value, too, for "without intelligence our complex modern world cannot subsist; still less can it make progress."[17] Other objectives proposed by Russell include vitality, courage, and sensitiveness.

Even though Russell argues, as did Whitehead, that all good education is useful he did not mean this in the pragmatic sense. For example, the study of good literature may have little utility in the strict sense of the word but it is practical in the sense that "it gives a man a mental possession which he would be sorry to be without, and makes him in some sense a more excellent human being. . . ."[18]

On the negative side of the ledger, Russell was violently opposed to the priority so many countries in the world were giving to citizenship education in their schools. In his reply to Bode's criticism of his own insistence upon the development of *individual intelligence*, he contends that making community living (social living or national

---

[16] F. Breed, *Education and the New Realism* (New York: Macmillan Co., 1939), p. 198 ff.

[17] B. Russell, *Education and the Good Life*, p. 74.

[18] *Ibid.*, pp. 23–24. Russell uses Shakespeare's plays as an example. They may have little utility unless one wishes to kill one's uncle but they are practical because they train in expression of thought.

aims) the goal of education is the cause of tyranny, statism, and dictatorship.[19] As a realist, however, he did recognize that unbridled individualism is completely impracticable in modern society[20] Russell's advocacy of socialism bears witness to his beliefs in regard to the limitations of individualism in economics and politics.

Whitehead, who appears to make some concessions to instrumentalism in the area of educational aims, insists that "utility" should be the goal of education. But, he adds, education must be useful only in the sense that "understanding is useful." A perusal of Whitehead's *Aims of Education* seems to point to the development of intelligence or understanding as the primary goal of the entire educational enterprise. The end result of this process will be the dispelling of "inert ideas" and bringing ideas to life by putting them into new and fresh combinations. Whitehead applies this theme to the different levels of education and the subject-matter areas. He prefaces the discussion of aims with the statement: "The purpose of education is to stimulate and guide their [students'] self-development . . . the whole book is a protest against dead knowledge, that is to say, against inert ideas." Thus Whitehead is not against giving students knowledge, but he is opposed to making education the vehicle for cramming the student's mind with "scraps of information" which will remain forever "inert."[21]

Harry Broudy, a contemporary realist, proposes that the "good life" should be the ultimate aim of education since it is the final goal of all human activity. But he recognizes the great difficulty involved in translating this general objective into operational terms for guiding the activities under the direction of the school — the many subjective judgments of the pupils, teachers, parents, and administrators, all combined, make it extremely difficult to state a general objective which will satisfy all.[22] But a perusal of the remaining chapters of Broudy's book will suggest to the reader that the author is in agreement with Russell and Whitehead that the development of intelligence and the acquisition of living (not inert) ideas and knowledge should be the primary concern of the school. The modern

---

[19] P. A. Schilpp, *The Philosophy of Bertrand Russell* (Evanston: Northwestern University Press, 1944), pp. 730–734.

[20] B. Russell, *Education and the Good Life*, pp. 38 f., 236 f.

[21] A. N. Whitehead, *The Aims of Education*, pp. 11, 13, and *passim*.

[22] H. Broudy, *op. cit.*, Chap. II. Broudy's book is not a statement of "new realism" but a modernized version of classical realism. However he does hold some views in common with the new realists.

school, he avers, should not neglect secondary aims such as development of character, vocational competence, physical fitness, and citizenship.

One belief of all realists in connection with educational aims, albeit a negative one, is the rejection of the instrumentalist notion that "social living" is the primary purpose of the entire educational enterprise. In fact, most realists begin their discussion of objectives with a critique of instrumentalist concern for democratic living, adjustment, and group dynamics.

ACADEMIC FREEDOM

Any discussion of academic freedom within the realist framework must take into account the notion of truth held by its advocates. Since the new realists believe that truth has an objective criterion (see section on "Epistemology"), in order for statements to be true they must correspond to things as they are. Therefore, no teacher is free to make any statement he pleases about the world unless he has sound empirical evidence to demonstrate the truth of his statement. Nor is he "free" to reject truths which are held by those who are trained in a specialized field unless he has legitimate grounds for questioning such truths. A corollary of this limitation of academic freedom is derived from the definition of an hypothesis. A teacher should never present an hypothesis as "verified truth," but he should present it for what it is, namely, a *tentative* theory to explain certain facts and to guide the investigation of others. Too many teachers equate hypotheses with verified truth and indoctrinate their students instead of enlightening them.

However, Whitehead warns that administrators should not kill the imaginative abilities of their teachers and researchers. If the frontiers of knowledge are to be pushed forward, teachers and researchers "must be free to think rightly and wrongly, and free to appreciate the variousness of the universe undisturbed by its perils." If teachers are forced, by community or administrative pressure, to study and teach only that which is "safe," the spirit of intellectual adventure will be stifled and society will be the loser. This approach to academic freedom should hold true not only for science and mathematics, but also in politics, economics, business, the humanities, and religion.[23]

---

[23] A. N. Whitehead, *The Aims of Education*, p. 98 f.

Breed gives yet another reason for advocating academic freedom for all teachers and researchers. He grants that truth is objectively determined, yet holds it is difficult to make "any claim for the *absolute* truths of any proposition relating to the nature of the external world." Therefore experts in any field must be given the freedom to question the most "sacred" truths in the world of scholarship so that their validity constantly will be put to the empirical test.

All realists, however, do recognize the responsibility which accompanies academic freedom. No teacher can claim the rights of academic freedom without making the transmission of and the search for truth the goal of his professional activities. He is never free to teach falsehood as truth.

INDOCTRINATION

Should teachers indoctrinate students? To this question the realist answers "yes" and "no." To the extent to which the subject matter being taught is known to be true, to that extent the teacher is warranted in indoctrinating his students with that truth. Where there is doubt among the experts about what is true, indoctrination is out of place. For example, in the field of natural science the teacher can be very definite because of the relatively high degree of certainty achieved in this field. Similarly, if a teacher of mathematics is teaching Euclidean geometry, he can be quite dogmatic about its postulates, definitions, and theorems. In teaching the social sciences, on the other hand, one must avoid indoctrination simply because these areas lack the definiteness of the natural and mathematical sciences. Thus teachers should present all points of view objectively.[24]

Throughout the educational writings of Russell and Whitehead one finds indirect references to the problem of indoctrination. The giving of "scraps of information and inert ideas" would constitute indoctrination for Whitehead. Russell suggests that the teacher avoid indoctrination by developing within his students the scientific attitude which will encourage them to seek answers to problems which provoke their curiosity. This attitude includes such facets as the desire to find the truth, initial uncertainty as to the outcome of one's search for the truth, and willingness to revise one's notions when new findings are presented. The teacher who does not develop this attitude in his students is encouraging a dangerous credulity in his

---

[24] F. Breed, *op. cit.*, p. 68 f.

charges. Breed believes that the teacher should not identify himself with any side of a controversial issue in his classes. The bright students do not care what the teacher believes and the less intelligent ones would take the teacher's point of view uncritically.[25]

Another important consideration in the realist's views on the problem of indoctrination is the maturity level of the learner. Even the most iconoclastic realist would not recommend that grade school children be presented with all points of view in the subjects they are learning. On the other hand, there is no reason why the college student should not be encouraged to consider all views, even the most unpopular and "dangerous." Whitehead admonishes university educators to introduce young minds to ideas when they are at the most imaginative stage in their life. "Universities should be homes of adventure shared in common by young and old."[26]

PERMANENCE AND CHANGE

As one might expect, the modern realist does not deny the existence of change. But he does reject the instrumentalist notion that everything is in a state of flux, even the laws of change. The realist affirms that change is indeed a very real thing — but all changes occur according to fixed laws. Change, then, is not haphazard and the world is not completely indeterminate. Without positing some regularity in the world, scientific investigation would be impossible. Otherwise one would no sooner learn something about the world around him than it would change and be something else. The evolutionary process, although it is one of change, takes place according to certain laws.[27] And the scientific realist certainly would agree that the world of today and the people in it are quite different from those of millions of years ago. Nor is the world as we know it today a completely finished world; more changes will take place. However, we always seek to discover things as they are and the knowledge acquired has a sufficient degree of stability.

Thus, in the view of the realist, changes are occurring according to definite laws and patterns. As man discovers these most important

25 B. Russell, *Education and the Good Life*, p. 290, and F. Breed, *Education and the New Realism*, p. 186 ff.

26 A. N. Whitehead, *Aims of Education*, p. 102.

27 F. Breed, *Education and the New Realism*, pp. 47–49. Also F. Breed, "Education and the Realistic Outlook," *Philosophies of Education*, p. 108.

laws he can predict, with greater and greater accuracy, the changes that will take place and the manner in which they will take place.

Another important argument used by the realist against the instrumentalist notion of change as the prime metaphysical reality is associated with the meaning of progress. Recall that the instrumentalist viewed change as the foundation stone of progress. The realist argues that progress does not consist in change but in "retentiveness." Santayana, for instance, contends that "When change is absolute, there remains no being to improve and no direction is set for possible improvement; and when experience is not retained, as among savages, infancy is perpetual. . . . "[28] He continues this line of reasoning by asserting that human nature is limited in the direction that evolutionary variations might take. Certain changes in human nature would destroy it. In order to remain "human," it must retain all which now constitutes it. Certain changes would result in the destruction of the human species. If, for example, man's advanced reasoning faculties were to be lost due to evolutionary changes he would cease to be man.[29]

The implications of the realist position on permanence and change for educational theory can be derived from this fundamental view of the world. One can expect to find both permanent and changing elements in educational aims, objectives, and the curriculum. But change alone cannot be the sole guide for educational theory and practice, as it is for the instrumentalist. The educational realist is dealing with both facets of reality, permanence and change. The young are expected to learn what others have discovered about the world. All knowledge of the past should not be cast aside simply because some new discoveries have been made. For this reason Russell chides American educators for paying insufficient heed to the values and tradition of the old world in favor of concentration on current problems and knowledge.[30]

SUPERNATURALISM VS. NATURALISM

Earlier in this chapter it was pointed out that the scientific realists are sometimes called naturalistic realists. The adjective "naturalistic" pretty well sums up the new realists' attitude toward the supernatural

---

[28] G. Santayana, *The Life of Reason*, p. 82.
[29] *Ibid.*, p. 83 ff.
[30] B. Russell, *Education and the Good Life*, pp. 74–77.

realm. Here is one of the fundamental differences between the scholastic realist and the new realists. Since they make no claim to a special kind of method which might provide them with a grasp of transempirical realities, they can be considered, at best, agnostics in regard to some of the most important beliefs of the scholastics about God, angels, the human soul, and immortality. None of these beliefs are capable of proof by empirical methods or scientific hypotheses. Most realists of this brand consider the doctrines of the traditional religions as organized superstitions. Some, among them Bertrand Russell[31] and George Santayana, have been quite militant in their opposition to religious beliefs. Santayana granted that the liturgy of the Catholic Church possessed aesthetic value or beauty but held that its dogmas had no roots in reality and were, therefore, not to be considered true.

That the new realist discredits or at least disregards the claims of the supernaturalist will be evident in the section on "Epistemology." Here we can note that his basic metaphysical presupposition is naturalistic. He is concerned with the biology and chemistry of plants, animals, men, and the chemistry and physics of the earth, the planets, the stars, and space. Any consideration beyond these is, in the words of Breed, an attempt "to unscrew the 'unscrutable.' "[32] And Breed does not hesitate to align himself with the instrumentalists in their denial or disregard of the realm of the supernatural. "Both of the philosophies mentioned are of the experience type," he says.[33]

NATURE OF MAN AND SOCIETY

Most new realists reject the body-soul dualism of Aristotle and the scholastics. "It is perfectly clear that life is definable in terms of chemical process. . . . Life is some sort of chemical process and nothing further." To this statement of E. B. Holt, Breed adds: "Neither pragmatist nor neo-realist looks upon the material of the body and that of the mind as different in kind. They no more invoke the dualistic hypothesis in describing mind and body relationships than in describing an idea and its object."[34] If realists appeal to no spiritual element in man as the basis for intelligence, how do they define

---

[31] Russell says: "Religion encourages stupidity, and an insufficient sense of reality," *Education and the Modern World* (New York: Norton Co., 1932), p. 239 f.

[32] F. Breed, "Education and the Realistic Outlook," *op. cit.,* p. 91.

[33] *Ibid.,* p. 97.

[34] F. Breed, *Education and the New Realism,* pp. 256, 89.

this function which is so important for the educator? Breed argues that both the ability to learn and the ability to abstract are essential to the definition of intelligence. With these two elements operative, human intelligence involves the ability to respond selectively to elements or combination of elements of the world of objects as well as to attach meanings to them. Attaching meanings to certain responses is to be regarded as "abstraction." The other function of intelligence, learning, seems to consist in the selective responses of the organism to the objects of the environment. At any rate, intellectual activities are rooted in the organic functions of the person rather than in the powers of an immortal soul.[35]

In a manner similar to that of Breed, Russell finds the foundation of human intelligence in curiosity which is present in its elementary forms in animals. Human curiosity is but an advanced form of that found in animals but is characterized by a love of knowledge. In its highest stage of development intelligence is reflected in curiosity about general propositions and theories rather than about particular facts or interests associated with personal advantage. Human intelligence begins to deteriorate when the person no longer displays that natural curiosity toward the novel but is satisfied with the existing state of affairs.[36] One should not infer, however, that Russell wishes to throw out everything from the past. In fact he criticizes American educators for their neglect and even disparagement of the values and traditions of the old world.[37]

Another traditional view of man's nature which the realist rejects has reference to the belief that man is tainted with evil tendencies and desires. Russell contends that man is not inclined to evil or good at birth. He is born with instincts and reflexes which can be directed toward good or evil. Herein lies the task of education.[38]

The scholastic realist holds that man is free, that he has free will. We have seen how the neo-realist has radically modified the traditional notion of intelligence. Does his view of the function of human will involve as great a modification? His answer to this question will be of great significance for modern education because of the contemporary educator's concern for preparing the young to live the good life.

[35] *Ibid.,* pp. 86–88.
[36] B. Russell, *Education and the Good Life,* pp. 74–77.
[37] *Ibid.,* pp. 55–57.
[38] B. Russell, *Education and the Good Life,* p. 41.

In general, new realists are determinists. Some of them go to the extreme of maintaining that all of man's choices and actions are completely determined by environmental forces beyond his control. Such a view indeed follows from their belief that all reality, including man, is governed by inexorable laws of nature. The sole task of man is to discover these laws, thus enabling him to explain the cause-effect relationship between environmental and hereditary forces and man's choices. This deterministic attitude is very evident in modern scientific psychology which (using rats, rabbits, and pigeons) attempts to reduce all choice to reward or reinforcement (usually food) and punishment (usually an electric shock). Rigid scientific controls are applied as in the physical sciences and the results are considered just as accurate as those in the physical sciences. The information gathered and the theories constructed on the basis of these experiments with animals are used as the guide for inferences concerning human choice and the rules governing them. Therefore when enough evidence is gathered and adequate theories developed the psychologist will be able to predict what choices a human being will make under a given set of conditions, just as he is able to predict what turn a hungry rat will make in the T-maze in order to reach the food.

However, Russell argues that simply because the psychologist can predict what a human being will do under a set of given conditions (determinism) one cannot conclude that the person was *forced* to act in such a manner. What Russell means is that determinism and freedom of the will are not contradictory. The contradictory of freedom is not determinism but fatalism. Thus, he contends, the only occasion when man is *not free,* arises when there is sufficient evidence to indicate that physical or psychological force was exerted by an external agent, thereby removing any opportunity for individual choice. Individuals, then, cannot claim immunity from responsibility for their actions on the basis of a deterministic conception of will.[39] Russell's long and turbulent life has been witness to the belief that the individual need not be pushed along by the tide of custom, social pressure, or the fear of being unpopular. One cannot infer, however, that Russell believes that man, by reason of his spiritual soul, can rise above hereditary and environmental forces to make free choices.

---

[39] See B. Russell, "The Free-Will Problem," in *Readings in Philosophy of Science* (New York: Appleton-Century-Crofts, 1953), p. 387–408.

Once the nature of the individual has been defined it is necessary to determine the realist's view of the proper relationship that exists between men or, in other words, the nature of society. Some modern philosophies, especially instrumentalism and reconstructionism, view the individual as a spark of society. The new realists, on the contrary, are constantly warring against the forces which threaten to engulf the individual in society. For them, the ultimate value of society rests on the value of the individuals composing it. A good society is one made up of good individuals; a good society does not make good individuals. The latter, they believe, is the fatal error of totalitarianism. As Breed points out, "Respect for the individual is the first principle of democracy." All of the other "freedoms" (speech, press, assembly, religion) are derived from this fundamental one.[40]

Santayana and Russell also contend that man does not receive his "nature" from the social group. Human nature is a "functional unity" in each man, not a derivative of the common type.[41] As one would expect, then, the new realists emphasize the development and good of the individual in their educational theory. But at the same time they see the necessity of harmonizing individual needs and desires in order to achieve enough social unity to enable individuals to achieve maximum happiness. Minimum harmony should be achieved by persuasion rather than force, but unbridled individualism can lead only to chaos.

Breed, in rejecting the radical *laissez-faire* outlook of many Americans, says it fails to take into account the realities of modern life. One may dream of a world free from external interferences fulfilling the individual's desire to do as he pleases. But as soon as other individuals become a part of one's environment they, too, have rights which *ipso facto* limit one's freedom. The principle of equality itself limits the application of the principle of freedom. Thus, Breed argues, there must be authority, obedience to law, and recognition of the truth both in and out of school. Any educational theory which fails to recognize these "realities" of life is doomed to failure.[42]

In respect to the emphasis on the authority of truth and law the

---

40 F. Breed, "Education and the Realistic Outlook," *op. cit.*, p. 131 f.
41 G. Santayana, *The Life of Reason*, p. 80.
42 F. Breed, "Education and the Realistic Outlook," *op. cit.*, p. 133 f. Also see C. Weber, *Basic Philosophies of Education* (New York: Holt, Rinehart Co., 1960), p. 73 f.

realist position represents a reaction against both the extreme individualism of early progressivism and the child-centered school (lunatic fringe) and the later society-centered forms of pragmatism. The realist wishes to preserve the "sanctity of the individual" and avoid the "sanctity of the state," while still recognizing the need for social harmony and cooperation.

EPISTEMOLOGY

Whereas the classical realism of Aristotle and the medieval schoolmen centered their philosophizing around metaphysics, the study of being, the new realists concern themselves chiefly with the knowing process. Their preoccupation with the analysis and description of knowing is common to other modern schools of philosophy. But this very concern with knowing makes this school of thought very relevant to education. After all, the school historically has made knowledge at least one of its major objectives.

Starting from the assumption that the world of objects and elements does not depend upon a knower for its existence, the realist asks the fundamental question: "How does the knower come to know his environment?" The answer to this question is somewhat simpler for the scientific realist than for his scholastic counterpart, since the former does not posit the existence of a dual nature in man. Since the knower is made of the same stuff as the world around him no explanations are needed to bridge the gap between the material object and the immaterial idea or concept as the scholastic must do.[43] Their fundamental appeal is to simple common sense. For them transempirical realities, if existent, are unknowable. Man comes to know his world by coming in contact with it. In the age of science, this uncomplicated mode of knowing has been augmented greatly by the tools of an advanced technology. But even the highly complex theories of modern science have not changed the notion of the new realists, that the knower and what he knows are of the same nature. The extensive studies of the learning process by E. L. Thorndike (usually considered a realist) are based upon this view of the knowing process.

Knowing, then, is a mechanistic process whereby the objects outside the knower act as stimuli upon the senses and call for some response on the part of the organism.

[43] F. Breed, *Education and the New Realism*, p. 89 f.

In response to the query "What are the sources of our knowledge?" Bertrand Russell says that "sensation, immediate expectation, immediate memory, and true memory all give knowledge. . . ."[44] Of course, the realist admits that there is an element of uncertainty in all our knowledge except that derived from mathematics and logic. The latter two give certain knowledge because of their formal and public nature. All other forms of knowledge which originate in sensation lack the characteristic of certainty. Russell admits, though, that we can accept what we read in books and hear from authorities in certain fields since this is public knowledge and each individual can, if he wishes, check the statements for himself by delving into the primary sources or by doing the experiment for himself. Similarly the knowledge "stored" in the memory (which also had its origin in sensations) cannot be considered completely reliable but it, too, can be checked against other sources.[45]

The kind of knowledge which is the most reliable is scientific since it represents what has been discovered by the "collective intellect of mankind" and is wholly impersonal. Scientific knowledge is least susceptible to personal biases, faulty individual sensations and memories.[46] But even the knowledge acquired by the exact sciences does not bear the stamp of absolute certainty for the new realist. Only logic and mathematics, as mentioned before, yield "certain" knowledge. But this certainty is based upon the *formal* structure of mathematics and a mathematically ordered logic, not upon the facts of the case.

Does the realist deny "truth"? Certainly not! This was evident in Russell's controversy with Dewey concerning the nature and criterion of truth. Dewey had argued for abandoning the concept "truth" and substituting "warranted assertability" in its stead. He maintained that the traditional notion of truth was so associated with "certainty and absoluteness" that the term was wholly inaccurate. Russell rejected Dewey's view and reaffirmed the "correspondence theory of truth," asserting that a statement is true when it corresponds to things "as they are." Simply because man makes errors in his search for truth or does not have complete knowledge of his universe one

[44] B. Russell, *Human Knowledge: Its Scope and Limits* (New York: S. Schuster, 1948), p. 96 f.

[45] B. Russell, *An Inquiry Into Meaning and Truth* (New York: W. Norton Co., 1940), pp. 15–18.

[46] B. Russell, *Human Knowledge*, p. 3.

cannot say there is no truth.[47] Breed likewise holds the same theory of truth. In rejecting the instrumentalist theory of truth (workability), he says, "ideas are true when they work, but when they work they do so because they conform to a definite order of things beyond them."[48] Neither Russell nor Breed implies that knowledge has no utilitarian value. On the contrary, Russell argues that the science and mathematics he learned in school "was not only of immense utility but also of great intrinsic value as affording subjects of contemplation and reflection and touchstones of truth in a deceitful world."[49]

It is worth noting that in this entire discussion about the origin and nature of truth and knowledge the truths of revelation and traditional metaphysics have not even been mentioned. The reason for the absence of such considerations is quite simple: these "truths" are outside the realm of sense-knowledge and scientific experimentation, even though Breed claims that the new realism "does not deny a place to religion in the world." But he is quick to add that "it is a foe of superstition in every form,"[50] and for him "religion" pretty much means "superstition." It seems quite safe to assert, then, as was done in the section on "Supernaturalism," that there is no place in the philosophy of new realism for truths other than those of an empirical nature. Consequently, educational aims and curricula will be this-worldly and completely devoid of any connection with the realm of the supernatural.

In the 1920's, a significant difference of opinion arose among realists concerning the manner in which one comes to know the world outside the knower. The realists split into two major camps, the neo-realists and the critical realists. As yet, these two groups of realists have not settled their differences. But the educational significance of this difference is not great enough to warrant inclusion in this text. The issue is highly technical and the interested reader can study its various facets in a philosophical treatise on the subject.

THE SEARCH FOR VALUES

The discussion of the philosophical basis of the new realism has

[47] B. Russell, *An Inquiry Into Meaning and Truth* (London: G. Allen & Unwin Ltd., 1940), pp. 318–326.

[48] F. Breed, *Education and the New Realism*, p. 88 f.

[49] B. Russell, *Education and the Good Life* (New York: Boni & Liveright, 1926), p. 28 f.   [50] F. Breed, *Education and the New Realism*, p. 88 f.

shown, thus far, a striking degree of unanimity among its advocates. All have agreed that permanence and change are twin aspects of reality; there has been quite general agreement in the rejection or nonrelevance of the supernatural sphere, at least as a concern of philosophy; their notions of the nature of man and society have been surprisingly similar; they have been quite well agreed upon how we arrive at knowledge and what is the nature of truth.

Such agreement, however, is not easily detected in the realist's view of the nature and origin of values. Therefore an attempt will be made in this section to reflect the divergence of opinion in the axiological beliefs of these philosophers.

Breed, for example, seems to grant values the same objective quality as he recognizes in other "reals." He asserts that "Value in the last analysis, rests on the *facts* of human interest." Knowledge of the facts of human preference will determine what is politically, economically, socially, or educationally worthwhile. He cites the value of democracy as an example of a "natural value" derived from the "facts of experience" rather than from any transcendental source.[51] Values, then, for Breed are rooted in human nature and expressed in human interests and desires. The fact that there is great disagreement among men as to which values are "best" does not alter the fact that they are rooted in nature and, thus, objective. For him, "good" consists in accepting and conforming to the laws of nature discovered in an orderly universe. Good is not variable, mysterious, or mystical. Evil is simply the rejection of the laws of nature. The moral law is just as much a part of nature as the laws of physics, genetics, etc.

Russell, on the other hand, holds that ultimate values are essentially subjective. In other words, he believes that no goal or object is bad or good in itself. Only the means for acquiring such goals or objects can be judged good or bad insofar as they enable the individual or the group to attain them. Thus a certain set of actions may achieve the goal of universal peace whereas another set of actions may not achieve it. Those actions which do achieve the goal may be judged objectively good but the ultimate goal itself remains subjective. The only "objective" aspect of the goal itself is that it actually is desired by some people and that they want others to have the same desire. Russell, then, does not root ultimate values in nature

---

[51] F. Breed, "Education and the Realistic Outlook," *op. cit.,* p. 136.

itself but in men's preferences and choices. Science can be of assistance in selecting the means to ends, but not the ultimate ends themselves. Science can only objectively determine, by a study of the consequences, just how successful certain means have been in the achievement of subjectively accepted goals.

If Breed grants objectivity to the moral law, it would seem consistent for him to recognize an objective order by which to discern beauty and ugliness. Those products of the art forms which faithfully reflect the world *as it is* would be considered beautiful. Ugliness, on the other hand, would consist in that which does not correspond to the order and harmony found in the universe of objects and events.

On the other side of the coin, it seems that the Russell camp would have to admit the subjectivity of all judgments of beauty and ugliness and limit itself to saying that such and such a piece of art has succeeded in conveying what the author wished it to convey. Santayana seems to prefer Russell's side of the coin since he maintains that the criterion for aesthetic taste is nothing more than the taste itself refined by intellectual reflection. It is, in other words, the expression of "conscious preferences" put into exquisite language. For Santayana, aesthetic value lies in "making people happy, first in the practicing of the art and then in possessing the product."[52]

Because of this basic difference of opinion about the origin and nature of values within the realist camp, it is difficult to specify how the educational program would reflect their different views. Furthermore, since none of the advocates of the different views have ever been responsible for the construction of elementary and secondary curricula (or college programs) one cannot point to a specific program which is truly representative of either the Breed or Russell brands of realism applied to the fine arts or moral training.[53] The only instance of scientific realism applied to morals and art is found in Soviet culture and education.

EVALUATION OF REALISM

Of the non-Catholic systems discussed in this text, the school of scientific realism has the most in common with the philosophy of a Christian educator, both in its philosophical bases and its educational theory and practices. Realists and Christian thinkers agree in accepting the independent existence of the world outside the knower. The

---

[52] G. Santayana, *The Life of Reason*, p. 375.
[53] See sections on "Aims" and "Curriculum" above.

objective nature of truth and the "correspondence theory" of truth are acceptable in both camps. Some of the new realists also posit the objectivity of the moral law, as do their scholastic brethren.

However, there are essential differences worth noting:

1. The scientific realist either rejects the world of supernature or takes an agnostic attitude toward it.

2. In general, most of the propositions of Christian educators are considered outmoded by the new realists. For example, they view as naïve any metaphysical explanations of motion. For them, science is to answer this question. Hence any quest for "Unmoved Mover" is not properly philosophical.

3. Their denial of man's dual nature (body-soul) is, of course, unacceptable to Christian educators.

4. The epistemology of the new realist is to be considered inadequate at least, since only empirical knowledge is recognized as valid within their system. Also, the passive aspects of the knowing process are overemphasized by most scientific realists. One reason for this emphasis flows from the monistic assumption that the known and the knower are of the same nature. Also their rejection of revelation as a legitimate source of truth is not in harmony with the beliefs of Christian educators.

5. Those realists who reject the objectivity of moral judgments divorce knowing from doing and do violence to the organic unity of man. Furthermore, they give no logical reasons for rejecting the objective nature of knowledge about values.

In educational theory and practice, scientific realism might be criticized by Christian educators for some of the following reasons:

1. Too much emphasis is placed upon the individual in the educational program. Such preoccupation with the individual flouts the reality of the complexity and interdependence of modern society and the Christian concept of the brotherhood of man and corporate destiny of mankind.

2. Some Christian educators might argue that the scientific realist's curriculum is one-sided since empirical knowledge holds a position superior to that of the humanistic studies. Such emphasis is extremely dangerous at the present time. Witness the almost complete lack of respect for the person fostered in Soviet Russia where the schools have adopted the extreme (and perhaps the most logical) form of scientific realism.

3. The scientific realists, with the exception of Russell, stress content much more than the methods of acquiring knowledge. Students are forced thereby to rote memorization, one of the major weaknesses of the program of the traditional school. Teachers who follow this approach to learning may pay lip service to the goals of developing critical thinking, understanding, and other complex intellectual functions. But a close scrutiny of their course syllabi, the texts they use, and the examinations they give will provide ample evidence that rote memorization is about the only criterion of student success.

4. Of course, the Christian educator must object to the complete and apriori exclusion of religious studies from the curriculum of the new realists.

5. Some Christian educators, chiefly the "holists," would object to making development of intelligence and mastery of subject matter the primary goals of the school. The development of moral character (the perfect Christian) is viewed by the Christian holist as equal or even superior to the goals of intellectual development and mastery of content.

SUMMARY

The scientific realists are much less concerned with methods than the progressivists and more concerned with content. This they hold to be determined by the advances in science, for science is the guiding star of modern civilization and education's task is to help initiate youth into modern civilization. Thus the curriculum will stress studies in the mathematical and physical sciences and in the humanities to the extent that humanistic disciplines help provide clues for civilized man regarding the *human* use of scientific procedures.

Along with other modern philosophies, scientific realism rejects or disregards the supernatural, and likewise denies any duality in man's nature or any distinction of cognitive powers into sensory and intellectual. Scientific realists hold that man can know reality, and that he does so through inductive experience.

BIBLIOGRAPHY

Breed, Frederick, *Education and the New Realism* (New York: Macmillan Co., 1939).
——— "Education and the Realistic Outlook," 41st Yearbook, N.S.S.E., edited by Nelson B. Henry (Chicago: University of Chicago Press, 1942).
Broudy, H. S., *Building a Philosophy of Education* (New York: Prentice-Hall Co., 1961).
Creative Intelligence, by Dewey, Moore, Brown, Mead, Bode, Stuart, Tufts, Kallen (New York. Henry Holt & Co., 1917).

Essays in Critical Realism, by Drake, Lovejoy, Pratt, Rogers, Santayana, Sellers, Strong (London: Macmillan and Co., 1920).

Feibleman, J. K., *Inside the Great Mirror* (The Hague: Martinus Nighoff, 1958).

Hansen, Kenneth H., *Philosophy for American Education* (Englewood Cliffs, New Jersey: Prentice-Hall, Inc., 1960).

Kinney, Sister M. Cyril Edwin, O.P., M.A., *A Critique of the Philosophy of George Santayana in the Light of Thomistic Principles* (Washington, D. C.: Catholic University of America Press, 1942).

Morris, Van Cleve, *Philosophy and the American School* (Boston: Houghton Mifflin Co., 1961), Chaps. 3–10.

Russell, Bertrand, *Education and the Good Life* (New York: Boni & Liveright, 1926).

———— *Education and the Modern World* (New York: Norton Co., 1932).

———— "The Free-will Problem," in *Readings in Philosophy of Science* (New York: Appleton-Century-Crofts, 1953), pp. 387–408.

———— *Human Knowledge: Its Scope and Limits* (New York: Simon & Schuster, 1948).

———— *An Inquiry into Meaning and Truth* (New York: W. W. Norton & Co., 1940).

Santayana, George, *The Life of Reason* (London: Constable & Co., Ltd., 1954; New York: Mentor Books, 1960).

Schilpp, P. A., *The Philosophy of Bertrand Russell* (Evanston: Northwestern University Press, 1944).

Weber, Christian O., *Basic Philosophies of Education* (New York: Holt, Rinehart & Winston, 1960).

Whitehead, Alfred North, *The Aims of Education* (New York: Mentor Books, 1949, 1957).

Wild, John, "Education and Human Society; A Realistic View," *Modern Philosophies and Education,* 54th N.S.S.E. Yearbook (Chicago: University of Chicago Press, 1955).

CHAPTER NINE

Marxism and Education

INTRODUCTION

WITHOUT a doubt, Communism is the most powerful competitor of Catholicism in the struggle for man's mind. It is true that its rapid spread is due, to some extent, to the use of force. But the same accusation is made about the spread of early Christianity and later of Protestantism. Every student of history is well aware that ideas are not accepted because of force alone. Therefore, an understanding of the ideological roots of Communism is most necessary in the Christian's struggle against it. One cannot fight effectively what he does not know! Furthermore, Communism is one of the few philosophies mentioned in this book which has been applied in such a thoroughgoing fashion to education in so many countries. Indeed, education is the most powerful weapon, even more powerful than the sword, for the spread of Communism.

Throughout the chapter most frequent reference is made to the brand of Communism (and communistic education) found in the Soviet Union. Space does not allow for descriptions of Titoism or Chinese Communism, or that found in the satellite countries. Also, it does not seem necessary to indicate the minor differences which might exist, since the Soviet Union is the ideological center for the entire worldwide movement. Even the present temporary rift between the Chinese Communists and the Soviet Union is of no philosophical significance since it involves only a difference of opinion on *how* Communism should be spread throughout the world, not *that* it should be spread.

METHODOLOGY

As one might expect, Marx made no specific recommendations for teaching schoolchildren. Nor did the early leaders of the revolution concern themselves with such matters. During the educational chaos which followed the revolution, educators tried all kinds of methods, exerting special care to avoid using methods in vogue prior to the "people's liberation." For a time, they even gave serious thought to adapting progressive methods to the Russian schools. But this experiment was short-lived since progressive methods granted too much freedom to pupils and failed to "discipline them" in obedience and conformity.

Recent visitors to the Soviet Union noted:

> The classes we observed (academic classes in math, science, etc.) were conducted exclusively by the lecture-recitation method. The teacher would discuss the lesson for the day and then call upon the pupils to recite, or to work out problems at the blackboard in front of the class, or to perform a demonstration. At the conclusion of his recitation or performance, the pupil would receive a mark which would be recorded in the teacher's record books and in the pupil's notebook as well.[1]

Instructors in polytechnic institutes use a great variety of methods (even the lecture-recitation method is still employed); both group and individual techniques are used. In the industrial arts classes — which they try to keep to fifteen students — the teacher states the aim of the course, lectures to the students on the theory of the machine, etc., and demonstrates the processes involved. When the students begin working on the machines the class is divided into smaller groups and their work is closely supervised by the instructor. The teachers use audio-visual aids and texts when available. Whenever possible individual instruction is used (and this method seems to be the most popular among polytechnic instructors). The teacher explains and demonstrates the process to each student and then observes the student's work. This procedure is repeated until the student masters the skill. A standard manual serves as a guide for both teacher and student. In most respects the methods and materials of Soviet polytechnic education are quite similar to those used in this country.

At the university level, the lecture method is used almost exclusively. Of course, in the sciences, laboratory work plays an important role in the teaching-learning process.

Underlying the externals of the methods described above, one finds the theoretical basis for all methodology in Communist schools,

---

[1] Wm. Medlin, *et al., Soviet Education Programs* (Washington, D. C.: U. S. Department of Health, Welfare, and Education, 1960), p. 45.

namely discipline. As indicated below in the section on values, discipline ranks high in the family of values which make up Communist morality. It seems correct to say that Communist educators are not overly concerned with teaching methods or techniques. Any method or technique is acceptable so long as it contributes to the general aim of producing a disciplined member of the collective. Yesipov and Goncharov, two well-known Communist educational theorists, maintain that discipline must be an "inner condition." Even when fear and punishment are used these should not be considered the best means of achieving true inner discipline. Rather, the pupil must live the disciplined life in school so that he will live it in adult life.

> The discipline of pupils is nurtured by the general practice and the whole content of the work of the school: skillful teaching of school subjects, strict regimen for the entire school life, unwavering observation by each pupil of the Rules for School Children, firm organization of the children's collective, and rational use of measures and rewards and punishments. The leading role in this work belongs to the teacher.[2]

The "Rules for School Children" mentioned in the quotation form an integral part of all teaching-learning methods. The student should study well, be on time for classes, pay attention to the teacher's lecture and fellow pupils' recitations, and do his own homework well. When a pupil is reciting he should stand erectly and remain standing until the teacher gives him permission to be seated. If he wishes to answer a question he should raise his hand and wait for the teacher to call him. All students must rise when the teacher (or visitor) enters or leaves the room. The "Rules" also cover dress, health habits, use of language on playground, courtesy to visitors at school, and deportment to and from school. In short, they control the behavior of school children during all their waking hours.[3]

One final theoretical consideration in connection with teaching methods is the relationship that exists between method and habit formation. The building of good habits which will make the student an effective member of the collective appears to be a primary goal of all teaching methods. Early in his school career the pupil must

[2] B. P. Yesipov and N. K. Goncharov, *Pedagogy,* translated and abridged under the title *I Want to Be Like Stalin* by G. S. Counts and N. P. Lodge (New York: John Day Co., 1947), p. 97.

[3] For a more detailed list of the "Rules," see Yesipov and Goncharov, *op. cit.,* pp. 97–102.

form habits that will enable him to perform most actions without having to ponder over them. By so doing he will "free himself" for more significant tasks. But a person who has been properly adjusted to life in the collective must be able to put aside old habits and acquire new ones when those in authority or the situation call for a change. Thus a university student will have to abandon some habits he acquired in the university collective when he becomes a member of the armed forces. This change will call for a relatively quick removal of some habits and a rapid acquisition of new habits. "Adjustment to the collective" is a habit which all good Communists should possess.

The teacher's role in habit formation is crucial according to Soviet educational theorists. First, the teacher teaches more by example than by precept (especially with younger children). In all his words and actions the teacher must be a perfect example of the ideal Communist so that his pupils will emulate him. The teacher who does not reflect true Soviet morality has no place in the educational system. Because of the Soviet recognition of the power of good example, children are expected to attend nursery schools when they are three years old. At this tender age a well-disciplined cadre of Communist teachers can mold the personality of the child to fit the pattern of behavior drawn up by the leaders of the party. And those parents with bourgeois sympathies and tendencies will have little opportunity to influence their children against the party program. Even though there seems to be a good deal of psychological research about the effectiveness of teaching methods going on in the Soviet Union, the educational psychologists have been unsuccessful in getting new methods adopted by those who control the schools.[4]

In summary, it seems safe to assert that the controlling idea in all teaching-learning methods is discipline in and for Communist morality. Any method or technique which detracts from this central concept is unacceptable; any method or technique which fosters it is highly desirable.

CURRICULUM

It is not the purpose of this section to give a detailed account of the curriculum of Communist schools from the nursery through the university since such a description would require approximately

---

[4] Medlin, *et al., op. cit.,* p. 11.

sixty-five printed pages. It seems more advisable to point to the general-content areas emphasized in the schools and give the rationale for their presence in the curriculum.[5]

Since the school is the arm of the state, indoctrination in Communist ideology has a predominant place in the curriculum at all educational levels. At the University of Moscow, even a student specializing in physics must take three courses in Communist doctrine: Foundations of Marxism-Leninism, Political Economy, and Dialectical and Historical Materialism. All students in teacher-education programs, regardless of their specialty, must take History of the Communist Party and the Soviet Union, Political Economy, and Dialectical and Historical Materialism. Also, as one might expect, all courses in the humanities and social sciences, especially history, serve a political purpose. In the elementary and secondary schools (the ten-year school), indoctrination in Marxist ideology is integrated in the classes in Russian history, literature, and geography. More significant perhaps than actual courses at this level of education are the indirect means of political indoctrination effected through the program of discipline. The "Rules for School Children" and "training in Communist morality" permeate all the activities of the school, including such neutral subjects as mathematics and astronomy. It seems fair to assert, then, that even if the number of hours devoted to specific courses in Communist doctrine is not as large as that given to other subjects, certainly it is the most important part of the curriculum.

Next to political education, science and mathematics receive the greatest amount of consideration in the curriculum. The emphasis on sciences jibes with Lenin's view that "science is the only path to truth." (See, below, section on "Epistemology.")

Bear in mind that Communism was born in the scientific age. Science spells power and control especially when applied via technology. Science raises the standard of living; it wins wars and conquers space. This power must be put to the use of the people's revolution.

Mathematics, the tool of science and technology, is taken by all students for all ten years of the ten-year school (Grades 1 to 10 inclusive). Geography (as a science) and biology are begun in the

---

[5] For a full description of Communist curricula cf. W. K. Medlin, *et al., op. cit.,* pp. 217–281.

fourth year and continued throughout the remaining years. Physics is given in the sixth through the tenth years. Chemistry is taken for the last four years. Astronomy and psychology are given in the last year. Technical drawing, fundamentals of production, and applied science (technology) are handled in formal classes for three or four years and the students are expected to apply their learning in out-of-class activities under the supervision of experienced personnel.

The ten-year school devotes a relatively small amount of time to the humanities. Of course, Russian language and literature are taken by all students every year of the ten-year school. They take six years of a foreign language and six years of singing and drawing.[6]

When a student has completed the ten-year school (elementary and secondary) he is eligible for admission to the university or professional schools. However, the number attending the institutions of higher learning is quite limited, and admission is based on achievement in the lower schools and upon highly competitive examinations (a very unsocialistic policy, indeed). The curriculum at the university and professional schools depends upon the student's specialty. But each specialization has a required number and sequence of courses. Thus, if a student is specializing in physics at the university, that curriculum is completely prescribed — there are no electives. All professional and advanced curricula contain the three courses in political education mentioned above.

If a student is not able to gain admission to a university or professional school, there are many different kinds of technical institutes in which he can enroll. The graduates of these schools constitute the backbone of the specialized industrial and agricultural forces of the Soviet Union.

In many respects, the curriculum of the lower schools in Communist countries is very similar to that found in the schools of Western Europe. It is worth noting that the curricula of European and Soviet schools contain no "life-adjustment" experiences as we know them in the United States. In Communist countries, however, this phase of education is provided for by the youth organizations to which most of the youth belong. Schooling is only one aspect of the fabric of Communist education. Every phase of living is included in the overarching ideological program of Communist education.

---

[6] The Khrushchev reform of 1958 has not altered materially the course offerings of the ten-year school. Rather, this has been concentrated in an eight-year program leaving the two additional years for work experience.

EDUCATIONAL AGENCIES

In the Western democracies the three primary agencies, the family, state, and Church are accorded certain rights in education, The basic right of parents to select the kind of education they desire for their children is honored in theory, though not always in practice. Similarly, the rights of the Church in education as mother of the faithful is acknowledged, even by those who themselves do not accept the Church and her teaching. The state, too, is recognized as educator since its responsibility for civic education and maintenance of the common good requires its involvement in the educative process. All of these agencies have delegated certain functions to the school.

But in Communist countries the state is regarded as the sole educational agency. The leaders of the revolution recognized that education was the most powerful weapon at their disposal in their efforts to effect the radical change in society. In fact, they viewed education as the only means of transforming an individualistic capitalistic society to a socialistic, classless one. The ultimate aim of education was bluntly stated as "strengthening the Soviet state and the building of a classless society." All other goals arc subsidiary to this final one. (See, below, section on "Aims of Education.")

The leaders did much more than pay lip service to this aim. In order to destroy the influence of the family in the education of children, state-sponsored nursery schools were established as rapidly as possible. When a child was three years old he was placed in these nursery schools so that he could be given the "proper start" in his educational career and so that his mother could participate in productive labor and the political life of the nation. These nursery schools assumed the responsibility of the family in providing food, shelter, exercise, and the general physical development of the child. Character development, training of the will, and early intellectual development were given high priority in these preschool years. Habits of cleanliness, respect for his own belongings and for public property are coupled with training in cooperative activities with his fellow pupils. The whole program is designed to make the child a more effective member of the collective.

Finally, the nursery schools see to it that the child is instilled with the "love of the Soviet homeland, its leaders, the Soviet Army, the rich resources of the nation."[7]

Although it is not possible for all children to be placed in nursery schools and kindergartens, great efforts are expended to enroll as many as possible. Special attention is given to those children who might be turned against the Soviet state by parents who do not sympathize with the revolution. And once the child enrolls in the first grade his working hours are largely under the control of the school and Communist youth groups. Thus it appears that the Communists have been most successful in eliminating the family as an educational force in the life of the Soviet children.

Little proof is needed to show that the Church's influence in education has been negated completely. The Marxist dictum that "religion is the opiate of the people" is the key to the Communist attitude toward any Church (Russian Orthodox) involvement in education. One of the earliest Soviet decrees separated the Church from the school. The militant atheism of all Communist movements leaves little doubt about the fate of religion in any country under its domination. All kinds of devices are used to make it extremely difficult if not impossible for the Church to exercise its educational function through the liturgy, sermons, and organized religious instruction. Foreign observers may disagree regarding the effectiveness of the Communist program to eliminate the Church as an educational agency, but they all agree that this is the expressed intent of Communist policy.

With the family and the Church "out of the show" the state has a free hand in designing an educational program to serve its needs. The centralization of educational power in the state is absolute. "Schools are opened, approved and run by the state. The state determines the curriculum and methods of instruction to insure that education is in line with Party and State policy and that it can be planned and directed for the Nation as a whole."[8] All adult education is state owned and controlled. Even the few seminaries conducted by the Orthodox Church must follow state curricula and methods.

----

[7] Division of International Education, *Education in the USSR* (Washington, D. C.: U. S. Department of Health, Education, and Welfare), Bulletin No. 14, 1957, p. 43.
[8] *Ibid.*, p. 15.

Some countries of the non-Communist world such as France have centralized control of education. But this control is in the hands of educators. In the Communist countries, the party leaders decree what the schools shall teach, when they shall teach it, and how it shall be taught. Centers for educational research exist, such as the Russian Academy of Pedagogical Sciences, but their findings can be applied in the schools only when they are approved by party authorities. The only criterion applied to such research regarding its acceptability is whether or not it serves the needs of the state and is in harmony with Marxist ideology.[9]

In this modern technological age, mass-communication media (radio, television, newspapers, periodicals) can be considered important educational agencies. In the Western democracies a significant amount of political, aesthetic, and intellectual education is carried on by these means. Even when the state owns or controls these media (British Broadcasting Company) different points of view are presented. But in Communist countries all broadcasts and publications have one basic purpose, the service of the state. The Gordian knot has been tied again by the all-powerful dictatorship of the proletariat: there is only one educational agency, the state.

STUDENTS

The equalization of educational opportunity is one aspect of the Communist program which has been most successful. The achievements of the Communists in making the benefits of education available to all at little or no cost to the individual have been the more startling since prior to the revolution education in those countries was limited to the upper socioeconomic classes. Article 121 of the Soviet constitution states that all citizens have the "guaranteed" right to free, universal, compulsory primary and secondary education. Those citizens who have talents which make them of greater service to the state are assured of higher and professional education by a system of scholarships which include the cost of schooling, materials, room and board and a stipend, recreation, travel, and the like. For

[9] The educational research of Anton Makarenko is representative of the work which has been done by Soviet educators. But only those aspects of his theory of education have been incorporated in the education program which further the aim of Communism. For example, the "establishment and maintenance of collective discipline" proved most useful. See James Bowen, *Soviet Education: Anton Makarenko and the Years of Experiment* (Madison: University of Wisconsin Press, 1962).

those who are not able to pass the entrance examinations for the universities and professional schools a multiplicity of technical institutes and adult-education programs is available to all who wish to enroll. The Soviets boast that their free educational programs cover the span from the cradle to the grave.

Another aspect of the equalization of educational opportunity consisted in offering to women the same chances for lower and higher education offered to men. In general, the Communists seem to have been consistent in this policy, and within two decades after the revolution the percentage of men and women in universities and professional schools was almost the same. In some schools, the directors were quite scrupulous about the application of this principle and admitted the same number of women as men even to all those programs, such as medicine and engineering, which formerly had been open to men only. At mid-century the percentage of women in higher education is equal to that of men except in elementary education and medical-nursing services where women outnumber men. Programs for military careers, of course, are for men only. During World War II (the great "patriotic war") women received military training but primarily as an emergency measure.

Free, compulsory education for both sexes has its roots in Marxist egalitarianism. It is, however, fostered for very pragmatic reasons as well. It was mentioned in another context that Marxism has recognized that education is the most powerful weapon at the disposal of the state for the reconstruction of society according to socialist principles. It would be most unwise on the part of the leaders of the revolution to exclude women from the program of indoctrination which the schools were expected to carry out. If women were not encouraged to participate in the socialist revolution they might well become a force for reactionism. Therefore women as well as men must be involved in changing "the school from a weapon of bourgeois class rule into a weapon for complete destruction of this class divided society and into a weapon for communist transformation of society."[10]

In conclusion, the Communist had no choice but to liquidate illiteracy. One who could not read or understand the language was beyond the reach of Communist propaganda. It was an easy matter to see to it that only the right things were read and heard since

[10] A. G. Kalashnikov, *People's Education* (Moscow, 1946), p. 10 ff.

the party controlled all media of communication. The revolutionaries had everything to gain by raising the educational level of all the people (young and old), and raise it they did. At the time of the revolution nearly three fourths of the population of Russia was illiterate. Forty years later, Russia had one of the best literacy records in the world. The history of education has recorded no feat as astonishing as this. The same thing seems to be happening in China today. *Reaching primary consideration of all people*.

AIMS OF EDUCATION

Unlike their American counterparts who can agree upon no ultimate goal, Communist educators are in perfect accord that the ultimate purpose of education is "strengthening the Soviet state and the building of a classless society."[11] All other objectives are subsidiary. This central aim supplies the rationale for the curriculum, teaching methods, teacher-pupil freedom and discipline in the schools, which agency shall have responsibility for education, and who shall be educated. Also, the official espousal of this aim accounts for the almost unimaginable centralization of the control of education in all Communist countries. Perhaps, too, this aim serves as the primary motivation for the vast amount of money spent on education in Communist countries (two or three times more than is spent in the U. S.).

It is worth noting that this ultimate aim of education is derived from and is wholly in harmony with the Marxist conception of change and morality (see, below, sections on "Permanence and Change" and "The Search for Values"). All change is directed toward achieving a classless society in the Communist millennium: Communist morality also has the same end insofar as the criterion of all morality is the extent to which behavior contributes to or detracts from the attainment of a classless society.

Obviously, the classroom teacher needs some "down-to-earth" objectives as guides for his daily lessons. Scattered throughout Communist literature on professional education one can locate some of the proximate goals which guide the teacher.

1. The development of knowledge in the academic areas such as mathematics, science, foreign language, and history. But knowledge or science for its own sake must be abhorred. All knowledge has a social purpose, the service of the state.

[11] Yesipov and Goncharov, *op. cit.*, p. 14.

2. Competence in those vocational fields for which the greatest demand exists, such as technology and agriculture.

3. Respect for public property. Great emphasis is placed on this objective since youth are inclined to be careless with things which do not belong to them. All socialist countries have had to emphasize this objective (just as it has to be emphasized in our country).

4. Development of good health habits. Youth can be of little service to society if they are not physically fit and do not possess habits which will protect themselves and society from disease. The importance of physical fitness for military service gives this objective added significance in Soviet education.

5. Training of the will of students so that they will understand and conform to party discipline for the good of socialist society.

6. Development of habits of industriousness which will motivate the person to put forth maximum effort for the common good.

7. Creation of a courageous spirit in every Communist to enable him to fight for Communism and against capitalism in both hot and cold wars. Death "for the cause" of Communism is an honorable and desirable achievement for true apostles of Marx and Lenin.

8. The promotion and spread of atheism in Communist lands and throughout the world. Only when men's minds are *freed from* the superstitions of theism with all its capitalistic connotations will they be freed for the work of international Communism.

9. Development of aesthetic perception to enable the student to distinguish the beautiful and the harmonious from the ugly and the vulgar.

10. Acquisition of habits governing manners, dress, and social behavior.

11. Developing "initiative and independent thought" in harmony with the goals of Marxist-Leninist ideology. This goal seems to have acquired greater significance in recent years after Soviet educators realized that the strict discipline and intellectual conformity in the schools squelched the initiative of those who should be able to contribute most to society.[12]

This rather lengthy list of educational objectives should dispel the notion that schools in Communist countries are narrowly academic.

---

[12] See M. J. Shore, *Soviet Education* (New York: Philosophical Library, 1947), p. 137 ff. G. Counts, *The Challenge of Soviet Education* (New York: McGraw-Hill, 1957), Chap. III.

In fact, since Khrushchev came to power, Soviet educators have been openly critical of the intellectualistic goals of education during the Stalin era.[13]

With the exception of "political indoctrination," these objectives are essentially the same as those proposed by Herbert Spencer and the Educational Policies Commission of the N.E.A. Clearly, the Communist conceives of the role of the school as one which should develop the "whole child," not merely his intellectual powers.

ACADEMIC FREEDOM

From the discussions on aims, methods, and curriculum, it is quite evident that academic freedom, in the sense that it is understood in the Western democracies, is nonexistent in Marxist countries. In the lower and secondary schools the teacher has no freedom in regard to course content, the way the content is to be taught, or when it is to be taught. Textbooks and syllabi are uniform throughout the Soviet Union, for example. Such uniformity in content and method is quite incomprehensible to the average American educator. But it is a reality. An American college professor who toured the Soviet Union several years ago visited a science class in a Moscow school. The same afternoon he took a one-thousand mile jet plane flight to another town and visited a science class the next day. Both classes were on the same lesson, on the same page in the text, had the same assignment, and the like.

The teachers are not allowed to mention other "points of view" in their discussion of assigned topics: there is only one point of view on any issue — that handed down by party officials. It seems that the indoctrination given elementary and secondary teachers is so effective that there are few breaches of this rigid discipline by teachers of these levels. But one wonders how the Communist countries, especially the Soviet Union, can be so advanced in research in the sciences if no academic freedom is granted to university professors involved in such research. The answer to this question seems to be that adequate freedom is given in those areas which do not touch upon politics or ideology. Thus the physicist, mathematician, astronomer, and chemist are given financial support and freedom to pursue their researches, for there is little chance that their findings

[13] See R. Renfield, "The Soviets Are Criticizing Their Schools," *N.E.A. Journal,* XL (March, 1959), pp. 22–25, 78.

will suggest changes in Communist philosophy. Of course, the economist, historian, political scientist, and even the biologist are not so fortunate. T. D. Lysenko, the biologist, had to have the approval of the Central Committee of the party for the contents of an address, "On the Situation in Biological Science." In this address, Lysenko stated the official Communist doctrine on genetics, asserting that all theories of inheritance which allow for chance are false. After this official position was made public, another geneticist, Zhebrak, wrote the following to *Pravda:*

> As long as our Party recognized both tendencies in Soviet genetics and as long as debates between them were regarded as a creative discussion of theoretical questions of contemporary science facilitating the discovery of truth, I persistently defended my views which at some points differed from the views of Academician Lysenko. But now, since it has become clear to me that the basic theses of the Michurin school in Soviet genetics are approved by the Central Committee of the All-Union Communist Party, I, as a member of the Party, cannot defend positions which have been declared mistaken by the Central Committee of our Party.[14]

If the biological theories are so closely scrutinized, certainly the social scientist enjoys no academic freedom.

Perhaps there is another explanation for the relatively large amount of pure research going on behind the Iron Curtain. The college teacher and researcher is encouraged to search for knowledge, especially that kind which will assist the nation to reach its goals in agriculture, production, space, and military preparedness. The results of such experimentation are submitted to the party and either accepted or rejected for theoretical or practical reasons. For example, the Russian Academy of Pedagogical Sciences, American observers say, is carrying on basic research in education very similar to that done in the United States and Britain. Those doing the research are quite free in their choice of techniques, etc., but only when the party officials examine and approve their findings can the schools put them into practice.

The American scientist or teacher often is amazed that his Communist counterpart can achieve so much with so little academic freedom. It may be well to note, however, that in many of the Iron Curtain countries, especially Russia, academic freedom never was a reality. Prior to the dictatorship of the proletariat, the Russian

---

[14] *Pravda,* August 10, 1948, quoted in G. Counts and N. Lodge, *Country of the Blind* (Boston: Houghton Mifflin, 1949), p. 212.

intellectuals were accustomed to the dictatorship of the Tsars. One type of tyranny was replaced by another. Perhaps this fact explains why so many Russian intellectuals made great contributions in the "value-free" sciences, such as mathematics and physics, under the Tsars. One could not be beheaded as a traitor for deriving a new mathematical formula.

INDOCTRINATION

It seems quite clear from the above that teachers enjoy very little academic freedom in Communist countries. If teachers have no freedom, it would be foolhardy to deny that indoctrination of pupils in Communist principles is standard procedure in schools. As noted above, a relatively large portion of the curriculum from kindergarten through the university is devoted to indoctrination in Marxist-Leninist principles. The lecture-recitation method, which is used in all academic classes, lends itself most effectively to in-doctrination techniques. School discipline is another effective, though indirect, method of indoctrination. All the informal means of educa-tion — youth organizations, radio, TV, and printed matter — are un-der the absolute control of the party and are used for indoctrination purposes. Thus it is correct to say that indoctrination in Marxism is carried on from the cradle to the grave.

But Soviet educators, and perhaps even some political leaders, recognize the need to develop habits of creative thinking in those areas of a nonpolitical nature. They need young people who can devise new ways of improving agricultural and industrial production. Genius in physics, chemistry, mathematics, space research, and mili-tary science is not developed by lockstep educational programs and lifeless indoctrination. Moreover, new means of spreading Com-munism throughout the world must come from the minds of youth. To achieve this end the Pedagogical Research Institutes now are seeking new ways of "developing individual thinking in pupils," especially in the areas mentioned. The institute in Leningrad, for example, considers experimentation in this aspect of teaching one of its major projects. But up to this time, opportunities for pupils' voluntary expression and creative thinking are very limited. Secon-dary school pupils do a few individual projects in the sciences and in the applied sciences such as agriculture and technology. It appears that the greatest opportunity for self-expression and activities related to pupil interests is afforded by the extensive programs outside school. Such extracurricular activities are under the direction of experienced teachers and often result in spectacular creative works by the pupils. Training for future leadership in the spread of Communism is also carried on chiefly in the well-organized programs of the Pioneers and Young Communists. Rewards, such as certificates of merit and medals, are awarded to those students who produce outstanding work in extracurricular and class activities. Teachers encourage students to go beyond the basic requirements set down for all pupils. The *Pedagogy* of Yesipov and Goncharov gives pupil initiative special consideration:

> The tasks of communist education require that our pupils leave school as people of initiative. Citizens of our Soviet Union are expected not only to execute consciously and perseveringly the will of their leaders, but also to show personal resourcefulness of their own and to contribute a spark of personal creativeness directed toward the welfare of the Motherland. Only people of initiative are able to extricate themselves successfully from a difficult situation under any conditions or solve creatively some new problem presented by life.[15]

These educators insist that creative potentialities in children be developed from their early school days. Group games and socially useful activities are considered excellent means of developing initiative. Teachers are encouraged to be alert for suggestions from children regarding excursions, holiday plans, assemblies, and club organizations. All of these will develop creative abilities and leadership qualities in youth.

It is easy, therefore, to understand the dilemma of the Soviet educator who must indoctrinate the pupils in all the tenets of Communism but still is expected to graduate creative persons who will take the leadership in making the Communist lands superior to the enemy in technology, agriculture, art, and military strength.

PERMANENCE AND CHANGE

Like other modern philosophies Marxism is assuredly to be placed in the category of the "philosophies of change." Engels attested to this classification of Marx at the oration he delivered at Marx's funeral when he compared him to Darwin. Darwin, he said, discovered the laws of biological change; Marx, the laws of change applied to

---

[15] Yesipov and Goncharov, *Pedagogy*, trans. by Counts and Lodge, *op. cit.*, p. 128.

historical development of human kind.[16] Basically Marxists accept the Darwinian notion of change and add the dimension of social change to that of the biological. Further, they insist upon the inevitability of change in human events because of the "dialectic of history." This view, of course, is an adaptation of the well-known Hegelian triad: thesis-antithesis-synthesis. (See Chapter Eleven, "Idealism.") It is an adaptation of Hegel since his world was a spiritual or mental one whereas Marx's world is purely material. Thus the term *dialectical materialism* is used to describe the Marxist system.

Engels recognized the use to which Hegel's dialectic could be put to explain the phenomena of change:

> In this [Hegel's] system — and herein lies its great merit — for the first time the whole world, natural, historical and intellectual, is represented as a process, i.e., as in constant motion, change, transformation, development and the attempt is made to trace out the internal connection that makes a continuous whole of all this movement and development.[17]

The Marxist uses dialectic to explain the changes of the past and predict the events of the future in all areas, politics, economics, and education. But these changes are gradual and the new forms always contain some of the old. For example, a certain economic system such as nineteenth-century capitalism contains certain elements of past economic systems; it is not completely new. To apply the dialectic to economic systems, let us begin with capitalism as the thesis. Capitalism generates its own antithesis, competition. The thesis and antithesis combine to form the synthesis, perhaps a controlled economy. This synthesis becomes the new thesis which, in turn, will generate another antithesis and the fusion of the two will be the new synthesis. Those Marxists who demand the complete break with every trace of the past are not following the dialectical process but are introducing a novel interpretation of it. Lenin himself insisted that "We can build communism only on the stock of knowledge, organizations, institutions, human forces and means left to us from the old society."[18] Apply the same dialectic to social institutions and you have (1) the social institution in existence (thesis); (2) the

---

16 Marx and Engels, *Selected Works* (Moscow: Foreign Language Publishing House), Vol. I, p. 142.

17 F. Engels, *Socialism: Utopian and Scientific* (Chicago: C. H. Kerr Co., n.d.), p. 85.

18 V. Lenin, *Works* (Moscow: Gospolitzdat, 1950), Vol. 31, p. 251 ff.

human needs and demands which this institution produces (antithesis); (3) the new social institution which arises because of the relation and interaction of the existing social institutions and the human needs and demands it produced (synthesis). To illustrate this dialectic process, let us start with feudalism as the thesis. Feudalism, because of the independence of each feudal lord, lacked any kind of political unity which might provide protection for the people. Thus feudalism generated in the people the need for unity to assure their safety and provision for common wants — the antithesis. The synthesis of these two opposites resulted in a new social form, monarchy, or strong central control of some type. Monarchy, then, becomes the new thesis which in turn generates its own antithesis from which a new synthesis will result. And so the process will continue until the final synthesis is reached, the Communist millennium in which no government will be necessary. This is why Khrushchev can say, "We will bury you." His belief in the inexorable dialectic of history convinces him that eventually Communism must win. Note that all changes show unity between the two phases since some features of the thesis are retained. Also, certain essential differences appear since certain elements of the old form are destroyed. Finally, the synthesis is essentially new since the combination of the old and novel aspects form a qualitatively novel state of affairs.

In summary, then, the Marxist view involves the following beliefs about change:

1. The physical and biological realms are in a state of constant flux. These states are guided by the dialectical process which leads them inevitably from one stage of development to another.

2. The social, political, economic, and educational realms, too, are changing according to the rules of the dialectic. One type of structure must give way inevitably to another until the final synthesis is realized.

3. All change is gradual, and at times imperceptible, since every new synthesis contains elements of the previous thesis and antithesis.

4. The only thing that does not change is the schema of development — the dialectical process according to which change takes place.

NATURALISM VS. SUPERNATURALISM

In some of the areas discussed in this chapter, the Communists have been somewhat ambivalent in their acceptance or rejection of traditional beliefs. In the areas of curriculum and methodology, they have reinstated much from prerevolutionary times. Even their rejection of capitalism has not been absolute since they have retained the modes of production and even some of the aims of the capitalistic system. In the realm of values, Communism holds many of the ancient beliefs such as patriotism, love and respect for parents and elders, honesty, and distributive justice.

Such is not the case in connection with the existence of the supernatural. Marxists deny the traditional belief in any form of religion. Both Marx and Lenin left no doubt about it when they said that religion was the opiate of the people, a spiritual intoxicant used by the oppressors to keep the workers in slavery. Religion, they averred, was used to keep the worker passive and patient in the acceptance of his unhappy lot by promising him a reward in the hereafter.

Theoretically, of course, the Communist has only the choice to reject supernaturalism in all its forms. Dialectical materialism connotes exactly what it says — matter alone exists. All forms of reality are manifestations of matter. Mind itself is only the highest product of matter. The dialectical process, thesis-antithesis-synthesis, is rooted in matter. All the different brands of Communism agreed on this point — Bolshevism, Trotskyism, Leninism, Stalinism, and "Khrushchevism" — all belief in the supernatural must be "liquidated."

Upon coming to power in any country, the Communists immediately launch a full-scale attack upon all forms of religious institutions and beliefs. They withdraw financial support from all religious institutions or organizations, confiscate church property, close religious schools, forbid the teaching of religion in state-supported schools, prohibit religious instruction in groups (even in church), destroy the influence of the clergy by accusing them of traitorous acts, usually following this with imprisonment or death.

The next line of attack concentrates on removing the indirect influence coming from the cultural heritage of the past. Museums, libraries, textbooks, and the like are purged of any religious influence. In place of these influences, Communists enthrone atheistic and materialistic values designed to fill the void left by the removal of religious values.

Militantly atheistic organizations are formed to occupy the leisure time of the young and old alike. One such Russian organization, the League of Militant Godless, has organized a most comprehensive program for "stamping out God." It conducts classes, seminars, and lectures on atheism, prints antireligious materials of all kinds, floods museums, libraries, the theater, radio, and TV with the philosophy of godlessness. In a similar way the Young Communists and Pioneers gear their programs to liquidation of religious beliefs. The state schools integrate antireligious teachings in all subjects, even in "neutral" ones such as mathematics and science. No stone is left unturned in the attempt to wipe out all traces of the belief in the supernatural.

Since religion is a reality in all cultures Marxists need some way of explaining its presence in society. Marx believed that religion was simply an immature way of dealing with production and consumption of goods in the different types of societies.[19] Engels felt that primitive men (who knew no science) could not explain certain phenomena of their own experience, such as dreams, thought, and sensation, and hence placed the source of these activities in a spiritual soul. Since these activities were not bodily they would not die with the body, but live on. Thus arose the idea of immortality of the soul. The idea of God evolved from the personification of natural forces which ignorant men could not explain by natural means. Eventually, by rationalistic (nonscientific) means, the belief in one God was created by men.[20] Lenin finds the basis of religion in modern capitalistic societies in the "social oppression of the working classes." Religion supports the "rights of the rich" to retain what they own; it teaches the poor to accept their lot as the "will of God"; it holds out to the oppressed a state of heavenly bliss where all injustices will be "righted."[21]

One final consideration of the Marxist war on religion is necessary for an understanding of Marxist education. The leaders of both the early and modern revolutions realize that you cannot pluck the heart out of a people and expect it to live. In all the societies where Communism has taken over, religion was the very heart of human existence. To fill this void the Communist leadership introduces the new religion of materialism. In place of the Christian heaven the

---

[19] K. Marx, *Capital,* trans. by E. Untermann (Chicago: Charles Kerr Co., 1906), Vol. I, Chap. 1, Sect. 4.

[20] F. Engels, *Ludwig Feuerbach* (New York: International Publishers, 1934), p. 30 ff.; Engels, *Anti-Dühring* (New York: International Publishers, 1935), p. 353 ff.

[21] V. Lenin, *Religion* (New York: International Publishers, 1933), p. 7.

people are offered the "Communist millennium" which will be free
from all trials, tribulations, oppressions, and sickness. The doctrines
and dogmas of the churches are replaced by those of Communism.
The prophets and messiah are Marx, Engels, Lenin, Stalin, Khrushchev, and their successors. The sacred scriptures of Communism
were written by Marx, Engels, and the early "apostles" (Lenin, etc.).
The Central Committee (Politburo) assumes the function of the
synod or council of the Christian Churches. The premier (or the
equivalent) has more power than any pope, patriarch, or bishop ever
possessed. Top party officials and their subordinates become the
hierarchy and clergy to manage all the affairs of men and machines.
No "heresy" is tolerated and all deviationists are assisted in their
return to the "true faith" by being given the opportunity to recant
doctrinal errors.

Thus the new religion of materialism covers all the traditional
phases of man's association with God plus the added attraction of
gettting all these "benefits" in a hurry. The void here has been filled!
Man has been offered new and immediate goals and he seeks these
goals with a religious fervor equal to that of the early Christians.
Students of society have pointed to this characteristic of Communism
as one of the major reasons for its success. Some of the other philosophies we have discussed in this book (naturalism, instrumentalism,
and atheistic existentialism) do not offer "social man" any such goals.
Perhaps for this reason they have never become the dominant
philosophy of any worldwide movement. Theodore Brameld, a pragmatist, has pointed to the "goallessness" of instrumentalism as one
of its major weaknesses. In his own version of pragmatism (called
Reconstructionism) he attempts to remedy this shortcoming by
proposing very definite goals for society which will appeal to the
social-minded man of today.[22] Perhaps, too, this is why religious
people who have lost their fervor and commitment are the first to
fall prey to the new religion of Communism.

NATURE OF MAN AND SOCIETY

Although Marxist principles found no educational application until
the second and third decades of the twentieth century, there are

---

[22] T. Brameld, *Toward a Reconstructed Philosophy of Education* (New York:
Dryden Press, 1956), Chap. I.

many basic philosophical views held in common with some of the philosophers mentioned in preceding chapters. This is especially true regarding the Marxist's view of the nature of man.

As everyone knows, Marxism's descriptive title, *Dialectical Materialism,* indicates that the source of all life is found in matter, crass matter. Thus it is right to say with F. Engels, Marx's coauthor of the *Manifesto,* that "man is what he eats." Man, then, is purely a product of nature, and not a result of any force outside nature. In reality, he is not even a product of evolution, but of his own making. Marx avers that "men begin to differentiate themselves from animals as soon as they begin to produce their own means of subsistence. . . ."[23] Thus his essence is defined in terms of productivity, i.e., man is a productive animal. Matter and productivity are the two key concepts relating to man's nature. His need for clothing, shelter, sex are purely material needs modified by a desire for social acceptance. But basically it is a change in material conditions which effects changes in man's ideas, views, and conceptions.[24]

Obviously, Marxism rejects mind-body or spirit-matter dualism as an interpretation of man's behavior. The origin of life, the reality of death have no bearing on and are not related to any supernatural order but are delicate and complex forms of matter. Mind itself is simply a product of matter and merely represents a difference in the organization of matter. Like other naturalists, the Marxist explains man's clinging to belief in the supernatural in terms of material needs. Thus, in religion, man projects his natural needs into the realm of the spiritual (or supernatural) hoping to obtain satisfaction from such projection. However, the Marxist says, man creates a conflict within himself because he has transferred to God that which is proper to his own nature. This internal conflict can be resolved only when man recognizes that he is his own god and the only true faith is the religion of humanity.

In spite of the denial of the dual nature of man, Marx did not deny that "human nature" is a reality. On the contrary Marx's starting point in all discussion about man assumes that man is an entity distinguishable from other organisms, who should be studied *as man.*

---

[23] K. Marx, *Gesamtausgabe,* Sect. 1, Vol. V, p. 10.

[24] See H. Parkes, *Marxism: An Autopsy* (Boston: Houghton Mifflin Co., 1939), p. 158.

He says we "must first deal with human nature in general and then with human nature as modified in each historical epoch."[25] Of course the human nature of which Marx speaks is not the changeless "essence" of man used by the scholastics. But there are some changeless drives and needs in man such as the needs for food, shelter, and procreation. The changing drives are those which owe their origin to certain societal structures such as the drive to accumulate wealth. Thus Marx found in man "a general human nature" (basic, changeless drives) and an historical man (basic human nature plus the additives of a certain kind of society). It is the historical man that makes himself. He starts with the raw materials of general human nature and by his works makes the nineteenth-century man or the fifth-century man and so on.

If, then, man is a purely material being, how does the Marxist explain freedom of the will? The answer is quite simple — there is no freedom of the individual will. Man's personality is not of his own making but a product of social production and the tensions of the class struggle. Marx says: "In the social production which men carry on they enter into definite relations that are indispensable and independent of their will. . . . It is not the consciousness of men that determines their being, but, on the contrary, their social being that determines their consciousness. . . . At a certain stage of their development the material forces of production in society come in conflict with the existing relations of production. Then begins the epoch of social revolution."[26] The individual man's true freedom is achieved when he adjusts to the "collective will of the people." The best expression of individual freedom is realized when the person knows he must act according to the laws of the collectivity and actually follows these laws. Knowledge of this concept of freedom is essential for an understanding of Marxist education. Whereas education in the Western democracies generally encourages the individual to think for himself and express his thoughts in a creative manner, the educators of the Communist countries place a premium on thinking and acting *with* the collective mind and will. This phenomenon is very obvious to visitors in schools behind the Iron Curtain. The *same* questions are asked and the *same* answers

---

[25] K. Marx, *Capital* (Chicago: C. H. Kerr & Co., 1906), p. 668.

[26] Marx, *A Contribution to the Critique of Political Economy* (Chicago: C. H. Kerr & Co., 1904), p. 11 ff.

are received to the questions in all schools — there is no choice of answers, even to "controversial" questions.

In summary, the Marxist's basic belief about the nature of man includes the following: (1) man is a purely material being with a natural origin and destiny; (2) man is not composed of body and mind or body and soul — mind is simply a complex function of the material body; (3) man possesses no personal or individual freedom but finds his freedom in following the collective will of "the people" (party); (4) all knowledge of man's nature is derived from scientific sources. Philosophy and theology yield no valid knowledge about man's essence; (5) the science of man is subsumed under the science of society; that is, one cannot speak of the science of man but of men.

On the basis of what has been said above it is meaningless to speak of the nature of man since the Marxist view of the nature of society determines what the nature of man should be. Individuals *per se* are of no significance since they never exist in themselves, but only in groups. But society itself and the groups within society are subject to the changes dictated by the dialectic of history. One societal form is in opposition to another; the ensuing struggle results in a new form which contain elements of both conflicting forms. Thus each new society creates a new man who is different from, yet similar to, the old man in some respects. The feudal man, the mercantile man, the factory man are all different because the societies which gave them birth are different.

In theory, at least, the instrumentalist and the Marxist agree that society creates individuals and that individuals will change as society changes. But whereas the instrumentalist feels that the state is a legitimate (and even necessary) arm of society, the Marxist feels that the state is intrinsically evil. Since this notion has had great influence on education, further explanation of the relation of society to state is necessary.

The Marxists, unlike the scholastics, believe that the state is not a natural institution, but one which arose in society when social classes began to form. Certain classes created the state as a means of protecting what they had acquired against the attempts, on the part of those who did not have any private property, to restore ownership to all the members of society. The state, then, is a creation of the greedy "haves," to maintain their ownership of the means of producing wealth. Had society never formed any classes which possessed wealth, there would have been no class struggle. A state would never have come into existence. The state then becomes a power outside of society — above it. It does not represent "the people" but the class of "haves."

If, then, the state is not the true representative of society, what should be done with it? The working class (proletariat) must seize the power of the state and abolish all private ownership. When this has been accomplished the proletariat itself will disappear as a class (as well as all other classes). When a classless society is realized, the class struggle will be at an end and the state will have no reason for existing. Society will be in perfect harmony since no one will have to fight with his fellowman either to defend what he owns or to acquire what he does not have. All the people will own all the natural resources and the means of production. As the world nears this ideal condition the state gradually will wither away. Even the democratic state of the Western world will suffer the same fate, for Engels insists that "the state is nothing more than a machine for the oppression of one class by another, in a democratic republic no less than in a monarchy."[27] Lenin and Stalin held the same view that the state should eventually disappear.

However, the first fifty years of Communist domination indicate a strengthening of the "evil state" to a point even beyond that of the autocratic regimes of the tsars. The world has not seen any state system as centralized, rigid, and impersonal as the Communist states. And the Marxists do not deny that their existing states are dictatorial. But, they argue, the dictatorship of the proletariat is a necessary phase in the dialectic of history. It is essential for the working class to establish a dictatorship to insure the destruction of the privileged classes who have exploited them throughout history. It is this political arrangement, the dictatorship of the masses, which Marxists equate with democracy. Obviously they are not using the term in the same sense that it is used in non-Communist circles. Thus they are quite consistent with their basic assumption about the evil nature of the state when they assert that democracy too, will pass away since it represents the power structure of one class, the proletariat.[28]

---

[27] K. Marx and F. Engels, *Selected Works* (Moscow: Foreign Languages Publishing House, 1955), Vol. I, p. 416 ff.

[28] For an analysis of the meaning of democracy in Communist literature and the

When all classes including the proletariat have disappeared the Communist millennium (heaven on earth) will be at hand. Strife, physical discomfort, and moral evil will no longer plague man; society will be in a state of perfect equilibrium.

This promise of perfect happiness on earth is perhaps the point which had the greatest appeal to the downtrodden, impoverished masses of industrial Europe.[29] The utopian intellectuals who sided with the working class in their struggle against oppressive employers were attracted to this ideal just as much as the workers. It also offered them an end to the social conflicts which had bloodied the pages of history; it was a means of removing the scourge of war from the face of the earth. Why should man wait for life after death to see justice done? It could never be verified by experience that wrongdoers received their just deserts or that those who lived in misery and sorrow would receive comfort and joy in the afterlife. Therefore, build a perfectly classless society — one that will supply all the needs and wants of man here on earth. Then man can forget the myth of heaven.

The educational implications of the Marxist doctrines on the nature of man and society are evident to the world. The denial of man's dual nature explicitly affects teaching methods, curricular content, and educational objectives. The belief that man is a product of society is evident in all the formal and informal educational activities emphasizing group allegiances, cooperativeness, and conformity. The doctrines of the desirability of dictatorship of the proletariat as the means of achieving a classless (economic) society are both preached and practiced in the schools.

EPISTEMOLOGY

The philosophy of Marxism, unlike other modern philosophies, such as logical positivism and pragmatism, is not overly concerned with theory of knowledge. For the Marxist, the nature or origin of truth, the modes of knowing are not major problems. However,

---

essential differences between that definition and some of the Western nations of democracy, see R. N. Carew Hunt, *Marxism — Past and Present* (New York: Macmillan Co., 1955), Chap. X.

[29] It is worth noting that the only period during which Communism achieved some success in the United States was in the great depression of the 1930's. An improved standard of living among the workers brought about by full employment and high pay has made Communism very unpalatable to the American working class.

the Marxist view on some major issues in the theory of knowledge is available. First, knowing does not consist in an apprehension of the "thing in itself," but rather a grasp of the thing as it exists for us. McFadden interprets the knowing process of Marxist epistemology as a combination of active and passive aspects of mind. On the one hand, the outside world acts upon man's sense organs and thus provides a continual flow of stimuli to the knowing organism. On the other hand, the mind itself, since it is an integral part of the world (matter), partakes of the same active nature as the world and is itself active in the knowing process.[30] In some ways this active-passive aspect of knowing is similar to that of instrumentalism. In the process of acquiring knowledge, man is simultaneously changed by the knowledge he acquires and changes the world by the knowledge acquired.[31] True knowledge of the world, then, consists in more than a comprehension of isolated things. To understand the world, the knower must perceive the relations which exist among the things of the real world and between himself and these external objects. Therefore Marxist theory of knowledge cannot be classified as either realistic or idealistic but rather as a mixture of both. Consequently truth can never be objective or absolute, for it is a "relative experience" which does not have set laws.[32] If this be the case it is easy to understand why the "truths" contained in textbooks are frequently changed by Marxists.

There seems to be no doubt that Marxists have placed a priority on the scientific mode of knowing and understandably so, since in this age of science such knowledge gives power. In fact any knowledge which does not give power to its possessor is not worthy of the name. Lenin himself held "that the only path to truth is science which holds the materialist point of view."[33]

It is evident from the section on the "Curriculum" that Communists have applied Lenin's view: after political indoctrination, science dominates the course of study at the elementary and postelementary school level. And it is through the medium of science and technology that Russia has achieved power.

[30] C. J. McFadden, The Philosophy of Communism (New York: Benziger Bros., 1939), p. 60.

[31] Ibid., p. 69.

[32] The Communist Manifesto, p. 35.

[33] V. Lenin, "Materialism and Empiric Criticisms," Selected Works (New York: International Publishers, 1943), p. 205.

Because of the major role science plays in Marxist schools one might be led to believe that radical empiricism is the only epistemological position amenable to Marxists. Such, however, is not the case, for there is a strong strain of rationalism within the system. This rationalistic strain is derived from the Hegelian notion of mind as both the source and unifying principle of experiences. Hegel imposed upon the world of things and events a certain rationalistic structure by which both things and events were to be understood and interpreted. This structure, which itself is a result of his formalized "dialectic," presumes that the world is inexorably moving through the three states, thesis, antithesis, and synthesis. (See section above on "Permanence and Change.")

True, the Marxists gave a materialistic (economic) twist to the Hegelian triad, but changing the nature of the substance involved in change did not alter the rationalistic origin of the doctrine of change. This hard-nosed rationalism is very obvious in the unwavering belief that regardless of what non-Marxists do to prevent the ultimate triumph of Communism, it will win out. "It's in the cards." "There's no way out — it *must* come to pass."

Thus, in spite of their verbal espousal of exclusively materialistic and empirical modes of knowing, Marxists cannot deny the rationalistic underpinnings of their epistemology. The educational system belies their commitment to such rationalistic views, especially in the realm of political and economic instruction. The educational theorists see what they want to see and disregard the brute facts of the political and economic world. If the facts don't fit the theory, so much the worse for the facts. The world is viewed through the colored glasses of dialectical materialism.

THE SEARCH FOR VALUES

In spite of the many statements that Marxists have no concern for values (especially moral values) a perusal of Communist technical and educational literature reveals that more attention is paid to the moral behavior of the "faithful Communist" than any other aspect of life. The school, for example, is given the major responsibility for developing "ethical character" in pupils so that they will be law-abiding, productive citizens of the communities in which they live. Only by living the good life can they contribute to the ultimate triumph of Marxism. It is true that the leaders of Marxism rejected the traditional foundations of morality and subordinated all value theory to the interests of the working class in its struggle against the oppressors. The final criterion of all value must be the extent to which the holding of certain values furthers the purposes of the revolution.[34]

In the field of aesthetics, the great interest and productivity of the people of Communist countries in the fine arts puts the American to shame. But a more detailed description of the Marxist view of value is necessary for an understanding of their educational philosophy.

ETHICAL VALUES

It is well known that, shortly after the Bolshevik revolution, the Marxists threw out all the moral standards of prerevolutionary days. In most respects, this attitude is true of all revolutionary movements including that of progressivists in American education. "Do away with all vestiges of the old regime" is the cry of the revolutionary. In so doing, they "throw out the baby with the bath." But it does not take very long for the folly of such an attitude to become evident, even to the leaders of the revolution. And in the case of Marxism, it was contrary to the very doctrine of change (the dialectic) upon which the system was constructed. It was noted above in the discussion of permanence and change that every new form of social organization must of necessity contain certain elements of the old. It is, therefore, not in harmony with theoretical Marxism to destroy utterly all beliefs, moral standards, economic and political structures of the system displaced by the revolution. It was, then, to be expected that the revolutionaries soon would recognize the anarchical nature of the moral code (or lack of a code) of the Bolsheviks and propose a very definite code of behavior. This new code is contained in the official textbook for teachers, *Pedagogy,* by B. P. Yesipov and N. K. Goncharov (1946). George Counts and Nucia Lodge translated those sections which are of the greatest import for philosophy of education under the title, *I Want to Be Like Stalin.* It could just as well be titled, "I Want to Be Like Khrushchev or Any Other Leader," since the same ethical principles hold. This and other sources will be used to construct the theory of Communist ethics.

---

[34] See V. Lenin, "The Tasks of Youth Leagues," *Selected Works of Lenin* (New York: International Publishers, 1943), Vol. 9, p. 475 ff.

1. Moral Character.   A person with proper moral training is one who subordinates all his actions, interests, and desires to the service of the Communist state and the "people." In order to achieve this perfect moral state, the child must learn to hate all that is contrary to the principles of Communism, including the nations which hold these principles. Furthermore, the morally perfect Communist must be willing to sacrifice everything, including his life, to defend the doctrines of Communism.

One of the first moral principles children must learn is the respect for public property (of course, all property is public). Teachers should inculcate this principle by using stories from history but, above all, by example. If neither of these approaches succeeds in convincing the pupil, the teacher must use force to convince him of his error. The child should not be allowed to harm others by his lack of conformity to rules demanding respect for public property.

Respect for authority is another moral principle which children must learn early in life. This respect is not to be based upon fear of punishment (except in extreme cases of nonconformity) for, as Anton Makarenko says, cruelty begets cruelty in children. Rather, the child should learn to respect the authority of the teacher and others because these people have been helpful, understanding, fair, and firm. "True authority is founded on the making of reasonable demands on the child, combined with respect for his personality, devotion to his interests, ability to help him, clarity, firmness of educational purposes, and worthiness of personal example."[35]

2. Patriotism.   The development of good moral character is essential to Communist philosophy, but these virtues must be expressed in an unwavering devotion to the motherland. This devotion begins with love of parents, relatives and friends, the local community, and local environs. From these immediate attachments the child can be led to an ardent devotion to the Communist party and the great prophets of Communism, Marx, Lenin, Stalin at least until recently, and Khrushchev, and a passionate hatred of their enemies.

Another aspect of the moral virtue of patriotism rests on the pride all good citizens must manifest in the achievements of Communism in the areas of production, politics, economics, art, and education. This pride should not be limited to the achievements of Communists in the Soviet Republics but should extend to those of the

[35] B. Yesipov and N. K. Goncharov, *op. cit.,* p. 48.

workers' parties throughout the world in the battle for the destruction of capitalism. Ultimately, then, patriotism will take on an international hue, for it will involve devotion to all people fighting for true equality.

Yet another by-product of the virtue of patriotism is heroism. This virtue is expressed in bravery on the battlefield as well as in the efforts put forth to bring about the triumph of Communism throughout the world. Of course, the Russians go to great lengths in rewriting history to prove that Communists were the prime causes in bringing about the defeat of Fascism and Nazism.[36] Others (capitalists) were fighting for their personal possessions, not for the good of humanity:

> The services of the Russian people are exceptionally great, not only to the peoples of the Soviet Union, but also to all mankind. The Soviet Union by its example inspires the workers of the entire world for the struggle against exploiters and ravishers. The history of the Russian people proves to all mankind their political wisdom, their military valor and their genius.[37]

Finally, the student must demonstrate his patriotism by deeds, the most important of which is realized in his mastery of military skills of all kinds.

3. Love and Respect for Parents, Elders, and All Workers.   As mentioned above, patriotism is based upon the immediate attachment to parents, friends, relatives, and local environment. But the love of persons is a value worth cultivating for its own sake. Stalin insisted that people (persons) are the "most valuable and most decisive" capital. And only in Communism can the person be granted his true worth. In order to achieve a state of affairs in which true humanism (Communism) will thrive, those opposed to socialism not only must be hated, but also destroyed.

Education must play the important part in fostering love and respect for people. Children should be taught these noble sentiments through literature, good example, and the practice of manners expressing in word and deed the true essence of these basic values. Children should never be allowed to get away with rudeness or disobedience toward parents, elders and teachers or one another. This kind of behavior is "capitalistic" and unbecoming to socialist youth of good character. However, in teaching love and respect, the

---

[36] *Ibid.*, p. 62.
[37] *Ibid.*, p. 61.

negative aspects should not be overemphasized. Rather, proper training will result in the positive virtue of responsibility. This virtue can be taught best by giving the student responsibility for tasks in accordance with his ability and by expecting him to complete such assignments.

Another aspect of developing respect for persons is found in the respect for truth and contempt for lying. From early childhood, children should learn to tell the truth and refrain from cheating and lying not only because these acts harm others but because they destroy the person's own integrity. If he has made a mistake, the child should admit it and bear the responsibility for his own errors.

The virtues of justice and integrity are inextricably involved with the other virtues mentioned above. Yesipov and Goncharov say:

> A person possessing a feeling of honor and personal dignity demands justice for himself and is just to others, refuses both to submit to insult and to insult others, and overpraises neither himself nor others. A person reared in a spirit of honor and personal dignity is revolted by every manifestation of sycophancy, servility, officiousness, flattery, and other such vices. On the other hand, respect for oneself and personal dignity are irreconcilable with peacockery, conceit, hard egotism and self-love. Genuine dignity is identified with that modesty which permits the individual to judge himself properly and to respect the honor and dignity of others.[38]

4. The Common Good. For obvious reasons the common good is ranked high among moral values inculcated in Marxist countries. Public ownership of all land, resources, instruments of production, housing, recreation, and education are basic in the philosophy of Communism. The first steps toward the full realization of this abstract good are found in comradeship and friendship. Comradeship is developed in early years by kindness to one's classmates and by the "community of interest and action." Friendship is a more intimate and personal relationship between persons. But it should never be permitted to displace cooperation between all members of the collective. The priority of cooperation for the common good over personal friendships is emphasized by the strong pressure brought to bear upon youth to participate actively in the many organizations such as Pioneers and Komsomol. "Our children must be indoctrinated with the spirit of collectivism, because a strong collective is the foundation of foundations of the Soviet educational system. . . . The entire secret of [his] success is found in the simple fact that

---

[38] *Ibid.,* p. 80.

he formed a genuine collective which set the tone of the [youth] colony, mastered the most incorrigible individuals, and by habituating them to discipline cultivated the will."[39]

Sharing, cooperation, discharging social obligations, respect for school property, group work and play, coeducational projects, all are specific applications of the broader virtue, cultivation of the common good.

5. Discipline. In the Marxist system, discipline is conceived as a virtue essential to achieve the goals of Communism. The school must insist on discipline not only because it is necessary for successful study and learning but also because it is necessary for life. Yesipov and Goncharov affirm:

> Before the teacher stands a much deeper task: the cultivation in children of a state of discipline as a high quality of communist morality and one of the most important traits of character. The development of this quality in children is linked with the task of preparing future citizens of the Soviet state who will act from a sense of public duty and will possess a feeling of responsibility before the socialist Motherland. Without discipline one cannot achieve high productivity of labor in production. Without discipline one cannot conquer in war.
> From early years we must educate children so that a state of discipline will remain as their permanent possession.[40]

The characteristics of true Communist discipline are: (1) It must be based on an understanding of the necessity for norms of conduct. (2) It must be self-discipline, not one of obedience for obedience' sake. The person will have so disciplined his will that he will always be ready to perform his duty in the best possible manner without waiting for the command to do so. (3) In its most perfect form, discipline will reflect a state of unquestioned obedience to authority when the situation demands that orders be given. (4) Discipline must habituate the individual to the performance of group (collective) activities. (5) True discipline must be founded on mutual respect for all members of the collective. (6) Finally, discipline is "resolute, that is, it surmounts difficulties, prompts the completion of every task, subjects conduct to high purposes and conquers motives of low degree."[41]

6. Sex Morality. After the Russian revolution, the Communists, in their eagerness to discard all ties with "bourgeois morality," went

[39] *Ibid.*, p. 84 ff.
[40] *Ibid.*, p. 94.
[41] *Ibid.*, p. 95.

on a free-love binge unparalleled in modern history. The Marxist penchant for order and discipline, however, soon made such a course untenable. Also Marx himself rejected the communization of sex relations by considering such a view as the point of "infinite degradation" of the humanized man. It represents, to his mind, a state in which man seeks to satisfy his biological, animal needs rather than social needs. And, after all, it is the expression of social needs and their fulfillment which humanizes man.[42]

One might look for a clue to the Communist attitude toward sexual behavior for youth in the shift from segregation of the sexes to coeducation in Communist schools. But the reason for the change is based upon the Marxist view of the equality of all human beings rather than upon the desire to promote promiscuity. Perhaps the best answer to the question is given by Frank S. Meyer, a man well versed in Communism, when he affirms that the Communist party has no official views on sexual behavior. But it does try to channel these natural desires for the good of the party. And, as long as the fulfillment of such desires does not interfere with party discipline or the achievement of party objectives, the officials neither frown upon nor approve illicit sexual behavior.[43] Moreover, the present laws governing marriage and divorce seem to be based on a desire to maintain order rather than any ethical norms concerning the rightness or wrongness of keeping or breaking marriage contracts.

Other values, such as courage, strength, equality, and international understanding (for workers) are held in high esteem. But these might be considered as subvalues to those discussed above. One very important value which has not been mentioned specifically above, the value of labor, is of great significance for education.

7. The Value of Labor. The Marxist believes that the true value of any object is to be measured by the amount of human labor which has been expended in its production.[44] Labor, then, is not to be viewed as something distasteful or burdensome. On the contrary, in Communist countries work is conceived as an expression, the highest aspiration of the human person. It is a matter of "honor,

---

[42] See Erich Fromm, *Marx's Concept of Man* (New York: Frederick Ungar Co., 1961), p. 30 ff.

[43] Frank S. Meyer, *The Moulding of Communists* (New York: Harcourt, Brace & Co., 1961), pp. 47, 81.

[44] See Sidney Hook, *Towards the Understanding of Karl Marx* (London: V. Gollancy Ltd., 1933), p. 171 ff.

glory, valor, and heroism." It offers man the opportunity to serve his fellowman, thus promoting the common good. Such could not be the case in capitalist countries, Marxists argue, since labor is performed for the benefit of the employer or owner. But in Communist countries, it is performed for all since there is no private ownership or personal profit.

As the educational level of the Soviet people rose, youth of school age began to lose sight of this most important socialist value. In reality, Soviet youth vied for the opportunity to attend institutions of higher learning so they would not have to work at manual tasks. But Premier Khrushchev noted this serious defection from "Communist morality" when he said: "A portion of those who finish the ten-year school unwillingly go to work in factories, plants, and collective and state farms, and some even consider it an insult to them."[45]

To correct this diversionist, "capitalistic" attitude the Khrushchev reform of 1958 required all young people who completed the first eight grades to work at productive labor before going on to higher education. The only exception to this rigid rule applied to exceptionally talented students in science and fine arts.

This Communist attitude toward labor is closely entwined with the values of discipline, patriotism, the common good, love of one's fellow worker, and Communist morality in general. Some Marxists, in reality, consider the Communist view of labor as the highest value in the hierarchy of values.

AESTHETIC VALUES

The handling of the artist and the development of a theory of art presented early Marxist revolutionaries with a nearly insoluble problem: the prerevolutionary despots had been patrons of the arts and the art works of that period could hardly be used as propaganda media for Communist doctrines because of their bourgeois tone. On the other hand, the Bolsheviks recognized the almost innate love of the Russian people for drama, literature, music, and painting. Two points of view developed among the early revolutionaries. One group of extremists demanded that all art works, especially literature, preach the party line. In other words, the arts should be considered as vehicles of Communist doctrines and no deviation

---

[45] *Izvestia,* September 21, 1958.

from these doctrines should be tolerated. The more moderate group, which included Trotsky and Bukharin, felt that the arts could thrive only when the artist is given sufficient freedom to produce creative works; creativity is stifled if the artist is made to produce according to political specifications. The engineer, the agricultural expert, and the economist could be bound by Communist doctrines but the artist could not be so bound. Of course, the artist could never be permitted to use his art as a political weapon against the revolution. But the artist was accustomed to this limitation of his freedom of expression since the tsars had tolerated no political opposition from artists.

These two groups vied for control of the art world until Stalin decided to wipe out all vestiges of both Tsarism and Trotskyism. Then an official theory of art called "socialist realism" was promulgated and the artist had his choice of conforming to the theory or spending the rest of his days in a Siberian labor camp. The official organ of the party clarified the meaning of socialist realism as follows:

> Socialist realism, resting on the tradition of classical realism, establishes as the foundation of artistic creation, not the subjective-arbitrary fancies of the artist, but his comprehension of objective reality. The degree of artistic representation of Soviet realistic writers is determined first of all by the degree to which they produce accurately and faithfully in artistic forms the course of the life processes. . . .
>
> In their creative works Soviet writers are *guided by the policy of the Bolshevik party and the Soviet state.* This constitutes the strength of Soviet literature, because it gives to writers the opportunity *to understand the course of reality more profoundly and to reflect it truly.* Also, it opens before the writer the perspective of active participation through his work in the building of a new life, inspired by the ideal of Communism. The best works of Soviet literature *assist actively in the reeducation of the broad masses of the people in the spirit of Communism* and in the liberation of the consciousness of the toilers from the vestiges of capitalism. *The most important task of Soviet writers is to propagate the idea of Communism.* . . .[46]

Although the reference in this proclamation is aimed primarily at writers, the same rules hold for painters, sculptors, and musicians. Obviously, the written art forms lend themselves more readily to indoctrination and much more rigid control is necessary than in those forms less susceptible to it. Certainly, then, this official statement put an end to freedom in the arts. And, with the exception of

---

[46] Taken from the periodical *Bolshevik* of May 15, 1948, No. 9, p. 45 ff. (Italics mine.) Quoted in G. Counts, *The Challenge of Soviet Education,* p. 199.

occasional relaxation of these rules (for ulterior motives), the artist in Communist lands has had to follow the party line. Witness the treatment which Boris Pasternak received for his *Doctor Zhivago*. Further, note the official banning of "capitalistic art forms," including jazz music, imported from Western countries. Khrushchev has attacked Stalinism, but he has not given one inch of ground to the weakening of the Stalinist proclamation on the arts. In March, 1963, Premier Khrushchev bluntly told Soviet writers and artists that all artistic works must be used as weapons of the class struggle and that all Western forms of abstract art will be purged from the Soviet world. Socialist realism cannot coexist with bourgeois art forms. The Premier attacked the writer Ilya Ehrenburg for defending modern art. Ilyichev, chief propagandist for the party, said, "The very essence of socialist realism is in seeking new and beautiful features in art that are true to life and justified from the standpoint of the Communist world outlook."[47] They still remain the tool and weapon of Communist ideology.

In summary, the following generalizations about Communist axiology are offered:

1. All values are rooted in the class struggle of the proletariat against the oppressing classes.

2. Values have no independent existence; that is, there is no appeal to a realm of value independent of the Marxist-Leninist ideology such as "natural law," the decalogue.

3. The ultimate source of values is not found outside the realm of socialistic human experience.

4. The criterion of values is depicted best by the dictum, "Whatever aids Communism is good; whatever hinders it is evil."

5. Values are in a state of flux since each new synthesis will create new values.

6. All values must reflect devotion to the party, its leaders, and the motherland.

7. All values must develop the love and esteem for labor so essential for the triumph of Communism over capitalism.

EVALUATION OF MARXISM

An evaluation of Marxism from the Christian point of view could be made by any intelligent graduate of a Christian high school. Its

[47] Quoted in the March 10, 1963, *Milwaukee Journal* from *Tass*, Soviet news agency.

basic philosophy so obviously contradicts the teaching of the Church that a simple listing of the main points is all that is needed.

1. The crass materialism of Marxism cannot account for the realities around us. Its interpretation of the world of knowledge and experience is wholly inadequate since it recognizes no distinction between mind and matter and soul and body.

2. The absolute denial of the existence of a supernatural realm is, of course, unacceptable to a Christian.

3. The militant atheism of Communism proposes to destroy the very foundations of civilized society. Not only are Judaism and Christianity rejected but also the religions of the oriental world. All of these religions make man responsible to a higher power, thereby enabling him to appeal to some source of authority outside society.

4. The acceptance of science and Marxist ideology as the only valid sources of knowledge excludes two basic modes of knowing accepted by a Christian, namely faith and humanistic studies. Communist education, therefore, concerns itself with only "half of the man" (the physical aspect) and neglects his higher faculties, mind and spirit.

5. The Marxist application of the dialectic to all reality and values destroys the belief in any permanent states in the natural and supernatural world. Truth, goodness, and beauty have no norms or standards and are but a result of the whims of man and/or the party leaders. Furthermore, there is no evidence that the dialectic is operative in all natural and human events. History itself does not say that all things *must* follow this pattern. In reality, many changes of the past have not been a synthesis of the old and the new, but actually have been a return to some older structure. The dictatorships in Communist countries are prime examples of this phenomenon. Their political structure is similar to that found in the absolute autocracies of the ancient world.

6. The Marxist assumption that values are dependent entirely on the context of society must be rejected by the Christian, who also recognizes *objective* values in things

7. The rejection of freedom of the will by Marxists is, of course, contrary to Christian belief. Such a position destroys the very foundation of morality and responsibility.

The educational limitations of Communism lie chiefly in the more theoretical areas.

1. To make the state the end of education, to put all education in the hands of the political leadership, to prohibit any other agency from participating in the educational enterprise is to destroy education's very foundations.

2. The overemphasis on science and mathematics resulting in a neglect of the humanistic disciplines devitalizes the curriculum. Man cannot be prepared for full living by science and mathematics.

3. The lecture-recitation-test method of teaching does not allow for independent or creative thinking on the part of pupils. It emphasizes memory rather than understanding; it encourages passivity rather than engages the knowing powers of the student by activity.

4. The absence of academic freedom among Communist teachers, especially at the higher educational levels, weakens the very foundations of true scholarship. Unless teachers are free to seek the truth and publicize the results of their research, an educational system will eventually destroy itself.

5. The complete indoctrination of youth found in Communist countries can only create "a land of the blind." It may serve the immediate purposes of the party, but in the long run a nation will become educationally stunted by such spoon feeding.

But not all is evil in Communist education. Any educational system which can advance from one of the lowest to one of the highest literacy levels in a few short decades must have something to offer. Perhaps other systems might learn a few lessons.

1. Communist countries have taken the whole business of education most seriously. They spend proportionately more of their national income on education than the Western democracies.

2. This seriousness of purpose is reflected in the attitude of youth toward education. In general, Communist youth take their studies very seriously and consider it a privilege and a duty to attend school and do their very best to promote the "common good." There is no time wasted. Students finish elementary and secondary school in less time than the American student.

3. By expanding educational opportunity to all people, including adults, Communist educators have made full use of the abilities of the citizens. No talent "goes to waste" because the individual cannot afford to attend school.

4. Although there appears to be too great an emphasis on science, as mentioned above, one feels that a Communist youth leaves secondary school with a thorough knowledge of the basic sciences. In a "scientific age," this seems to be a very realistic goal and one which can be achieved in democratic lands.

5. In Communist countries all educational activities are directed to an ultimate purpose. One may not agree with the ultimate goal of Communism, but one must admit that the possession of such a purpose gives direction to all activities.

6. Although there are certain disadvantages in having nationwide standards, curricula, textbooks, educational time schedules, and the like, some things are to be gained from such uniformity. For example, studies of teacher effectiveness, comparison of achievement between schools or districts, pressure to cover certain content areas are all possible when all schools are doing the same thing, in the same way, at the same time for the same purpose.

SUMMARY

Marxists make education a tool of the state in initiating youth to the requisites of a classless society. Teaching methods are centered around the teacher rather than the student, with the lecture-recitation-test pattern predominating. The curricular content is determined exclusively by the needs of the Communist society, with heavy emphasis on training in those skills necessary for making dedicated, intelligent workers, capable of transforming an agrarian economy into a strong modern society. Discipline is essential, and students are taught the value of co-operative labor, respect for authority and the goods of the state.

BIBLIOGRAPHY

Bowen, James, *Soviet Education: Anton Makarenko and the Years of Experiment* (Madison: University of Wisconsin Press, 1962).

Brameld, T., *Toward a Reconstructed Philosophy of Education* (New York: Dryden Press, 1956).

Counts, George, *The Challenge of Soviet Education* (New York: McGraw-Hill Book Co., 1957).

Division of International Education, *Education in the USSR* (Washington, D. C.: U. S. Dept. of Health, Education, and Welfare Bulletin No. 14, 1957).

Engels, F., *Anti-Dühring* (New York: International Publishers, 1935).

——— *Ludwig Feuerbach* (New York: International Publishers, 1934).

——— *Socialism: Utopian and Scientific* (Chicago: C. H. Kerr Co., n. d.).

Fromm, Erich, *Marx's Concept of Man* (New York: Frederick Ungar Publishing Co., 1961).

Hook, Sidney, *Marx and Marxists* (New York: D. Van Nostrand Co., 1955). Contains selected readings from leading Marxists.

――― *Towards the Understanding of Karl Marx* (London: Victor Gollancy Ltd., 1933).

Hunt, R. N. Carew, *Marxism Past and Present* (New York: Macmillan Co., 1955).

Kalashnikov, A. G., *People's Education* (Moscow, 1946).

Lenin, V., "Materialism and Empiric Criticisms," *Selected Works* (New York: International Publishers, 1943).

――― *Religion* (New York: International Publishers, 1933).

――― "The Tasks of Youth Leagues," *Selected Works of Lenin* (New York: International Publishers, 1943), Vol. 9.

――― *Works* (Moscow: Gospolitzdat, 1950), Vol. 31.

McFadden, Charles J., *The Philosophy of Communism* (New York: Benziger Brothers, 1939).

Marx, K., *Capital,* translated by E. Untermann (Chicago: Charles Kerr Co., 1906), Vol. I.

――― *A Contribution to the Critique of Political Economy* (Chicago: C. H. Kerr & Co., 1904).

――― *Gesamtausgabe,* Vol. V.

Marx, Karl, and Engels, F., *Manifesto of the Communist Party* (New York: International Publishers, 1948).

――― *Selected Works* (Moscow: Foreign Language Publishing House), Vol. I.

Medlin, W. K., *et. al.,* *Soviet Education Programs* (Washington, D. C.: U. S. Department of Health, Education, and Welfare Bulletin No. 17, 1960).

Meyer, Frank S., *The Moulding of Communists* (New York: Harcourt, Brace & Co., 1961).

Parkes, H., *Marxism: An Autopsy* (Boston: Houghton Mifflin Co., 1939).

Renfield, R., "The Soviets Are Criticizing Their Schools," *N.E.A. Journal,* XL (March, 1959).

Shore, M. J., *Soviet Education* (New York: Philosophical Library, 1947).

Soviet Education (New York: International Arts and Sciences Press, published monthly since 1959).

Yesipov (Esipov), B. P., and Goncharov, N. K., *Pedagogy,* translated and abridged under the title *I Want to Be Like Stalin* by G. S. Counts and N. P. Lodge (New York: John Day Co., 1947).

CHAPTER TEN

Atheistic Existentialism

INTRODUCTION

IT MIGHT be argued that existentialism is so remote from educational theory and practice that it does not deserve serious consideration in a book on philosophy of education. But if one keeps in mind that existentialism represents a reaction against both traditional and modern philosophies, at least it has the appeal of "being different." It is true that Christian existentialism, described in Chapter Five, has had little influence on Christian educational theory and practice. But it does not follow that existentialist ideas will have no impact on education in general.

Although the rise of existentialism antedates World War II, it was not until that time that it gained any popularity. Young thinkers chafed under the kind of conformity demanded by Fascism, Nazism, Communism, scientism, and the organized religions. They wished to be freed from the doctrines and practices of all of these "faiths": they wished to "create themselves" according to their own personal desires and interests. They did not want to be told what they were supposed to be. Rather, they felt that they should be what they *wanted to be* — they wanted to be their own creators. Such unlimited freedom was possible only within the context of atheism since belief in a personal God would of necessity limit man's context of freedom.

Thus atheistic existentialism will be a force to be reckoned with in public education, especially at the higher levels in the near future. In fact, the cry of the educational liberal today calls for freeing the individual from the lockstep pattern of American education. Greater emphasis is being given to the role the student must play in *making himself* as opposed to *being made* by his environment. Even those who reject existentialism feel that it might serve this one purpose, the heightening of individual responsibility for one's own choices and actions.

Rather than attempt to define existentialism (which existentialists themselves maintain is futile)[1] it might be better to determine what the task of philosophy is according to the proponents of this school of thought. First of all, the existentialist does not concern himself with problems concerning the nature, origin, and destiny of the physical universe. This task, he believes, falls to the scientist. He must develop the tools and methods for discovering, explaining, and predicting the universe of things, celestial movements, or the like. The philosopher should not even concern himself with the basic assumptions of the physical or biological sciences. This, too, is the business of the scientist. In general, the entire subject matter of epistemology, so highly esteemed by most traditional and modern philosophers, should not occupy the labors of the philosopher.

What, then, should engage the philosopher? Very simply, the philosopher's search is *man* — man as a choosing, valuing, living, and dying being. Not man as an object of study by psychologists or biologists but man as a free agent involved in that most serious process, *existing*. Consequently, ethics and aesthetics constitute the two major areas of philosophic concern for the existentialist.

Unlike other modern philosophers, the existentialist has used the fine arts as a mode of communicating his philosophy to his fellow-man. One can expect, therefore, to find the philosophic works of these thinkers to be much more poetic and literary than those of the instrumentalists, realists, or idealists. This characteristic of their work will call for quite an adjustment on the part of the student in attempting to understand their writings. But this might come as a refreshing change to one accustomed to the cold, detached literature of technical philosophy.

Some of the "greats" of atheistic existentialism with which the student is most familiar are Nietzsche, Sartre, and Heidegger. (Nietzsche is regarded by most philosophers as a forerunner to con-temporary existentialists, but he is rightly reckoned as "existential"

---

[1] See J. P. Sartre, *Existentialism and Humanism* (London: Methuen and Co., Ltd., 1948), p. 25 ff.

in his approach and in his appraisal of culture. Walter Kaufmann of Princeton University could be called a modern-day Nietzsche.) Frequent reference will be made to their works especially in the sections treating the philosophical bases of existentialism.

METHODOLOGY

Naturalists like Rousseau and Pestalozzi have been very specific in their recommendations on teaching methods. The instrumentalists center their educational practices around the problem-solving method. Even the modern adaptations of classical philosophies to educational theory have been "method-conscious." Such preoccupation, however, is not found among existentialists. Yet, some inferences about educational methodology might be drawn from their works on general philosophy. In reality, the way in which subject matter is handled seems to be more important to the existentialist than the subject matter itself.

Perhaps the most significant assumption or underlying belief regarding educational methodology is that any teaching method must place the responsibility for choosing what to learn and actually learning it upon the individual. This assumption is entirely in harmony with the existentialist's insistence upon the absolute freedom of the individual. Obviously, no self-respecting existentialist would employ the traditional lecture-recite-assign-test method. He would reject with equal zeal the problem-solving method of instrumentalism because of its social emphasis. Any method which fosters group thinking or group action would be alien to the existentialist.

Perhaps, then, the only criterion for method is that the teacher show by his example that education is a concentration on personal freedom — one which encourages the student to accept the facts and beliefs which have relevance for him. Nietzsche states this position very vigorously in criticizing the traditional method (historico-scholastic method) of teaching the mother tongue:

> People deal with it as if it were a dead language and as if the present and the future were under no obligation to it whatsoever. The historical method has become so universal in our time, that even the living body of language is sacrificed for the sake of anatomical study. . . . The historical method may certainly be a considerably easier and more comfortable one for the teacher; it also seems to be compatible with a much lower grade of

ability and, in general, with a smaller display of energy and will on his part. But we shall find that this observation holds good in every department of pedagogical life.[2]

With equal force Nietzsche criticizes the teaching of German composition in the public schools:

> Owing to the very fact that in this department it is almost always the most gifted pupils who display the greatest eagerness, it ought to have been made clear how dangerously stimulating, precisely here, the task of the teacher must be. German composition makes an appeal to the individual, and the more strongly a pupil is conscious of his various qualities, the more personally will he do his German composition.[3]

Nietzsche then goes on to tell what the typical teacher in the public school does with the pupil's first attempt at expressing his individuality in composition.

> What does he [the teacher] hold most reprehensible in this class of work? What does he call his pupil's attention to? To all excesses in form or thought — that is to say, to all that which, at their age, is essentially characteristic of the individual. . . . In short, their individuality is reproved and rejected by the teacher in favor of an unoriginal decent average. On the other hand, uniform mediocrity gets peevish praise.[4]

Thus far the emphasis has been on what the existentialist *does not like* in teaching methods. George Kneller offers some specific approaches to methodology which would be congenial to the existentialist. For example, in teaching ancient history to a seventh-grade class the teacher does not present certain events and their causes but encourages "a reenactment in the imagination of great and critical moments. . . . I stress the men themselves who were responsible for these events. I consider them as actors playing out their respective roles in the great encounters of politics. I divide the different parts among my class — Julius Caesar, Pompey the Great, Brutus, Mark Antony, Cicero, Octavianus. To relive the past we must cease to be its spectators and become instead its agents."[5]

Thus history must "come alive"; it must be a human adventure in which the student becomes involved. The student actually experiences what each of these great individuals experienced in creating their own being — their essence.

---

[2] F. Nietzsche, *The Future of Educational Institutions* (London: T. N. Foulis, Ltd., 1909), p. 60.

[3] *Ibid.*, p. 52.

[4] *Ibid.*, p. 53.

[5] George Kneller, "Education, Knowledge and the Problem of Existence," *Proceedings of the Philosophy of Education Society*, 1961, p. 137.

Similarly, a science should be considered a personal, human activity in which the student relives the great moments of discovery in the history of science. It should not be taught as an exercise in laboratory technique nor as a cold lifeless body of content to be mastered. The existential way to teach science is to have the students live it. This approach to teaching proposed by Kneller seems to be the same as that which Nietzsche implied in his criticism of traditional methods.

AGENCIES OF EDUCATION

From what has been said about the role individuality should play in the development and application of educational methodology, it is quite evident that none of the traditional agencies of education (family, Church, and state) can claim the primary right to educate. We shall later (in the sections on "The Nature of Man and Society," "Epistemology," and "Value Theory") make it quite clear that the individual, the personification of absolute freedom, is the sole "agency" responsible for creating his own essence or being. To be consistent, the existentialist cannot permit any agency "outside the individual" to usurp this primary right and responsibility.

Nietzsche's attack on public education is based upon his conviction that the public schools in his country (during the late nineteenth century) destroyed individual freedom and responsibility and replaced them with a state-enforced conformity.[6] Since mass education (always compulsory) has been initiated by the state or in some instances by the Church, many existentialists feel that both of these organizations have overstepped their bounds. The best examples of the modern misuse of education by the state can be found in Communist countries where the state is the sole educational agency and the primary aim of education. George Kneller, an expositor of existentialism, has expressed similar misgivings about public education:

> But who will persuade me that today's (public) schools have an absolute right to their existence? . . . I am not convinced that in itself the school is necessarily a good thing. It is at best a benevolent, well-meaning concentration camp. It denies in its actual make-up the very emancipation and enfranchisement of youth that it is established to cherish. . . . Deny, if you can, the dreadful similarity between the mass education of children in a school and the mass production of goods in a factory.[7]

[6] Nietzsche, *op. cit.,* pp. 44, 46, 47, 49.
[7] George Kneller, *op. cit.,* p. 136.

Some of the younger (beatnik) class have shown their scorn for this intrusion upon their freedom by refusing to attend institutions of higher learning.

Certainly, the atheistic existentialist has an additional reason for denying the rights of the Church in educational matters, since he considers the entire theological-administrative structure of the churches as a grand and fraudulent imposition on the individual's freedom of choice and action. It (the Church) has demanded that the individual conform to a code of behavior, a system of beliefs, and a set of rules for group life. It has used the schools as the agency for achieving this conformity. The existentialist would point to parochial education as an example of the Church's denial of the individual's right to determine his own proximate and ultimate goals in life. Such misuse of education can only be resisted by the existentialist.

The family, too, should not be considered the chief agency of education. The authoritarian structure of European (and some American) families has crushed the individuality of the young. Simply because the parents have provided the biological components of the child, they are not entitled to dictate what the child shall make of himself.

Consequently, we are left with only one conclusion: the individual is the sole "agency" of education. The family, Church, and state should provide an atmosphere conducive to the individual's creation of his own essence. Their only role in the educative process is an auxiliary one — a service role. These agencies should cooperate in "freeing the individual" from the artificial restraints of organized society so that he will be able to choose and act as he wishes.

CURRICULUM

From the foregoing sections on methodology and aims, one can conclude that the *existence of individuals* must constitute the "core of studies" both in and out of school. It is worth noting, however, that Nietzsche, Kneller, and Ralph Harper do not demand that history, science, mathematics, and the like be thrown out of the curriculum. Their criticism is leveled at the impersonal, cold, and dry-as-dust approach to subject matter found in the schools. It is safe to assume, then, that both traditional and modern subject matter would be found in the existentialist schools. But subject matter would not be learned "for its own sake." The views that one should teach subject matter for its own sake, or for training the pupil's intellect, or for adjusting the student to his environment are foreign to existentialist thought.

Would the existentialist curriculum be mainly prescribed or elective? In all probability, great freedom of choice would be encouraged. After all "man is freedom" — he is not granted freedom by some authority. Therefore, the student should select those areas of knowledge with which he feels personally involved and through which he can best develop his own potentialities, his own being or existence.

There is one feature of the existentialist curriculum which should differentiate it sharply from most existing elementary, secondary, and college programs. Most of these programs are devoid of content designed to offer the educand the opportunity to express his individuality in moral and artistic ways. As explained below, in the section on "Value Theory," the existentialists have made extensive use of the art forms as the media for conveying their beliefs about philosophical matters. It certainly would be in harmony with this emphasis on values to provide the broadest possible curricular offerings in the value-laden areas. Early in the elementary school, the child should be given the opportunity to express himself in any art form which he chooses. Also, the school program should afford myriads of opportunities for the young pupil to make his own decisions in ethical matters. If this emphasis is continued throughout the secondary and college programs, then the student will be truly "educated to freedom."

It seems, then, as suggested above, that the existentialist is not so much concerned with the actual courses or subjects in a curriculum as he is with what the teacher and (most especially) the pupil does with them. The exercise of existential freedom *within* a curriculum is more important than the curriculum content. George Kneller takes each area of the curriculum, history, science, citizenship, music, art, dramatics, poetry, biography, and shows how the "existential approach" can be applied to each one. In each instance the student "lives" the subject or, better, becomes *personally* involved in the life of the material under consideration.[8]

---

[8] G. Kneller, *op. cit.*, pp. 137–142.

STUDENTS

The question "Who should be educated?" would appear to be a rather simple one for the existentialist. One might expect him to answer that anyone who so desired should be given all the education he wants. This response is probably correct as far as education in general is concerned, since the broad meaning of education includes more than schooling. In other words, a person can educate himself in many ways such as by reading, by working, and perhaps, most important, by living — by willing and acting.

However, some existentialists have been quite clear in advocating a culture and education for the elite. Nietzsche was very outspoken in his scorn of "equality of opportunity" for all the children of all the people.

> The education of the masses cannot, therefore, be our aim; but rather the education of a few picked men for great and lasting works. . . . What is called the "education of the masses" cannot be accomplished except with difficulty; and even if a system of universal compulsory education be applied, they can only be realized outwardly: those individuals of lower levels where, generally speaking, the masses come into contact with culture — all these levels can scarcely be reached by direct means. . . .[9]

In this context Nietzsche was not speaking only of college or university education but of the lower levels, elementary and secondary. He felt that public education, which attempted to educate the masses, was bound to fall short of the aim of true education simply because the masses were involved.[10]

George Kneller does not object to universal education, at least at the lower levels. But he does point to the grave danger that compulsory public education might well engulf the individual in the sea of complete, depersonalized anonymity. Also, the "compulsory" aspect of public education seems to cause him concern since it removes completely the individual's freedom of choice in educational matters.[11]

It appears that American existentialists would not campaign against "equality of educational opportunity" for all the children of all the people. Their platform would rather be one of reform in public (and private) education, a reform calling for the release of

[9] F. Nietzsche, op. cit., p. 75.

[10] Ibid., pp. 46–51.

[11] G. Kneller, Existentialism and Education, p. 91, and "Education, Knowledge and the Problem of Existence," op. cit., p. 136.

the individual from the captivity of an "educational system." Even though children are expected to attend school, they would be given time and encouragement to contemplate what all their activities are about. They would be afforded the opportunity to build themselves to their own liking rather than conform to the mold arbitrarily made by society. What could be more "American"? Is not this the true spirit of 1776?

AIMS

Existentialists have been quite consistent in their recommendation of educational aims which are in harmony with their philosophic views. Ralph Harper says:

> Thus, the end of education for an existentialist is making individuals aware of the meaning of homelessness, of being at home, and of the ways of returning. In the strict sense, this means that existentialism is concerned principally with liberal education, *freeing man from his isolation and his anonymity, freeing his mind* from the confusions that prevent him from seeing his situations and his powers. So much it has in common with psychiatric therapy. No philosopher today is more concerned with education in this sense than an existential philosopher. Every existential philosopher is a doctor and a missionary . . . for the purpose of *encouraging individuals* of all kinds and conditions *to understand their situations* and themselves. And it is the starting point of every existentialist that *no other modern philosophy has taken the self and its situation seriously enough* to make that situation the subject matter of its inquiry. . . . All existentialists start with the individual who chooses his course and who dies in disquietude. And all of them protest against the forces within man and his contemporary situation that discourage him from being-at-home, or, worse, from seeing himself as both mortal and responsible.[12]

Prior to stating this general objective for education, Harper had pointed up that the existentialist wants to educate the "whole child," not just one side. This "whole-child" concept has been utilized by others, among them the instrumentalists. But the existentialist proposes a more *individualistic* notion, that is, the "unfolding of the *individual* as a whole in the situation in which he finds himself."[13] Whereas the instrumentalist desires that the individual locate himself within a social context and adjust to the process of socialization, the existentialist emphasizes those situations such as tragedy, guilt, suf-

---

[12] Ralph Harper, "Significance of Existence and Recognition for Education," *Modern Philosophies and Education,* 54th NSSE Yearbook (Chicago: University of Chicago Press, 1955), p. 227. (Italics mine.)

[13] *Ibid.,* p. 223.

fering, and death which happen to the individual rather than the group.

Nietzsche voices the same view against "the general topsy-turvifica-tion of all genuine aims for education" in which the individual is lost sight of _as an individual._[14]

ACADEMIC FREEDOM AND INDOCTRINATION

A perusal of the section on the nature of man and value theory will suggest a quick answer to the age-old educational problems of academic freedom and indoctrination. If man is "freedom person-ified," as the existentialist maintains, obviously no teacher has the right to indoctrinate his students, and no community, administrator, or outside authority has the right to restrict the academic freedom of the teacher.

Another way of clarifying the existentialist position on the ques-tion of teacher and pupil freedom might be stated in the form of a more basic question namely: "Why is the question asked at all?" Those who ask the question surely do not understand the true nature of freedom. They already have surrendered their own freedom in exchange for the "security of the crowd." They are afraid to make their own choices and suffer the consequences of these choices. They are men no longer, but merely "things."

To corroborate the view that existentialists demand unrestricted freedom for teacher and pupil one need only refer to their state-ments of educational aims, the content of the curriculum, and the teaching methods they espouse. In all of these educational areas freedom, absolute and unrestricted, is the touchstone. Nietzsche at-tacked the public school system of his country because it restricted the freedom of creative teachers and their pupils. Kneller expresses the fear that the American public schools are performing the same dis-service to teacher and pupil even though the "spirit of America" would suggest the opposite approach. Sartre lashed out against all "dogmatisms," religious, political, and moral, which deter man from creating his own essence. Kierkegaard fought against organized (formalized) Christianity (though he remained a Christian) because he, a teacher and preacher, was denied the freedom to teach the truth as he saw it. Thus one could go through the complete roster

---

14 F. Nietzsche, *op. cit.,* p. 41.

of existentialists and find this same theme dominating all their thinking: man's freedom must not be denied him.

PERMANENCE AND CHANGE

The philosophy of Aristotle and the scholastics explains change in such a way that change is impossible without something *stable* which endures throughout the process of change. When a child changes to a man, *becomes* a man, there is continuity of past with present, as it is the same person who once was a child and is now a man. In his essence as rational animal the child-become-a-man abides. Existence then is not prior to essence; man is born with an essence. As soon as he exists he has a predetermined essence.

The existentialists, on the contrary, deny the *preeminence of essence.* They reject the notion that there is a predetermined nature for every human being. Man is not born with a rational soul which "forms the matter," the body. Man has no essence at birth; he must create his own essence. And with Darwin, the existentialist would concur that no living beings will remain the same — all are in the process of changing. Consequently, existentialism is to be classified as one of the philosophies of change. In this one respect, at least, it is like the other modern philosophies discussed in this book.

Since most readers will find the notion that existence is prior to essence somewhat new, it might be well to discuss it further. Moreover, since the existentialist's primary concern is with human beings we shall limit the discussion to this level of being. In the first place, since the atheistic wing of existentialism repudiates any belief in a supreme God as the first cause and maker of all beings, one cannot point to a prototype or pattern according to which all men are created. Man is not made to the image and likeness of anybody or anything. At birth he is merely a living mass of flesh and blood — he is just here. He is not anything or anybody in particular. It is true that, legally, this bundle of human flesh is someone's son or daughter with some of the physical characteristics of the parents, but their resemblance in no way determines what the child will become. The child simply exists! Sartre states this position very succinctly:

> If man as the existentialist sees him is not definable it is because to begin with he is nothing. He will not be anything until later, and then he will be what he makes himself. Thus, there is no human nature, because

there is no God to have a conception of it. Man simply is. Not that he is simply what he conceives himself to be, but he is what he wills, and as he conceives himself after already existing — as he wills to be after that leap towards existence. Man is nothing else but that which he makes himself. That is the first principle of existentialism. . . . Man will only attain existence when he is what he purposes to be.[15]

In some respects, the existentialist commitment to change as a fundamental characteristic of all reality is similar to that of the pragmatist since he, too, denies that nature or man has any definable essence. The earlier forms of pragmatism, especially that of William James, emphasized the completely indeterminate character of man's being. He will make of himself what he wishes; he will create his own religious experiences and decide which are most workable for him. Even though the later forms of pragmatism, such as instrumentalism and reconstructionism, are more socially oriented, man as a member of society must make the new man and the new society by his intelligent interaction with an ever changing physical and social universe.

NATURALISM VS. SUPERNATURALISM

Frederich Nietzsche's statement, "God is dead," succinctly expresses the atheistic existentialist's view on the issue of the existence of a supernatural realm. Neither Nietzsche, Heidegger, nor Sartre makes any attempt to refute the traditional arguments for the existence of God presented by the scholastics or those who use the "ontological argument." Rather, they simply begin with the assumption that God does not exist and proceed to construct their philosophical views on this postulate. Nietzsche says:

Where is God gone? . . . I mean to tell you! We have killed him — you and I! . . . Do we not hear the noise of the grave-diggers who are burying God? God is dead! God remains dead! And we have killed! . . . the holiest and the mightiest that the world has hitherto possessed, has bled to death under our knife — . . . What are our churches now, if they are not the tombs and monuments of God.[16]

Martin Heidegger does not quarrel with Nietzsche's postulate that God is nonexistent or at least need not exist. He feels that man

---

[15] J. P. Sartre, *Existentialism and Humanism*, p. 28.
[16] F. Nietzsche, *Joyful Wisdom*, in *The Complete Works of Frederich Nietzsche* (London: Allen and Unwin, Ltd., 1909), Section 125.

does not need to seek answers in divine revelation since philosophy can solve the basic riddles of human existence. For Heidegger, then, the existence or nonexistence of God and supernatural values is irrelevant to man's major task, that of creating himself.

Sartre's atheism is more thoroughgoing than either that of Heidegger or Nietzsche. Whereas Nietzsche felt that God was dead and Heidegger that God's existence was irrelevant, Sartre maintains that man can never comprehend the true meaning of his own existence unless he presupposes there is no God. For when we begin with the premise that there is a God, then we must conclude that man possesses an essence which precedes personal existence. Sartre says:

> Atheistic existentialism, of which I am a representative, declares with greater consistency that if God does not exist, there is at least one being whose existence comes before its essence, a being which exists before it can be defined by any conception of it. That being is man or, as Heidegger has it, the human reality.[17]

Thus Sartre rejects classical atheism which suppresses the idea of God but retains the notion that men possess a common, rational nature or essence. This position, Sartre believes, is inconsistent with atheism because it retains all the significant elements of theism and refuses to accept the individual responsibility for self-creation which all true atheism implies.

A corollary of this argument for Sartre's postulatory atheism is found in his voluntaristic interpretation of human action. Again, Sartre argues that it is inconsistent to speak of free will in man if one accepts the existence of God. Only when one rejects God can one be said to be "in possession of himself as he is. . . ." Only then does the responsibility for one's own existence, decisions, and acts rest squarely on one's own shoulders. Only then can man be considered truly free since he is no longer hamstrung by precepts "from above" or by a nature imposed upon him by a creator.

THE NATURE OF MAN AND SOCIETY

The very question of the nature of man is a meaningless one for the existentialist. In both of the sections above it was emphasized that man has no "nature" as such but rather that he must create his own essence. Man is nothing more than what he makes of himself. Perhaps, then, it might be more accurate to speak of certain char-

---

[17] J. P. Sartre, *Existentialism and Humanism*, pp. 27–28.

acteristics, states, or conditions which man creates for himself or into which he is thrown.

The most important of these characteristics is freedom. Man is condemned to freedom. "Human freedom is not a part of human existence," Sartre says, "it precedes human existence and makes it possible. The freedom of man cannot be separated from the being of man. It is the being of man's consciousness. It is not a human attribute but it is the raw material of my being. I owe my being to my freedom."[18]

Man, then, does not possess free will as a part of his essential nature (as the scholastic believes), but rather he exists in a state of *absolute freedom*. None of the environmental or hereditary forces are considered strong enough (by the existentialist) to impair man's freedom. When a person selects a certain advisor or counselor, this very choice represents his freedom. To illustrate, if a young man goes to a priest for advice he knows what kind of counseling he will receive since the priest represents a certain value orientation. The young man is freely choosing this way of life by his initial choice of seeking advice from one who represents that way of life. If the young man were to seek advice regarding the same problem from a Freudian he realizes that he is committing himself to a naturalistic rather than a supernaturalistic point of view. Either of the choices is his own to make. And he is still free to accept or reject the counsel of either.

The most important characteristic of existentialist freedom, then, is that it is absolute. It does not consist, as some traditional philosophers hold, in the freedom to choose among alternative goods. Man has no guideposts by which to make his choices. He must simply *make choices* and these choices will determine his being. He is completely responsible for his own decisions and the effects they will have upon him and others.

It is this condition of absolute freedom in which man finds himself and the responsibility entailed by it that creates the condition in man called *anguish*. Sartre describes this condition as one which necessarily arises when a man commits himself to a course of action fully realizing that he is deciding not only what he will be but also what effect his decision will have on others. Every decision adds

---

[18] J. P. Sartre, *To Freedom Condemned,* J. Streller, ed. (New York: Philosophical Library, 1960), p. 32.

something to one's being; every decision affects other human beings. The realization of this responsibility causes existential anguish. Sartre remarks that those persons who conceal their anxiety perhaps have more of it than those who do not conceal it. They are in flight from anxiety which itself produces greater anxiety.[19]

To illustrate this existential anguish, Sartre points to the state of mind found in people who bear great responsibility. For example, an army officer who must take upon himself the responsibility for dispatching a number of men on an assignment which might mean death to some or all of them. Even when the officer acts under orders from a superior, the decision is still his own. It does not prevent him from giving the order but it is the very condition of his action. He realizes that many different possibilities exist and that no one result can be predicted. But he must make a decision which will affect him and all those under his command. Even the decision not to give an order to attack does not relieve him of his anguish; it only intensifies the anguish.[20]

Existentialists make it very clear, however, that true anguish does not lead to inaction. On the contrary, the behavior of all great leaders is characterized by intense anguish. They are the people who realize the great responsibility entailed by their decisions both for their own existence and for the effect their decisions will have on their fellowmen.

A second condition brought upon man by absolute freedom is abandonment. By abandonment, the atheistic existentialist means that since God does not exist, man is left to his own deserts in creating himself and the kind of world in which he will live. There are no *apriori* values according to which he can make his decisions; there are no transcendental codes of behavior; there is no moral law in "nature" to be discovered and followed by man. Since neither God nor the "natural law" exist, man cannot find any source outside himself by which he can judge his decisions or actions to be right or wrong — all is permitted. Man is abandoned to his own decisions — *he must do what he wills; he must create his own essence.*[21]

The reader might be helped to understand this condition of abandonment by imagining himself on the vast expanse of a desert.

[19] J. P. Sartre, *Existentialism and Humanism,* p. 30.
[20] *Ibid.,* pp. 31–32.
[21] *Ibid.,* p. 32 ff.

There are no landmarks, trees, signs giving directions, no reference points of any kind which he can interpret. Yet he wants to get himself and any others who might be with him out of the desert. To emphasize the loneliness of the situation, let us assume that he does not know why he is in the desert nor how he got there. The sum total of all the feelings that well up within his being under such conditions might be compared to existentialist abandonment. Every choice has to be made without the assistance of anything outside himself. He is completely "on his own." Thus anguish and abandonment go hand in hand; they are correlative states resulting from absolute freedom.

Despair is another condition resulting from absolute freedom. Sartre describes this condition in these words: "It [despair] merely means that we limit ourselves to a reliance upon that which is within our wills, or within the sum of the probabilities which render our action possible."[22] Thus, when one makes a decision to act, he never can be sure what the result will be for himself or others. There is no certainty whatsoever that events will turn out as we will them. Nevertheless, one must make decisions and act in spite of all the uncertainty involved. Man must decide and act *without hope*. This willing and doing without any certain hope that what we wish or do will be as we would like it, is existentialist despair.

For the atheistic existentialist the despair is much more frightful than for his theistic brethren who seek an escape from final despair by placing their trust in God. The atheist must live with his despair; he must continue making decisions and action in spite of despair; he must rely upon himself.

The condition of existentialist despair is important since it places upon each man the sole responsibility for creating his own essence. If he had some certainty that his decisions and deeds would have the desired outcomes, either in this life or the next, his freedom would be limited since actions would have a predetermined outcome. Under such conditions, the existentialist argues, both the world of events and man would be determined. This state of affairs, of course, would contradict the basic assumption of existentialism, absolute freedom.

In a discussion on existentialism, the task of defining the nature of society is much more difficult than it was for other philosophies. For the instrumentalist or the Marxist, the nature of society is

---

[22] *Ibid.*, p. 39.

specifically defined. Man's place in society and the effects of society on man's nature are clearly spelled out. Such, however, is not the case for existentialism. If man has no predetermined nature, certainly society must have none. In other words, there is no place in existentialist philosophy for social theory as developed within the other philosophies treated in this book. The existentialist often is accused of being "antisocial" in his behavior as well as in his philosophy. This position is understandable if one keeps in mind that existentialism represents a reaction against the society-centered political philosophies of the pre-World War II era. Nazism, Fascism, Communism, and Socialism were anti-individualistic. In these systems individual perfection consisted in conformity of one's will and actions to that of society (the state). Also, the atheistic existentialist revolted against the moral and doctrinal conformity demanded by the great religious bodies, chiefly Catholicism and Lutheranism. All of these systems, they argue, limit man's freedom in the process of creating his own being and essence. All of them put society, the state, the Church, or the party above man; all make man a slave to a predetermined pattern of behavior and belief.

If existentialists have no theory of society, it might be more accurate to ask *how they view other men.* First, they would grant to others the same existential freedom which they demand for themselves. That is, man is never to be viewed as a means but rather as an end. It is on this very point (man as means) that Fascism, Communism, and Nazism have erred since they made of man a means for the realization of national, political, social, or racial goals.

Second, individual man is not bound to other men by any predetermined notion of brotherhood or by allegiance to a certain group. On the contrary, each man should express his freedom in the creation of his own selfhood, first by "withdrawing from the crowd," and then by communicating only with those whom he personally chooses as kindred spirits. Sartre is most emphatic on this point. He carries to its logical conclusion Kierkegaard's fight for the individual against the crowd, social institutions, or the system. Sartre feels that the entire network of social life is *anti-individual.* Churches, schools, political parties, and even the family tend to militate against man's absolute freedom.

This antisocial outlook seems to be one of the facets of existentialism which the "lunatic fringe" of the movement has given major emphasis. Nonconformity is the watchword of the beatnik wing of existentialism. They are against membership in churches, clubs, or any organization with rules; they dislike attending formal educational institutions since these, too, limit one's freedom by holding the student to very specific requirements, class attendance, examinations, and the like. However, most existentialists do not go to such extremes. They are realistic enough to recognize that groups and institutions exist and that without them life would be well-nigh impossible. Nevertheless they insist that the individual does not exist for the group, the institution, or society. Rather, all social forms exist for the individual; they are mere means for creating his own being!

To summarize, the main points in the existentialist beliefs about the nature of man and society hinge on the basic assumption that *man is absolute freedom*. This existential freedom generates anguish, abandonment, and despair. Because man is a lonely being, he cannot seek solace in social relations but must choose and act as an individual rather than as a member of society. A person who wills and acts in accordance with the notion of absolute freedom will never be swayed by the "will of the mob" or by the demands of social institutions. He will do as he wishes; he will create himself "according to his own image and likeness."

EPISTEMOLOGY

In general, the modern philosophies discussed in this book give the greatest priority to the scientific mode of knowing. Naturalism, instrumentalism, Marxism, and naturalistic realism have placed their trust in the power of science. In these systems, truth is equated with the findings of science.

Existentialists, however, have given little attention to inductive reasoning. Science, they believe, has been one of the major dehumanizing forces in the modern world. It is not that existentialists want to put an abrupt halt to all scientific work. Rather, they argue, the philosopher should not concern himself with such matters. It should be quite evident from the section above that "philosophizing" is performed on such topics as the nature and importance of freedom, man's mental states, decisions, and action. The nature of scientific method, the nature of the physical universe, and similar topics are conspicuously absent from their philosophical treatises.

The existentialist approach to philosophy, then, calls for a new epistemology. This new approach to knowledge is known as the *phenomenological method*. The atheistic existentialists inherited this method from Husserl. It was adapted further by Heidegger and Sartre to suit their philosophy of "will and action," especially as it concerns the individual. There is neither the time nor the need for a discussion of Husserl's complex phenomenology in a book on philosophy of education. However, a nontechnical description of the phenomenological method of knowing might clarify the relationship of this method to the teacher-learning process. The first step consists in an intuitive grasp of one's conscious experiences with objects, people, and events. This phase of the knowing process is closely allied to the existentialists' insistence that "existence precedes essence" (see above, "Permanence and Change"). Then the subjectivity of this aspect of knowing is evident since man does not begin with a ready-made knowing mechanism, but chooses subjectively (as an individual) that which goes into the making of his being.

The second step in the phenomenological method consists in the expression of the experiences of my consciousness through the media of ordinary language, the fine arts, and, when need be, through the language of technical philosophy. George Kneller gives this description of the method:

> . . . I describe in detail the appearance of things and events as they present themselves to my consciousness; I interpret them in their subjective reality, after the manner of the poet or novelist, without being bound by logical analysis or scientific empiricism. The latter I regard as means, not ends, by which corporeal existence may be explained (as contrasted with personal experience). . . . I regard scientific empiricism as a means to the understanding of the structure of rocks and atoms, and the behavior of rats, lice and guinea pigs. But I agree with Berdyaev that in the long run such "objectivity" can only cool the fire of human individuality.[23]

Clearly, then, the existentialist is not so concerned as are other modes of thinking with the kind of knowledge found in the empirical sciences. Such knowledge is not concerned with choices of values, modes of living, and acting. Scientific knowledge is objective (must be capable of test by all scientists); it must be removed from the

---

[23] George Kneller, "Education, Knowledge and the Problem of Existence," *op. cit.*, p. 142.

realm of value-judgment and commitment; it becomes meaningful only when all personal, subjective elements are removed.

In opposition to this cold impersonal approach to knowledge, the existentialist argues that true knowledge is "choosing, acting, living, and dying." Let the scientist continue his pursuit of cold, lifeless fact and theory, but let the philosopher concern himself with the aspects of the world which involve personal, subjective experience. Sartre considers this latter approach true humanism.[24]

SEARCH FOR VALUES

Ethics. From what has been said above in connection with the nature of man and the knowing process it is quite evident that the atheistic existentialist cannot subscribe to any value theory which purports to be objective, absolute, universal, or social. If there were a preexistent moral law which detailed general or specific behavioral patterns for all men, true existential freedom would be a mockery as well as an impossibility. Also, since man himself has no specific nature, and man is the only living being who makes choice of "good or evil," one cannot argue that a good man will make certain choices and an evil man will make other choices. Furthermore, since society has no independent existence (that is, independent of the persons who make it up) it cannot claim any rights over the moral choices and behavior of individuals. Values, then, do not exist except in conjunction with the freely chosen acts of individuals.

Truly, it is because of this lack of an external moral authority that the individual finds himself in the states of anguish, abandonment, and despair. In fact, even those individuals who have committed themselves to the assumedly "objective systems" of morality (the decalogue, Catholic, Protestant, or Moslem ethical codes) have done so of their own free choice. They have not made this choice because these ethical systems are "objective"; rather, by choosing this or that code of behavior, they have "objectified" for themselves their own subjective choices.[25]

If there are no objective or societal norms for behavior, how does the existentialist decide what is right or wrong? There seems to be only one possible answer to this most important question. Each choice is for the good! The fact that I choose this way of acting

[24] Sartre, *Existentialism and Humanism*, p. 24.
[25] J. P. Sartre, *op. cit.*, p. 36 ff.

rather than another makes it good, for, in choosing, I am exercising my absolute freedom.[26]

All choices must be good, at least for the nonce. At a later date, I might regret having made such a choice but that is beside the point. The very essence of good is choosing.

It seems then, that man never chooses evil. If one is to speak of evil at all, it would be in the sense that not making a choice is evil. If one makes no choice one is not creating his own essence. This is how animals behave — their masters choose for them. But animals are not free so they cannot be accused of good or evil. But man, who is "condemned to freedom," must choose if he wishes to consider himself more than an animal. A man "becomes a man" when he makes choices. When he makes choices he creates his own values. When he creates his own values, he creates his own being or essence.

But the nonexistentialist says, what motivates one to make this choice rather than another? Does the physical environment determine or even suggest the choice? Does the social and cultural milieu surreptitiously or unconsciously direct me to my choice? Do hereditary factors predetermine my choice? To these queries, the existentialist gives a categorical "No!" The only recourse left to the existentialist is that one's own subjective feelings, impulses, "mental states" are the moving forces in making choices.

Of all the doctrines proposed by the existentialists, this view of the nature of value probably has the greatest effect on educational theory. All other educational philosophies, traditional and modern, purport to give the young a certain set of values by which they can guide their choices. The Hebrew-Christian ethic serves as the guide for the majority of the educators of the Western world. Marxists have a very definite set of values which are taught to all pupils and which are enforced by rigorous discipline. Even the instrumentalist, who is avowedly an ethical relativist, indoctrinates youth in democratic social values. But the existentialist must forego the security of any of these systems of morals. He must emphasize the *necessity of making choices* without providing the young with any guide for making them.

The effects of this view on educational aims, objectives, methods, and curricula have been discussed above. Academic freedom and

---

[26] Norman Greene, *Jean-Paul Sartre, The Existentialist Ethic* (Ann Arbor: University of Michigan Press, 1960), Chap. IV.

indoctrination assume entirely different theoretical and practical meanings for the existentialist. In general, it seems that existentialism would demand far more radical changes in education than even those inaugurated by progressivism.

Aesthetics. For most of the philosophies discussed in this book, art has no *raison d'être* of its own. For the Marxist it is a medium of social reform. The instrumentalist views it as a way of spending leisure time. Philosophers with a predominantly scientific orientation, such as positivism and scientific realism, place little stock in the value of philosophizing because their concern is with the findings of the empirical sciences. The existentialist, however, considers the development of aesthetic theory as one of the major concerns of the philosopher. Perhaps the only other area to which he gives greater emphasis is ethics.

Another distinctive feature of the aesthetical views of existentialists lies in their use of the art forms, especially literature, drama, and painting, as media for communicating philosophical doctrines. The history of philosophy records no parallel of a school of thought which uses the arts as the avenue for putting their beliefs into the cultural stream of the age. It is true that Plato, St. Augustine, and others have produced works which are considered great literature. Also, great artists such as Michelangelo, Dante, and Shakespeare have reflected certain metaphysical beliefs in their masterpieces. But in both instances these great thinkers or artists were not attempting to be both professional artist and philosopher.[27]

It is this very feature of existentialist philosophy that makes it difficult to understand, namely, the use of poetic language (and other art forms) to express the ideas of technical philosophy. The neophyte, in his first attempt at reading the existentialists, is completely baffled by the terminology and the concepts. A good background in scholastic philosophy, for example, seems to be of little help. In fact, a student of modern literature is much more "at home" with existentialist philosophy than is the student of philosophy.

What are the main characteristics of the existentialist theory of art? First and foremost it must be noted that there are no rationalistic or empirical criteria for art. Nor can social, political, or re-

---

[27] Because the existentialist fuses the activities of the artist and the philosopher, some of their opponents have argued that they (existentialists) should be classified as artists rather than philosophers. That argument cannot and need not be settled here.

ligious norms be applied to the art forms. Art is purely subjective
—it is its own master — it is its own criterion. Stated negatively,
this view means that the artist is not bound by such criteria as
symmetry, unity, harmony, or definiteness. Nor is he expected to
portray the "real world" as it exists independent of his own perception of it. Also, his art products need not promote socialism,
democracy, religion, or a philosophy of life. What guidelines does
the artist use? None! He simply expresses in his novel, play, or painting his own feelings, his own choices — whatever these may be. All
he has to say to the critic who does not understand is: "I like what
I have done. I have chosen to express myself in this manner. None
of your traditional criteria move me!" The most important thing
for the artist is that he express (in some art form) those feelings
and impressions about situations in which he himself is personally
engaged. He is expressing true (existential) freedom.[28]

It might be worth noting that artistic expression is somehow tied
in with the phenomenological method described above. What the
existentialist artist seems to be doing is looking in upon (intuiting)
his innermost desires and feelings and expressing these through the
medium of the arts.

The themes of existentialist art are most interesting since they
give live portrayal to the conditions of "existent man" mentioned
above in the section on "Epistemology." Their plays and novels
depict anguish, abandonment, despair, nausea, and death. For example, the ballet *Le Jeune Homme et la Mort* (*The Young Man
and Death*) portrays a bored and disillusioned young man struggling
with melancholy and death. His anguish is evident from the antics
which go into the dance; his despair can be noted from the futile
fight which he wages against Death. The novels and plays of Jean-
Paul Sartre, such as *The Flies* and *In Camera,* express the same
themes, anguish, despair, abandonment, and death. The works of
the French novelist, Camus, carry these same messages. Some
American novelists have been incorporating existentialist notions in
their work; J. D. Salinger's *Catcher in the Rye* often is cited as an
example of this influence on American literature. Some critics say
that the whole trend in American literature today is existentialist.

As noted in the introduction, existentialism has little influence on
American education at the present time. Perhaps it will have some

---

[28] See J. P. Sartre, *What Is Literature?* (New York: Philosophical Library, 1949).

influence in the relatively near future through the medium of the arts (especially literature and drama) as these forms themselves become more predominant in college and high school education. As the mid-century emphasis on science seems to be waning and as more and more teachers and students become interested and involved in the arts we might find the seeds of existentialism flourishing in the schools.

EVALUATION OF EXISTENTIALISM

The reader, no doubt, has spotted the major deficiencies in atheistic existentialism when viewed from the perspective of Christian education. Some of the most fundamental differences are:

1. Atheism, with all the implications the existentialist draws from it, is wholly unacceptable to the Christian.

2. The Christian thinker believes that man's essence or nature is something definite, something determined to be what it is by God. Every man born into this world has a "human nature," he does not have to create it. He possesses a body and a soul, an intellect and a will. What the individual does with this "ready-made" equipment is his own concern — he may use it for good or evil. Therein lies his freedom.

3. The Christian accepts other sources of knowledge besides "personal experience." Revelation and pure reason provide valid knowledge — these the existentialist does not accept.

4. The doctrine of absolute freedom espoused by the atheistic existentialist must be qualified by the Christian. Man's freedom is limited, first of all, by his nature insofar as he can act only in accordance with his nature. Second, the Creator-creature relationship which exists between God and man limits man's freedom. Only God is absolutely free.

5. To assert, as the existentialist does, that values have no existence independent of human choices contradicts the Christian notion of the objectivity of the eternal and natural law. It is not for man to make the moral law, but to discover it by the use of the God-given faculty of reason.

Other limitations of existentialism which perhaps are not so basic as those mentioned above lessen the acceptability of this school of thought as a philosophy for modern man. The most glaring one seems to be the naïve view that existentialists take of the "social realities" of the modern industrial, urban world. They offer no social theory for solving the complex problems of our scientific age. Thus proposals for "individual living" might appeal to the hermit or the frontiersman but they are of little help to the people who must spend their lives in large cities, work for large companies, worship in large congregations, and even recreate in crowds. The very real interdependence among human beings contradicts the extreme individualism or personalism of atheistic existentialism. Man is responsible, not only for himself but for his fellowmen.

Yet another weakness might be noted in existentialist philosophy which limits its application to the modern world, namely, the neglect of the scientific mode of knowing in their general theory of knowledge. After all, this is the "age of science" and any complete philosophy of life cannot relegate the philosophy of science to a position of minor importance.

As an educational philosophy, existentialism, at least in its present form, does not provide an adequate basis for educational theory. Perhaps this state of affairs is due to the fact that most existentialists have given no serious consideration to the development of the educational implications of their fundamental philosophical tenets. However, the existentialists are not the only modern philosophers who have not considered it necessary to philosophize about education. The logical positivists, for example, have shown a similar distaste for the practical concerns of the professional educators. However, as these two thought systems extend their realm of influence to all areas of practical concern, one can expect to find increased interest in educational theory. In fact, educational philosophers are beginning to derive certain educational principles from existentialist literature.

Thus far, the evaluation of existentialism has been quite negative. Some even view it as an antiphilosophical movement. Others, however, do not take such a dismal view of it. James Collins believes that it is:

. . . a challenging and instructive philosophy. It embodies a legitimate continuation of several important European traditions and addresses itself to vital problems of the greatest contemporary moment for both philosophy and life. . . . Perhaps the somewhat morbid popular interest in the personality of Sartre may be advanced as an excuse for not giving careful hearing to the arguments of the existentialists. . . . Yet in point of fact, the existentialists have a good deal to say about the movements fashionable today in English-speaking countries. . . . Common courtesy, if not prudent open-mindedness, recommends that we give the existentialists, in turn, a fair hearing.[29]

The reader already might have detected some of the areas in which existentialism has "words of wisdom" for the modern world. The preoccupation of many thinkers with cold and value-free "science" has contributed to a large extent to the mechanistic view of man so prevalent today. The emphasis upon social unity has engendered a type of conformity unprecedented in human history. Group responsibility has been substituted for human responsibility; personal, individual freedom has succumbed to freedom to work with and for the group. Modern man finds security by "joining" as many organizations and clubs as he can rather than by developing his own choice-making faculties. He will not act unless he has the backing of a party, an organization, or a strong following; he fears independent action.

The school itself has become a place where the individual is "socialized" so that he can be a good group member, a good citizen rather than a good person. If existentialism does nothing else but bring about a proper balance between the individual and society, it will have merited the praise of educators.

SUMMARY

Existentialism is the most individualistic of all modern philosophies. Its overriding concern is with the individual and its primary value is the absolute freedom of the person, who *is* only what he makes himself to be, and who is the final and exclusive arbiter of the values he freely determines for himself. Great emphasis is placed on art, on literature, and the humanistic studies, for it is in these areas that man finds himself and discovers what values he will seek to attain.

BIBLIOGRAPHY

Collins, James, *The Existentialists* (Chicago: Henry Regnery Co., 1952).

Greene, Marjorie, *Introduction to Existentialism* (Chicago: University of Chicago Press, 1959).

Greene, Norman N., *Jean-Paul Sartre — The Existentialist Ethic* (Ann Arbor: University of Michigan Press, 1960).

Harper, Ralph, "Significance of Existence and Recognition for Education," *Modern Philosophies and Education,* 54th N.S.S.E. Yearbook (Chicago: University of Chicago Press, 1955), Chap. VII.

Heidegger, Martin, *Existence and Being* (London: Vision Press, 1949).

---

[29] James Collins, *The Existentialists,* p. vii ff.

Kaufmann, Walter, *Nietzsche* (New York: Meridian Books, 1956).

Kingston, F. Temple, *French Existentialism: A Christian Critique* (Toronto: University of Toronto Press, 1961).

Kneller, George F., "Education, Knowledge and the Problem of Existence," *Proceedings of the Philosophy of Education Society,* 1961.

—————— *Existentialism and Education* (New York: Philosophical Library, 1958).

Morris, Van Cleve, "An Overview: Existentialism and Education," *Educational Theory* (October, 1954), Vol. 4, No. 4.

—————— *Philosophy and the American School* (Boston: Houghton Mifflin Co., 1961), Chaps. 3–10 and 13.

Nietzsche, F. R., *The Future of Our Educational Institutions,* Vol. 6 of *The Complete Works of Frederich Nietzsche* (London: T. N. Foulis, 1909).

—————— *Joyful Wisdom,* in *The Complete Works of Frederich Nietzsche* (London: Allen and Unwin, Ltd., 1909).

Roberts, David E., *Existentialism and Religious Belief* (New York: Oxford University Press, 1957).

Sartre, Jean-Paul, *Existentialism and Humanism* (London: Methuen & Co., Ltd., 1948).

—————— *Literary and Philosophical Essays* (New York: Criterion Book, Inc., 1955).

—————— *To Freedom Condemned,* J. Streller, ed. (New York: Philosophical Library, 1960).

—————— *The Transcendence of the Ego* (New York: Noonday Press, 1957).

—————— *What Is Literature?* (New York: Philosophical Library, 1949).

Salvan, Jacques, *To Be and Not to Be* (Detroit: Wayne State University Press, 1962).

Wahl, Jean, *A Short History of Existentialism* (New York: Philosophical Library, 1949).

CHAPTER ELEVEN

Idealism

IN ONE sense, idealism is a name applied to any belief that the world is governed by an idea or plan. In this sense, Plato, Aristotle, and the major scholastics were idealists, although they accepted the material world as fact. In the more usual sense, however, idealism is the theory that nothing exists but mind or spirit. The dualist sees a division running through the whole universe of being, expressed in various facets as matter and mind, existence and essence, substance and accident, and so forth. The monist accepts no such division. If he is a materialist, he seizes upon matter and its motion as the sole reality; if an idealist, spirit and its thought.

Idealism is a difficult philosophy about which to generalize because it takes many forms. Idealists are usually classed as "subjective" and "objective." The former starts, like Descartes, with the individual's experience. Unlike Descartes, he never gets beyond it, but claims that nothing exists except the self, or at least that nothing else can be known with certitude. The mind, he believes, is turned inward upon itself and can only know its own states. The objective idealist stays with mind as the sole reality, but does not limit his cosmos to any one finite mind. Rather, he thinks of the universe as a kind of spiritual Absolute engaged in knowing itself, and is apt to regard the individual man somewhat as a thought in the mind of God.

This chapter will look at educational methods, agencies, curriculum, students, aims, academic freedom, and indoctrination under idealism, as well as problems of permanence and change, naturalism and supernaturalism, the nature of man and society, and moral and aesthetic values. An overall evaluation of idealism will then be attempted. In concluding, we shall consider some philosophies of education which, while not idealistic in the proper sense, are closely related.

This will not be a very "American" chapter, for idealism is historically and logically a rather German product, and mostly a nineteenth-century phenomenon. It has never had much impact upon American thought or education, probably because it does not suit our national temperament. The typical American has no time to spare for the notion that the material world is not "there." He uses too much time and energy every day wrestling with what certainly *seems* like a material world! His attitude is expressed in the limerick:

> There was an old mystic of Beal
> Who said, "Although pain isn't real,
> When I sit on a pin
> And it prickles my skin
> I dislike what I *fancy* I feel!"

Nevertheless, idealism is one of the few fundamental positions on the nature of reality for which a serious philosophical case can be made. It has had its great upholders: Berkeley, Fichte, Schelling, Hegel. It has had its great protagonists among educators: Horne, Froebel, Mann, Royce, Calkins, and others. It is still a recognizable "movement" in American education and deserves to be taken seriously.

METHODS

We cannot look to idealists to speak with one voice on educational methods, since there are so many kinds of idealism. Objective idealists tend toward an emphasis upon formal logic of some sort, usually not so involved and militantly nonempirical as Hegel's dialectic of mind. They thus lean toward an intellectualistic approach to teaching.

There has been a tendency for idealists, however, to insist on some openness in the student's reasoning process, to view any prespecified course of logical reasoning as too constricting. In general, idealists have steered a middle course between rationalistic instruction and a learn-by-doing approach. Most of their methodological prescriptions, while possibly sound from an empirical standpoint, do not seem to flow with syllogistic necessity from their theories of being and of knowledge.

Idealist educators are likely to seek to derive their methods from their epistemology. After all, the idealist makes a claim unique to

himself: Comprehend the nature of knowledge and you will comprehend reality. What, then, is the idealist's answer to Pilate's question?
To the realist, truth is a *correspondence* between thought and its
object. To the pragmatist, truth lies in *consequences,* the results of
acting on an idea. For the idealist, truth is *coherence* or consistency
within the total body of experience and thought. He cites two objections to the realists's theory: (1) We cannot transcend experience.
A man who lived in a windowless house and had never left it would
have no basis for saying what was "out there." We must simply
judge each idea, each sense-impression, each recollection, etc., by
how well it *fits* into a context provided by all the others. For instance,
a man dreams of a voyage, then awakens. How does he know that
the voyage was "only a dream"? It seemed real enough while it
lasted. But it does not fall harmoniously within the context of earlier
and later experiences. But you cannot, says the idealist, say anything
about how the dream relates to something *outside* experience, because
experience is all that we have. (2) The realist theory tends to place
great stress on isolated facts, e.g., "This clock is five minutes slow." In
objective idealism, the cosmos is a sort of giant echo chamber where
everything reverberates forever and touches everything else. There
are no closed systems, no isolated facts. An isolated fact is, to that
extent, a distorted fact, an untruth if you like.

This is not to say that experience is irrelevant to learning truth.
What sort of peace the idealist makes with experience as a criterion
depends upon what sort of idealist he is. Mary W. Calkins, for
example, wrote that, by experience, she established the fact of the
self and that the self is limited by something beyond itself.[1]

AGENCIES

Again there is no essential "idealist position." Philosophers of
this group have tended to acknowledge the state as the supreme
educational agency on the grounds that it speaks for ultimate, spiritual reality. The confusions that can arise as one moves from one
level of abstraction to another, however, are illustrated in the intellectual gaps between metaphysical idealism and its sociopolitical applica-

---

[1] Mary W. Calkins, "The Philosophical Credo of an Absolutistic Personalist," in
George P. Adams and William P. Montague, *Contemporary American Philosophy*
(New York: Macmillan Co., 1930), V. I, p. 201.

tions. One of the great disappointments in the history of thought is the breach between Hegel the philosopher and Hegel the politician. Everything from virtual anarchy to totalitarianism has been advocated in the name of idealism.

CURRICULUM

Idealist educators have tended to stress factors of imitation, interest, effort, discipline, and self-activity rather than prescribe any given curriculum. William E. Hocking, however, is among those who hold, in the name of idealism, that the school must offer something definite.[2] Horne suggests this way to build the curriculum: First, conceive the ideal character of man and the characteristics of an ideal society. Then "select those experiences, activities, life-situations, and studies that, according to one's best judgment, best contribute to those ideal ends."[3] He further suggests that a curriculum should include equivalents of three aspects of the pupil's environment: intellect, emotion, and will. Accordingly, there should be some science, some art, and some volition.

Bogoslovsky has proposed a curriculum for his *ideal school*. There should be four interrelated areas of study: the universe (physical science), civilization (social sciences), culture (philosophy, art, literature, religion, etc.), and personality (behavioral sciences).[4]

In view of the coherence theory of truth, one might expect idealist educators to advocate so-called broad-fields curricula, and other means of integrating subject matter. Mostly they have done so. To this extent they are in agreement with Christian thought on the point:

> Anyone who is conversant with school problems knows that there is nothing so harmful as knowledge accumulated confusedly and without order, knowledge which is not co-related and integrated; bits of knowledge, rather, which often are opposed to, and contradict, each other.

> It frequently happens that the teaching and study of scientific matters proceed in complete abstraction and without regarding the necessity for a complete formation of the mind. By serious philosophical study the mind must continually acquire a capacity for synthesis and thorough investigation. Therefore, science and philosophy must be integrated and brought to each

[2] William E. Hocking, *The Meaning of God in Human Experience* (New Haven: Yale University Press, 1928), pp. 259–261.

[3] Herman H. Horne, *This New Education* (New York: Abingdon Press, 1931), p. 90.

[4] B. B. Bogoslovsky, *The Ideal School* (New York: Macmillan Co., 1936), p. 133.

other's aid where the more intimate and profound structure of matter is studied, and where a wider and loftier order of harmony must be produced or discovered.[5]

An idealist, of course, would change "the profound structure of matter" to mind. By the same token, idealists have usually been more sympathetic with liberal arts and humanities courses than with scientific and technical ones.

STUDENTS

As we shall see later in discussing the idealist's view of man, he sees the student or pupil primarily as a conscious self. He is a spiritual being, "the temple of the Holy Ghost."[6] He is not created by his environment so much as he creates it. And the pupil is, to use a phrase in current popularity, "becoming." The pupil has a soul, but that soul is capable of evil as well as of good. The idealist is neither so optimistic as Rousseau nor so pessimistic as Calvin, but sees the pupil as morally neutral in his essential nature, capable at any time of going in any moral direction.

AIMS

An idealist tends to see the purpose of education in terms of individual or of social development, according as he belongs to the subjective or objective branch of idealism. Social aims have been stressed. Friedrich Froebel (1782–1852), a German, saw the school's goal as seeking closer unity between the pupil and the Absolute. The "natural" way for children to do this is through play. Drawing, clay-modeling, painting, coloring, singing, dancing, block-building, stories were pressed into service to that end. These materials and activities were seemingly valued as much for their symbolism as for their substance.

But how can one judge the degree of his unity with this spiritual ultimate, with his "lost, larger self"? Not the least of idealism's difficulties is that its lofty metaphysical conceptions become equated with not-so-lofty political and social arrangements. Generally the culture comes to be regarded approximately as the voice of God. The school, in turn, becomes "the mind of society," a sort of mouthpiece for

---

[5] Pius XII, "The Bases of Sound Education," an address to the students of Rome, *The Pope Speaks,* IV (Summer, 1957), 17.

[6] Herman H. Horne, *The Philosophy of Education* (rev. ed.) (New York: Macmillan Co., 1927), p. 37.

the Absolute. There is an obvious danger in this sort of ventriloquizing.

Some idealists have stressed individualism as a goal. Giovanni Gentile lent his idealistic philosophy of education to the service of the fascist state. Nevertthless, he wrote of self-realization as the ultimate educational aim, and further characterized this as spiritual becoming.

Herman H. Horne (1874–1946), thirty-three years at New York University, is probably the leading American idealist educator. Horne, descriptively, agrees with many nonidealists in specifying truth, beauty, and goodness as proper goals. The school should adjust the child to "these essential realities that the history of the race has disclosed."[7] Horne once provided a list of thirty-three traits which should characterize the educated man. Among them: he can play with children and have a truly fine time, he can enjoy a vacation. Somewhat loftier is Horne's rather well-known definition: "Education is the eternal process of superior adjustment of the physically and mentally developed, free, conscious, human being to God, as manifested in the intellectual, emotional, and volitional environment of man."[8]

Theodore M. Greene has presented what he calls a liberal Christian idealist philosophy of education.[9] He urged "students' maximum freedom of choice" as an aim, qualifying it with some references to the spirit of liberalism.

ACADEMIC FREEDOM, INDOCTRINATION

Theodore Greene declared, "every student should, so far as possible, be encouraged to explore all available points of view, all of man's generic experiences, all serious accounts of nature, man, and God, as sympathetically, eagerly, and open-mindedly as possible."[10] This typifies the idealist's usual reaction against any form of in-

---

[7] *Ibid.*, p. 102. Horne, a prolific writer, produced *The Psychological Principles of Education* (1908), *Idealism in Education* (1910), *Free Will and Human Responsibility* (1912), *Jesus, the Master Teacher* (1920), *Christ in Man-Making* (1926), *Philosophy of Education* (1927), *This New Education* (1931), *The Democratic Philosophy of Education* (1932), *The Philosophy of Christian Education* (1937), and other works.

[8] *Ibid.*, p. 285.

[9] Theodore M. Greene, "A Liberal Christian Idealist Philosophy of Education," Chap. IV in *Modern Philosophies and Education,* 54th Yearbook of the National Society for the Study of Education, ed. by Nelson B. Henry (Chicago: University of Chicago Press, 1955), esp. pp. 107–111.

[10] Greene, *op. cit.,* p. 109.

doctrination. There are, however, as noted under another heading, exceptions. The subjective idealist has good reason to favor academic freedom on the grounds that there is no objective truth, anyway. By the same token, if he is consistent, he has little reason to place any special value on academic freedom. The objective idealist, logically, should favor academic freedom on the grounds that his coherence theory of truth allows for an ever expanding intellectual horizon. On the other hand, coherence argues for limits in this expanding: each new element should fit comfortably with what is already there.

PERMANENCE AND CHANGE

The idealist must face, in his own way, the problem of the one and the many. If he insists uncompromisingly on the reality of individual minds, then the Absolute becomes merely their arbitrary sum, not much of a reality in its own right. Conversely, if he holds out militantly for his Absolute, individual minds are swallowed up within it. The objective idealist sees the Absolute as permanent in its total self, but changing in its finite expressions and manifestations. Yet these changes do not, for most idealists, rule out the immortality of individual finite minds. Bosanquet and Hegel are examples of idealists who stress the unity of the Absolute at the expense of swallowing up the individual mind, while Leighton and Hoernle are idealists who stress the individual mind and let the Absolute redeem itself as best it can.

NATURALISM AND SUPERNATURALISM

It might seem that idealism would accommodate itself comfortably to religious beliefs, since it insists upon a purposive, nonmechanistic reality. But idealism is not very compatible with theism, since the latter is dualistic in the sense of insisting upon an irreduceable difference between God and all created beings. For the idealist, God is no longer the Creator and governor of the universe; He *is* the universe. This means that He *becomes;* He is dependent upon everyone and everything; He is finite. But the classical proofs for God's existence argue to an unchanging, indivisible God who is *prior* in every sense to nature and its laws. A God such as Hegel's Absolute is not the God of theistic belief. Baruch Spinoza (1632–1677) may be taken as an example of the pantheism that grows out of idealism. For Spinoza there was but one substance, which he equated with God. God's two chief attributes are extension and thought. These are reflected in man, since man has body and mind. There is no immortality in the sense of the survival of individual souls; for, after death, the soul is reabsorbed into the totality of God. This is similar to the pantheism of many oriental religions.

NATURE OF MAN AND SOCIETY

Like other monists, the idealist bases his argument chiefly upon the difficulties inherent in dichotomizing reality and then trying to glue it together again. It is significant that idealism gained favor after the absolute dualism of Descartes. The carefully qualified dualism of the Aristotelian-Thomistic tradition does not make so radical a split. In the wake of absolute dualisms, most philosophers felt they had to seize one or the other horn of the mind-matter dilemma, so they became either materialists or idealists. The nature of man, then, is for the idealist in any case spiritual. The reality of an individual, spiritual self is a cornerstone of idealist thought.

But if the individual is a spiritual self, the reality surrounding him, so the idealist argues, is of the same sort. Bosanquet has suggested that, instead of saying, "I think," Descartes should have said of the Absolute, "It thinks in me."[11] That is, reality is a thinking Being of which (or of Whom) I am a part. Thus society is regarded as somewhat more real, somewhat more concrete, than the individual mind. The writing of Hegel illustrates this viewpoint very well.

MORAL AND AESTHETIC VALUES

Objective idealists agree that values, moral and aesthetic, are "real," and independent of man's perception, though they disagree considerably as to what those values are. The coherence theory of truth suggests a certain way of looking at values, and implies that one way by which the individual can realize values is by effectively relating parts and wholes — means and ends, perhaps. Mary Calkins suggested that "the ultimately real relations are those of whole and part, of including and being included," and added that one can enlarge his experience by trying to see all phases of life in harmonious relation to its totality.[12]

[11] Bernard Bosanquet, "Life and Philosophy," in J. H. Muirhead (ed.), *Contemporary British Philosophy,* Series II (New York: Macmillan Co., n.d.), p. 61.

[12] Calkins, *op. cit.,* V. I, pp. 210–211.

In the aesthetic realm, Schopenhauer is probably the greatest idealist thinker. Schopenhauer saw art as "the flower of life."[13] Schopenhauer had little sympathy with anything involved in being individual. Like many oriental philosophers, he saw this as the root of desire, struggle, striving, pain, and all evil. The whole value of art, he said, is that it raises the individual above individuality. Music is the highest of the arts because least dependent upon the forms of nature. Music tends to tell us in a mysterious way what is *behind* nature, and thus comes closer than anything else to expressing the will and nature of the Absolute.

EVALUATION OF IDEALISM

If everything reduces to one principle, it does not seem to matter much what you call it. If everything is X, then clearly there is nothing to fall into a not-X category, and, therefore, no comparisons to help to define X. The idealist has good reasons for calling X spirit, however. First, he opposes any mechanical theory of the origin and governance of the universe. This is perhaps his greatest insight. Second, he rejects realism, or belief in any extramental world.

All philosophers, like all artists, seek unity. The idealist's fundamental difficulty is that he is looking for a good thing in the wrong place. He finds his unity too soon, as it were, short of where it really is. He finds unity in the world's *nature,* whereas such ultimate unity can be found only in the world's *Source.* Thus matter becomes in his world an embarrassment, a metaphysical fugitive, an unallowable phenomenon. The common experience and judgment of mankind that a material world exists must be rather heavy-handedly shut out.

The idealist epistemology is stimulating in some ways. The role of context in judgments is probably the facet of knowledge that Thomism needs most to develop. Nevertheless, certain weaknesses in the idealist theory of knowledge can be detected. Instead of asserting that we can never transcend experience, it might describe the situation better to say we cannot know the world except *by* experience. If we assume objective knowledge to be impossible, we are driven into a self-contradictory position. As regards isolated judg-

---

[13] Arthur Schopenhauer, *The World as Will and Idea,* trans. by R. B. Haldane and J. Kemp, 4 ed., V. I (London: Kegan, Paul, Trench, Trubner, and Co., Ltd., 1896), p. 345.

ments being distorted ones, this is true chiefly on questions of causality. To deal in cause and effect is to enter a realm far more complex than most people, even scientists, realize. Most medieval scholastics had a tendency to underplay efficient and material causes. Today the tables are turned; final and formal causality are widely neglected or even denied. Nearly all statements of "why" something happened or some condition obtains are oversimplified. It is here that the danger of isolated judgments arises. It is doubly unfortunate when heirs of the Aristotelian heritage make such naïve judgments. While Aristotle's "four causes" probably do not exhaust the possible types, they give a comprehensive schema that, until now, has not been improved upon. Chardin's insistence upon examining both "the inside of things" (formal and final causality) and "the outside of things" (material and efficient causality) is a clarion call to a fuller, more balanced approach.

Two other difficulties about the coherence theory of truth should be noted: (1) This is not the criterion anyone really uses. When the idealist himself says that his theory is true or valid, he does not mean simply that it agrees with something larger; he means "this is the way things are." (2) *What is left for the coherence theory to be coherent with?* What is the context that judges *it?* That is, it is, itself, incomplete and abstract, and therefore inadequate by its own criterion. Yet there is nothing beyond itself to which to appeal within a framework of idealist thought.

Idealists often feel that their system is more flexible and expandable than realist philosophies. Perhaps they are right. Yet, precisely idealism's difficulty is that *it makes the idea a closed object rather than an open relation.* Idealism makes the mind a *measure of* reality instead of the thing *measured by* reality. It thereby cuts itself off from the possibility of verifying its own tenets.

OFFSHOOTS OF IDEALISM

Philosophic labels become less reliable as the centuries roll on. In the past two generations we have had a number of monistic systems that more or less defy specific classification. Science has influenced this situation; for, as matter proves surprisingly elusive and — by nineteenth-century conceptions, at least — curiously nonmaterial, the meaning of "materialism" or "idealism" is less clear.

One offshoot of idealism (perhaps of materialism) is *dynamism.*

This philosophy is monistic but conceives of matter in a rather up-to-date way. Curiously, it "made the scene" prior to the newer conceptions in physics, in the philosophies of such men an Henri Bergson (1859–1941), whose *élan vital* was the talk of sophisticated parlors in the early part of this century.[14]

Closely related are various systems of thought (both in philosophy and psychology) which have emphasized the wholeness and indivisibility of reality, and are variously called organic, organismic, "field theory," etc. Peter F. Drucker, in *Harper's Magazine,* recently summarized the impact of this way of thinking upon practical endeavors, in an article titled, "The New Philosophy Comes to Life."[15] He spoke of a "new foundation," said it is "something we have acquired, all of a sudden, within the past fifteen or twenty years."[16] He discussed how it stresses configurations and patterns rather than "elements," the qualitative rather than the quantitative, purpose rather than efficient causality.

WHITEHEAD'S "PHILOSOPHY OF ORGANISM"

The late Alfred North Whitehead developed a system of thought which he called "the philosophy of organism," and which is probably rivaled only by Thomism and Hegelianism in the sweep and grandeur of its vision. Whether Whitehead was metaphysically wrong or right, one must grant him his architectural genius. Whitehead also had some things to say about education, although there is room for doubt as to whether they follow from his philosophy.

Unfortunately Whitehead was one of those writers who insist upon inventing new terms for meanings for which old terms seem to be available. Because of this and because of the complexity and profundity of his thought, it is always difficult to be sure that one has understood him. The essential idea, however, is that *everything permeates everything else.* There are no closed systems in reality. Whitehead was also a mathematician and conversant with the work of Einstein and other modern physicists. One must be prepared to think in mathematical terms, often, to go along with the argument.

---

[14] This was conceived as a sort of life force, the interior creative principle in all organisms. All nature, in turn, shared this force, was in some sense alive.

[15] Peter F. Drucker, "The New Philosophy Comes to Life," *Harper's Magazine,* CCXV, No. 1287 (August, 1957), 36. Commentary on this article from a Thomistic standpoint: R. B. Nordberg, "The March to Holism — Where Are We?" *Catholic Educational Review,* LVIII, No. 4 (April, 1960), 240–247.

[16] Drucker, *op. cit.,* p. 36.

Whitehead begins by criticizing the picture of the universe that seventeenth-century science provided. Science bifurcated cause from effect, mind from matter, substance from qualities. These are false dichotomies. Science also sought to give us a world without values, and, by the same token, without very much meaning.

All of this came about, says Whitehead, because science deals in abstractions. The trouble is, scientists forgot that you cannot "say all" about anything; *they confused their abstractions for concrete reality*. This is the point he never tires of making, the key to his elaborate analyses of specific problems. Science, in short, misplaces its concreteness. Here we are reminded strongly of Hegel's arguments which gave rise to the coherence theory of truth.

Science has succeeded well enough, for its purposes, in thus dividing the seamless coat of the universe. But it is becoming ever harder to maintain these inert abstractions. Science has gone about as far as it can go until it becomes more *conscious of abstracting*. And how can we correct the errors of analytical bifurcation? Simply by putting together again what should never have been divided in this fashion. Instead of cause and effect, for example, we simply postulate process, and heroically resist all efforts to break this process into units or entities of any kind. The universe is a giant organism, which implies that what happens to part of it affects all of it, and that all of it participates in anything that any of it does. This position takes some thinking about, and is bound to be "frightening"! It means that I am at the mercy of the whole universe; but it also means that, in some measure, the universe is at *my* mercy.

In this cosmic organism, argued Whitehead, all bodies are sensitive to one another, somewhat in the sense suggested by Sir Francis Bacon. This is not a mechanistic sensitivity such as expressed by the law of gravity; it is more *a living attraction,* a la Bergson. Someone said rather aptly that Whitehead "biologizes the world." In *Process and Reality,* his most difficult but most essential work, Whitehead suggested that the forms of energy described in physics are typical scientific abstractions from what, in ourselves, we recognize as types of emotion. This amounts almost to animism!

Intelligibility in Whitehead's World

By now, however, Whitehead has got himself in several difficulties. One important one is the intelligibility of the world. It takes little reflection to see that, in such a cosmos as he proposes, all finite knowledge would be distorted and untrustworthy. What is there to know in a world of pure becoming? Whitehead solves the problem in a curious way, by postulating what he calls Eternal Objects (caps are his). These Eternal Objects "ingress into" the flux of spatiotemporal events. In short, we have here something unmistakably like the Platonic Forms, and the man who set out to be the most uncompromising of monists becomes the most Platonic of dualists.

This is a most serious defect, it would seem, of Whitehead's system. He cannot have it both ways at once. If the Eternal Objects are the governing agencies of change and development, real in their own right, then Whitehead's trenchant criticisms of a "bifurcated universe" must be retracted. Conversely, if he wishes to stick with his "seamless universe," he is inconsistent in postulating the Eternal Objects.

What would a Thomist have to say about all this? He could not accept Whitehead's equation of God and the cosmos. The concrete interdependence of all things in nature may well be a theme that could use more elaboration in scholastic thought. Much of this theme is found in de Chardin.

Whitehead's criticism of philosophical bifurcation must be carefully examined, however, if one is to avoid various pitfalls. There is little of the bifurcating mentality in Aristotle's treatment of the four kinds of causes, and he was the first major philosopher to insist emphatically that we never find qualities apart from substances. A Thomist insists, however, that mind and matter are essentially different, although not in such a way that they cannot coinhabit the world.

There is much reason for agreeing with and profiting from Whitehead's criticism of failing to be conscious of abstracting, hence confusing our abstractions with the concrete. Thomists have not, on the whole, been exempt from that serious kind of error. It is not inherent in their philosophical system; it is simply a careless way of thinking that one can easily enough fall into. Finally, we should be happy enough about Whitehead's Eternal Objects, suggesting only that the rest of his philosophy needs drastic alteration to be brought into harmony with this postulate.

Organismic Philosophies of Education

Various organismic philosophies of education have been developed. Frank C. Wegener, borrowing from Whitehead, has produced one such system.[17] The most serious contender, however, is that of Whitehead himself. The chief educational ideas of the late Harvard professor are set forth chiefly in a celebrated essay, "The Aims of Education."[18]

Whitehead's educational theories follow in a very general way from his philosophy of organism, but not with irresistible force. His basic message, consistently with his thesis of a unified cosmos, is, *Tie things together!*

> In training a child to activity of thought, above all things we must beware of what I will call "inert ideas" — that is to say, ideas that are merely received into the mind without being utilized, or tested, or thrown into fresh combinations.[19]

(Recall our earlier quotation from Pius XII on the importance of integrating knowledge.) Introduce into the student's thinking, urges Whitehead, only a few main ideas. Throw these into every combination possible, and make the child understand "their application here and now in the circumstances of his actual life."[20]

Professor Whitehead rejects the pragmatist's idea that proof of an idea comes only through its utilization. Nevertheless, he urges that what is proved should be utilized, and *vice versa*. He insists on the child's inability to grasp applications that are not proximate to his present concerns, sounding at this point very much like John Dewey.

While urging the importance of basic principles in teaching, Whitehead warns, "There is no royal road to learning through an airy path of brilliant generalizations."[21] That is, there must be many specific applications and relations pointed out, if effective transfer is to occur. (There is some empirical evidence to the contrary.)

Remove, urges Whitehead, the "fatal disconnection of subjects" which kills the vitality of a curriculum. "There is only one subject-

---

[17] Frank C. Wegener, *The Organic Philosophy of Education* (Dubuque, Iowa: Wm. C. Brown Co., 1957).

[18] Alfred North Whitehead, *The Aims of Education and Other Essays* (New York: Mentor Books, 1951).

[19] *Ibid.,* p. 13.

[20] *Ibid.,* p. 14.

[21] *Ibid.,* p. 18.

matter for education, and that is Life in all its manifestations."[22]

Nevertheless, the mathematician's love of his field shows through, and one gathers from Whitehead's remarks on mathematics that he does not want it to come out on the short end of any curricular integration!

Whitehead's essay is written with style, argues a certain viewpoint effectively, and deserves to be read in its entirety. Nevertheless, his philosophy of education, like his general philosophy, may well create more difficulties than it resolves. His vision of the nigh-infinite possibilities of education seems at curious variance with his little-faithed insistence upon starting with matters the learner now considers important. In place of Aristotle's shrewd observation that all men *by nature* desire to know, he borrows too much of Dewey's "blockage theory." Also, "Life in all its manifestations" has a way of being an unintelligible mishmash. One has to select and organize, like any good novelist. Little case can be made for the view of subjects as essentially unrelated entities, planets with no sun, occasionally bumping one another by accident. This view, while formally accepted by few, seems to prevail widely in practice. No better case can be made, however, for obliterating all distinctions, robbing every discipline of the formal object that defines its purpose and procedures, dumping everything into "Life in all its manifestations." One wonders whether Whitehead had his Eternal Objects clearly in mind when he wanted to do that!

SUMMARY

This chapter has examined idealism, subjective and objective, and the organismic philosophy that is one of its offshoots. We have sought to trace the implications of idealism for education as to aims, methods, curriculum, and so forth, and to evaluate both the philosophy and the implications. Despite the slight influence of idealism in American life and education, it is a basic metaphysical system which has had distinguished defenders. Some form of it may yet succeed Deweyism as the "official" philosophy of American public schools.

Idealism, it was noted, reduces all reality to mind or spirit, but may or may not go beyond the limits of the individual mind to a spiritual Absolute that encompasses all things. The educational implications of idealism were found to vary a great deal, but to follow in some fashion the implications of the coherence theory of truth.

----
[22] *Ibid.,* p. 18.

Probably the greatest thing idealists in education have contributed is their keen sense of the importance of interrelating all learning experiences, all phases of the curriculum. While this sort of integration is something of a catchword by now, we may be pardoned for continuing to stress it so long as it receives such scant honor in practice, even from some of its enthusiasts. If coherence is taken, not as an epistemological ultimate, but as a guideline for organizing learning and teaching, it may well be that the idealists have much of value to tell us.

BIBLIOGRAPHY

Bogoslovsky, B. B., *The Ideal School* (New York: Macmillan Co., 1936).

Bosanquet, Bernard, "Life and Philosophy," in J. H. Muirhead (ed.), *Contemporary British Philosophy*, Series II (New York: Macmillan Co., n. d.).

Calkins, Mary W., *The Persistent Problems of Philosophy*, 4 rev. ed. (New York: Macmillan Co., 1917).

———— "The Philosophical Credo of an Absolutistic Personalist," in George P. Adams and William P. Montague, *Contemporary American Philosophy* (New York: Macmillan Co., 1930).

Drucker, Peter F., "The New Philosophy Comes to Life," *Harper's Magazine*, CCXV, No. 1287 (August, 1957), 36.

Gentile, Giovanni, *The Reform of Education*, trans. by Dion Bigongiari (New York: Harcourt, Brace, 1922).

Greene, Theodore M., "A Liberal Christian Idealist Philosophy of Education," Chap. IV in *Modern Philosophies and Education*, 54th N.S.S.E. Yearbook, ed. by Nelson B. Henry (Chicago: University of Chicago Press, 1955).

Hegel, G. W. F., *Selections*, ed. by J. Loewenberg (New York: Charles Scribner's Sons, 1929).

Hocking, William E., *The Meaning of God in Human Experience* (New Haven: Yale University Press, 1928).

Horne, Herman H., *Idealism in Education* (New York: Macmillan Co., 1910).

———— *The Philosophy of Education* (New York: Macmillan Co., 1930).

———— *This New Education* (New York: Abingdon Press, 1931).

Leibniz, G. W. von, *Selections*, edited by Philip Wiener (New York: Scribners, 1949).

Nordberg, R. B., "The March to Holism — Where Are We?" *Catholic Educational Review*, LVIII, No. 4 (April, 1960).

Pius XII, "The Bases of Sound Education," an address to the students of Rome, *The Pope Speaks*, IV (Summer, 1957).

Schopenhauer, Arthur, *The World as Will and Idea*, trans. by R. B. Haldane and J. Kemp (London: Kegan, Paul, Trench, Trubner, and Co., 1896).

Urban, W. M., *The Intelligible World* (New York: Macmillan Co., 1929).

Wegener, Frank C., *The Organic Philosophy of Education* (Dubuque, Iowa: Wm. C. Brown Co., 1957).

Whitehead, Alfred N., *The Aims of Education and Other Essays* (New York: Mentor Books, 1951).

CHAPTER TWELVE

Role of Philosophy of Education in Building the Future

SURELY there is nowhere so determined an optimist as will not admit that grave perils face civilization today. We cannot explain or wish away nuclear weapons, worldwide anxiety, the enslavement of over half the world to a totalitarian system. It is almost universally agreed that education has had much to do with our present plight and will have much to do with making it better or worse. People may disagree radically as to what *sort* of education we need, but America, the Soviet Union, all the world powers involved in the Cold War are eyeing their school systems with unprecedented care.

Education, in turn, is fairly (though imperfectly) responsive to whatever philosophy it is based upon. The teacher, of course, is always limited by reality itself. You cannot consistently carry out an error. Nevertheless, most teachers in Communist-run schools undoubtedly do a great deal to take their aims and methods from Marxism, as currently interpreted by its high priests. There has also been a great deal of honest effort to tailor Western education to the cause of democratic freedom, even if this is conceived in varying and sometimes confused ways.

It is not excessive, therefore, to say that a carefully built and well-heeded philosophy of education could go far to change the world. Philosophy changes classroom practice, which changes the world into which graduates go. Lest we forget, these changes have been, over the sweep of the centuries, for woe as often as for weal! We have much historical precedent for believing that philosophy of education "matters," as does general philosophy. The Nietzsche of today sketches in the Hitler of tomorrow; today's Marx is tomorrow's

Stalin. A John Dewey or a Robert Hutchins leaves his mark in the lives of millions of schoolchildren, though these influences be too subtle and complex to trace.

NEED FOR GREATER UNITY

Let us, therefore, inquire into the role of philosophy of education in building the future. It seems clear that there is presently a cultural, economic, and political need for greater unity among educational systems. We need not all think alike on every issue, but now we have discord and even hatred over the roles of private and church-related schools and colleges; we have waste of personnel and resources on a tremendous scale because institutions cannot cooperate beyond the typical modicum; we have confusion and suspicions because they cannot articulate their goals and reasons for them in a way that will win sympathy outside their ranks, even though not agreement.

We live, in the United States, in a religiously pluralistic society, and, in a larger sense, one of cultural pluralism. It is not necessary for the Catholics to become Deweyites, the Jews to become Catholics, and so forth. Still, if we can find areas of agreement within our basic reference frames, sacrificing no convictions, are we not all the better for it?

What are some possible areas of agreement among the divergent educational systems and viewpoints? The most important one, perhaps, is *fact*. While we often use phrases such as "the fact that" rather cavalierly, not just any assertion qualifies. A fact is a proposition that all observers (possibly excepting the psychotic or mentally defective) can agree upon after appropriate observation. A statement can be true without meeting this criterion; it can even belong to established knowledge and still be inferential. Nevertheless, facts have a "public" quality that uniquely qualifies them as arbiters of disagreements. Facts in themselves are meaningless, we can readily admit, and science involves interpretation as well as data-gathering. But theories *without* facts are empty, sterile.

Empiricists have frequently charged that facts and observation make no difference in metaphysical discourse. This must be assigned as an argument of ignorance. Metaphysics differs from descriptive science in its level of abstractness and in the type of questions it asks, but not in having experiential roots. To know St. Thomas at all is to note his insistence that knowledge begins in the senses. This is even true of metaphysical knowledge, except that the concepts it entails cannot be traced to observations in the same direct fashion as in empirical science.

Debates are currently heard about Catholic intellectualism or its opposite in the United States, about the caliber of Catholic schools, colleges, and seminaries. Often the controversy proceeds in a vacuum because not enough "hard facts" are fed into it. In matters of this sort, we might stand to learn quite a bit from the phenomenalists. Without accepting the "pure becoming" metaphysics that usually underlies phenomenology as a method, one can use this method to describe data. A first area for divergent educational philosophers to come together might well lie in *describing the environment*. Let us all learn more about how to measure, how to weigh, how to observe, how to check, how to distinguish facts from opinions. A student recently stated about another student: "He ratted on me." This was stated as matter-of-factly as if the statement had been, "He drank a glass of water." The accuser could not see that a great variety of behaviors might be interpreted as "ratting on" somebody, and that different observers could quite reasonably invoke different criteria here. Catholic scholarship has too often been marked by this same seeming inability to discern hard fact from soft interpretation. Sometimes we write of people's motives as if they could not possibly have been otherwise than as we suggest, as when one study stated flatly that a certain action was taken toward a Catholic school "due to bigotry on the town board." Sometimes we treat of complex, cause-effect matters as if nobody in his right mind could disagree that X was the sole, complete, simple cause of Y. This scarcely does credit to a group which holds the elaborate Aristotelian-Thomistic treatment of varieties and modes of causality as part of its intellectual legacy.

There is probably as much offending on other pastures. "Science proves" is a phrase that springs entirely too quickly to the lips of positivists and pragmatists. A quotation from Dewey or Kilpatrick seems to have the same status as an experimental discovery. Here, then, is a place where all philosophers can renew their humility and sharpen their analytical equipment: Learn to tell facts from opinions and inferences.

A second sphere for cooperation is *action*. If Mr. Jones and Mr. Brown are both opposed to alcoholism, but for different reasons, there is usually broad scope for them to act jointly in fighting this evil. Who is in favor of disease? Who favors ignorance? grinding poverty? prejudice? Thomists may chide instrumentalists for having *no* valid reasons for opposing these things; instrumentalists may scold Thomists for opposing these things for *wrong* reasons; nevertheless, why cannot they work together to eliminate what both hold as evil? Sometimes it is difficult to avoid the conclusion that many of us are less concerned to rid the world of its woes than to blame them on people who do not believe as we do.

Are there, however, any significant chances for real agreement on philosophical issues? The writer, to be frank, doubts it. It would be much pleasanter to report that we seem to be on the brink of a great philosophical consensus which could embrace believers and unbelievers, theists and pantheists, Christians and Jews, Catholics and Protestants, Dominicans and Zen Buddhists; but history gives no mandate for the prognosis nor do present conditions. Further, the thing is rather clearly a self-contradiction. The only way a monist and a dualist, a realist and a pragmatist, a naturalist and a supernaturalist can agree philosophically is for one of them to cease believing as he has believed hitherto. This is not a compromise, but a flat change of position on somebody's part.

There are undoubtedly encouraging omens in the "interfaith dialogue" that started chiefly in Germany and has been pursued considerably in this country. Such dialogue has its dangers as well, however, and we have probably already felt a number of them. There is, for instance, the chance for superficial, *semantic* agreement that simply obscures deep diversities. If general semanticists and Thomists can agree that "dead-level abstracting" is wrong, this should not blind either side of the fact that they mean radically different things when they talk of "abstracting." Different modes of exposition present a further problem, the habitual Catholic preference for Aristotle's orderly ways being pitted against a contemporary preference for an "unstructured" approach. Above all, there is the danger of a climate in which one idea comes to seem automatically on a par with all other ideas — skepticism.

Perhaps "the facts" as discussed earlier can help us here, but this seems debatable, too. When the scientist and the philosopher ask, "What is man?" they are not asking the same question. The latter is looking for a real, essential definition, a statement of man's "pure essence." The scientist is asking, What *data* on man can we get? As Maritain writes, "The purely scientific idea of man is, and must be, a phenomenalized idea without reference to ultimate reality."[1] The scientist is not "wrong" for doing this, but those are wrong who expect that his data can, *in themselves,* answer the philosopher's question. It is valuable to learn things "about" man, but if all the data from all behavioral and social sciences were somehow collated and presented, something important would be left out. This would not be because a fact was missing here or there or because some specialized point of view had been forgotten; it would be because man is a whole which is not the sum of its parts and needs a philosophical statement of the exact and final character of that whole. It is true that many are trying to resolve questions of value and of ontological principles from psychology and sociology, but the procedure yields "a spurious metaphysics disguised as science and yet deprived of any really philosophical insight. . . ."[2] Our idea of man must also be religious, and it is simply nonsense to suppose that, for example, atheists and Christians will find room for significant agreement upon this.

Indeed, we may well be on the threshold of a new "Dark Age" in this respect. A survey of a magazine such as *Contemporary Psychology,* whose reviews and comments provide a ready index to the pulse of psychological science, points to such contemporary developments as operant conditioning, programed instruction, teaching machines, Osgood's "semantic differential," and other thoroughly materialistic devices and orientations. If it is true that holism and atomism alternate through the ages, psychology seems to be entering a new atomistic phase.

The further progress of science is also going to make for increasingly "tough sledding" for all transempirical views of human nature. As scientists can predict better and better how people, at least in the aggregate, will behave in various types of situations, there will seem (to casual observation) less and less reason to "slip into a nonphysical level of discourse," as one critic sternly put it. This arises from a confusion of the roles and natures of science and philosophy, respectively. It is widely accepted among empiricists that science is a *substitute* for philosophy, a new and better way of

[1] Jacques Maritain, *Education at the Crossroads* (New Haven: Yale University Press, 1960), p. 5.

[2] *Ibid.,* p. 6.

describing and predicting human behavior. They simply do not yet get the point that philosophy was never *intended* to describe and predict human behavior. The comparisons that *deserve* to be made here, that would "make sense" and be valid, are between medieval science and contemporary science, *not* between contemporary science and medieval philosophy. Again, however, history provides little ground for encouragement that, on the sudden, the issues will be clearly perceived and the whole difficulty straightened out.

What are the prospects for more widespread agreement in epistemology? The history of philosophy shows a tableau of changing labels attached to unchanging philosophies. It is not as if there were a thousand basic ways of conceiving of ultimate reality! In criteriology, one sees empiricism and intellectualism, two or three fundamental varieties of each, threading their ways down the centuries. If this pattern suddenly changes, it will be contrary to all the usages of the past. One could argue that the psychology of perception and of cognition keeps feeding new data into the discussion. These should be helpful, but they cannot force the ultimate decision. Does man have a spiritual intellect, irreducible to material components and functions, or doesn't he? Can we know things as they are independent of ourselves, or can't we? Such questions are still being answered divergently despite present-day knowledge of perception and learning, and the divergence will doubtless continue. There is room for progress, though, and no reason to suppose it cannot be made, as regards better mutual understanding of one another's positions.

Take, for instance, the principle of identity, or of contradiction, in its epistemological applications. A dynamist[3] may deny universals or essences. A Thomist may say, "You can't take that position, because that logically requires you to deny identity itself." The Thomist may think that thus he has refuted the dynamist, while the latter is thinking, "Yes, but I deny identity, too!" There is little point in criticizing an opponent's position on the grounds that it commits him to another position which he admits taking. The Thomist may, of course, be victim of the same sort of fallacious reasoning. Again and again Thomistic arguments on particular subjects are criticized by empiricists on grounds that they depend upon a criterion other than observation, which the Thomists would cheerfully admit to be

---

[3] One who believes nothing exists or can exist except energy.

the case. The least philosophers should do is understand and acknowledge each other's basic tenets. We can show that most modern philosophy is self-contradictory by requiring knowledge to be simultaneously possible and impossible in the same way. Nevertheless, if the
modernist admits, as he often does, that he does not mind being
self-contradictory in the least, there is simply no way to pursue the
argument any further!

The philosophical area that seems to the writer to hold most
promise of agreement among educators concerns, strangely enough,
purposes of education. Ultimate purposes will doubtless continue to
provide a bone for contention, but we can have many agreements
on *proximate* purposes. Consider, for instance, intellectual cultivation as a proximate aim. At a fairly operational level, there are
and have been very few educators and classroom teachers who do
not favor and seek to develop the minds of their students. They
have, of course, differing conceptions of what sort of knowledge
accomplishes this, but the differences are not nearly so drastic as
they might be. The teacher who announces on ceremonial occasions,
"I don't teach subjects; I teach children," might quietly add, "I teach
children algebra." Again, nearly all experts agree that both facts
and principles are part of an education. Those who insist that all
principles are subjective or relative are nonetheless insistent, as a
rule, upon pupils learning them.

It is equally difficult to find anyone who, in practice, opposes
character and personality training. Only a few extremists seriously
propose that you can develop a child's mind and leave his personality
untouched, or vice versa. The guidance function, to personalize and
individualize education, is clearly here to stay, and has always been
with us in some form. It is now in a young phase as regards its
formal movement. Nevertheless, those who oppose educational guidance are usually quick enough to protest if the school turns out
juvenile delinquents or conspicuous neurotics. At this proximate
level, at least, nearly all of us can find some common purposes.

BUILDING A PHILOSOPHY OF EDUCATION

Working together at a practical level and agreeing on minor issues
does not, however, take the place of building an educational philosophy. How can one do the latter? How can *you*, as a teacher
and/or citizen, build a philosophy that your own educational efforts

will be based upon and that you will try to propagate so far as possible? Let us consider this question. We shall do so by means of the same categories that have been employed in our analysis of various ancient, medieval, and modern educational philosophies.

Methodology. "How to teach" depends quite directly upon the nature of knowledge, which depends quite directly upon the nature of man. The methods that psychology and technology have produced for teachers are, in themselves, mostly good, clearly superior to some methods of the past. Their very efficiency becomes a sort of blinder, though, threatening to eclipse the issue of what they are for.

We have encountered various methodological issues in preceding chapters, but the basic one that crops up perennially concerns the relative roles of experience and of reason in learning and in teaching. If man were a physical organism *and nothing more,* if his "intellect" were merely a name for certain neurophysiological functions of cor-relating and connecting sense-data, then experience, mostly direct, would be not merely the ideal way to learn, but the only way. If, again, man were a soul somewhat haphazardly materialized, remembering things from a past experience, then Plato's prescription would apply: Pure reason. If man is, as Catholic thought affirms, a composite of matter and spiritual soul, then he learns by sensations and images and, most importantly, by abstracting from them with his intellect and employing these abstractions in judgments and deductions.

Aside from theology, how can you prove to yourself that you have an intellect? One way is by introspection, by noticing what you do when you think, when you solve problems, and by indirectly observing what other people seem to do. The Thomistic account of abstracting, judging, deducing is *drawn from experience.* It is strange that empiricists so often do not notice this!

We have treated elsewhere of how the teacher takes the pupil from known to unknown by a sort of rational discourse, pointing out new relationships among elements the pupil already "knows." This you can prove or disprove by trying it for a reasonable time. No matter how much or little structuring a teacher does, what he is usually concerned to accomplish is for the pupil *to grasp important ideas, to reason.*

Agencies of Education.   Amid contention and bitterness, how can one decide what agencies have what rights and duties in education?

We have already discussed Catholic thought on this matter; our present concern is to outline an approach to the question which anyone can take. Philosophy here can be guided by the homely maxim, "Cobbler, stick to your last!" or by the more technical axiom, "Essence is prior to operation." That is, if things have natures, these natures establish what the things can and should do.

To decide the proper educational concerns of family, Church, and state, therefore, we need but examine the essential character of each. Some sociologists and others nowadays view the individual as existing for the family and the family for the state or society, an inversion of Christian conviction. The rearing of children is often held to be a minor concern, and the rather obvious end of the sexual act, the procreating of children, is held to be an incidental relation. Few persons deny, however, that the family is a group, as distinct from a collection of individuals, and few deny that parents owe more to their children than bringing them into the world, feeding, clothing, and housing them. Even the beasts watch over their young and teach them. In this spirit the United States Supreme Court declared about the Oregon Act:

> We think it entirely plain that the Act of 1922 unreasonably interferes with the liberty of parents and guardians to direct the upbringing and education of children under their control. . . . Rights guaranteed by the Contitution may not be abridged by legislation which has no reasonable relation to some purpose within the competency of the state. The fundamental theory upon which all governments in this union repose excludes any general power of the state to standardize its children by forcing them to accept instruction from public teachers only. The child is not the mere creature of the state; those who nurture him and direct his destiny have the right coupled with the high duty to recognize and prepare for additional obligations.[4]

If the family were a derivative of the state and possessed of no role or function save those with which the state might choose to endow it, the family would have no educational rights or obligations toward the children. If the family is the first, most natural type of human society, with an intrinsic role not bestowed by the state, then it has both rights and duties toward children's schooling.

We can approach the educational rights and obligations of the Church with the same formula: operation follows essence. If the

---

[4] Cited by Charles N. Lischka, *Private Schools and State Laws* (Washington, D. C.: National Catholic Welfare Conference, 1926), p. 292. The act in question would have required parents in Oregon to send their children to public schools.

Catholic Church is not what it claims to be, if it is a totally natural and human group, then it has no educational rights beyond those any group with pedagogical purposes has, although a case of limited scope could still be made upon that basis. If, however, the Catholic Church is the visible society founded by the Son of God to teach and to sanctify, then its nature and its Source demand that it have and fulfill this right. The right is limited and directed by the proper end of the Church, the spiritual good of man. McGucken wrote, in this connection, "It is worth noting, in view of the widespread misunderstanding of the Church's position on her educational rights, that the Church has no jurisdiction over those that are not baptized, nor does she exercise any authority in matters of education over those not of her fold."[5]

Finally, what of the state? Its nature dictates its prerogatives. These must always be differentiated from its *powers*. Most governments exercise many powers that do not rest on any clearly established *rights*. If Hegel was right, if the state is the Absolute or the closest expression of it man can recognize, then its educational warrant is unlimited. If, however, the state is one society among others, a natural society whose proper end is man's temporal good, its educational rights and duties are limited accordingly. We have commented elsewhere on these rights and duties on that basis.

Curriculum.   Our treatments of educational philosophies have encountered quite a few curricular issues and varieties. Basically, though, the question is, where should the curriculum come from? We can concede without argument that it must be limited and shaped to at least a minor extent by the limits of the learner at any given stage. Still, why have a curriculum at all? What demands it, if anything? The traditionalist, who is still content to define curriculum as "a course of study," sees it as resting largely upon *reality itself*. Certainly any course of studies has its arbitrary, man-chosen aspect, but even these are means of accomplishing certain things in a world that is as it is.

A philosophical realist will say, "Teach arithmetic because the world has arithmetical aspects." A pragmatist will say, "Teach arithmetic because, and only insofar as, it has proved a useful tool in solving practical problems." The realist thinks of the curriculum as

[5] William J. McGucken, *Catholic Education: Its Philosophy, Its Fundamentals, Its Objectives* (New York: America Press, n.d.), p. 35.

Anyone who is influence or influences it can form the ph

having a certain status and structure in the abstract, in potentiality; the teacher's job is to help the pupil actualize that structure in himself. The pragmatist will more likely see the curriculum as having no status at all except in the concrete; teacher and pupil together produce it *ex nihilo,* or out of their interactions and "felt needs."

If you believe in objective truth, you are logically committed to believe in some sort of fixed, perhaps required, curriculum. Pius XII, in *Humani Generis,* wrote of "the mind's ability to attain certain and unchangeable truth."[6] If the mind has, indeed, this power, it seems inescapable that the cumulative culture and wisdom of its past exercise should not be preserved in a curriculum that is, in part, unchanging and prescribed.

The respective roles of experience and intellect, or of faith and reason, likewise are clearly pertinent to curriculum. The "experience curriculum" is the child of empiricism, while a moderate intellectualism dictates that children must be taught to reason about the data presented to them, and argues for a methodical, orderly procedure in exposition of subject matter. Again, if God has revealed important truths of His nature and plan for men, these obviously should be taught to the young; while, if there is no such revelation, equally obviously it follows that it should not be taught.

Students. Among the points in debate here, the chief one is: Shall schooling, especially at higher levels, be for everyone who wants it, or for a selected minority? If the latter, what shall be the basis of selection? Insofar as education stresses "organismic adjustment," the understandable tendency is for its institutions to welcome all who wish to come. Insofar as intellectual cultivation or development of specific talents, such as art or music, is stressed, there must be some screening; not all can profit substantially from it. The fairly inevitable basis for this screening is specific talent or general academic potential, that is, intelligence. Much emotionalism has been attached to some discussions by life-adjustment theorists on this problem. They see it as undemocratic to educate a minority, and often wax vehement about the development of an American elite, seeing this as a great evil. Of course, elitism is apt to connote social and political favoritism, as well as superiority in specifically academic matters.

---

6 Pius XII, *Humani Generis* (Washington, D. C.: National Catholic Welfare Conference, 1950), p. 13.

That connotation has been rather gratuitously attacked by the life adjusters, however. There is, as Thomas Jefferson suggested, a natural aristocracy of brains. Some people are brighter than others. We may evaluate this fact as we like, but in the end we must accommodate it.

The nature of man is partly at issue here. If there is no fixed human nature, if man is indefinitely perfectible, if genetic inheritance sets no insurmountable limits, then a case can be made for giving everyone as many years of schooling as he wishes. If there is a fixed human nature, if intelligence is largely fixed by heredity (the first issue is ontological; the second, empirical), then it is appropriate to expose only the more intelligent students to intellectually demanding courses. Also, if man is, in the technical sense intended by Catholic theologians, a rational creature, then an education that helps him develop his nature must be aimed at expanding his mental horizons. Such an education must needs be limited by the quantitative potentialities in this respect of each learner.

Aims. Education is for whatever life is for. These days we hear much speculation to the effect that human life is not "for" anything, that, in the popular term, it is "meaningless." The nature of this assertion has probably not been examined thoroughly by some of those who make it. We find meanings in parts of situations, relative to the whole situation. We find meaning in situations, goals, and so forth, relative to life *as a whole*. Can life as a whole be said to have "meaning" in the same sense that its *parts* do? The answer seems to depend upon whether there is any *larger, rational whole* into which human life fits. To ask this is to ask the final metaphysical question, "What is?" The existentialist, for example, as an atheist, denies that any conscious, rational Being designed, created, sustains, governs, or has any plan for man. Therefore he denies that life taken as a whole can possibly have any meaning, except the meanings each person arbitrarily assigns to it. If the existentialist were right that life has no rational context beyond itself, one could still make a strong case that each person should simply *imbue* his life with meanings by what he does, thinks, and feels. To do something challenging but possible, to do it well, this is the essence of art. But art envisions nothing beyond itself. The believer in God and in the afterlife will want to put art in a context, to make it serve ethical ends.

Art (in the broad sense) has compensations in its sheer process, but the product (again in the broadest possible sense) must serve man's supernatural destiny, "for they are all made for man's use."[7]

The Catholic, therefore, need have no hesitancy in saying education is for man's Christian perfection in time and eternity, as the Marxist has no trouble saying it is for economic gain and the triumph of the proletariat. Dewey held that the educational process has no goal beyond itself because he conceived it as largely synonymous with art, which was largely synonymous with life, which had no meaning *beyond* itself, only miscellaneous meanings *within* itself.

Academic Freedom and Indoctrination.   Teachers through the ages, and perhaps more so their supervisors, have been searching for definite criteria for deciding how free the teacher should be to teach whatever and however he wants. No thoughtful person could say the problem is even now fully solved. At one extreme, some teachers and professors have been discharged and even persecuted for teaching conclusions that were demonstrably true, simply because someone in a powerful position found them discomfiting. The vigilance with which some communities scrutinize textbooks for sentences and phrases that might sound "socialistic" illustrates this mentality at its extreme. At the other extreme, some teachers have held that they have a right to teach whatsoever they choose, whether it is demonstrably true or even if it is demonstrably false, and even if they do not, themselves, believe it. Some people suggest that those who believe in academic freedom are Communists, while others say that those who do not believe in it are Fascists. Obviously, the thing has frequently been discussed with more heat than light!

We need, as always, some philosophical criterion. The question can be approached in various ways, but seems to be mainly an epistemological one. If no conclusions are beyond reasonable doubt, then no conclusion or even "fact" deserves a monopoly over others competing with it. By the same token, however, it is difficult to say, then, why it is of great importance to stress any given line of thought. If, however, certain things can be known beyond reasonable doubt, then the teacher has no justifiable option as to whether they shall be taught. A certain freedom of inquiry and of expression is necessary to scholars, but in the end the mind of teacher and pupil alike must be determined by what is.

---

[7] St. Thomas Aquinas, *Summa Contra Gentiles*, III, 36.

Questions of indoctrination hinge on the same epistemological question. If all is open to legitimate doubt, anyone is indoctrinating who does more than indicate various possible alternative beliefs, and such indoctrination is not justified. If, however, there is objective knowledge, the teacher should present it *as* knowledge, and opinion as opinion. To present either as the other is wrong. Now and then teachers present established truth as if it were merely personal belief, which is just as misleading as presenting the latter as the former.

The division of causality in the teaching-learning process as analyzed in our Chapter Four is also relevant here. If the pupil is the principal cause of his own learning and the teacher an instrumental cause, the heart of indoctrination's evil lies in the "Because I say so" sort of answer. The teacher is presumed — sometimes on scant evidence — to be an expert in a field, but his status as such does not justify his operating behind a smokescreen of alleged personal infallibility. *Experts must be held accountable.* The teacher's job is not simply to say, "This is the way it is," but to help the learner to *see why it is this way*.

How Not to Build a Philosophy

To become conscious of one's assumptions about the ultimate principles and causes of things, to evaluate these assumptions for clarity and consistency, to restructure them in that light, to apply the consequences where they fit, this is the philosophic enterprise. Many key tenets of an educational philosophy can be deduced from analysis of the problem of change, as treated in our second chapter. Aristotle's study of change led him, you will recall, to postulate potentiality between being and nonbeing. One of St. Thomas' basic tenets was that nothing can pass from potentiality to act — from possible to actual existence — except by the help of something else already in act. From this premise, denial of which obliges denial of the principles of identity and contradiction, he deduced most of the pillars of his system of thought. Either something always existed or the universe began *ex nihilo*. This eternal Something must, moreover, be adequate to produce its effects. Thus was he led by natural reason to the existence of God and something of His nature. God, being Pure Act, is in every way prior to, superior to, and independent of nature. A God who could not work miracles would not be much of a God. Thus reason leads us to the possibility of a supernatural order, which history marks as actual. As McGucken lucidly summarized:

> With his philosophy of supernaturalism, the Catholic rests his case for education and for everything else in the world. Reactionary he may be, even dangerous to modern life, but at least in the light of his first principles he believes that he is consistent.[8]

Note that the Catholic philosopher does not *begin* with God and the supernatural order; he does not arbitrarily postulate these things. They are *conclusions* to which observation and reason lead him. Some philosophers, to be sure, have reasoned to other conclusions. An alarming and widespread tendency today, however, is for many secularist philosophers to *start* with certain beliefs and values, and simply find a way to rationalize them. Sometimes they even admit that they are doing this. The most frequently cited educational goal is "democracy," conceived in a great variety of ways. This is taken as an absolute (self-sustaining) value or goal, not as a secondary or derivative one. This is a bit embarrassing for authors who declare that there must be no absolutes, but they often solve the problem semantically by speaking of "consummatory goals," "the democratic faith," or something of the sort. Philosophy deteriorates into apologetics when one simply takes his values as he feels them, then finds good reasons for accepting them.

Neither can we look to science to provide values in the practical sense or to demonstrate them to be such. Science is concerned to describe the world; it has no means to say how things are ultimately or how anything ought to be. One writer on the role of empirical science in establishing values produced this passage:

> Our hope is that all men, disciplined in democratic and scientific methodologies and commonly committed to the values inherent in these methodologies, can seek and find common and valid bases for cooperative planning without destroying the substantive differences in individual and group normative orientations that contemporary society incorporates.[9]

The passage illustrates, for one thing, recent attempts to bring science and democracy within a single genus, which seems a very

---

[8] McGucken, *op. cit.*, p. 40.

[9] Warren G. Bennis, Kenneth D. Benne, and Robert Chin, *The Planning of Change: Readings in the Applied Behavioral Sciences* (New York: Holt, Rinehart, and Winston, 1961), p. 98. The entire volume illustrates the ethical "scientism" in question.

strained and, thus far, unsuccessful attempt. The passage does not suggest what *are* "the values inherent in these methodologies" or why these values, if such there be, should without question take precedence over other values from other sources. At the same time, the desire is expressed that all of this can be done "without destroying the substantive differences in individual and group normative orientations that contemporary society incorporates." One is left wondering what orientations the writer has in mind, just how "substantive" in what sense are the differences that he wants to endure, and, above all, how we can all manage to agree and disagree at the same time. Of course, the whole thing is expressed as a "hope," so one could argue that the statement is correct as a subjective report of its writer's feelings. If this is what it is, however, one should not mistake it for an argument. Even as a subjective report, it seems to contradict itself.

SUMMARY

Our last chapter, while not attempting a résumé of the whole book, has tried to borrow from its substance to consider the role of philosophy of education in building the future. Philosophy of education makes a big difference to education, which makes a big difference to the condition of the world; this was our central premise, for which some historical precedents were offered.

The cultural, economic, and political need for greater unity among educational systems and, to an extent, their philosophies was discussed. Possible areas of such agreement were cited, including sheer factual description, mutual action on concrete problems, and theories of man, of knowledge, of the purposes of education. Issues and procedures for building one's philosophy of education were then discussed with respect to methodology, agencies, curriculum, students, aims, and academic freedom and indoctrination. It is hoped that this volume, in sum, has given the reader a basis for building for himself a philosophy of education which can command his conviction and be reflected in his pedagogical endeavors. For, as Aristotle argued, you must philosophize, even if you are only trying to prove that man should not philosophize. It is surely more comfortable, however, to take a policy toward philosophizing which is in conformity with its own logical requirements.

BIBLIOGRAPHY

Aquinas, St. Thomas, *Summa Contra Gentiles,* III.
Bennis, Warren G., Benne, Kenneth D., and Chin, Robert, *The Planning of Change: Readings in the Applied Behavioral Sciences* (New York: Holt, Rinehart, and Winston, 1961).

Articulation - smooth esculated flow of students from one year to another by course material.

Bestor, Arthur, Jr., *Restoration of Learning* (New York: A. Knopf Co., 1955).

Butler, J. Donald, *Four Philosophies and Their Practice in Education and Religion* (New York: Harper and Bros., 1957).

Dupuis, Adrian M., and Craig, Robert C., *American Education* (Milwaukee: The Bruce Publishing Co., 1963).

Lischka, Charles N., *Private Schools and State Laws* (Washington, D. C.: National Catholic Welfare Conference, 1926).

McGucken, William J., *Catholic Education: Its Philosophy, Its Fundamentals, Its Objectives* (New York: America Press, n. d.).

Maritain, Jacques, *Education at the Crossroads* (New Haven: Yale University Press, 1960).

Mayer, Martin, *The Schools* (New York: Harper and Bros., 1961).

Molnar, Thomas, *The Future of Education* (New York: Fleet Publishing Co., 1961).

Pius XII, *Humani Generis* (Washington, D. C.: National Catholic Welfare Conference, 1950).

Van Dalen, D. B., and Brittell, R. W., *Looking Ahead to Teaching* (Boston: Allyn and Bacon, 1959).

Woelfel, Norman, *Molders of the American Mind* (New York: Columbia University Press, 1933).

Index